Introductory Guide
to the Old Testament

Zondervan's Christian Textbook Contest

INTRODUCTORY
Guide
to the
Old
Testament

MERRILL F. UNGER

13935

ZONDERVAN PUBLISHING HOUSE
Grand Rapids 2, Michigan

To My Mother
"The ordinances of the Lord are true
and righteous altogether.
More to be desired are they than
gold, yea, than much fine gold;
Sweeter also than honey and
droppings of the honeycomb."

Psalm 19:9, 10.

PREFACE

There is today a recognized need for conservative, evangelical textbooks designed for use in Bible institutes, Christian colleges and theological seminaries. While there is no dearth of so-called "scholarly" material in many of the fields of study pursued in Christian institutions, much of this material from the student point of view is either too technical and detailed for general use or too negative and destructive from a Biblical point of view. Accordingly, in the present volume the writer has aimed at simplicity and conciseness of treatment. No attempt has been made to be exhaustive or to appeal to the merely technical scholar. Discussion has been limited to what the author considers essentials. The volume does not profess to be an Old Testament Introduction in the strict sense of the term, but merely a guidebook to conduct the Christian student through the labyrinth and past the pitfalls of modern destructive criticism.

No apology is made for including a chapter on the inspiration of the Old Testament, nor for taking a firm stand for the plenary verbal view in a day when such a position is openly scouted even by some professing evangelicals, and commonly regarded as no longer tenable. Matters of general introduction are dealt with—the canon, the text, the Apocrypha and the various versions. Matters of specific introduction are also treated, including a defense of the Mosaic authenticity of the Pentateuch against the fallacies of the Wellhausen hypothesis. A short introduction to each of the individual books of the Old Testament in the order in which they occur in the Hebrew canon is also presented. In dealing with matters both of general and specific introduction the latest contributions of archeology have been utilized. The aim has been to present in one volume a text which might serve for a one or two-semester course in Old Testament Introduction.

The author sends forth *Introductory Guide to the Old Testament* with a prayer that God may use it to enlighten the understanding of Christian people everywhere, build them up in the faith and give them a finer appreciation of the Old Testament, in a time when the world never more desperately needed the regenerating and purifying power of the Word of God.

Merrill F. Unger

CONTENTS

Part I
GENERAL INTRODUCTION

Part II
THE PENTATEUCH

Part III
THE PROPHETS

PART IV
THE WRITINGS

Part I
GENERAL INTRODUCTION

Chapter I

THE UNIQUENESS
OF THE OLD TESTAMENT

From whatever angle it is considered, the Bible, of which the Old Testament is a vital and inseparable part, is a unique book. In describing it, it is difficult not to deal in superlatives. Incontestably it is the Book of books, the incomparably excellent and inestimably valuable book. With ample reason it has been called "the best gift God has given to man."[1]

Despite the fact that it is the greatest book ever written and the world's best seller, the Bible is easily the most abused piece of literature in existence. Again and again it has faced hatred, persecution, fire and sword, but always it has emerged triumphant. Out of each furnace experience it has come forth more resplendent than before. Although its most effective foes are neglect and indifference, the Bible has undoubtedly endured greatest abuse and misunderstanding from rationalistic higher criticism and skepticism. No small part of the mischief has arisen from the field of Biblical introduction.

The tendency has been to narrow the science of Bible introduction to a consideration of purely critical questions. Too frequently the internal evidence of order, symmetry, purpose and meaning of the books individually and in their collective relationship has been completely set aside by radical hypotheses based on unwarranted assumptions. The result is that many Biblical introductions are almost totally negative and de-

[1] Abraham Lincoln, **Reply to Committee of Colored People**, September 7, 1864.

structive and, in consequence, unconsciously miss or deliberately ignore the genius and spirit of the Scriptural narratives. This is particularly true of Old Testament introductions.

It need scarcely be said that critical questions and radical arguments ought to be fairly faced and adequately answered, at least insofar as the present status of knowledge allows. But it is nevertheless a serious mistake, highly inimical to sound progress in Biblical studies, to confine Biblical introduction to criticism alone. For, after all, the task of disposing of destructive theories and refuting radical arguments directed against the integrity and authenticity of the Scriptural Records, while quite indispensable in an age of rationalistic skepticism, merely clears the way for a positive and constructive treatment of the Sacred Record, and is not an end in itself.

Biblical introduction which fails to recognize the uniqueness of the Sacred Record, attested by both internal and external evidence, cannot avoid the just censure of being called unscientific, nor escape the danger of doing the Ancient Writings gross injustice and wrong. In what, then, does the uniqueness of the Old Testament consist?

I. The Old Testament Is Unique In Its Relation To the Bible As a Book of Books

The thirty-nine books of the Old Testament and the twenty-seven books of the New make up the divine library of sixty-six books, which is nevertheless, in a vital sense, *one* Book. In the light of the unity of the Book the separate books may be considered as chapters. Yet in its individual aspect each book is complete in itself with its own distinctive purpose and theme contributing to the unity of the whole.

The development of the expression "The Bible" to denote the Book of books is evidently providential. As a quasi-technical term it would be difficult to find a more apt designation to capture the vital idea of the essential oneness of the sixty-six books comprising "The Book" *par excellence.*

It is a matter of common knowledge that our English word "Bible" came originally from the name of the papyrus or *byblus* reed, used extensively in antiquity for making scrolls and books. Quite naturally the Greeks came to term a book *biblos* or small book *biblion.* By the second century A. D. Greek Christians began to refer to their Sacred Scriptures under the designation *Ta Biblia,* "the books." When this title was subsequently transferred to the Latin, it was significantly treated as if it were a feminine singular *Biblia,* which reappears in English as *Bible.* Accordingly, this most appropriate name not only emphasizes the unity of the collection of books, but stresses their selection from a larger literature for their present position of pre-eminent authority.

II. THE OLD TESTAMENT IS UNIQUE IN ITS RELATIONSHIP TO THE NEW TESTAMENT

The Bible, although consisting of two testaments, is nevertheless, as we have already noted, *one* book. The two testaments no more detract from its unity than do the sixty-six different books of which it is composed. The Old Testament is a vital and inseparable part of that *one* Book. It is foundational and preparatory to the New Testament. There could have been no New Testament without it, and the New Testament is meaningless apart from it. One is a counterpart of the other. Since the New Testament is *enfolded* in the Old, and the Old Testament is *unfolded* in the New, to separate the two and to treat each as an isolated unconnected unit has resulted in irreparable harm and confusion.

Judaism in rejecting Christ and the New Testament revelation not only set aside Him Whose coming and redemptive work its Scriptures clearly foretold, but also, at the same time, refused the final momentous chapters which conclude the thrilling story of redemption.

The practice in our schools and theological seminaries of separating the Old and New Testaments into different departments, while doubtless mandatory because of the bulkiness of the subject matter handled in each department, is nevertheless an artificial device attended with the gravest peril unless the essential unity of the Bible as a whole is kept constantly in mind.

The usage of the term "Old and New Testaments" was popularized by the Latin Fathers, and did not come into vogue until the "Christian Scriptures" were complete, serving as a device to distinguish them from the "Jewish Scriptures." A testament (Hebrew *berith*) signifies primarily a pact or covenant especially that made between God and the Hebrew nation and ratified through the nation's representative, Moses, on Mount Sinai. The Pentateuch preserves the record of the origin and early history of that covenant. The prophets interpret its obligations in the life of the nation. The sages urge its requirements upon the life of the individual. The historical books sketch its practical outworking.

The New Testament is erected on the failure and ruin of the Old Covenant. It is an agreement between God the Father and mankind sealed by the blood of man's representative, Jesus Christ, on Calvary. The Jew who would now enjoy God's favor, must come by "a new and living way" (Hebrews 10:20), that is, Christ (John 14:6).

III. The Old Testament Is Unique In Its Origin and Preservation as Inspired Scripture

Together with its inseparable counterpart, the New Testament, it is essentially incomparable with any other written book, because it is the Word of God. God, revealing Himself to His ancient people, is its principal author. The sacred writers, or hagiographers, so guided and wrought upon by the Holy Spirit that they were enabled to receive and record the divine message in its fullness and with infallible accuracy, are its instrumental cause.

Everywhere in the Old Testament there is abundant evidence of its divine origin. The sacred penmen were prophets in a most emphatic sense. They received the divine Word immediately and spoke it directly to the people. Over and over they prefix their messages with such commanding expressions as, "Thus saith the Lord . . ." (Exodus 4:22), "Hear the word of the Lord . . ." (Isaiah 1:10). Often they were commanded to write down their oracles (Exodus 17:14; 24:4, 7; Jeremiah 30:1,2). Moreover, there is every evidence to believe that their literary accomplishments were owned as God's Word by the obedient and the faithful from the start.

Then, too, those who spoke of future events like Isaiah, Jeremiah and Daniel had their predictions verified by time. Added to this cumulative internal evidence are the explicit New Testament declarations of the inspiration of the Old Testament books (II Timothy 3:16; II Peter 1:20, 21).

Almost as unique as the inspiration of the Old Testament Scriptures is their providential preservation. Solomon complained in his day that "of making many books there is no end" (Ecclesiastes 12:12). Early in the history of Israel there must have been a substantial literature of high caliber. Echoes of this early literary efflorescence have survived in the Scriptural references to such productions as the "Book of Jasher" (Joshua 10:13, II Samuel 1:18) and the "book of the wars of the Lord" (Numbers 21:14). Human writings apparently competed with inspired documents.

All of these early works have perished, except the Inspired Oracles, which were miraculously preserved through fire and sword and the vicissitudes of centuries.[2] Later writings of a high order, but not inspired, have survived in writings now known as the Apocrypha. Much sorting had to be done.

2 Solomon Goldman, **The Book of Books: An Introduction** (New York, 1948), p. 27; Max I. Margolis, **The Hebrew Scriptures in the Making** (Philadelphia, 1922), p. 27.

Divine guidance made possible the right selection. Men of sincere purpose, enjoying spiritual illumination and direction, became instruments in God's hands for preserving His revealed Word. The eventual result was the canon of inspired Scripture, invested with an intrinsic authority as God's message to man.

IV. THE OLD TESTAMENT IS UNIQUE IN ITS POSITION AND PURPOSE IN THE SACRED CANON

It comes before the New Testament because it is preliminary and preparatory to all that is unfolded there. It catalogues the creation, the fall of man and the beginning of the history of redemption. Its central unifying theme (as is the case of all inspired Scripture) is the person and work of Jesus Christ, the Redeemer. Everywhere He is to be traced in type, symbol, promise and prophecy. His person and work form the warp and woof of the narrative from the "seed of the woman," the promised Redeemer, in Genesis 3:15, to the "sun of righteousness," seed of David, Israel's King, in Malachi 4:2, returning in glory to dispel the darkness of Israel's unbelief and rejection, and as the "Prince of Peace" (Isaiah 9:6) to usher in the resplendent millennial day.

Critics who fail to see that Christ is the *one* pre-eminent and all prevailing theme of the Bible and that the Old Testament is the preparation for His first coming and a prophecy of His second coming to set up the millennial kingdom and to consummate the promises made to Israel (Acts 1:6), miss the unique place and purpose of the Old Testament narratives in the history of redemption.

V. THE OLD TESTAMENT IS UNIQUE IN ITS CHARACTER AS A DIVINE-HUMAN BOOK OF ABIDING VALUE

It is a divine book because it is divinely inspired and miraculously preserved as God's message to man. It is no less a human book,[3] because it is for men as they are, where they are.

3 Cf. G. Mains, **Divine Inspiration** (New York, 1915), pp. 93-99.

It is, in short, *God's Book for man*. It reveals God's mind and will on problems that reach the soul of humanity. Like all Scripture, it possesses a quality of universality and omni-temporality. It belongs to every age. It meets the needs of every people. Concerned with issues of time and eternity, it responds to the deepest heart cry and deals with the most vexing problems of the human soul. Its message reaches beyond the times to which it was originally directed. Today God is writing His Word in human hearts and in regenerated and purified lives as of old He wrote upon the hearts and lives of the Hebrew people. His Word, which is "very pure" (Psalm 119:140), perennially has the matchless power of cleansing the hearts and lives of those who believe and receive it. "Its present fruits" are "the proof of its inspired authority."[4] It is inspired because it inspires. It is superlatively great because, like the New Testament, although divine, it is intensely human.

It is this high moral and spiritual value and singleness of religious purpose which makes the Old Testament consistently current, perpetually up-to-date, and always contemporaneous. Its message "is essentially religious."[5] As the ultimate source of the basic doctrines of Christianity, as well as Judaism, it intrinsically possesses the quality of permanency. In the present age of the outcalling of the Christian Church (Acts 15:14), it is the indispensable introduction to the New Testament revelation. In the millennial age to come it will be the charter manual of a reinstated Judaism, grounded in the finished work of Christ, spiritually vitalized, and fulfilling all the covenants and promises made to Israel in the blessings of the Davidic Kingdom (Isaiah 2:1-4; 60:7; Ezekiel 40-48; Zechariah 14:16-21).

Recognizing the essential uniqueness of the Old Testament

---

4 Charles F. Kent, The Origin and Permanent Value of the Old Testament (New York, 1911), p. 27.
5 H. H. Rowley, The Rediscovery of the Old Testament (Philadelphia, 1946), p. 26.

and understanding the real nature and purpose of these Ancient Oracles constitute the best preventive against contamination from the injurious and unsound theories and views which have plagued the field of Biblical introduction. As long as men are willing to take the Old Testament for what it is, and for what it has proved itself to be in history and human experience, and as long as they continue to test its teachings in the laboratory of life and to know them by their fruits, nothing can permanently endanger their position in the Christian Church or in the life of humanity. Only man's indifference, neglect, and proud unbelief can hinder the Ancient Oracles from proving themselves to be what they actually are in deed and in truth—the Word of God.

"The world has always needed God's message, but we cannot help but believe it needs it now as never before. We should do our very best to understand that message aright and to present it effectively to the men and needs of our age."[6]

Literature On the Uniqueness of the Old Testament

Ladd, G. T., *What Is The Bible?* (New York, 1888).

Mounton, R., J. Peters, A. Bruce, *The Bible As Literature* (New York, 1896).

Kent, C. F., *The Origin and Permanent Value of the Old Testament* (New York, 1912).

Peake, A. S., *The Bible, Its Origin, Its Significance, And Its Abiding Worth* (New York, 1914).

Eckman, G. E., *The Literary Primacy of the Bible* (New York, 1915).

Rice, J. A., *The Old Testament in the Life of Today* (New York, 1920).

Martin, H., *The Meaning of the Old Testament* (London, 1922).

McCaig, A., *The Grand Old Book* (London, 1923).

Sands, P. C., *Literary Genius of the Old Testament* (Oxford, 1926).

Price, W. J., *The One Book* (Philadelphia, 1928).

Sprau, G., *Literature in the Bible* (New York, 1932).

Rowley, H. H., *The Rediscovery of the Old Testament* (Philadelphia, 1946).

6 Samuel A. Cartledge, **A Conservative Introduction To The Old Testament** (Athens, Ga., 1944), p. 10.

Tasker, R. V. G., *The Old Testament in the New Testament* (Philadelphia, 1947).

Grant, R. M., *The Bible in the Church* (New York, 1948).

Goldman, S., *The Book of Books: An Introduction* (New York, 1948), pp. 1-12.

Smith, C. R., *What Is The Old Testament? An Introductory Study* (Rev. ed., London, 1949).

CHAPTER **II**

THE INSPIRATION
OF THE OLD TESTAMENT

ALTHOUGH THE DOCTRINE of the inspiration of the Bible is frequently considered as a purely theological subject and commonly omitted altogether in studies in Biblical introduction, this procedure is fraught with the utmost hazard. The reason is obvious. Since all evangelical Christian doctrines are developed from the Bible and rest upon it for authority, the correct Biblical teaching of inspiration is, as it were, "the mother and guardian of all the others."[1] A faulty view of the inspiration of Scripture is bound to produce unsound views and foster radical hypotheses.

I. THE SCRIPTURAL DEFINITION OF INSPIRATION

In defining *inspiration* in the distinctive sense in which it is employed in the Holy Scriptures it is necessary first to distinguish between revelation, inspiration and illumination.

1. The Definition of Revelation.

Revelation is the divine act of communicating to man truth which otherwise man could not know. Revelation may be oral or written. Most commonly God spoke His revelation audibly or communicated His message by supersensory impressions upon the human agent (inspiration). In rare instances He Himself wrote His revelation, as He did upon the tables of stone on Sinai in the case of the first draft of the Ten Com-

1 L. Boettner, **Studies In Theology** (Grand Rapids, 1947), p. 48.

22

mandments (Exodus 34: 28, Deuteronomy 4:13; 5:22, 10:4). Since, however, God's spoken message was usually soon written down, revelation is most generally understood to be the communication in its written form.

Man being created in God's image and endowed with capacity to commune with God, it is reasonable to expect that God would communicate Himself and His mind to man. If unfallen man, being a finite creature, needed divine revelation and instruction (Genesis 2:16, 17; 3:8), how much more fallen man, completely undone and incapacitated by sin! Hence, revelation may be defined as an act of God whereby He communicates to the mind of man truth unknown and unknowable to the mind of man unaided.

2. *The Definition of Inspiration.*

Inspiration is "a supernatural influence exerted on the sacred writers by the Spirit of God, by virtue of which their writings are given Divine trustworthiness."[2] Three factors must constantly be kept in mind in defining the doctrine of the inspiration of Scripture. First, there is the primary efficient *Cause*, the Holy Spirit, who acts upon man. Secondly, there is the subject of inspiration, man, the *agent*, upon whom the Holy Spirit acts directly. Finally, there is the *result* of inspiration, *a written revelation once for all given and thoroughly accredited*, attested by miracle and fulfilled prophecy.[3]

It is manifest that this method of an objective, once-for-all revelation is far superior to an immediate revelation to each person, which would interfere with human free-will, involve endless repetition and open the way for contradiction and imposture. It is, moreover, demonstrably more certain, satisfactory and permanent than oral tradition. Such a record or report of revelation, inerrant and thoroughly accredited, as the Bible is, is one of God's greatest benefits to man and the

---

2 B. B. Warfield, "Inspiration," **International Standard Bible Encyclopedia,** p. 1473.

3 Cf. John E. Steinmueller, **Companion To Scripture Studies** (New York, 1941), Vol. I, pp. 5, 14.

most priceless heritage of the human race. Yet this gift is not at all incommensurate with the vast importance of the subject of revelation.

3. The Definition of Illumination.

Illumination is that influence or ministry of the Holy Spirit which enables all who are in right relation with God to understand the objective written revelation.

4. The Contrast Between Revelation, Inspiration and Illumination.

Revelation comprehends God *giving* truth. Inspiration embraces man, under divine control, accurately *receiving* the truth thus given. Revelation on God's part involves the *origin* of truth; inspiration on man's part deals with the inerrant reduction of that truth into writing under the influence of the Holy Spirit. In brief, inspiration is help from God to keep the report of divine revelation free from error.

Both revelation and inspiration, which concern the origin and accurate reception and recording of the divine message, may be clearly distinguished from illumination, in that the last named "is promised to all believers; that it admits of degrees, since it increases or decreases; that it depends not on sovereign choice but rather on personal adjustment to the Spirit of God, and without it none is ever able to come to personal salvation (I Corinthians 2:14), or the knowledge of God's revealed truth."[4]

Revelation, as it concerns the Holy Scriptures, had a specific time period and involved the inspiration of certain sovereignly chosen individuals as the recipients of the revelation. Both of these divine operations have ceased, whereas illumination is continuously operative in behalf of all who qualify for this ministry of the Holy Spirit.

In summary, it may be said, revelation involves *origin,*

4 Lewis Sperry Chafer, Systematic Theology, (Dallas, 1947), Vol. I, p. 51.

inspiration relates to *reception* and *recording* and illumination concerns *understanding* or *comprehension* of the written objective revelation.

II. The Scriptural Doctrine of Inspiration

1. The Fact of the Inspiration of the Old Testament.

a. The Fact of the Inspiration of the Old Testament Stated (II Timothy 3:16, 17).

"All scripture is given by inspiration of God, and is profitable for doctrine, for reproof, for correction, for instruction in righteousness: that the man of God may be perfect, thoroughly furnished unto all good works" (II Timothy 3:16, 17, A.V.). This pivotal passage in the plainest possible terms teaches five great truths: first, the plenary inspiration of the Bible—"all"; secondly, the plenary inspiration specifically of the Old Testament (later when the Sacred Canon was completed, the New Testament also) "all scripture"; thirdly, the divine authorship of Scripture—"given by inspiration of God" ("God-breathed"); fourthly, the supreme value of all Scripture to the spiritual life because of its inspiration and consequent authority—"profitable for doctrine, for reproof, for correction, for instruction in righteousness"; fifthly, the holy purpose of Scripture, "that the man of God may be perfect (complete), thoroughly furnished unto all good works."

Two possible translations are commonly made of verse 16. The first, "All scripture is given by inspiration of God" ("God-breathed," theopneustos) "and is profitable" (Athanius, Chrysostom, Gregory of Nyssa, Calvin, Conybeare, A.V. and others). The second, "Every scripture inspired of God is also profitable" (Origen, Theodoret, Grotius, Erasmus, Vulgate, Luther, R.V., Weymouth). For a number of reasons the *second* rendering is decisively to be rejected. It is *exegetically weak and meaningless*. One does not have to be told that "every scripture inspired of God is profitable." That such is the case is obvious. It is *syntactically objectionable*. The normal easy rendering of the Greek requires the first translation, as is proved by the Revised Version's rendering the same construction (a subject and two predicate adjectives joined by a co-ordinate conjunction) in Hebrews 4:12, 13, I Corinthians 11:30 and II Corinthians 10:10. It is *critically precarious.* The Greek Fathers, adept at the language, did not adopt it. Several prominent members of the Revision Committee (1881-1885) including Archbishop Trench, Bishop Moberley, Bishop Wordsworth, Dr. Tregelles and others opposed it and refused responsibility for its insertion in the Revised Version. It is condemned by many modern scholars, even by rationalists and liberalists. Finally, it is *doctrinally dangerous.* It suggests a subtle and erroneous notion that some Scripture may not be inspired, hence, not profitable, thus privileging human judgment and reason to decide what is and what is not Scripture. It permits unsound theological views, such as those of Barthianism and Neo-orthodoxy, that the Bible contains the Word of God, but not all that is in the Bible is necessarily the inspired Word of God.

Thus, what the Apostle says is, "All Scripture is *God-breathed* and is profitable." Moreover, he is saying not so much that it is divinely "breathed in" (*inspirare*), as B. B. Warfield notes, but "divinely breathed-out."[5] The "breath of God" in Scripture is the symbol of His almighty power, the bearer of His omnipotent Word (Psalm 33:6). Accordingly, the statement that "all scripture" is the product of the divine breath ("God-breathed") is as emphatic a declaration of a specifically divine operation as it is possible to make.

b. The Fact of the Inspiration of the Old Testament Implied.

Although the Old Testament nowhere explicitly states that it is inspired, that it is, is everywhere assumed and most definitely implied. In fact, the cumulative evidence for inspiration is incontrovertible.

5 Op. cit., p. 1474; **Revelation and Inspiration,** p. 280.

(1) *The Sacred Authors Were Prophets or Speakers of God's Word in the Highest Sense of the Term.*

"But the prophet, which shall presume to speak a word in my name, which I have not commanded him to speak, or that shall speak in the name of other gods, even that prophet shall die" (Deuteronomy 18:20). Concerning Aaron, Moses' mouthpiece, Jehovah said, "And thou shalt speak unto him, and put words in his mouth: and I will be with thy mouth, and with his mouth, and will teach you what ye shall do. And he shall be thy spokesman unto the people: and he shall be, even he shall be to thee instead of a mouth, and thou shalt be to him instead of God" (Exodus 4:15, 16). "And the Lord said unto Moses, See, I have made thee a god to Pharaoh: and Aaron thy brother shall be thy prophet" (Exodus 7:1).

Continually the Old Testament appraises itself as a supernaturally inspired book in language transparently clear. Its pages are filled with such expressions as "Then the word of the Lord came . . . saying . . ." (I Kings 16:1). "Hear ye the word of the Lord: thus saith the Lord" (II Kings 7:1). "Thus said the Lord unto me . . ." (Jeremiah 13:1). "The word of the Lord came expressly unto Ezekiel . . . " (Ezekiel 1:3).

(2) *Other Prophets Spoke of Future Events and Their Predictions Have Been and are Still Being Verified.*

Moses foretold the coming of Christ, the Prophet *par excellence* (Deuteronomy 18:15-18). David (Psalm 22) and Isaiah (Isaiah 53) prophesied the sufferings, death and resurrection of the Messiah. Daniel previewed the rise of Persia, Greece and Rome (Daniel 2:37-40; 7:4-7). Jeremiah foresaw the seventy-year captivity in Babylon (Jeremiah 25:11; 29:10). All of these events transpired in due course of time precisely as predicted.

(3) *Other Prophets Had Their Messages Authenticated by Divine Power and Miracle.*

28 *Introductory Guide to the Old Testament*

Moses wrought signs and wonders in Egypt. Elijah called down fire from heaven, and withheld rain from the sky for three-and-one-half years. Elisha performed even more miracles than Elijah.

(4) *Some Had a Divine Irresistable Compulsion to Speak the Word of God Revealed to Them.*

Jeremiah complained, "Then I said, I will not make mention of him nor speak any more in his name. But his word was in mine heart as a burning fire shut up in my bones, and I was weary with forbearing, and I could not stay" (Jeremiah 20:9).

(5) *These Prophets Were Often Commanded To Write Down Their Utterances.*

More than once Moses is said to have written down what God had revealed to him. "And Moses wrote all the words of the Lord . . ." (Exodus 24:4). "And thou shalt write upon the stones all the words of this law very plainly" Deuteronomy (27:8). Isaiah (30:8), Jeremiah (30:2) and other prophets were commanded to write their messages.

2. *The Nature of the Inspiration of the Old Testament.*

"Knowing this first, that no prophecy of scripture is of any private interpretation. For the prophecy came not in old time by the will of man: but holy men of God spake as they were moved by the Holy Ghost" (II Peter 1:20, 21). This decisively important passage is as direct an assertion of the divine origin of Scripture (the Old Testament) as II Timothy 3:16, but it proceeds to deal with the question *how* the Scriptures were inspired. The terms "prophecy of scripture" and "prophecy" in this passage are certainly equivalent to the word "scripture" (Scripture in a general sense, particularly the Old Testament) as in II Timothy 3:16, and can scarcely refer to mere predictive portions of the Bible.

First, these verses declare *how* the Bible (the Old Testament) did *not* originate. It is not of "private interpretation," that is, it is neither the result of human research nor the product of the writer's own thought. It did not "come into being by the will of man." Man did not purpose to write it, determine its subject matter or plan its arrangement.

Second, these verses outline *how* the ancient Scriptures *did* originate. "Men," that is, certain chosen men, "spake from God," the Source, spoke as with the voice of God, as ambassadors from God. These men spoke because they were being borne or carried along by the Holy Spirit (as a ship is propelled forward by the wind). A strong, definite operation of the Holy Spirit upon man is indicated, making the message *His, not theirs*. Hence, if it can be proved that we have the words they spoke and wrote, transmitted substantially in identical form with the autographa (and the science of textual criticism enables this to be done), then a charge of error is a charge against God, not against man, except where the supposed "error" may be due to corruption of the text in the course of millennia of transmission. Where the text has unquestionably suffered in transmission, the labors of devoted scholars are directed to its restoration through the study of ancient versions, textual variants and other linguistic and historical evidence continually being brought to light by archeology and various phases of Oriental research.

3. *Other Scriptural Proofs of the Inspiration of the Old Testament.*

a. God Spoke Through the Old Testament Prophets:

"God, who at sundry times and in divers manners spake in time past unto the fathers by the prophets, hath in these last days spoken unto us by his Son . . ." (Hebrews 1:1, 2). The reference is to the entire Old Testament period in which God is declared to have spoken through the prophets as He now has spoken in His Son, "The Prophet" *par excellence*. The truth of the inspiration of the Old Testament is inescapable from this text.

b. The Old Testament Scriptures Are Inviolable.

"Jesus answered them, Is it not written in your law, I said,

Ye are gods? If he called them gods, unto whom the word of God came, and the scripture cannot be broken: say ye of him, whom the Father hath sanctified, and sent into the world, Thou blasphemest; because I said, I am the Son of God?" (John 10:34-36). In this passage our Lord asserts the supreme authoritative trustworthiness and certain fulfilment of the Old Testament Scriptures under the general term "law." The Scripture cannot be luthenai, "annulled" or "abrogated." As the Word of God, possessing God's authority, it cannot fail. It must be fulfilled for His infinitely holy character and truthfulness are bound up with it. The indefectibility and certainty of Old Testament promise and prophecy are clearly seen in the oft-recurring expression "that it might be fulfilled" (Matthew 1:22; 2:15, 23; 8:17; 12:17, etc.). "Heaven and earth shall pass away, but my words shall not pass away" (Matthew 24:35).

c. Jesus Used the Old Testament As Authoritative.

"It is written . . ." (Matthew 4:4, 7, 10). Three times appeal was made to the authority of the Old Testament to rout the tempter. It is significant, too, that in each instance our Lord drew His citation from Deuteronomy, the book under ceaseless fire from the higher critics.

d. The Holy Spirit In the Old Testament Prophets Equipped Them For Their Ministry.

"Of which salvation the prophets have enquired and searched diligently, who prophesied of the grace that should come unto you: searching what, or what manner of time the Spirit of Christ which was in them did signify . . ." (I Peter 1:10, 11). Accordingly, it was "the Spirit of Christ" (the Holy Spirit) in the Old Testament prophets who enabled them to prophesy. This is the unvarying qualification of a prophet in the Old Testament narratives. Joshua was so filled with the Spirit for his ministry (Deuteronomy 34:9), as was David (II Samuel 23:2, Acts 1:16-20); Ezekiel (Ezekiel 2:2-7; 3:12-14 etc.); and Micah (Micah 3:8).

e. The Spirit of God Spoke Through David.

"Now these be the last words of David . . . The Spirit of the Lord spake by me, and his word was in my tongue." (II Samuel 23:1, 2). This statement, from David himself, is unequivocal as to the manner in which "the sweet psalmist of Israel" received his messages. The "Spirit of the Lord" actually spoke through him, and God put His Word in his tongue. There could not possibly be a plainer statement of divine inspiration.

4. Proof of the Inspiration of the Old Testament from Tradition.

Although sacred tradition is *not* another source of revelation in addition to the Bible as the Roman Catholic Church teaches,[6] yet the witness of the ancient Jews, the testimony of the church fathers and theologians, together with the decisions of church councils and the firm conviction of humble Spirit-taught believers in every century of the history of the Christian Church may be viewed as offering corollary proof that the Scriptures were written under a special divine influence and have God as their author.

a. The Witness of the Jews.

The Jews have always regarded the Old Testament as of divine origin. *The Writers of the Old Testament Apocrypha* recognized the canonical books of the Old Testament as inspired, God-given, and authoritative. They referred to the Sacred Oracles as "the holy books" of Scripture (I Maccabees 12:9). The Torah was specially sacred, the source of all wisdom and incorruptible light. Moses was a "holy prophet," God's mouthpiece (Wisdom 11:1; Baruch 2:28). The prophets were likewise God's spokesmen. Isaiah "saw by an excellent spirit." Jeremiah spoke "from the mouth of the Lord" (Ecclesiasticus 48:22-24; I Esdras 1:28; Baruch 2:20-24).

Philo, the Jewish Alexandrian philosopher, who died about

6 See A. A. Hodge, Outlines of Theology (New York, 1891), p. 82 for the doctrine of the Church of Rome on this point.

50 A.D., held "divine inspiration in the most absolute degree" for the Pentateuch.[7] He viewed inspiration as a sort of ecstasy, having "various degrees, the greatest of which was given to Moses."[8]

Josephus, the Jewish Palestinian historian, who died about 100 A.D., also declared himself strongly in support of the divine inspiration and authority of the Old Testament Scriptures. He says of Moses, "Whatsoever he pronounced, you would think you heard the voice of God Himself" (Antiquities IV, 8, 49). Isaiah he regarded with his countrymen as "a divine and wonderful man in speaking truth" (Antiquities X, 2, 2). To him the entire Hebrew canon was alike "sacred scriptures" (Against Apion I:6, 7, 8; II:4).

Early Rabinnical Schools admitted the divine origin of the Scriptures, but attributed revelation solely to the Torah or Pentateuch. According to some of the rabbis, God orally taught Moses everything he was to write. According to others, God gave Moses the completed Torah or dictated it to him in its entirety. According to these same rabbis, the Nebiim (prophets) and Kethubim (writings) were inspired through God's presence (Shekinah), or were written by the sacred writers from traditions handed down to them from the Mosaic period (at which time God was believed to have revealed the contents of these books to the great lawgiver). Plenary inspiration was attributed to Moses. Other sacred writers were inspired, but in lesser degree. Modern Jewish theologians have abandoned literal dictation or mechanical inspiration, but maintain that "the Spirit of God" was in the sacred writers. Biblical inspiration thus differs, they hold, from purely human inspiration.[9]

b. The Testimony Of the Christian Church.

The Christian Church throughout its entire history has consistently taught the inspiration of the Sacred Scriptures. How-

7 H. E. Ryle, **The Canon of the Old Testament** (New York, 1892), p. 148.
8 Steinmueller, **op. cit.,** p. 12.
9 Steinmueller, **op. cit.,** p. 13.

ever much the Fathers may have differed in other doctrines, they all were, with perhaps some trivial variation in detail "unanimous in this one great doctrine."[10] The early Church Fathers, Barnabas, Clement of Rome, Ignatius and Justin Martyr quote extensively from the Old Testament in such terms as to preclude all doubt that they held these Ancient Oracles to be the divinely inspired and authoritative Word of God. The same is true of Irenaeus, Origen, Tertullian, Jerome, Augustine and John Chrysostom.[11]

The *early Protestants* were particularly zealous in their doctrine of inspiration, and some went to extremes. The Helvetian Formula of Consent (1675) taught that the vowel points and accents had been revealed to the sacred writers. There is a trend in the opposite direction toward natural inspiration in modern liberalism. But the vital regenerative and purifying power of the Holy Scriptures in the lives of countless thousands of earnest believers today, and in every age since the Bible was first given to minister to man's moral and spiritual needs, is evidence of its supernatural origin, and an unanswerable argument against the sterility and spiritual bankruptcy of the higher critical views.

5. *The True Biblical Doctrine of Inspiration.*

Although nowhere in Scripture is the nature of inspiration *fully* explained—that is, the *precise modus operandi,* so to speak, yet it is possible to formulate a doctrine which accords with all the plain and sufficient Scriptural facts vouchsafed to us. This is called *verbal, plenary inspiration.* Sometimes called the "Dynamic View," this teaching, as the name suggests, concedes power sufficient for all the facts. While it maintains the superintendency of the Holy Spirit, rendering the writers of Scripture infallible in their communications of truth and inerrant in their literary productions, yet leaves

10 H. S. Miller, **General Biblical Introduction** (Houghton, N. Y., 1940), p. 62.
11 Steinmueller, **op. cit.**, p. 9.

room for the fullest play of personality, style and educational and cultural background of the individual authors.

By *verbal* inspiration is meant that in the original writings the Holy Spirit guided in the actual choice of the words used (I Corinthians 2:13). On the other hand, the human authorship is preserved to the extent that the writers' style, vocabulary and individual differences are preserved, but without the intrusion of error.

By *plenary* inspiration is signified that the accuracy, which verbal inspiration assures, is extended *to every portion* of the Bible, so that it is, as a whole and in all its constituent parts, *infallible* as to truth and *final* as to divine authority.

This is the traditional teaching of the Church and is that doctrine set forth by Christ and the apostles. This view preserves the dual authorship of Scripture (the divine and the human) in perfect balance, ascribing to each that consideration which is accorded it in the Bible.

III. INADEQUATE AND ERRONEOUS THEORIES OF BIBLICAL INSPIRATION

1. *The Mechanical or Dictational Theory.*

This hypothesis maintains that the human authors were passive instruments and unconscious penmen of the Holy Spirit. As Mains shows, this view is "distinctively neither Hebrew nor Christian" but pagan.[12] It is manifestly lopsided in that it emphasizes the divine authorship almost to the complete eclipse of the human agent, who is reduced to a mere tool or automaton. It is easily disproved. For example, had God mechanically dictated the Scriptures to men, the style and writing would be uniform. Special interests (cf. Romans 9:1-3) and idiosyncrasies of men (cf. II Peter 3:15, 16) would be ruled out. Such a varied report of the wording of the superscription over the cross, as occurs, for instance, would

12 G. Mains, **Divine Inspiration,** p. 72 f.

be impossible. "THIS IS JESUS THE KING OF THE JEWS" (Matthew 27:37); "THE KING OF THE JEWS" (Mark 15:26); "THIS IS THE KING OF THE JEWS" (Luke 23:38); "JESUS OF NAZARETH, THE KING OF THE JEWS" (John 19:19).

2. The Conceptual Theory.

The thoughts, it is contended, not the words of Holy Writ are inspired. God imparted ideas to the human author who clothed them in his own language. Even if it were possible to separate ideas from words, this contention is opposed to the clear teaching of Scripture that God's message is given in *words* (not concepts) which the Holy Spirit teaches (I Corinthians 2:13). Jesus said, "The *words* that I speak unto you, they are spirit, and they are life" (John 6:63). Apart from inspiration embracing the words of Scripture, there could be no exegetical study of the Bible. Its value and authority would be greatly impaired.

3. The Theory of Partial Inspiration.

Protagonists of this view insist that inspiration extends only to truths unknowable by human reason or research, that is, moral and spiritual doctrines and precepts. It is claimed that the Bible is not an inerrant and infallible book in its "literary, historic and scientific features."[13]

Although, it is true, Holy Scripture is not a discourse on history or science, yet as an inspired book, written wholly and entirely, and in all its parts under the superintendency of the Holy Spirit, it may be expected to be accurate where in the history of redemption, it happens to touch upon these subjects. It is impossible that error can coexist with inspiration. The two are incompatible. God, the supreme Truth, cannot utter or condone falsehood. Devout scholars have throughout the centuries expended their skill as well as their reverent faith to reconcile numerous passages, which seem at variance, and to solve disturbing problems. Phenomenal progress has

13 Mains, op. cit., p. 103 f.

been made. Numerous seeming discrepancies and difficulties have been solved by advances in linguistics, textual criticism and historical and archeological research. As a result the view that the divine writings, as they left the hands of the hagiographers, were free from all error is not a naive dogma of blind faith and religious enthusiasm, which refuses to face facts, but a rational and scientifically defensible position.

4. *Natural Inspiration.*

Like exceptional musicians, artists and poets who have produced masterpieces in the fields of music, art and literature, so in the spiritual realm, the advocates of this theory hold, there have been men of pre-eminent spiritual genius, who, in and of themselves, were able to write Holy Scripture. Contrary to the clear and uniform teaching of the Bible of the unique ministry of the Holy Spirit in Biblical Inspiration, this position admits of little more than a superlative degree of genius such as Beethoven, Titian or Shakespeare possessed.

5. *The Mystical or Illuminational Theory.*

By virtue of spiritual equipment granted to all Christians for special service, this position assumes that human authors were, in like manner, enabled to write the Scriptures. Schleiermacher helped to popularize it, and it has assumed various forms. One of its manifestations is a tendency among many people "to acknowledge from God only such Scripture as 'finds them'"[14] It is dangerous in that it fails to see the true doctrine of inspiration upon which the authority of the Bible rests, and to note that such inspiration ceased with the closing of the canon. Moreover, it offers a basis for the formation of new cults based on a supposed new authoritative revelation.

IV. THE RESULTS OF INSPIRATION

Since the Bible was brought into existence by the supernatural action of the Holy Spirit upon the sacred writers,

---

14 B. B. Warfield, Bibliotheca Sacra, 51, 623-4, 1894.

what is the result of this divine process in the product itself—the written, objective revelation, once for all given and thoroughly attested by miracle and fulfilled prophecy?

1. The Absolute Inerrancy of the Autographa.

This absolute freedom from error must be directly attributed to the original copies of the inspired writings, since inaccuracy and mistake cannot coexist with inspiration, any more than that God Himself, the supreme Truth, can speak that which is untrue. The claim of verbal plenary inspiration is made only for the original writings, however, and does not extend to the multitudinous transcriptions or to the various translations. Inerrancy applies to transcriptions (as the Massoretic Text and the Greek New Testament Text) and translations (as the Septuagint, Vulgate, Syriac, Luther's Bible etc. and the various English Versions) only insofar as they reproduce exactly the original autographic manuscripts.

It hardly need be mentioned that none of the autographa either of the Old or New Testament are known to exist at the present day. They likely perished within several generations after they were written. Copies, however, were made of them. The earliest manuscript copies of the Massoretic text go back no farther than the ninth century A.D. (except for the sensational recently discovered manuscript of Isaiah, which W. F. Albright dates around 100 B.C.).[15] Greek manuscripts of the New Testament go back to the fourth century A.D.

Mains erroneously rejects the inerrancy of the autographa as "an assumption for which probably there is no warrant in sound reason."[16] But the fact and the truth rest not upon "reason," but upon the clear revelation of the Scriptures themselves (II Timothy 3:16; II Peter 1:20, 21).

2. The Providential Preservation of Scripture With Regard to Its Substance.

[15] **Biblical Archeologist**, Vol XI, no. 2 (May, 1948), p. 22. no. 3 (September, 1948), p. 55.
[16] **Op. cit.**, p. 109.

Although inspiration does not *per se* exclude possible error from the literary transmission of the text, yet actually divine providence has faithfully preserved the Sacred Scriptures with regard to their substance. Important differences do exist, for example, between the Massoretic text and the Septuagint version. The former is demonstrably superior to the latter, due to the hand of providence manifest in the extreme veneration of the ancient Jews for the Sacred Text, resulting in their miraculously meticulous and highly accurate copying of it throughout the centuries. From about the seventh to the ninth centuries A.D. the Massoretes standardized and froze the Old Testament text, so that the Hebrew Old Testament *is* the Massoretic tradition.

Copied and recopied endlessly by hand for almost two millennia before the discovery of printing in the middle of the fifteenth century A.D. changed the situation, it was inevitable that copyists' errors should creep into the transmitted text, despite extreme precautions taken to avoid them. But owing to scholarly researches, prodigious and devout, coupled with great strides in linguistic and archeological science and progress in textual criticism in the last one hundred years, the present generation is in possession of the nearest approach to the original Scriptures that has ever thus far been possible in human history.

There is no field of research in which more consecrated, exhaustive and competent labor has been bestowed than in the effort on the part of a multitude of scholars to reproduce from all available sources the original form and expression of our Holy Scriptures. From these distributed and combined labors immensely valuable results have come. Critically important editions of the Hebrew Old Testament, indispensable to scholarly study, have appeared in the Bibles of Rudolf Kittel[17] and C. D. Ginsburg (1894 and 1926). Moreover, into

17 Rudolf Kittel, **Biblia Hebraica** (first edition 1905; second ed., 1912; **third ed., 1945**)

the hands of the ordinary reader of the Bible have been placed highly accurate and most trustworthy renderings of the original records of Divine Revelation, which, we have every reason to believe, are practically identical with the original autographs.

3. *Scriptural Inerrancy Embraces Scientific Features.*

The Bible, first and foremost a religious book, intended by God to teach moral and spiritual truth, is emphatically not a treatise on the natural sciences, or any phase of them. Having the least connection with God's plans and purposes for human salvation, natural sciences are mentioned in Scripture only in the most casual way and only insofar as they may chance to bear upon the story of creation or redemption. No pretension is made to penetrate the secrets of nature or to set forth the mysteries of the physical universe in ˙technically precise language.

Frequently employing poetical and figurative expressions and drawing pictures and similitudes from nature to illustrate spiritual truths, sacred writers were often concerned with the external appearance of natural objects and not with their essential and intrinsic character. To have encumbered themselves and their sacred narrative with the latter and to have used precisely scientific and of necessity highly technical language in their simple and "unscientific" age would have been consummate folly, understood by nobody until the rise of our modern-day scientific expert. Surely we, who believe that *God wrote* the Scriptures through human agency for the *common man* would not suspect the Omniscient One of such crass stupidity as some modern critics seemingly would, who prate about the "scientific inaccuracy" of the Bible, and act as if it were a "high-brow" book for a handful of super-intellectuals.

Moreover, is the Bible to be berated as "scientifically inaccurate" because the sacred writers employed terms which were in common use at that time, and which in many instances are still in daily idiomatic use in our own scientifically enlightened day? Is it such a scientific blunder to say the "sun rose" or the "sun set" (Ecclesiastes 1:5) or "the dew fell" (Numbers 11:9) when we all constantly say so in a day when every schoolboy knows that the sun does not rotate around the earth, but the earth rotates on its own axis and also around the sun, and that the dew does not "fall"? Are the hagiographers to be mocked as fools or commended for their common sense in delivering a popular account and accommodating themselves to the environment and intelligence of their audience?

Moreover, is the Bible to be branded as not inerrant and not infallible if God, who inspired it, saw fit to withhold revelation *in part* in a realm where natural reason and human research in time would yield vast secrets? But we say only *in part*, if that concession *must* be made, for who can deny the amazing evidences of supernatural inspiration in the purely scientific features of Scripture? One need go no farther than the account of creation in the first two chapters of Genesis for a brilliant illustration of this.[18] Or how could Job, in an age of gross ignorance concerning the size, shape and extent of the physical world around him, have written the marvelously accurate statement that God "hangeth the earth upon nothing" (Job 26:7)? Because the Bible frequently does not speak of natural phenomena scientifically or exactly, but accommodates itself to the popular way of thinking, is no reason to doubt its accuracy. Suppose God *had* chosen to write out beforehand answers to all the perplexing questions of the physical universe. Would not men then have missed the thrill of using their God-given faculties to discover them? And, at the same time, would they not have lost the thrill of the discovery itself? Might not life in that case have been unbearably dull and prosaic?

18 For a popularized, but nevertheless, valuable study of this subject see Harry Rimmer, *Modern Science and the Genesis Record* (Grand Rapids, 1946), 292 pp.

4. *Inerrancy of Scripture Extends to Its Historical and Literary Features.*

Where the Bible touches history, we may expect it to be strictly accurate. An inspired account of redemption inaccurate in its historical details would be anomalous and contradictory. Unlike the literature of other religions, the Bible does not deal in legends or myths. It speaks with concrete precision regarding geographical locations, dates, events and persons. It is, in short, objective, authentic history, clear-cut and factual, in striking contrast to the incoherent gibberish of the Koran or the fantastic mythologies of the Vedas. The utter candor of its biographical characterizations is another pre-eminent element in its historicity. It catalogues the bad as well as the good traits of its "heroes." It is thoroughly honest and realistic, furnishing abundant proof of its unfictitious character.

In no feature of its content has the Bible been subject to more hostile scrutiny than the historical. It is a lamentable fact that some scholars at great expense of labor, conduct and publish investigations into linguistic and archeological antiquities whose evident chief purpose is to find mistakes in the Ancient Oracles, and thereby to discredit and destroy their authority. Some display not only extreme hostility but the most biased unfairness. A profane book or document is accepted without hesitation, while the Scriptural Record, if it contains the slightest suspicion of error, is summarily dismissed as unreliable with little or no discussion.

When the subject of the inerrancy of the historical features of the Bible is considered in its own merits, it must be confessed that critical methods employed by modern historians in writing history are not always minutely verified in the ancient documents. The Old Testament does not aim or profess to be a scientific history of the ancient Jews. In recording events the Bible may omit some facts, important to a pure historian, but unnecessary in a specialized account of redemption. Also, strict chonological order may be neglected, abbreviated genealogies may be employed or the lengths of kings' reigns reckoned anomalously, according to some now-unknown factors. But these limitations do not make Biblical history false or lead men into error. They belong to the genius of the Bible, and are to be interpreted in the light of ancient Oriental literary practices and in the spirit and purpose of the book.

Despite the fact that numerous historical difficulties and seeming discrepancies in the Biblical text have in a most amazing manner been solved by modern archeology and linguistic research and the accuracy of the Bible vindicated in the face of critical censure, vexing problems still exist, such as the date of the Exodus from Egypt,[19] the fall of Ai (Joshua 7),[20] the presence of Philistines in Genesis (21:22, 33; 26:1f.),[21] the chronology of the kings of Judah and Israel,[22] the historicity of Darius, The Mede (Daniel 5:31)[23] and others. Further advance in archeological and philological research may be expected to shed light on these perplexing questions and perhaps offer a complete solution.

The story of how archeology in numerous instances is vindicating the Bible historically is a thrilling one. No longer, for instance, can higher critics dissolve the Hebrew patriarchs in the mists of myth and legend. Archeology furnishes concrete evidence of their historicity.[24] The famous Ras Shamra tablets discovered at Ugarit in North Syria (1929-1937), recovering a religious epic literature written in an alphabetic dialect closely allied to Hebrew and coeval with the age of Moses,

19 Jack Finegan, **Light from the Ancient Past** (Princeton, N. J., 1946), pp. 105-108.

20 Millar Burrows, **What Mean These Stones?** (New Haven, 1941), p. 272 f.

21 J. McKee Adams, Ancient Records and the Bible (Nashville, 1946), pp. 284-293.

22 Edwin R. Thiele, "The Chronology of the Kings of Judah and Israel," **Journal of Near Eastern Studies**, III, 1944, pp. 137-186; W. F. Albright, "The Chronology of the Divided Monarchy of Israel," **Bull. of Am. Schools of Or. Res.** 100, p. 16 f.

23 Burrows, op. cit., p. 277; H. H. Rowley, **Darius the Mede and the Four World Empires** in the Book of Daniel, 1934.

24 R. P. R. De Vaux, **Revue Biblique** 53, no. 3, pp. 321-328.

offer evidence that Israel's great lawgiver could have written the Pentateuch in the current *Hebrew* language of his day.

Modern archeology in resurrecting the buried history of whole nations like the Hittites,[25] and more recently the Hurrians (Biblical Horites),[26] has freed the Bible of the grave critical suspicion which rested upon it because it mentioned these peoples heretofore unknown to secular history.

A final concrete example of how archeology is clarifying ancient history and at the same time attesting the historical accuracy of the Bible is furnished by the recent discovery of the so-called Melcarth Stela of Benhadad I (I Kings 15:18) north of Aleppo in North Syria. This important monument, published in 1941 by M. Maurice Dunand,[27] offers evidence that Benhadad I, contemporary of Asa and Baasha, was identical with the so-called "Benhadad II," contemporary of Elijah and Elisha, thus solving a vexing perplexity of long standing, and clarifying the whole period from the death of Solomon about 922 B.C. to the rise of Jehu 842 B.C.[28]

LITERATURE ON THE INSPIRATION OF THE OLD TESTAMENT

Smith, H. B., *The Inspiration of the Holy Scriptures* (New York, 1855, rev. ed. Cincinnati, 1891).

Hodge, C., *Systematic Theology* (New York, 1871), Vol. I, pp. 151-186.

Haldane, R., *The Verbal Inspiration of the Scriptures Established* (Edinburgh, 1830).

Gaussen, S. R. L., *The Plenary Inspiration of the Holy Scriptures* (London, 1888) and Chicago, Moody Press, 1949.

Lee, W., *The Inspiration of the Holy Scriptures, Donellan Lecture,* 1852 (New York, 1857).

Bannerman, J., *Inspiration. The Infallible Truth and Divine Authority of the Holy Scriptures* (Edinburgh, 1865).

25 Sir Frederic Kenyon, The Bible and Archeology (New York, 1940), p. 81 f.
26 W. F. Albright, From the Stone Age to Christianity (Baltimore, 1940), pp. 109-112.
27 Bulletin du Musee de Beyrouth, Vol. III, pp. 65-76.
28 See the author's discussion, "Archeology and the Israelite-Aramaean Wars." Bibliotheca-Sacra 106 (Apr.—June 1949), pp. 178-186.

Patton, F. L., *The Inspiration of the Scriptures* (Philadelphia, 1869).

Elliott, C., *A Treatise on the Inspiration of the Holy Scriptures* (Edinburgh, 1877).

Hodge, A. A., and B. B. Warfield, *"Inspiration"*, Presbyterian Review (April 1881).

Cave, A., *The Inspiration of the Old Testament Considered Inductively* (London, 1888).

Manly, B., *The Bible Doctrine of Inspiration* (New York, 1888).

Dieckhoff, A. W., *Die Inspiration und Irrthumlosigkeit der heiligen Schrift* (Leipzig, 1891).

Rohnert, W., *Die Inspiration der heiligen Schrift und ihre Bestreiter* (Leipzig, 1889).

MacGregor, J., *The Revelation and the Record* (Edinburgh, 1893).

Urquhart, J., *The Inspiration and Accuracy of the Holy Scriptures* (London, 1895).

Burgon, J. B., *Inspiration and Interpretation* (London, 1905).

Orr, J., *Revelation and Inspiration* (London, 1910).

Mains, G. P., *Divine Inspiration* (New York, 1915).

Warfield, B. B., Revelation and Inspiration (New York, 1927).

Manley, G. R., *New Bible Handbook* (Chicago, 2nd ed. 1949).

LITERATURE ON REVELATION IN THE OLD TESTAMENT

Hengstenberg, E. W.,*The Christology of the Old Testament* (Edinburgh, 1868), IV, appendix 6, pp. 396-444.

Oehler, G. F., *Theology of the Old Testament* (Edinburgh, 1874, I, part I), reprint Zondervan, Grand Rapids (1950).

Koenig, E., *Der Offenbarungsbegriff des Alten Testamentes* (Leipzig, 1882).

Fisher, G. P., *The Nature and Method of Revelation* (New York, 1890).

Orr, J., *The Christian View of God and The World* (1893) and reprint Eerdmans (1947).

Kuyper, A., *Encyclopaedia of Sacred Theology* (New York, 1898, div. III, ch. 11).

Davidson, A. B., *Old Testament Prophecy* (Edinburgh 1903).

Burrows, M., "Authority and Revelation" in *An Outline of Biblical Theology* (Philadelphia, 1946).

Warfield, B. B., "Revelation," *Int. Standard Bible Encyclopedia*, pp. 2573-82.

Rowley, H. H., "The Revelation of God and its Corollaries" in *Rediscovery of the Old Testament* (Philadelphia, 1946).

Heinisch, P., "Divine Revelation: The Source of Old Testament Religion," in *Theology of the Old Testament,* revised edition translated by W. G. Heidt (Collegeville, Minnesota).

Chafer, L. S., *Systematic Theology* (Dallas, 1947), Vol. I, pp. 48-60.

Chapter III

THE CANON
OF THE OLD TESTAMENT

THE FACT OF THE INSPIRATION of the Old Testament is basic to the study of the canon of the Old Testament. If the testimony of Scripture is accepted, that God is the Author of the Bible and that the Holy Spirit worked upon and through human instruments to receive and to record His Word inerrantly for future generations, the decisive question was bound to arise (since many religious books were written during the Old Testament period), *what particular books enjoy divine origin, and hence are divinely authoritative?* Other important questions arose out of this question. Who was responsible for collecting the various inspired and authoritative books? Who arranged them in their present order? When was this work done?

These and similar problems dealing with the subject, the origin of the thirty-nine books of the Old Testament Scripture, accordingly, constitute a historical inquiry dealing with man's response to God's operation in giving the Sacred Oracles. But the study, although mainly concerned with man's part in the process, is not entirely so. It would be highly unreasonable to suppose that God, who deigned to reveal Himself to man and so overshadowed and worked upon man that he might receive and record the revelation inerrantly, would not continue to exert His power providentially in preserving the precious documents from destruction and in guiding in their eventual collection and arrangement as a complete and authoritative whole. This we may confidently believe He did. The result was what we now know as the Old Testament "canon," consisting of twenty-four books in the Hebrew arrangement and thirty-nine in the English order.

I. THE MEANING OF THE TERM "CANON"

1. *The Christian Usage of the Term.*

The expression, of Greek derivation kanon and possibly a loan word from Semitic (Hebrew *qaneh,* Akkadian *qanu*), originally meant a reed or measuring rod. Actively it signifies "that which measures," that is, a standard, norm or rule: passively, "that which is measured" by that standard, norm or rule. In Alexandria, Egypt, the classic Greek authors were spoken of as the *kanones,* or models of excellence. Greek Christians by the fourth century A.D. had given the word a quasi-technical religious meaning, applying it to the Bible, especially to the Jewish books. Those books which were measured by the standard or test of divine inspiration and authority and were adjudged to be "God-breathed," were included in "the canon," the term which thus came to be applied to the catalogue or list of sacred books thus distinguished and honored as normative, sacred and binding.

Athanasius, the Greek Father, about 350 A.D., was the first person known with certainty to have applied the term canon (canonized, canonical) to the Sacred Scriptures. Thereafter the concept became general both in the Greek and Latin Churches.

2. *The Jewish Concept of the Term Canon.*

It is not known how the ancient Hebrews expressed the thought of canonicity. But that the idea existed is clear from the general attitude of prophet, king, priest and people toward the Sacred Scriptures, especially the deep reverence paid to the Torah from a very early period. From the first century

A.D. and following, it is known from the Talmud that the idea of canonicity prevailed among the Jews and was expressed technically in terms of a ritualistic formula known as "defiling the hands."

Many explanations of this enigmatic phrase have been attempted. The most likely seems to be that of George Robinson Smith, namely, that the hands which had touched the "sacred" writings, that is, those which were really God-inspired, were rendered "taboo" with regard to touching anything secular, somewhat like the high priest (Leviticus 16:24) washed not only when he put on the sacred garments on the day of Atonement, but also when he took them off.[1] One thing is sure. When writings "were holy, they were said to defile the hands, which was the same as saying that they were canonical."[2]

II. The Pre-requisites for the Formation of the Old Testament Canon

1. Pre-requisites from the Divine Side.

Obviously, if a body of Ancient Scriptures later to be known as the "Old Testament" was to come into existence, disclosing the mind and purposes of God, there first had to be a willingness on the part of the Creator to reveal Himself and a need for that revelation in the creature. The fall of man (Genesis 3) created the need, and the occasion immediately furnished evidence of God's gracious purposes of redemption centering in the promised Messiah (Genesis 3:15). If the revelation was to be consummated, there had to be men, nations or some select nation, whom God could and would choose, and to whom He was willing to disclose His redemptive purposes in Christ.

Certain individuals were chosen until God called the nation Israel to be the medium of His revelation and the recipient of

1 Int. Stand. Bible Encl., p. 554.
2 Solomon Goldman, **The Book of Books: An Introduction**, p. 29.

His Holy Oracles (Romans 9:4, 5). From this nation it was necessary for God to select His human instruments and work upon them so that they might clearly receive and infallibly record His divine message. But the divine requirement could not end here. God, Who had moved in man's behalf in revelation in giving the message, and in inspiration in causing the message to be inerrantly received and recorded, must so influence and guide His people as to cause them to recognize and receive His Word, rejecting that which laid spurious claim as inspired Scripture, and neglecting none that was genuine. Without this providential interposition the canon could never have been formed. Without further divine activity manifested in miraculously preserving the Sacred Writings the canon would never have been assembled, nor would it ever have been transmitted to us through the vicissitudes of many centuries.

2. *Pre-requisites from the Human Side.*

Since canonization presupposes divine inspiration and the latter involves dual authorship (the Divine-human), authentication on the human level is essential. There must be prophets, seers, men of God, accredited instruments to whom and through whom God could reveal Himself. Holy or canonical writings were those which were known or believed to be the work of a prophet to whom and through whom God spoke.

"It has not been the case with us," says Josephus, "that all alike were allowed to record the nation's history; nor is there with us any discrepancy in the histories recorded. No, the prophets alone obtained a knowledge of the earliest and most ancient things by virtue of the inspiration which was given to them from God, and they committed to writing a clear account of all the events of their own time just as they occurred."[3]

In these remarkable words the ancient Jewish historian stresses the importance of the accredited human agent (the prophet) and asserts the accuracy of the Hebrew Scriptures,

3 Contra Apionem (I:7); H. Ryle, *The Canon of the Old Testament*, p. 161.

resting the latter upon the ground of their divine inspiration. It is also noteworthy that Josephus includes in his statement two vital elements in the standard or test of canonicity. First, is the book *divinely inspired?* Second, is the book *authenticated on the human level?* Is it written, edited or endorsed by a prophet or an accredited representative of God? These two tests involving the divine-human elements are sufficient to prove canonicity. In consequence, a book or writing passing the test and admitted as canonical or authoritative may be expected to be true, authentic, historically and linguistically accurate, attested by Jewish and Christian tradition and supported by the ancient versions and secular history.

Strictly speaking, however, there is only *one* fundamentally basic criterion for canonicity; namely, is the book *divinely inspired?* If this is true, the question of authentication on the human side is really included. God's sovereign choice and the effective operation of His Spirit upon the human instrument automatically equipped the individual and constituted him a prophet, although previously he may not have been a prophet, as in the case of Amos (Amos 7:14, 15).

The human agent of inspiration, not considering his words his own, had no pride in personal authorship, and, unless perchance led otherwise by the Holy Spirit, who "bore him on" (II Peter 1:21), readily sank his name in anonymity. Nineteen of the thirty-nine books of the Old Testament canon mention no author, at either their beginning or ending. Although Goldman is most probably wrong when he says "the superscriptions and colophons in most of the remaining books are later additions" (using anonymity among Jewish authors down into the Middle-Ages as a parallel),[4] the fact remains that the mention of the author's name is *not* an absolute necessity for canonicity, either in the Old or the New Testament.

4 Goldman, **op. cit.,** p. 28.

3. Pre-requisites from a Literary Standpoint.

Necessary to the formation of the canon was a suitable language to serve as a medium for the reception and recording of the inspired message. Such a vehicle was providentially provided for the Hebrew people in the development of a simple *alphabetic* script rather than an unwieldy and cumbersome language like *Akkadian* with literally hundreds of hard-to-be-memorized cuneiform signs and symbols representing single syllables, or a number of syllables, or worse still, whole words.

From the testimony of the Pentateuch and the witness of archeology there is every reason to believe that Hebrew was already in spoken and written use by Moses and the Israelites who came out of Egypt about 1440 B.C. (using the early date of the Exodus).[5] The sensational discovery of a simple alphabetic Semitic script closely akin to Hebrew at Ugarit on the North Syrian coast (1929-1937), called from the ancient city "Ugaritic," and belonging to the Amarna Age (late fifteenth and fourteenth centuries B.C.),[6] adds new evidence that Hebrew was available as a literary vehicle for Moses, the first inspired penman of Scripture.

Not only was the provision of a suitable language imperative for the eventual formation of the canon, but there also had to exist the art and the practice of writing. Modern archeology has furnished overwhelming evidence that writing was hoary with age by the time of Moses. Although there is not the slightest need to suppose that Moses wrote the Pentateuch (Exodus 17:14; 24:4; Numbers 33:2 etc.) in any other script than the primitive wedge or prong-shaped alphabet of early Hebrew, notwithstanding, as an adopted son of the royal family, brought up in the Egyptian court (Exodus 2:10), he was assuredly well-versed in Egyptian hieroglyphics (Acts

5 Cf. M. S. Miller and J. L. Miller, Encyclopaedia of Bible Life (New York: 1944), p. 351.
6 Cyrus Gordon, The Living Past (New York, 1941), pp. 133-135.

7:22), and in Akkadian cuneiform, the *lingua franca* at that time of all Southwestern Asia, as is proved by the famous Amarna letters.[7] Accordingly, besides Hebrew, the great law-giver of Israel *could have written* the Pentateuch in Egyptian or Akkadian, had it been necessary to do so.

For centuries Hebrew continued as the medium for the writing of Holy Scripture. Practically all of the Old Testament is recorded in this language, except for small portions in a kindred language, Aramaic (Jeremiah 10:11; Daniel 2:4-7:28; Ezra 4:8-6:18; 7:12-26).

It is sometimes still supposed that the Old Testament is merely the complete collection of the national literature of the Jews. But this is actually far from the case. In order for the canon to be formed there was needed a literature extensive enough from which a selection might be made. That there was a large literature besides the inspired Scripture is suggested by sporadic references in the canonical books to more than fifteen extra-canonical works, which have perished. For example, we read of "The book of the wars of the Lord" (Numbers 21:14); "The book of Jasher" (Joshua 10:13; II Samuel 1:18); "The book of the acts of Solomon" (I Kings 11:41); "the history of Samuel the seer," "the history of Nathan the prophet," and "the history of Gad the seer" (I Chronicles 29:29), etc. Numbers of apocryphal books were also written between the close of the Old Testament canon and New Testament times.

4. Pre-requisites from the Necessity of the Case.

The actual need for an authorized and accredited list of inspired books was a decisive factor in the final formation of the canon. The Jews, especially during the exile and later, must have keenly felt the need of *defining the limits of the divine revelation* as vouchsafed to them. With a mass of un-inspired but worthy literature clamoring for canonical recog-

7 Garrow Duncan, **New Light On Hebrew Origins** (London, 1936), p. 108.

nition, it was necessary to determine precisely which books were genuine and which were not and which were to be read in the temple or the synagogue and which were to be omitted from public reading.

The Jews must also early have sensed the importance of *completing God's objective written revelation* to them. As Christians later recognized the whole Bible as a unity, in a real sense one book, with one theme, God's redemption of man, and recognized that God's revelation was incomplete until all the canonical books were collected and arranged in proper order, so the Jews evidently sensed in their Scriptures a unity or whole, at least as far as the Old Testament revelation extended, and were anxious to complete it.

In times of national calamity and persecution the Hebrew people of necessity were impressed with the need for a canon *to insure the preservation and defense of their Holy Books.* The fall of Samaria and the Northern Kingdom (722 B.C.), the destruction of Jerusalem and the Temple by the Babylonians (587 B.C.), the cruel persecutions under Antiochus Epiphanes (168 B.C.), when copies of the Sacred Scriptures were ruthlessly destroyed, all these and similar catastrophes made it mandatory for the Jews to know what books were "sacred" in order to defend and preserve them. Later in doctrinal collision with Christians, a precise delimitation of the Jewish canon was indispensable in an attempted defense of the foundations of Judaism against the superior claims of Christianity and the full divine revelation of Christ in the New Testament.

III. THE OLD TESTAMENT CANON AND THE THREE-FOLD HEBREW DIVISION

   1. Description of the Three-fold Division.
      a. The Twenty-Four Book Division.

The standard or Massoretic text of the Hebrew Old Testament contains twenty-four books, beginning with Genesis and ending with II Chronicles. The arrangement is such that there are only twenty-four books instead of thirty-nine as in our Protestant canon, but the subject matter is exactly the same. In other words the Old Testament canon of Protestantism is *identical* with that of the ancient Jews. The only variation is in the *order* and *division* of the books. In these matters the Protestant canon of the Old Testament has been influenced by the Septuagint, the translation of the Old Testament into Greek made about 250-160 B.C.

The Greek version divides the books of Samuel, Kings, Chronicles and Ezra-Nehemiah each into two (making eight, instead of four). The Twelve Minor Prophets are divided into twelve, instead of being counted as one. This totals fifteen additional books, explaining the thirty-nine. It is to be noted that *no new material* was added. Modern Hebrew Bibles from the year 1517 likewise have the books divided into thirty-nine, but the three-fold division, including the arrangement of the books, is the same as the ancient order. Genesis opens the canon. II Chronicles closes it.

The twenty-four book division is as follows:

First: *The Law* (5 books)
   Genesis, Exodus, Leviticus, Numbers, Deuteronomy
Second: *The Prophets* (8 books)
   1. The Former Prophets (4 books)
      Joshua, Judges, Samuel, Kings
   2. The Latter Prophets (4 books)
      (1) Major (3 books)
         Isaiah, Jeremiah, Ezekiel
      (2) Minor (1 book) The Twelve:
         Hosea, Joel, Amos, Obadiah, Jonah, Micah, Nahum, Habakkuk, Zephaniah, Haggai, Zechariah, Malachi
Third: *The Writings* (11 books)
   1. Poetical (3 books)
      Psalms, Proverbs, Job

2. Five Rolls (5 books)
   Song, Ruth, Lamentations, Ecclesiastes, Esther
3. Historical (3 books)
   Daniel, Ezra-Nehemiah, Chronicles
   b. The Twenty-two Book Division.

There is evidence of a twenty-two book arrangement of the ancient Hebrew Scriptures, which probably may be older than the twenty-four book plan. Josephus, a learned priest and Pharisee, whose career extended over the latter half of the first century A.D., places the number at twenty-two.[8] He apparently combined Ruth with Judges and Lamentations with Jeremiah.[9] Origen was the first to point out that this number was also that of the letters in the Hebrew alphabet,[10] and he was followed by Athanasius, Gregory of Nanzianus, Hilary of Poitiers and Epiphanius, as well as Jerome.[11]

There is reason to believe, despite Ryle's rejection of the twenty-two book tradition,[12] that Ruth was joined to Judges and Lamentations to Jeremiah in the second, instead of the third division of the Hebrew Scriptures, and that they were transferred to the Hagiographa after the second century A.D., because they were employed for liturgical reasons on special feast days.

c. Facts Concerning the Three-fold Division.

The Law (Torah) is identical with our Pentateuch. The Prophets (Nebhiim) are called "former" and "latter," probably in relation to the time period covered by each. The "Minor Prophets" are not inferior in quality or authority, but are shorter than the "Major Prophets," and therefore were grouped into one book. These eight books are called "Prophets" because they were written by men who had the prophetic gift

8 Contra Apionem, I:8; W. H. Green, **Old Testament Canon and Philology** (Princeton, 1889), p. 12.
9 Max I. Margolis, **The Hebrew Scriptures in the Making**, p. 24.
10 Ap. Eusebius, **Ecclesiastical History** VI: 25; Ryle, op. cit., p. 286 f.
11 **Prologus Galeatus**, cf. Ryle, op. cit., p. 287 f.
12 Ryle, op. cit., 220 f.

(inspiration) as well as the prophetic office (the official status of a prophet).

The Writings (Kethubhim) are mixed in character, and are thus grouped because the writers had the prophetic gift, but *not* the prophetic office (e.g. David, Solomon, Daniel and Ezra). Among the poetical books, Psalms, standing first, probably gave the popular name, "The Psalms" (Luke 24:44), to the whole third division. It is possible, though, that Jesus used the terminology in special reference to the Psalms only, as containing notable Messianic prophecies.

The Rolls (Megilloth) were grouped by themselves, and were so named because they were written each on a separate scroll to facilitate reading at the Hebrew feasts. The Song was read at Passover. Ruth was read at Pentecost, Ecclesiastes at Tabernacles, Esther at Purim and Lamentations on the Anniversary of the Destruction of Jerusalem.

The third section of the third division is unclassified as to subject matter, but it is mostly historical. Daniel is partly history and partly prophecy. Ezra-Nehemiah is history. Chronicles (*Paralipomenon,* "the remainder" in the Septuagint) is so named as though it supplemented the history recounted in Samuel and Kings.

2. *Determining Principle of the Three-fold Division.*

The closing and the ratification of the Hebrew canon are involved in considerable obscurity. Tradition, which is probably correct, attributes these notable achievements to the Men of The Great Assembly, a council organized during the generation which followed the foundation of the Second Temple (520 B.C.), and consisting of notables such as Ezra and Nehemiah. However, the history of this body, which is thought to have continued as a governing agency among the returned Jews until the time of Simon The Just (high priest around

300 B.C.) when it gave way to the Sanhedrin, is veiled in obscurity.[13]

Philo, Josephus and the New Testament, three important contemporary sources lying on the periphery of Jewish tradition, know the Hebrew Scriptures in their three-fold division, but none of them gives decisive information regarding the determining principle of the three-fold division. Various theories, however, have been offered to account for the arrangement.

a. The Division Represents Three Degrees of Inspiration.

The highest represents Moses, who, in the Pentateuch, spoke directly from God. The next highest embraces the prophets, who possessed the "Spirit of prophecy." The third comprises writers enjoying only the least degree of inspiration by the Holy Spirit. The notion of degrees of inspiration as the basis of the tripartite arrangement of the Hebrew canon was held notably by Maimonides and the rabbins of the Middle Ages.

The theory is untenable. Throughout the Bible, especially in the New Testament, the prophets enjoy equal inspiration and authority with Moses, and the other writers with the prophets. "All Scripture is God-breathed" (II Timothy 3:16; cf. John 1:45, Luke 24:27, 44). The Scripture also clearly intimates that the "Spirit of prophecy" is the Holy Spirit.

b. The Division Is Based on Differences In Material Content.

At first blush this theory seems to offer the key to the correct explanation. For example, the law stands by itself in the first section. The prophets, containing history and prediction, come in the second category. The writings, largely containing poetry, are arranged in the third division. But in the third section there are also history (Ezra-Nehemiah,

13 Cf. S. R. Driver, **An Introduction to the Literature of the Old Testament** (Edinburgh, 9th. ed., 1913), p. vii f. for a critical evaluation of the "Great Assembly."

Chronicles) and prophecy (Daniel). Lamentations (poetry) and Ruth (history) were doubtless originally in the second section. Moreover, large sections of Isaiah and the other Major and Minor Prophets are found to be poetry also, while extensive prophecy occurs in the Torah. Accordingly, the hypothesis of differences in subject matter as an explanation of the three-fold order is unsatisfactory.

c. The Division Is Due to Different Stages or Time-periods of Canonization.

This is the modern critical hypothesis. The process of canonization was gradual and extended over centuries, rather than confined to one man, or one set of men in one age. Diversity of opinion prevails in the details of dating, but the general idea is that *the Law* was first canonized before 432 B.C.[14] in Nehemiah's time, *the prophets* considerably later (300-200 B.C.)[15] and *the writings* last of all (160-105 B.C.),[16] being finally ratified with the completed canon in 90 A.D. at the council of Jamnia.[17]

This theory is an attempted explanation of the critics to account for the position of some books in the third section, which seemingly ought to belong in the second section. It is held that the second division was already closed before they were added, as in some cases (e.g. Daniel), before they were written.

Since, as Driver concludes, the age and authorship of the Old Testament books "can be determined (so far as this is possible) only upon the basis of the internal evidence supplied by the books themselves . . . no external evidence worthy of credence exists,"[18] it is not necessary to resort to the highly tenuous critical hypothesis. The problems created by the internal evidence can be explained otherwise more satis-

14 Ryle, op. cit., p. 93.
15 Ryle, op. cit., p. 113.
16 Ryle, op. cit., p. 178.
17 Robert Pfeiffer, Introduction to the Old Testament (New York, 1941), p. 64.
18 Driver, op cit., p. xi.

factorily, and without doing violence to the Scriptural teaching of inspiration, as the chronological hypothesis does.

d. The Division Is Determined By the Official Position or Status of the Writers.

This is the conservative (and we believe) the correct view. The Old Testament books were written with the definite purpose of being held sacred and divinely authoritative. Therefore, they possessed the stamp of canonicity from the moment of their appearance. The three-fold division is due to the official position and status of the writers and not to degrees of inspiration, differences of content or chronology.[19] This view is the simplest and most satisfactory of all, adequately accounts for all the facts, and is in agreement with the doctrine of plenary verbal inspiration as set forth in the Scriptures.

IV. THE CRITICAL VIEW OF THE GRADUAL DEVELOPMENT OF THE HEBREW CANON REVIEWED AND REFUTED

1. The First Claim: The Hebrew Canon First Consisted of the Pentateuch, and That Alone.

Critics admit that this is "nowhere directly affirmed," but insist that it "is implied by all the converging indirect evidence of which we can make use."[20]

a. It is Implied, It is Asserted, in the Earliest Reference to the Hebrew Canon in the Prologue to Ecclesiasticus (132 B.C.).

"The Law" is mentioned separately as a *distinct* group from "the prophets" and "the other writings." The phraseology is "my grandfather, Jesus, having much given himself to the reading of the Law and the Prophets, and the other books of our Fathers . . . gained great familiarity therein . . ." In the same context the tripartite division of the canon is referred to as "the Law itself, and the Prophets, and the rest of the books."

19 W. H. Green, General Introduction to the Old Testament (The Canon), p. 80 f.
20 Ryle, op. cit., p. 89.

Reply:

This is a valid argument that the prophets were by that time (132 B.C.) a recognized division of the Old Testament canon in distinction to the law, but it is not a sound argument that the prophets were necessarily canonized later than the law nor that the writings ("the other books") were canonized still later than the prophets. W. H. Green's words are to the point: "It has been alleged that the third division was then only in the process of formation, and did not yet contain all the books which were subsequently added to it. But the terms in which it is described are as definite and explicit as those applied to the other two divisions. There is no more reason to regard it as open to later additions than there is in the case of the law and the prophets. That it did not receive as equally descriptive designation is due to the somewhat miscellaneous character of its contents. The designations here used correspond precisely to those of later times—law, prophets, and k'thubhim (writings) or hagiographa (sacred writings)."[21]

b. It is Implied, the Critics Contend, in the Exceptional Reverence Paid to the Law of Moses in the Post-Exilic Writings.

The compiler of the Chronicles and Ezra-Nehemiah assumes the authority of the law in its finished form throughout the post-exilic history he narrates. Malachi (4:4) appeals to the law of Moses as the accredited standard of doctrine for all Israel.

Reply:

There is obvious reason for emphasis upon the law of Moses after the exile. The whole calamity of the fall of the Northern Kingdom (II Kings 17:13-41) and the later captivity of Judah are repeatedly traced to disobedience to the Law and the prophets, which are joined together as alike binding upon

21 Op. cit., pp. 79, 80.

Judah and Israel (Isaiah 5:24; 30:9; Amos 2:4-6). It would be natural after the restoration to give special attention to that to which former disobedience had brought suffering and ruin. It was not that the Law of Moses had not been recognized as authoritative or canonical centuries before the exile (cf. I Kings 2:3; II Kings 10:31, 14:6; 22:8, 13; 23:3; Jeremiah 6:19; 9:13; 16:11 etc., Ezekiel 22:26 etc). It was the familiar story of wilful apostasy in the face of stern prophetic warning based upon the authority of the Mosaic law.

It is a subtle error of modern criticism to identify the "book of the law," which Josiah bound the people to obey in 621 B.C. solely with Deuteronomy or a part of Deuteronomy, and to trace the beginning of Old Testament canonization from this episode, culminating in the canonization of the whole Pentateuch by Ezra (c. 444 B.C.). The transactions in both instances were simply the solemn recognition of a divine authority inherent in these ancient books from their first publication, in most cases, centuries before.

The very passages in the post-exilic writings recording the covenant engagements of the people to obey the law of Moses connect all the calamities that had overtaken them with their neglect of the Law and their abuse of the prophets. Compare Nehemiah (9:26-31). Zechariah does precisely the same thing (1:4; 7:7, 12), as does Malachi (3:7). These passages demonstrate that the words of the prophets were believed to have the same divine sanction as the statutes of the Mosaic law, and a similar divine penalty was meted out upon the transgression of the one as of the other.

The reason Ezra stresses the law of Moses is that the specific evils current in the young restored community—foreign marriages, Sabbath desecration and neglect of adequate temple worship (Nehemiah 10:29 ff.) were covered specifically and succinctly in the requirements of the law. The more general injunctions of the prophets, while in a most definite sense rooted in the Mosaic legislation, would not have been so direct and pointed.

c. It is Suggested in the Special Deference Accorded the Pentateuch in Later Times.

The Torah as the mainstay of Judaism was the object of Antiochus Ephiphanes' wrath in 168 B.C. (I Maccabees 1:57). The Pentateuch was not only the first installment of the translation of the Old Testament into Greek, but the only portion carried out with the care and precision demanded by an authoritative edition. Philo attributes to Moses and the Law the highest gift of Inspiration.

Reply:

It is true that the law is exclusively spoken of in I Maccabees as adhered to by the faithful and forsaken by the godless (1:52; 2:21, 26 f. etc.). But who, even among the critics, would be so bold as to assert on that account that there were no other books in the canon at that late date? As far as the evidence from the Septuagint is concerned, the fact of an inferior translation for all the other books (except the law) even if it could be fully proved, might rest upon any number of other factors, and not on a supposed non-canonization of the prophets or the writings. Philo's finespun theory of inspiration, like many things in later rabbinical lore, is a figment of the imagination and offers no proof at all.

d. It is Implied in the Use of the Torah in the Synagogue Service.

From the Torah alone were lessons systematically read in the public services of the synagogue. Not until later times (cf. Luke 4:17 f.) were lessons added from the prophets, and then only to supplement and illustrate the Torah.

Reply:

The synagogue lessons can readily be accounted for without resort to the critical hypothesis. The real explanation is that the readings were originally confined to the Law, not because it alone was at that time canonical, but because the divine covenant relation with Israel rested upon it and was conditioned upon its faithful observance. It would, accordingly, be natural that from the very first institution of the synagogue worship the Law should have a place in the worship.

Soon a need would be felt to enforce the Law by adding the historical-prophetical books, which record the blessings attendant upon obedience to the Law and penalty visited upon its infraction. The special use of the writings from early times is clear. In general they were less adapted to synagogue worship and were more appropriate for special occasions. The Psalms were sung in the Temple, and the five rolls were used on festal days. Selections from Job, Ezra-Nehemiah, Chronicles, Daniel and Proverbs were read throughout the entire night preceding the day of Atonement.[22]

e. It is Implied by the Subsequent Use of "The Law" to Designate the Whole Hebrew Canon.

This usage is assumed by critics to be a reminiscence of a much earlier usage, as well as a tribute to the higher esteem in which the law was held. In John 10:34 and 15:25 Jesus refers to the Psalms as "the law." In I Corinthians 14:21 the Apostle Paul alludes to Isaiah under the same designation.

Reply:

As the foundation of the whole Hebrew religious and liturgical system, it was natural for the name of the Pentateuch to be figuratively applied to the whole—a part denoting the entirety. The same figurative usage prevails in the term "the law and the prophets" (II Maccabees 15:9; Matthew 5:17; 7:12; 22:40; Luke 16:16, 29, 31; Acts 28:23; Romans 3:21). In no case must this usage be considered as a vestige of the time when first "the law," and later "the law and the prophets," composed the entire canon.

With perfect propriety all Scripture may be designated "the

22 F. Buhl, **Canon and Text of the Old Testament,** p. 15.

law" since it constitutes the revelation of God's purpose and will. The term doubtless reaches back long before the prophets wrote and it would be consonant with tradition to continue to call the inspired writings "the law" even after other inspired writings were added, which would properly not come under this category, although inspired and viewed as authoritative Scripture *at the time of their writing*.

f. The Samaritan Pentateuch Points at Least to the High Probability that Around 432 B.C. The Torah Alone was Canonical.

Why did the renegade priest, whose name was Manasseh according to Josephus (Antiquities 11:8), and who established the rival worship on Mt. Gerizim, only take the Torah? Why did he not take the prophets and the writings, had these been in the canon?[23] The critics see in this anomaly "presumptive evidence" that about 432 B.C. (cf. Nehemiah 13:28) the Torah alone was canonical among Jerusalem Jews.

Reply:

May not the mutilated canon of the Samaritans have had a similar origin with early heretical sects in the Christian Church? These groups accepted what suited their own peculiar views and particular purposes, arbitrarily rejecting the rest. This is ostensibly what the Samaritans did. It is a well-known fact that they altered Deuteronomy 27:4 to read Mount Gerizim instead of Mount Ebal, since they wanted divine sanction for building their rival temple there. If they deliberately did this, would they have hesitated to reject any part of the sacred canon which spoke approvingly of worship at Shiloh or Jerusalem?

Recognizing the force of this argument, Ryle[24] suggests the inclusion of isolated books like Joshua or Hosea, which would have been inoffensive to the purposes of the Samaritans, had these writings then enjoyed canonical authority. But would

23 Ryle, **op. cit.**, p. 93.
24 **Op. cit.**, p. 92 f.

choosing a few isolated books outside the Pentateuch have offered any advantage? Would it not rather have marred the unity and completeness, which the Pentateuch, as an important ancient entity cataloguing the foundation of the Jewish temple worship and ritual, afforded? They were thus, as Green correctly remarks, "necessarily limited to the Pentateuch irrespective of the extent of the Jewish canon at the time."[25]

Summary:

In epitomizing the critical arguments at this point the conclusion is clear. There is no unanswerable argument that the Hebrew canon first consisted of the Pentateuch, and the Pentateuch alone, except as the situation existed in the Mosaic age or shortly thereafter, *before any* of the prophetic writings were composed. From a historical point of view it is accordingly entirely possible that the prophets were already canonized at the time we definitely know from external evidence that the Law was (fifth century B.C.). Indeed, the view that they were accorded divine authority long before that date is the only conclusion that is not at variance with the internal evidence of the writings themselves and that does not do violence to the Scriptural doctrine of inspiration and the testimony of the Bible as a whole.

The basic mistake of the critical theory on the subject of the determining principle of the formation of the Old Testament canon is the false pre-supposition that the Ancient Oracles were not written with the avowed purpose of being held sacred and divinely authoritative and obligatory from the start, but that in the course of centuries came to be treated with a veneration which was not at first granted them.

In some cases, it is true, it may have taken time for inspired writings to have been received and recognized as authoritative. But to postulate extended time periods, running into centuries,

25 Op. cit., p. 100.

is totally unnecessary historically, and at variance with the internal evidence and tacit claims of the Scriptures themselves.

2. *The Second Claim: The Prophets Were Not Added to the Hebrew Canon Until Between 300 and 200 B.C.*

Critics admit that the steps by which the prophets became canonical over a century after the Law "are, indeed, in great measure hidden from our view" and that the evidence is "scanty."[26] However, they insist upon the claim.

a. *It Is Implied, Say They, By the Unpopularity of the Prophets During the Hebrew Monarchy.*

As long as the prophets were not well received, it is concluded that it was improbable, if not impossible, for their utterances, and their writings to have been regarded as possessing canonical authority. Not until the power and prestige of the prophets were enhanced towards the close of the exile and during the restoration were the prophetic writings collected and subsequently canonized.

This erroneous pre-supposition loses sight of the essential character of Biblical inspiration. Inspired Scripture possesses *intrinsic* binding authority and did not have to wait for either a long or short period of time to give it this quality, nor is this quality dependent on the popularity or non-popularity of the prophet, nor on the reception or rejection of his message.

In the critical argument there is thus involved the unsound and arbitrary assumption that "the incorporation of recent or almost contemporary work in the same collection with the older prophets" would not have been approved.[27] Why should it not have been approved if it were inspired and thus possessed intrinsic authority? Why would "many years have to slip away," for instance, before the book of Malachi, written about 445 B.C., would be received as worthy of canonical status, as Ryle contends?[28]

26 Ryle, op, cit., p. 95 f.
27 Ryle, op. cit., p. 106.
28 Loc. cit.

b. It is Suggested in the Date of the Compilation of the Book of Isaiah.

Chapters 1-35 are ascribed mainly to Isaiah (1-23; 28-33). Several chapters are put much later (34, 35 in the exile; 24-27 after the exile). Accordingly, the compilation of the first part of Isaiah is placed about the period of Nehemiah (444 B.C.). Chapters 40-66 (considered non-Isaianic and late post-exilic) were added when prophetical writings were being collected, and the authorship of this section being completely forgotten, they were appended to Isaiah's prophecies.

Reply:

Only the exigencies of the critical hypothesis (and not the internal evidence of the book itself considered as the genuine work of Isaiah) demand a long interval to attempt to offer some rational explanation for the unaccountable oblivion of the so-called "deutero-Isaiah." But the problem created by the critics still remains unanswerable. How could so eminent a prophet, writing such magnificent poems, flourishing, we are told, near the end of the exile, who so brilliantly stirred the imagination and zeal of the exiles, be so completely and incredibly forgotten that he was confounded with another, who lived at a different time and under entirely different circumstances?

c. It is Implied in the Date of the Composition of the Book of Daniel.

Wildeboer asserts the critical position succinctly: "At what time the division of the prophets was closed we are not informed. But on account of Daniel 9:2, whose author, living about 165 B.C., seems to know 'the books' as a collection with definite limits, and because the Book of Daniel itself was unable to obtain a place in the second section, we fix the *terminus ad quem* about 200 B.C."[29]

29 G. Wildeboer, **The Origin of the Canon of the Old Testament** (1895), p. 116.

Reply:

The late date of Daniel is determined to a large extent by critical pre-suppositions in regard to miracles and prophecy and must be rejected by enlightened faith. Apart from these arbitrary assumptions there is no valid reason to reject the claim of Danielic authorship, which the book makes for itself. It is untrue that the book was unable to obtain a place in the prophetic section of the canon. Its rightful place is where it is, in the third division. It belongs there quite apart from a consideration of the question whether the second division was open or closed at the time of its canonization.

But if the book of Daniel was not written until 168 B.C. how, it may be asked, did it gain credence in such a short time as to be quoted by Mattathias (died 167 B.C.), who encouraged his sons with a stirring example of fortitude drawn from the book (I Maccabees 2:59, 60)? Or, again it may be asked, why should it be translated into Greek with other canonical books in 130 B.C. when, according to the uniform admission of the critics, this book would not have found admission to the canon at all had it not been considered to be the *genuine* work of the prophet Daniel?

Summary:

Critics, of course, have no trouble assigning 200 B.C. as the *terminus ad quem* for the canonization of the prophets. Evidence from the book of Ecclesiasticus (about 170 B.C.) proves that the author of this apocryphal work was well acquainted with both the major and minor prophets in the second division of the canon. The specific mention of "the prophets" in the prologue to the same book (about 132 B.C.) as a well-defined section of the Hebrew Scriptures after the Law, supplies clear evidence.

The *weak* link, however, in the chain of critical arguments, is the *terminus a quo*. Because of insufficient and inconclusive evidence at this point, the critical notion that the prophets did not receive canonical status until 300 B.C., or later, almost a century and a half after the Law had been so honored, is to be rejected as untenable.

3. *The Third Claim*: *The Writings Were Not Canonized Until After the Prophets About* 160-105 B.C.

The general contention is that no steps were taken toward the formation of a third division and none of the books found in it were admitted to the canon until the second division had already been closed.[30] Reasons adduced to support this theory are as follows:

a. Considerable Time Had to Elapse After Malachi for the General Conviction to Crystallize that Prophecy had Ceased and No More Prophets Were to be Expected.

Otherwise, it is contended, Ezra, Nehemiah and Chronicles would have been placed with the other historical books, such as Samuel and Kings, and Daniel would have been inserted with other prophecies in the second section, if that division had not previously been closed, when they were finally adjudged canonical.

Reply:

The classification of the Hebrew canon is not based on the character of the contents of the various books, but on the official status or position of their authors. There is no need to assume that the prophets were closed and could not be reopened to admit these books.

b. The General Freedom and Inaccuracy of the Greek Rendering of the Writings is Evidence Against Their Canonization Before 160 B.C.

Dillmann,[31] for example, maintains that the additions to Esther and Daniel in the Greek, and the recasting of Chronicles and Ezra in the apocryphal Esdras, furnish evidence that

---

30 Robertson Smith, The Old Testament in the Jewish Church (New York, 1881), p. 167. L. Bertholdt, Einleitung in das Alte und Neue Testament, 1812, p. 81.
31 A. Dillmann, Ueber die Bildung der Sammlung heiliger Schriften Alten Testaments, in the Jahrbuecher fuer Deutsche Theologie, Vol. III (1858), p. 483.

these books were not regarded as sacrosanct as the Law and the Prophets.

Reply:

Later Targumic legends connected with the Law are answer enough that canonicity is no bar to imaginative additions conforming to popular taste. It would be strange, inneed, if stories so vivid and remarkable as Esther and Daniel did not arouse popular flights of fancy and lure romantic imagination to make melodramatic additions.

The general evidence of the Septuagint has doubtless been overdone, and has been variously employed to prove a late date for the canonization of the prophets and a still later date for that of the writings. But it is a subtle fallacy to assume that canonization always insures accurate translation or precludes the free play of imaginative fancy.

c. The Evidence of the Prologue to Ecclesiasticus Is Opposed to Canonization of the Writings Before About 160 B.C.

The supposed "vagueness" with which the writer of the prologue (about 132 B.C.) refers to the third division, in this the earliest extant testimony to the tripartite arrangement of the Hebrew Scriptures, is construed by Ryle[32] as evidence for the late canonization of the writings.

Reply:

The critics are patently hard pressed and labor to weaken the force of this definite testimony to the third division of the canon. Far from an imagined "vagueness" the language is remarkably precise and is exactly what would be expected had the canon been settled for three centuries. The designation of the third division by "the rest of the books" or "the other books of the fathers" is just as unambiguous, in the light of their miscellaneous contents, as the term "the law and the prophets."

In fact, the statement in the prologue is in full agreement

32 Op. cit., p. 143.

with the witness of Josephus, who, flatly denying the critical hypothesis, states that the canon was closed in the days of Artaxerxes (465-425 B.C.) and that since that time "not a soul has ventured to add, or to remove, or to alter a syllable" of the ancient records.[33] There is no proof whatever, despite the theorizings of the critics, that, in the long interval between Malachi and the son of Sirach, the third division of the canon was still in the process of formation, much less that it was not formed till 160 B.C. or later.

Summary:

a. Evidence Is Certain that the Hebrew Canon was Complete at Least a Century Before Christ.

Although critical conjectures as to the date of the final ratification of the Hebrew canon range whole centuries apart, all the way from the Maccabees (168-63 B.C.) down to the era of the Hadrianic persecutions (117-138 A.D.),[34] there is little doubt among most critics that the three-fold arrangement was completed at least a century before the Chrisian era. I Maccabees mentions Daniel and the Psalms. The New Testament adds further evidence of the existence of the tripartite division. Luke 24:44 refers to the Old Testament in terms of "the law of Moses, and the prophets, and the psalms . . ." Names and titles ascribed by the New Testament to the Old clearly imply canonicity, such as "the scripture" (John 10:35); "the holy scriptures" (Romans 1:2); "the sacred writings" (II Timothy 3:15); "Your law" (John 10:34) and "the law and the prophets" (Matthew 7:12).

Matthew 23:35 and Luke 11:51, which refer to "the blood of Abel unto the blood of Zacharias the son of Barachias" (II Chronicles 24:20, 21), can only have meaning if the final order and arrangement of the Hebrew canon is referred to. Every Old Testament book is quoted in

33 **Contra Apionem** I:8.
34 Goldman, **op. cit.** p. 33.

the New Testament except Esther, Ecclesiastes, Ezra-Nehemiah, Obadiah, Nahum and Zephaniah. But the last three were part of "The Twelve" and were treated as parts of a whole.

Josephus,[35] as noted, gives clear evidence of the three-fold division in his day (about 90 A.D.). The councils at Jamnia (90 and 118 A.D.) finally gave official sanction to such disputed books as Ecclesiastes and Canticles, but the canon had already been established in the hearts of the faithful with an authority that could not be shaken nor confirmed by the decisions of the schools. It was not a question of official sanction creating "public opinion" but rather confirming it.[36]

b. The Claim that the Writings Were not Accorded Canonical Status Before 160 B.C. Is Unsatisfactory and Inconclusive.

c. The Claim That the Prophets Were Not Granted Canonicity Till 300 B.C. Or Later is Also Devoid of Concrete Evidence.

d. The Claim That the Hebrew Canon At First Consisted of the Pentateuch Alone Is Likewise Not Conclusively Sustained by the Evidence Adduced.

e. Accordingly, the Critical Theory of the Gradual Formation of the Hebrew Canon; Namely, That the Law Was Recognized First (Before c. 444 B.C.). The Prophets Next Between 300 and 200 B.C. and the Writings Last Between 160 and 105 B.C. is To Be Rejected As Basically Unsound and Untenable.

V. The Correct and Conservative View of the Development of the Hebrew Canon Set Forth and Defended

1. *The Old Testament Books Were Written With the Immediate Idea of Being Held Sacred and Divinely Authoritative.*

Being divinely inspired they possessed the stamp of canon-

35 **Contra Apionem** I:8.
36 Cf. George L. Robinson, **op. cit.,** p. 560.

icity from the start. The prophets were evidently conscious that they were speaking the Word of God by inspiration and divine authority, for over and over again they prefix their spoken and written messages with an authoritative, "Thus saith the Lord God" (Ezekiel 32:3) or "The word of the Lord came unto me, saying" (Ezekiel 32:1), and similar expressions.

Early in the history of Israel God began the formation of the Book which was to be the revelation of Himself to man. The Ten Commandments were inscribed on stone (Deuteronomy 10:4, 5). Moses' laws, written in a book, were placed beside the ark (Deuteronomy 31:24-26). Copies of this book were made (Deuteronomy 17:18). Samuel also wrote in a book, and laid it up before God (I Samuel 10:25). The "book of the law" in the days of Josiah was recognized as the Word of God, possessing authority and entailing punishments because of its injunctions which had been neglected (II Kings 22:8-20). The prophets wrote their inspired messages (Jeremiah 36:32; Zechariah 1:4-6). Ezra read the law publicly (Nehemiah 8:3).

Precisely when or how the entire group of Old Testament books was set apart and definitely recognized as the Word of God is veiled in obscurity. As Goldman aptly observes, "Evidently, in the eyes of the ancients, the important thing was not how and when these extraordinary events in the history of religion and civilization occurred, but only that they had occurred."[37]

Jewish tradition attributes these remarkable achievements to Ezra and the Men of The Great Assembly. But the history of that body is itself wrapped in obscurity.[38] The simplest and best view, which does not run counter to the internal evidence and claims of the Hebrew Scriptures themselves, is that as these books were written by a prophet of God, usually with an established reputation (cf. Jeremiah 36), beginning with

37 Goldman, **op. cit.,** p. 32.
38 S. R. Driver, **op. cit.,** pp vii f.

Moses, they were at the time, recognized as inspired of God, and deposited in the Tabernacle or Temple, along with the accumulating store of Holy Oracles.

Official Tabernacle or Temple copies were jealously guarded and carefully copied as new scrolls were needed. When many copies were destroyed and scattered in the fall of Jerusalem to the Babylonians, it was Ezra who restored the Scriptures as a complete group to their place in the second Temple. In the post-exilic period other copies were made from Temple copies for use in widely dispersed synagogues.

Since the writings of the prophets, as soon as they were issued, had intrinsic authority as inspired Scripture, "no formal declaration of their canonicity was needed to give them sanction."[39] God, who had divinely inspired these writings, we may reasonably believe, moved providentially in behalf of their acceptance by the faithful and godly. However, their inspiration and consequent divine authority were *inherent*, and *not* dependent on human reception or lapse of time to give them prestige, or until there were no more living prophets, or *any other factor*.

The canon does not derive its authority from the sanction of Jewish priests and leaders, or from the Christian Church.[40] *That authority is in itself.* The collection of the canon is merely the assembling into one volume of those books whose sacred character and claim have already secured general acknowledgment.

2. *This View of the Formation of the Canon, However, Is Not Simply the History of the Production of the Various Books.*

Samuel Cartledge criticizes this view as "probably entirely too simple." "There are some," he writes, "who think that each author was fully conscious of his inspiration, and that

39 Green, **op. cit.** p. 35.
40 Cf. Green, **op. cit.** p. 110, and J. D. Davis, **Pres. and Reformed Review** (April, 1902), p. 182.

when he completed his book he deposited it in the Temple and it was immediately considered a part of the sacred canon. The history of the canon, then, is simply the history of the production of the various books."[41]

This criticism, although it does not affect the correctness of this view of the formation of the canon, which fully accords with the Biblical doctrine of inspiration, does sound a necessary warning. In rejecting the tenuous and unsound pre-suppositions and unsustained conclusions involved in the complexities of the critical hypothesis, requiring centuries for the canonization of the Old Testament and the formation of the three-fold division of the Hebrew Scriptures, the opposite extreme of naive over-simplification must be guarded against.

That the authors of Old Testament Scripture were fully conscious of their inspiration has been demonstrated by the internal evidence and claims of the books themselves. This by no means necessitates that the inspired writers simply deposited their oracles in the Temple and they were *immediately* considered a part of the sacred canon. Jeremiah gives us a close-up view of how inspired Scripture often met with hostile reception and even destruction. After having prophesied for some twenty-three years, the prophet is directed to write his prophecies in a book. It evidently took a year or so to dictate them to Baruch, who read them before the people, the princes and finally the king, Jehoiakim. Despite the fact that the Word of God had profoundly impressed some of the princes, the king defiantly burned the scroll. But Jeremiah was commanded by God to rewrite the book, and the new edition had many additions (Jeremiah 36:1-32).

Thus not all the inspired utterances of a prophet were received at once by the people, and not all his inspired words were divinely directed to be written down. That which was destined for Holy Scripture was commanded to be recorded, and despite the vicissitudes of its reception, was the Word of

41 A Conservative Introduction to the Old Testament, p. 22.

God, whether received or not. Moreover, it intrinsically possessed the stamp of canonicity. In addition it was the Word of God whether it was collected with other similar writings or groups of writings, and arranged in a particular fashion or not.

Canonization of books is not to be confounded with their collection. Books were not made canonical by reason of their collection. They were collected because they were canonical, i. e., possessed of divine authority by virtue of their inspired character. In consequence, the ancient Jews had a canon of Scripture long before their holy writings were *formally arranged in the three-fold division* and as a unified whole. It is at this point the critical theory transgresses. It makes canonicity dependent upon formal collection and arrangement, and fails to see the clear distinction which must be observed between the two concepts. Canonicity is quite independent of formal collection and arrangement. Formal collection and arrangement are *not,* however, independent of canonicity. To make canonicity dependent upon formal collection and arrangement is to foist upon ancient Jewish thought an idea which was manifestly foreign to it.

3. *The Real Basis of The Tripartite Division of the Hebrew Scriptures Is the Official Position or Status of the Individual Authors.*

The books of the first division were written by Moses, the great lawgiver and founder of the Old Testament economy. The writers included in the second division are those who possessed the prophetic office (the official status and calling of a prophet) as well as the prophetic gift (the endowment of inspiration). The authors in the third category had the prophetic gift but *not* the prophetic office. They were *not official prophets*. David, Solomon, Ezra, Nehemiah, Daniel— all were inspired writers of Scripture, but none of them had the prophetic office. David and Solomon were kings. Nehemiah was a civil governor. Ezra was a scribe. Daniel was a government official. None was an official prophet, yet each possessed the prophetic gift.

This view is the simplest and most satisfactory of all. It takes care of all the facts involved. It explains why certain books are in the third division, notably Daniel, and why, for instance, the Book of Kings is in the second and Chronicles in the third.

Objections faced:

a. Why Then Is a Work by a Writer of Both the Prophetic Gift and the Prophetic Office Placed in the Third Section?

Ought not Jeremiah's Lamentations, under this view, to have been arranged under the second division? Answer: Lamentations (as well as Ruth) was frequently found in the second section, the former being appended to Jeremiah's prophecies, and the latter counted with Judges. Josephus in the first century A.D. counts twenty-two books, and certainly numbers both of these writings in the second division. A similar view was held by some of the Church Fathers. In fact there is evidence that these books were originally in the second group until the second century A.D., when, apparently for liturgical reasons, they were transferred to the third section for use in public worship and on festal occasions.

b. Why is Daniel, the Prophet, in the Third Section When He Should Apparently Be in the Second?

Daniel is not called a "prophet" (*nabi*) in the Old Testament, but a seer (*hozeh*) and a wise man (*hakam*) (cf. Ezekiel 28:3). He had the prophetic gift, but not the prophetic office like his contemporary Ezekiel. His official position was that of a statesman, a prime minister at an Oriental court. His being called a prophet in the New Testament (Matthew 24:15) is in the same sense in which David is called a prophet (Acts 2:29, 30) because of his predictions. Daniel's office and ministry were exceptional under any consideration.

c. Why Is Amos In the Second Section, When By His Own Declaration That He Was Not a Prophet, He Should Be Placed In the Third Division?

Amos relates his call to the office of a prophet (7:14, 15). He was not a prophet nor the son of a prophet before his call. But God's clear call made him what he was not before. After his divine call, he received a prophet's commission, such as Daniel did not receive.

4. *The Three-fold Division of the Old Testament Canon, Accordingly, Contains No Indications of Having Been Formed At Widely Separated Periods, Nor of Being Arranged on the Basis of Differences In Degree of Inspiration Or On the Basis of Variation In Material Content.*

Each book is precisely where it ought to be, accurately classified upon a principle all its own. Since the Old Testament canon was fixed by the ancient Jews, the only consideration of moment is, what idea did the Jews have in mind when they thus arranged the three-fold division? Their idea, whether it appeals to the critical logic of our day or not, evidently is the official status of the prophet.

The higher critical theory of a gradual development of the Hebrew canon fails in that it overlooks three important facts. First, the fact of God revealing. Second, the fact of God inspiring the human agent to receive the revelation accurately. Third, the fact of the official position or status of the recipient. Failing to take these three facts into consideration results in placing the tests of admission to the canon on the plane of mere human judgment and choice.

In summary, three steps in canonization of the Scriptures may be stated. First, divine inspiration and consequent authority which make them canonical. Second, human recognition of this inspiration and authority by providential interposition. Third, eventual collection into a canon. It must be remembered, however, that canonicity was neither dependent on human recognition or eventual collection into an arranged grouping. It was something inherent, intrinsic and vital in the writings *themselves* by virtue of their being the inspired Word of God.

LITERATURE ON THE CANON

Haevernick, H. A. C., *Introduction to the Old Testament* (Edinburgh, 1852), pp. 17-80.

Fuerst, J., *Der Kanon des Alten Testaments* (Leipzig, 1868).

Davidson, S., *Canon of the Old Testament* (London, 1876).

Reuss, E., *History of the Canon* (Edinburgh, 1891).

Smith, W. R., *The Old Testament in the Jewish Church* (Edinburgh, 1881, 2nd ed., 1892, 3rd ed., 1895).

Ryle, H. E., *The Canon of the Old Testament* (New York, 1892, 2nd ed., 1895. *Philo and Holy Scripture,* London 1895).

Beecher, J., "The Alleged Triple Canon of the Old Testament," in *Journal of Biblical Literature,* 1896, pp. 118-28.

Wildeboer, G., *The Origin of the Canon of the Old Testament* (London, 1895).

Budde, K., "Canon: Old Testament" in *Encyclopaedia Biblica* I, 1899, 647-674.

Buhl, F., *Canon and Text of the Old Testament* (Edinburgh, 1892).

Green, W. H., *Old Testament Canon and Philology* (Princeton, 1889); *General Introduction to the Old Testament: The Canon* (New York, 1898).

Hoelscher, G., *Kanonisch und Apokryph* (1905).

Lofthouse, W. F., *The Making of the Old Testament* (London, 1915).

Raven, J. H., *Old Testament Introduction* (New York, 1906), pp. 17-42.

Strack, H. L., "Canon of Scripture," *New Schaff-Herzog Encyclopaedia of Religious Knowledge,* II, 1908, pp. 388-393.

Briggs, C. A., *General Introduction to the Study of Holy Scripture* (New York, 1899).

Margolis, M. L., *The Hebrew Scriptures in the Making* (Philadelphia, 1922).

Arnold, W. R., "Observations on the Origins of Holy Scripture" in *Journal of Biblical Literature,* 42, 1923, pp. 1-21.

Robinson, H. W., *The Old Testament: Its Making and Meaning* (Nashville, 1937), pp. 188-212.

Oesterley, W. O. E., and T. H. Robinson, *An Introduction to the Books of the Old Testament* (London, 1934), pp. 1-10.

Zeitlin, S., *A Historical Study of the Canonization of the Hebrew Scriptures* (Philadelphia, 1933).

Steinmueller, J. E., *Companion to Scripture Studies,* Vol. I (New York: 1941), pp. 44-117.

Robinson, G. L., "Canon of the Old Testament," in *The International Standard Bible Encyclopedia,* Vol. I, pp. 554-563.

Pfeiffer, R., *Introduction to the Old Testament* (New York, 1941), pp. 50-70.

Cartledge, S. A., *A Conservative Introduction to the Old Testament* (Athens, Ga., 1944), pp. 22-29.

Bostrom, O. H., "The Formation and Transmission of the Old Testament" in *Old Testament Commentary* (Philadelphia, 1948), pp. 10-19.

Goldman, S., *The Book of Books: An Introduction* (New York, 1948), pp. 27-38.

Bentzen, A., *Introduction to the Old Testament, Vol. I* (Copenhagen, 1948), pp. 20-41.

Manley, G. T., and G. C. Robinson, *The New Bible Handbook* (Chicago, 2nd ed., 1949), pp. 26-39.

Chapter IV

THE APOCRYPHA
OF THE OLD TESTAMENT

Old Testament prophecy terminated with Malachi some-time during the latter half of the fifth century B.C., or slightly later. At that time revelation, in its distinctive Biblical sense of a special act of God *giving* to man truth which otherwise man could not know, and inspiration in its precise Biblical usage of a direct operation of the Holy Spirit upon the human agent enabling him to *receive* and *record* inerrantly the message of God, *definitely ceased*. For over four hundred years until the rise of the New Testament revelation with the advent of Messiah and His subsequent death, burial and resurrection, revelation and inspiration, as they pertain to the formation of the canonical Scriptures, were in abeyance.

The result of the cessation of Old Testament prophecy was the completion and precise delimitation of the Hebrew canon. Scriptures which were divinely inspired and hence the authoritative Word of God and which had been collected and venerated as such for centuries since their publication, were now put in their final form and completed arrangement.

As we have seen in our study of the Canon of the Old Testament,[1] there is no decisive evidence either external or internal that necessitates viewing the process of the recognition of the sacred and authoritative character of the books as gradual, extending over hundreds of years from the canoni-

1 See chapter III.

zation of the Law in the fifth century B.C., that of the prophets in the third and that of the writings in the second century B.C. Nor is there any valid critical reason for not assigning completed canonization to the actual period when prophecy ceased, or at most to the generation or so following.

The close of the Old Testament canon, however, did not settle all questions of doubt concerning certain books *which had been admitted* as well as certain other books, written in the general period from the close of the Old Testament canon to the opening of the New Testament revelation, which were *laying claim to admission*. These latter writings are now known as the Apocrypha.

I. The Apocrypha of the Old Testament Defined

1. *The Connotation of the Term Apocrypha.*

The word *apocrypha*, a Greek adjective in the neuter plural (from *apokruphos* "hidden, concealed"), denotes strictly "things concealed." But, almost certainly, the noun *biblia* is understood, so that the real implication of the expression is "apocryphal books" or "writings." In its *final* developed quasi-technical meaning of "non-canonical," in common use since the Protestant Reformation, the term specifically refers to the fourteen books, written (we believe) after the Old Testament canon was closed, and which, being the least remote from the canonical books, laid strongest claim to canonicity.

The Greek adjective "apocryphal" (*apokruphos*) was first employed in the classical language in the original sense of "hidden" or "concealed," then "obscure, recondite, incomprehensible."[2] Among Jews as early as the first century A.D., and probably earlier,[3] and among early Christian writers it came to be used in connection with writings as we now use the term "apocalyptic" in the sense of "esoteric" or "mysterious," intended to be understood only by the initiated.

2 Euripides, **Herc. Fur.** 1070; Xenophon, **Memorabilia** 3:5, 14.
3 **II Esdras** 14:46-48.

From the thought of "secret" or "esoteric" came a derived meaning of "spurious" or "not genuine." Jerome, who died in 420 A.D., in the *Prologus Galeatus,* or preface to his Latin Version of the Bible, uses the word Apocrypha in the sense of "non-canonical." Having translated the thirty-nine books of the Old Testament, which he numbers as twenty-two (not twenty-four) of the Hebrew canon, evidently counting Ruth with Judges and Lamentations with Jeremiah, he says: "Anything outside of these must be placed within the Apocrypha," that is, among the uncanonical books.

Jerome's strong objections against the Apocrypha and his learned and scholarly plea for the recognition of only the Hebrew canon were disregarded in the Roman Catholic Church[4] in the confusion introduced by Augustine,[5] who beclouded the term "apocrypha" in connecting it with the idea of obscurity of origin or authorship. Not until the time of the Protestant Reformation was the confusion cleared up. Bodenstein of Carlstadt, an early reformer who died in 1541, was the first modern scholar to define Apocrypha precisely as writings excluded from the canon, irrespective of whether the true authors of the books are known or not. In this clear-cut definition, the Reformers not only went back to Jerome's correct position, but in their commendable zeal for the sole authority of the canonical Scriptures in matters of faith and practice laid a sure foundation to correct the errors and abuses which had crept into Christianity through the recognition of the Apocrypha as inspired Scripture and the unscriptural arrogation of authority by the so-called "Church."

It is thus to the Reformers that we are indebted for the sound and scholarly habit of employing the term Apocrypha to designate the collection of books appended to the Old Testament, which specifically did *not* possess canonical authority. Despite the fact that among the Reformers the adjective

4 R. Pfeiffer, **Introduction to the Old Testament,** p. 69.
5 **De Civitate Dei,** XV, 23.

"apocryphal" more and more developed a disparaging sense, Protestant Bibles up to 1827 included the Apocrypha, but as one collection at the end of the canonical Old Testament containing distinctly inferior writings. But in the Eastern and Western Churches, under the influence of the Greek Septuagint and the Latin Vulgate, the books of the Apocrypha formed an integral part of the canon and were scattered throughout the Old Testament, generally placed near books with which they seemed to have affinity.

2. *The Canon of the Old Testament and the Apocrypha.*

The close of the Old Testament canon did not completely settle all questions of doubt concerning other books besides the fourteen which laid closest claim to canonicity called Apocrypha. Other classes of books came into consideration. First, there were the *Homologoumena*. These were the books which were "confessed," that is, "were undisputed" (a present passive participle in the neuter plural, from the verb *homologeo* "to confess," the noun *biblia* "books" being implied). These were the writings which were not only received as canonical without dispute from the first, but whose right to a place in the canon was not subsequently challenged. They are thirty-four in number and comprise all the Old Testament books except the five which were disputed.

The *Antilegomena* (likewise a present passive participle in the neuter plural, from the verb *antilego* "to speak against") constitute those books whose right to a place in the canon, which they enjoyed, was challenged by certain rabbis in the second century A.D. They are Canticles, Ecclesiastes, Esther, Ezekiel and Proverbs. These objections were the opinions and doubts of individual Jewish rabbis and were such as would have no weight today. They did not affect the age or genuineness of the books nor any vital test of canonicity.

The objection to Canticles was that it seemed to be a poem of purely human love. Ecclesiastes was thought to tend toward atheism and to contain Sadducaical ideas. Esther was criticized because it omits any mention of God. Ezekiel in places was supposed to contradict certain requirements of the Mosaic Law, and Proverbs was said to contain certain contradictory maxims. All five of them survived attack and remained in the canon. After the Councils at Jamnia in 90 and 118 A.D., no further questions of any consequence were raised concerning any of the books of the Hebrew canon.

The *Pseudepigrapha* ("false writings") are religious compositions written under a false or unsubstantiated claim of authorship in the general era of the birth of Christ (200 B.C. to 200 A.D.), which were pawned off upon a gullible public as the genuine works of distinguished Bible characters. Old Testament Pseudepigrapha are Jewish in origin, and those of the New Testament are of Christian provenience. They are coeval with the Apocrypha. The Old Testament writings of this class were supposedly written in Hebrew (Aramaic), but today exist only in Greek, Syriac, Latin, Ethiopic and other languages.

These books were called Apocrypha by the early Church. They are now called Apocrypha by the Roman Catholic Church, which substantially accepts our Apocrypha as canonical Scripture. Protestant scholars sometimes call them the "Wider Apocrypha," but usually Pseudepigrapha or "Apocalyptic Literature." The latter designation is particularly appropriate since they are composed largely of visions and eschatological revelations. The Pseudepigrapha bear the same relation to the Apocrypha as the apocalyptic books of Ezekiel, Daniel and Zechariah bear to the Old Testament and the Revelation bears to the New Testament.

It is questionable whether the pseudonymous authorship furnishes evidence that the writers of these apocalypses intended to deceive. They were evidently men of piety and integrity, who in times of national calamity when Judaism was threatened with extinction imagined that they could make a greater appeal to the morale of the people and command better attention in their ministry of encouragement by using the names of some eminent person as author or by employing some notable event in Jewish history as background for their purpose.

Dealing with vision and prophecy of a bright future, with Messiah's Advent, the millennium and the like, the apocalyptic literature came into existence to comfort the nation which had suffered so agonizingly under the Seleucids, particularly, under the outrages of Antiochus Epiphanes (175-164 B.C.). Although the Maccabean victories to some extent alleviated the suffering, the Roman and Herodian yoke soon followed. In these times of deep distress writers arose to comfort and inspire hope in the people, like Ezekiel had done among the exiles and Zechariah among the returned remnant.

The Pseudepigraphical literature may be generally classified as either apocalyptic, legendary poetical or didactic. The more important apocalyptic books are the Book of Enoch, The Secrets of Enoch, The Apocalypse of Baruch, The Rest of the Words of Baruch, The Assumption of Moses, The Ascension of Isaiah, The Apocalypse of Zephaniah, The Apocalypse of Esdras and the Sibylline Oracles. Of the legendary books may be mentioned The Testament of Adam, The Book of Jubilees, The Testament of The Twelve Patriarchs, The Testament of Job, The Testament of Solomon and The Book of Noah. Poetical books consist of the Psalms of Solomon and a few additions to the Psalter. Didactic discourses include The Magical Book of Moses and the Story of Achiarcharus, cupbearer to Esarhaddon, king of Persia.

The Old Testament Pseudepigrapha, not accepted as canonical by the ancient Jews nor by any branch of the Christian Church, never seriously threatened to usurp a place in the Hebrew canon. However, the case was quite different with the Apocrypha. In the Bible of the Jews at Alexandria, Egypt, during the first century A.D. it seems certain that not only was the clear-cut separation between the prophets and the writings disregarded, with a topical and chronological arrangement of the books,[6] but interspersed among them were the Apocrypha.[7] The Jews never considered these canonical, except possibly, in some circles, Ben Sira's Ecclesiasticus.

Since the Septuagint Greek Bible containing the Apocryphal books was the Old Testament of the Christian Church from the beginning, and not the Hebrew Old Testament, it was inevitable that the Apocrypha should lay eventual (though invalid) claim to canonicity. This was the case despite the fact that there were always questions and doubts about the canonicity of some or all of the books of the Apocrypha. Accordingly, the Greek Church generally accepted the Apocrypha, although Origen and Melito of Sardis[8] were fully aware that they did not appear in the Bible of the Jews and that objections were voiced against their inclusion in the canon. Notwithstanding clear evidence to the contrary, the *Council in Trullo* (692) recognized the Apocrypha as canonical, but that of Jerusalem (1672) recognized only Tobit, Judith, Ecclesiasticus and the Wisdom of Solomon.

In the West the Roman Church likewise accepted the Apocrypha. Disregarding the scholarly objections of Jerome and following the usage of Augustine and the decisions of the synods of Hippo (393) and Carthage (397), Rome adopted the books of the Hellenistic Jewish Bible, including I Esdras, Wisdom of Solomon, Ecclesiasticus, Esther (with additions), Judith, Tobit, Baruch, The Epistle of Jeremy, The Song of The Three Children, The History of Susanna and Bel and The Dragon (with III-IV Esdras and I-II Maccabees at the end). The Council of Trent (1546), confirmed by the Vatican Council (1870), declared the Apocrypha canonical, but placed III-IV Esdras and the Prayer of Manasses in an appendix at the end of the New Testament.

6 Cf. Josephus, **Against Apion** I:8.
7 Cf. Pfeiffer, op. cit., p. 68 f.
8 Eusebius, **Ecclesiastical History** 4:25, 26.

Protestantism, emphasizing a return to the sole authority of inspired Scripture, of necessity rejected the Apocrypha, accepting only the books of the Hebrew canon. Luther in his translation relegated the Apocrypha to an inferior position to Holy Scriptures and placed them at the end of the Old Testament. Early English translations included the Apocrypha, but beginning with 1629 they were omitted in some editions, and since 1827 from practically all Protestant editions of Holy Scripture.

II. The Apocrypha of the Old Testament Catalogued and Classified

1. *The Catalogue of the Old Testament Apocrypha.*

The apocryphal Books are fourteen in number and appear in the following order in the English versions:

1. I Esdras
2. II Esdras
3. Tobit
4. Judith
5. The Remainder of Esther
6. The Wisdom of Solomon
7. Ecclesiasticus
8. Baruch (with Epistle of Jeremiah)
9. The Song of The Three Children
10. The History of Susanna
11. Bel and the Dragon
12. The Prayer of Manasses
13. I Maccabees
14. II Maccabees

Of these fourteen books the Roman Catholic Church recognizes eleven as canonical (Tobit, Judith, Wisdom of Solomon, Ecclesiasticus, Baruch, I and II Maccabees) with the remaining four added to other canonical books. The Song of the Three Holy Children, The History of Susanna and Bel and The Dragon are combined with canonical Daniel. The Rest of Esther is incorporated in canonical Esther. Thus the only apocryphal books rejected by Rome are III and IV Esdras (I and II Esdras of the Protestant list) and the Prayer of Manasses (Manasseh).

2. *The Classification of the Old Testament Apocrypha.*

a. Didactic or Wisdom Literature (2 books)

(1) The Wisdom of Solomon:

Swete calls this work "the solitary survival from the wreck of the earlier works of the philosophical school at Alexandria, which culminated in Philo, the contemporary of our Lord."[9] The object of the book is to protect Hellenistic Jews against paganistic influences of surrounding ungodliness and idolatry. The anonymous writer impersonates King Solomon in the style of wisdom literature of the Old Testament.

(2) Ecclesiasticus:

Called also "The Wisdom of Jesus, Son of Sirach," this long and valuable ethical treatise contains a wide range of instruction in general morality and practical godliness, patterned after the model of Proverbs, Ecclesiastes and Job. It was written originally in Hebrew about 180 B.C., and translated into Greek by a grandson of the original author about 132 B.C. Portions of the book in the original language have been discovered, and "about two-thirds of the Hebrew is now extant."[10]

b. Historical Literature: (3 books)

(1) I Esdras:

Sometimes called the "Greek Esdras" (in distinction to II Esdras of the Septuagint, which is the canonical Ezra-Nehemiah), I Esdras consists of an independent and somewhat free version of portions of II Chronicles and Ezra-Nehemiah, broken by an extended context which has no parallel in the Hebrew Bible. Swete Calls the context of

9 Henry B. Swete, **An Introduction to the Old Testament in Greek** (Cambridge, 1902), p. 269.
10 Richard R. Ottley, **A Handbook to the Septuagint** (London, 1920), p. 144.

I Esdras 3:1-5:6 "perhaps the most interesting of the contributions made by the Greek Bible to the legendary history of the Captivity and Return."[11] Despite the unauthentic character of some of its history, it is not wholy unreliable. Josephus,[12] although not unaware of its inaccuracies, used it in preference to the Greek version of the canonical Ezra-Nehemiah, probably because of the superiority of the Greek style.

(2) I Maccabees:

Covering a period of about forty years from the accession of Antiochus Epiphanes (175 B.C.) till the death of Simon Maccabeus (135 B.C.), or a little later, this generally reliable historical narrative is of first-rate importance as a source for the inter-Biblical period and gives a full and trustworthy account of the important Maccabean Wars and the struggle for Jewish independence. The writer was doubtless a Palestinian Jew, who wrote the original in Hebrew or Aramaic, as is evidenced by the clearly Semitic title Origen gives to the book, *Sarbeth Sabanaiel* (meaning, perhaps, "The Sceptre of The Old Man Are the Sons of God")[13] and by the fact that Jerome evidently saw a copy of this Hebrew or Aramaic text,[14] which has long since disappeared. The book is now extant only in versions.

(3) II Maccabees:

The second book of Maccabees covers a part of the same period as the first (B.C. 175-160), but offers a striking contrast to it. Instead of plain and for the most part trustworthy history it presents "a partly independent but rhetorical and inaccurate and to some extent mythical panegyric of the patriotic revolt."[15]

c. Religious Romance: (2 books)

11 Swete, op. cit., p. 266.
12 Antiquities X, 4, 4-XI.
13 Ryle, Canon of the Old Testament, p. 185. Swete, op. cit., p. 277.
14 Prologus Galeatus: "Maccabaeorum primum librum Hebraicum repperi."
15 Swete, op. cit., p. 278. So Martin Luther in his Preface to II Maccabees.

(1) Tobit:

This is a tale, devoid of concrete historical value, of a rich young Israelite captive in Nineveh under Shalmaneser (eighth century B.C.) although the story itself dates perhaps not earlier than the second century B.C.[16] It was apparently written for Jewish readers in Hebrew or Aramaic. Despite the fact that it was accepted by the Church and enjoyed great popularity among Christians, the Jews of Origen's time refused to recognize its authority or even include it among their Apocrypha.[17]

(2) Judith:

Judith, a rich, beautiful and devout Jewish widow, is the heroine of this romance with a pseudo-historical background, who, at the time of the Babylonian invasion of Judah, disguised herself as a traitress, and succeeded in beguiling and slaying the Babylonian general, thus saving her city. Some national heroine's deed may have served as the foundation for the story. The historical inaccuracies have been explained in part under the hypothesis that the names throughout stand for others of a later age. For example "Nebuchadnezzar king of the Assyrians" fictitiously stands for Antiochus Epiphanes, etc. This explanation is inadequate. The narrative is apparently intended to be religious fiction. Its morality, moreover, is questionable since it teaches that the end justifies the means. "The book probably dates from Maccabean times, and was almost certainly written in Hebrew."[18]

d. Prophetic Literature: (2 books)

(1) Baruch (and the Epistle of Jeremiah):

Consisting of prayers and confessions of the Jews in exile, with promises of restoration, purportedly written by Baruch, the scribe, this imitation of Jeremiah's language and style was regarded by the Church as an intrinsic part of the book of Jeremiah, in much the same way as Susanna and Bel and The

16 Cf. Ottley, op. cit., p. 135.
17 Swete. op. cit., Origen de. orat. 14.
18 Ottley, op cit., p. 138.

Dragon were considered to be authentic parts of Daniel. Both Baruch and The Epistle appear in lists which otherwise rigorously excluded the non-canonical books.[19] However, it never was included in the Hebrew Scriptures and is unquestionably uncanonical.

(2) II Esdras:

This book, Jewish in composition, but containing Christian additions, is apocalyptic in character and describes a series of visions. It is non-extant in Greek, but the existing Latin was clearly made from the Greek original. According to Ottley "the book is supposed to have been written about A.D. 100."[20] The Revised Version contains seventy additional verses in chapter VII, which were discovered in 1875.

e. Legendary Additions: (5 books)

(1) The Prayer of Manasseh:

Supposed to be the deeply penitential prayer of Manasseh, the wicked king of Judah, when he was carried away prisoner to Babylon by the Assyrians, it was thought to follow II Chronicles 33:18, 19, which outlines Manasseh's wicked reign and his repentance. Its date is uncertain. It is usually found only among the Odes in the Septuagint, but some editions have it elsewhere.[21]

(2) The Remainder of Esther:

Composed in Greek, this writing consists of passages which were interpolated throughout the canonical Esther of the Septuagint in the form of visions, letters and prayers designed to explain supposed difficulties and to show the hand of God in the narrative.

(3) The Song of The Three Holy Children:

This, the first of three unauthentic additions to the canonical book of Daniel, was inserted after the story of the fiery furnace in chapter 3, verse 23. It contains a prayer of Azariah

19 See Swete, op. cit., p. 274.
20 Op. cit., p. 135.
21 Ottley, op. cit., p. 147.

in the furnace, an account of the miraculous deliverance, together with an ode of praise of the three.

(4) The History of Susanna:

This amplification of the book of Daniel is in the form of a religious romance, narrating how the godly wife of a wealthy Jew in Babylon is cleared of the false charges of two immoral men by the wisdom of Daniel. In the Septuagint the narrative is placed before Daniel 1 and as Daniel 13 in the Vulgate.

(5) Bel and the Dragon:

A final spurious addition to Daniel, this melodramatic tale of which Daniel is the hero, narrates the destruction of the idols, Bel and the Dragon, two objects of Babylonian worship, and Daniel's rescue from the lions.

3. *The Composition and Date of the Old Testament Apocrypha.*

a. The Authors of the Apocrypha.

The writers were evidently for the most part Alexandrian Jews, with the notable exceptions of the authors of Ecclesiasticus and I Maccabees, who were most likely native Palestinians. As far as the writers themselves are concerned, their identity is entirely unknown, except in the case of Jesus, son of Sirach, who, in the Prologue to the Greek translation made about 132 B.C., is said by his grandson, the translator, to have written Ecclesiasticus.

Old Testament apocryphal writings and to some extent the books of the Hebrew canon, illustrate the principle of anonymity prevalent among Jewish writers. Such anonymity was practiced among Jews down into the Middle Ages. No tractate of the Talmud or Midrash can be set down as a whole and exclusively to one author. For the sake of authenticity of the tradition, the rabbins were solicitous to transmit the names of the authors of individual statements, but extensive compositions were collective efforts and the authorship remained anonymous. "When we do find a work attributed to one of them," says Goldman,[22] "it is, as a rule, not a book in our sense of the term, but a compilation, and he who is mentioned as its author is not really the author but the founder of a well-known school or one of its illustrious representatives."

Although this later practice may doubtless shed light on the difficult problems connected with the authorship of some of the canonical and apocryphal books of the Old Testament, yet there is no evidence to warrant the assumption that what we know was true of Talmudic times was "true in Biblical times as well," and that in dealing with the Bible " we must expand our conception of a book to embrace not only a coherent whole, but also a mere juxtaposition of parts related and otherwise, the result of a collective effort operative over a long period of time."[23]

However, whether we are able fully to explain the reason for the prevalence of anonymity of authorship among ancient Oriental writers or not, it is interesting to note that Jewish authors were apparently not concerned in revealing their identity as authors. Like the author of Hebrews in the New Testament, but in evident contrast to Paul in his Epistles, few, indeed, of the apocryphal writers, and not a very high percentage of even the canonical writers have attached their names to their writings.

b. The Language of the Apocrypha.

The original was predominantly Greek, the *lingua franca* of the Graeco-Roman world from 300 B.C. to 300 A.D., and most of the apocryphal writings at the beginning existed in that language alone. There is clear evidence, however, that Ecclesiasticus, Judith, Tobit, part of Baruch and I Maccabees were written in Hebrew, or in part at least, in Aramaic.[24] All except II Esdras are extant in Greek.[25]

22 **The Book of Books: An Introduction,** pp. 28f.
23 Goldman, **op. cit.,** p. 29.
24 Cf. Swete, **op. cit.,** pp. 270, 272-275, 277.
25 Ottley, **op. cit.,** p. 135.

c. The Date of the Apocrypha.

This varies in critical opinion from 300 B.C. to 200 A.D. However, extreme limits may safely be placed between 200 B.C. and 100 A.D. Apparently the oldest apocryphal book is Ecclesiasticus, which in its original Hebrew form is to be dated about 170 B.C.; its Greek form about 132 B.C. It is extremely unlikely that any may be placed later than 100 A.D., though II Esdras and others may be as late as that.

Higher critics are "quite certain that by far the greater part of the Apocrypha is of later date than the Old Testament,"[26] but upon the unsound and arbitrary assumptions involved in the higher critical view of the gradual development of the Hebrew canon[27] persist in refusing to admit that *all* the Apocrypha are later than the Old Testament canonical books, and that they were written after the closing of the Hebrew canon. Canonical Daniel and many of the Psalms are erroneously placed later than Ecclesiasticus and I Esdras. Esther is placed even later than Judith by some critics.

4. The Value of the Old Testament Apocrypha.

Although they are not inspired Scripture and consequently have no claim to authority, the Apocrypha as part of the religious literature of the ancient Jews have value and importance.

a. Their Biblical Importance.

Biblically they fill in the gap between the Old and New Testaments when prophecy had ceased and inspiration was in abeyance from the time of Malachi to the appearance of John the Baptist. They, accordingly, supply a connecting link and give information covering a period of over four and one-half centuries in the history of God's covenant people. As H. H. Rowley says, "In some respects, indeed, there is a hiatus between the Old Testament and the New, and the study of the Apocrypha and of other writings that issued from Jewish

26 T. W. Davies, "Apocrypha," Int. Stand. Bible Encyclopaedia, p. 183.
27 See chapter III.

circles in the last pre-Christian centuries and the century that saw the birth of Christianity may do something to fill the gap."[28]

b. Their Religious Importance.

Religiously the Apocrypha give a clear insight into the spiritual, philosophical and intellectual life of Judaism in the important intertestamental period. They supply evidence of the practical disappearance of idolatry, the growth of staunch monotheistic convictions, Messianic hopes and more widespread beliefs in resurrection and future rewards and punishments. At the same time they shed much light upon the progress of degenerating influences, especially the sterility of a spiritually bankrupt Judaism which rejected and crucified the Messiah. They furnish historical background and perspective for understanding such spiritually effete Jewish sects as the Pharisees and Sadducees of the first century of the Christian era.

c. Their Political Importance.

Politically the Apocrypha trace the history of the Jewish State throughout an important era. The books of Maccabees, especially the first book, outline in careful and reliable detail the fierce struggle of the Jews for religious and political freedom against the tyranny of Greek heathenism. They catalogue one of the most thrilling and heroic periods in all Jewish history.

d. Their Literary Importance.

As literature the Apocrypha have had a wide influence. Despite inaccuracies, contradictions, and absurdities due to their uninspired character, they nevertheless have been widely quoted and used to enrich secular literature. Although the New Testament does not quote from them nor recognize them, or any part of them, as Holy Scripture, yet New Testament writers show acquaintance with them. Hebrews 11:34-38 evidently refers to the heroes of the Maccabean era. Being

---

28 **Rediscovery of the Old Testament**, p. 12 f.

printed in all English editions of the Bible till 1629 and in most of them until 1827,[29] it was inevitable that they should be widely read and influential in a literary way. Shakespeare and other writers show familiarity with them, and a knowledge of the Apocrypha is necessary to understand some allusions in modern literature otherwise unintelligible.[30] To I Esdras, for instance, we owe the immortal proverb: *Magna est veritas et praevalet* (4:41). *Megale he aletheia kai huperis-chuei.* The value of the Apocrypha to a complete Biblical education is becoming increasingly apparent to modern scholars and teachers.

III. THE CANONICAL CLAIMS OF THE OLD TESTAMENT APOCRYPHA REFUTED

1. Canonical Claims of the Apocrypha Based on the Two-Canon Theory Refuted.

Because the Hebrew canon contains only twenty-four books (the thirty-nine of the Protestant canon), whereas the Septuagint version contains a larger canon including the Apocrypha, consisting of fourteen additional books or parts of books, many critics have erroneously assumed that there were two independent Canons, a "smaller" Hebrew or Palestinian canon and a so-called "larger" Greek or Alexandrian canon.[31]

Another theory, although it correctly defends the original unity of the two canons because of the intimate relationship which existed between the various Jewish communities, is equally erroneous in including the apocryphal books in it, and in maintaining that these were gradually eliminated until in the first century A.D. they were totally rejected from the Palestinian canon, by certain supposedly arbitrary and "invented" criteria of the Pharisees, which shortened canon was then followed by the Jewish dispersion.[32] This is manifestly a

29 Pfeiffer, op. cit., p. 70.
30 Cf. Swete, op. cit., p. 266; Ottley, op. cit. p. 135.
31 John E. Steinmueller, A Companion to Scripture Studies, Vol. I, p. 65.
32 This is the view of Zarb, Kaulen-Hoberg, and other Catholic scholars. Cf. Steinmueller, op. cit., pp. 65 f.

groundless and weak makeshift of Roman Catholic scholarship to attempt to defend the erroneous position of the Roman Church in accepting the Apocrypha as inspired authoritative Scripture. There is not a shred of evidence that the Apocrypha were ever taken out of the Hebrew canon. They could not have been "taken out" of the canon for the simple reason "they were never put into it."[33]

The only correct view is that not a single apocryphal book ever found its way into the Hebrew canon, which alone embraces *all* inspired Scripture of the Old Testament period and which was not only always accepted by all Jews everywhere unanimously from the beginning, but also that there were never two canons, a smaller or Palestinian-Jewish canon and a so-called "larger" or Alexandrian canon. The so-called "two-canon theory" (and with it the canonical claims of the Apocrypha) must be rejected for the following reasons:

a. There is No Manuscript Evidence For It.

The Alexandrian Greek version was made about 250-150 B.C. or possibly as early as 270-170 B.C. But the earliest extant manuscripts of the Septuagint do not date earlier than the fourth century A.D., which is at least six hundred years after the translation of the Septuagint had been begun or about five hundred years after the latest date for its completion. During this extended period of a half millennium or more, it is highly probable that these apocryphal books crept into the original Hebrew canon. It must be remembered that *all* the extant Greek manuscripts which contain the Apocrypha are of *Christian* and not of Hebrew origin. All of this only proves that the Apocrypha found favor with certain Christians.

b. The Jewish Religious Point of View is Against It.

Even scholars who defend the canonical authority of the Apocrypha feel constrained to abandon the vulnerable fortress of the "two-canon theory" on the strength of "the intimate relationship which existed between the various Jewish com-

33 H. S. Miller, **General Biblical Introduction**, p. 106.

munities."[34] It is obvious that it would be most unlikely for the Jews at Alexandria to alter or enlarge the Jewish canon. Such a drastic step would not only involve the basis of their religious faith, but would inevitably occasion a rift between them and their Palestinian brethren. Such a course would be contrary to their natural desire to strengthen their relation to their homeland and maintain their orthodox status.

c. Evidence from the Earliest Apocryphal Lists Is Opposed to It.

There is a notable lack of uniformity in the earliest lists of the Apocrypha in the oldest extant manuscripts containing them, which weakens the two-canon hypothesis. None of them includes exactly the same books which the Church of Rome decreed to be canonical. For example, the Vatican manuscript (350 A.D.) contains none of the books of the Maccabees, the first and second of which are received as canonical by Rome, but it *does* contain I Esdras, which is not received as canonical by the Roman Church.[35] The Sinaitic manuscript (350 A.D.) omits Baruch, which is deemed canonical, but includes IV Maccabees considered uncanonical by Rome. The Alexandrian manuscript (450 A.D.) contains I Esdras and III and IV Maccabees considered uncanonical by Rome.[36]

d. The Witness of Philo, Josephus and the Alexandrian Jews Militates Against It.

Philo, an Alexandrian Jew, was thoroughly acquainted with both canonical and apocryphal writings, but he confines his quotations strictly to the Hebrew canon.[37] Josephus writing about A.D. 90 and intelligently expressing the conviction of the Jews of that age definitely asserts that the canon was closed in the time of Artaxerxes I Longimanus 464-423 B.C.[38] and apparently knew nothing of a larger Alexandrian canon. His

34 See above, note 32.
35 Cf. Swete, op. cit., pp. 201. f.
36 Swete, loc. cit.
37 Cf. Pfeiffer, op. cit. p. 68.
38 **Against Apion**, I:8.

employment of the Septuagint and supposed use of apocryphal material (I Esdras, I Maccabees)[39] cannot be taken as proof that these books were in an "Alexandrian canon," or that he apparently regarded them as "equally authentic with the canonical books," as Pfeiffer contends,[40] when his testimony is in line with universal Jewish tradition, contained also in IV Esdras 14:45-46 and *Baba Bathra* 14b-15a, that all canonical Scripture was in existence in the time of Ezra. It is likewise significant that Aquila's Greek version made about 128 A.D. was adopted by the Alexandrian Jews and did *not* contain the Apocrypha.

e. The Witness of the New Testament Does Not Favor It.

Despite the fact that New Testament writers quote largely from the Septuagint rather than from the Hebrew Old Testament, there is not a single clear-cut case of citation from any of the fourteen apocryphal books, eleven of which Rome receives as canonical. The most that can be said is that the New Testament writers show acquaintance with these fourteen books and perhaps allude to them indirectly, but in no case do they quote them as inspired Scripture or cite them as authority. Even C. C. Torrey, who takes great pains to ferret out apocryphal quotations or allusions, must admit regarding the New Testament, that "in general, the apocryphal scriptures were left unnoticed."[41]

Alleged quotations are all from supposed sources outside of what we now know properly as the Apocrypha and concerning which no question of canonicity ever existed. For example Matthew 27:9 is supposed (on Jerome's word) to quote a now-unknown apocryphal writing of Jeremiah (cf. Zechariah 11:12, 13). I Corinthians 2:9 and Ephesians 5:14 are supposed (according to Jerome and Epiphanius) to

39 Swete, op. cit. p. 378; H. Bloch, Die Quellen des Fl. Josephus in seiner Archaeologia (Leipzig, 1879), pp. 8 ff.
40 Op. cit., pp. 67 f.
41 The Apocryphal Literature (New Haven, 1945), p. 18.

quote from The Apocalypse of Elijah, but Torrey must confess that "we have no means of verifying this."[42]

The nearest approach to a formal citation is Jude 1:14-16, which is supposed to stem from Enoch 1:9 (cf. 5:4 and 27:2). If this is a formal quotation (which is dubious), it is unique. It is not the case of the citation of an apocryphal book at all, but, strictly speaking, a pseudepigraphical work never recognized by anyone as canonical or laying any claim to canonicity. Thus when Torrey's cases of "actual citation of apocrypha"[43] are sifted, they are found to be non-existent.

With regard to supposed New Testament allusions to the Apocrypha, all they prove, if indeed they can be proved,[44] is that New Testament authors were acquainted with these writings. It would be strange indeed if such were not the case.

f. The Witness of the Eastern Church Does Not Support It.

The oldest catalogue of the canonical books of the Old Testament now extant is the second century list of Melito, Bishop of Sardis (about 170 A.D.). Melito expressly mentions his travels into Judea to make diligent research in order to arrive at certainty upon the subject of the canon. His enumeration does not contain the least evidence of a "larger canon," nor does it contain a single apocryphal book.

That the same canon prevailed at this early date in other parts of the Eastern Church is evidenced by Justin Martyr, who studied widely and traveled and wrote extensively. He quotes freely from canonical books, but does not make use of the Apocrypha. In a controversy with Trypho, an Ephesian Jew, in which the differences between Jews and Christians were aired, there is not the slightest indication of difference in their canon. Further evidence produced by the second century is supplied by the famous Peshitta or old Syriac

42 Op. cit., p. 19.
43 Op. cit., p. 20.
44 Cf. Torrey, op. cit., pp. 20-22.

version, which *originally* contained only the canonical and none of the apocryphal books of the Old Testament.

In the third century Origen (died (254), the most learned of the Greek fathers, left a catalog of twenty-two books preserved by Eusebius in his *Ecclesiastical History* (VI:25), and like Melito, clearly follows the Hebrew canon. He gives the books which he considers canonical. At the close he adds, "And apart from these (that is, not comprising a part of the canon) are the Books of Maccabees." Origen's canon agrees precisely with the canon we possess, except that he evidently includes in the Book of Jeremiah Lamentations and "his Epistle." If by this he means an apocryphal Epistle, bearing Jeremiah's name, which appears in the Vulgate as the last chapter of the Book of Baruch, he was betrayed into the belief that this forged letter was a genuine production of the prophet, for this apocryphal letter was never in the Hebrew canon, which Origen, like Melito, professly follows.

In the fourth century the Council of Laodicea (about 363 A.D.) strictly decreed that "books not admitted into the canon, but only the canonical books of the New and Old Testaments" are to be "read in the Church."[45] Basil the Great of Cappadocia[46] agreed with Josephus and Origen that the number of Old Testament books was twenty-two. Chrysostom[47] maintained that "all the books of the Old Testament were originally written in Hebrew, as all among us confess," thereby evidencing the fact that he followed the Jewish canon.

With a few minor exceptions like Athanasius (died 365) and Cyril of Jerusalem (died 386), who added to Jeremiah "Baruch and The Epistle," all the catalogs and evidence of the first four centuries testify in favor of one and the same canon, that of the ancient Jews, and that which received the

---

45 Cf. Green, **General Introduction to the Old Testament** (Canon), p. 164.
46 Philocalia, chap. III, Bishop Cosin, **A Scholastic History of the Canon** (1672), p. 66.
47 **Homil. IV** in Gen. Cosin, **op. cit.**, p. 70.

infallible sanction of Christ and the Apostles, and which Protestants now embrace.

Despite the clear-cut evidence in the East for the Hebrew canon over against apocryphal additions, the Greek Church, that is, the Holy Orthodox Eastern Church (officially "The Holy Orthodox Catholic Apostolic Eastern Church") like the Roman Church in the West, anomalously granted a degree of ecclesiastical recognition to the Apocrypha. Its position is inconsistent, wavering between the Roman Catholic and Protestant views on the extent of the canon.

The Septuagint version containing the Apocrypha is used. The Orthodox Confession cites them as authority. They were declared canonical in the Synods of Constantinople (1638), Jaffa (1642) and Jerusalem (1672). Notwithstanding, the Church refuses to employ them as canonical, and certain writers, as the Patriarch Metrophanes (died 1640) and the Larger Catechism (1839), the most authoritative standard of the Greek-Russian Church, expressly omits these writings because "they do not exist in the Hebrew."[48]

g. The Witness of the Western Church Does Not Support It.

In the Western or Latin Church, as in the Greek or Eastern Church, the early fathers subscribed strictly to the Hebrew canon. Tertullian (160-240/250), the first of the Latin fathers whose writings have been preserved, lists twenty-four as the number of the canonical books. Hilary of Poitiers, France (305-366), and Ruffinus of Aquileia, Italy (died 410), left complete lists of twenty-two books.

Jerome (340-420) the most accomplished and learned scholar and translator of his day, pled "for the recognition of only the Hebrew canon, excluding the Apocrypha."[49] He rejected the apocryphal books in the most unequivocal terms, limiting the number to twenty-two (the thirty-nine of our

48 H. S. Miller, op. cit., p. 114.
  49 Pfeiffer, op. cit., p. 69.

Protestant canon), as Gigot, the celebrated Romanist writer, frankly admits.[50]

Augustine (354-430), Bishop of Hippo in North Africa, although a contemporary of Jerome, and himself a great thinker, showed little critical ability or precision of treatment in the matter of the canon. He set forth a list of forty-four books, including the books Rome accounts canonical, omitting Baruch, which Rome accepts, and including II Esdras (evidently the English apocryphal I Esdras), which Rome rejects. Thus Romanists and other advocates of a "larger" or "two-canon theory" claim Augustine as their champion. But they do so unwarrantedly. Overlooking the cautions, limitations and distinctions which he made, they fail to interpret his witness embodied in the decisions of the Councils of Hippo (393) and Carthage (397 and 419) over which his influence predominated, in the light of the general voice of the Church, in this and the preceding centuries.

A careful survey of Augustine's terminology reveals that he used "canonical" in a wider and less precise sense, including, along with the divinely inspired books those that were not inspired, but sanctioned and commended by the Church as profitable and edifying religious books to be read privately and publicly in the churches.[51] Since Augustine, perhaps more than any other early theologian, molded the doctrines and practices of the Church in subsequent centuries, his infelicitous lack of precision in his pronouncements upon the canon (as his unhappy ideas of the Church as an earthly kingdom helped foster the invention of a papal hierarchy) interjected confusion into the thinking of the Church, which was to find its evil fruitage in the declaration of the canonicity of the apocryphal books by the Council of Trent (1546).

h. The Witness of the Church from Augustine to the Council of Trent Does Not Favor It.

50 F. E. Gigot, **General Introduction to the Holy Scriptures,** p. 56.
51 Cf. Green, op. cit., pp. 170-173.

Augustine's list was bound to lead to results he had not intended. In succeeding centuries some followed the accurate Hebrew canon of Jerome. Others subscribed to the "larger canon" of Augustine. The tendency was engendered to break down the distinction between "inspired" and "uninspired" by placing all the books on the same level. Cassiodorus, in his Institutes (556 A.D.) and Isidore of Seville (636 A.D.) placed the two lists side by side and did not attempt to decide between them.

Gregory the Great (640) and other distinguished men in the Western Church down to the sixteenth century recorded their decisions in favor of the Hebrew canon against the Apocrypha. Especially to be noted is the learned Cardinal Ximenes, Archbishop of Toledo in Spain, who, in the preface to his Complutensian Polyglot dedicated to Pope Leo X and approved by him, states that the Old Testament books printed in Greek only (Tobit, Judith, Wisdom of Solomon, Ecclesiasticus, Baruch, Maccabees, with the additions to Esther and Daniel) were not in the canon, but were received by the Church for the edification of the people rather than for the confirmation of doctrines.

Cardinal Cajetan (died 1534), a theologian of great eminence, commended Jerome for his clear-cut distinction between canonical and non-canonical books and interpreted Augustine in the light of that distinction. In dedicating his commentary on the Historical Books of the Old Testament to pope Clement VII he speaks of the Apocrypha thus: "These are not canonical books, that is, they do not belong to the rule for confirming those things which are of faith; yet they can be called canonical, that is, belonging to the rule for the edification of believers. With this distinction what is said by Augustine and written by the Council of Carthage can be rightly apprehended."[52]

i. The Witness of the Church from the Reformation to the Present Is Against It.

The Protestant Reformation shook Rome to its foundations. Luther gave the Scriptures to the people in the vernacular. He and the Reformers called the religious world to throw off the false authority arrogated by a hierarchical church and to return to faith in the true authority of inspired Scripture. Accordingly, the Apocrypha were separated from canonical Scripture and relegated to a subordinate place between the Testaments.

The Roman Church was practically forced to render a dogmatic decision on the canon and to settle its limits. This was done at the famous Council of Trent (1546). At one of the prolonged sessions, with only fifty-three prelates present, not one of whom was a scholar distinguished for historical learning, the Decree "Sacrosancta" was passed which declared that the Old Testament, including the Apocrypha, are of God. To boot, anyone was declared anathema who would not receive them as such.

Thus Rome, disregarding history, and forgetting that she was determining what she had no inherent right to determine, but that she was merely to hand down faithfully what was delivered to her, dogmatically decreed a so-called larger or Alexandrian canon based upon an erroneous and untenable "two-canon" theory. Despite these facts the Vatican Council (1869-1870) confirmed the Decree "Sacrosancta."

The Protestant Churches have from the first been unanimous in adhering to the Hebrew canon as the canon of Christ and the apostles and the canon of the Early Church. They differed only in the matter of the esteem in which they held

52 Cf. Green op. cit., p. 177.

the Apocrypha. The Church of England (1562) followed Jerome's words, "The Church doth read . . . " the Apocrypha "for example of life and instruction of manners; but yet doth it not apply them to establish any doctrine." The view of the Westminster Confession would logically banish them from the Bible altogether, "The books commonly called Apocrypha, not being of divine inspiration, are no part of the canon of Scripture; and therefore are of no authority in the Church of God, nor to be otherwise approved and made use of than other human writings."[53] This view may be said to have prevailed in Protestantism.

Beginning in 1629 the Apocrypha were omitted from some editions of English Bibles. Since 1827 they have been excluded from practically all editions. In the Revised Version (1885) and the American Standard Revision (1901) they were omitted entirely. In 1895 they were revised and published in a separate volume.

Summary:

It is apparent from abundant external evidence that canonical claims of the Old Testament Apocrypha based on a so-called "larger" or Alexandrian canon, according to the "two-canon" theory, are null and void. That there was only *one* canon of true, inspired Scripture, the Hebrew or Palestinian canon, and that the "larger" or so-called "Alexandrian canon" is a figment of the imagination is proved by a lack of manuscript evidence, by ancient Jewish tradition, by the Hebrew religious point of view, by the witness of the New Testament, by the unanimous testimony of both the Eastern and Western Churches in the first four centuries, and likewise by the general witness of the Church until the Council of Trent and from the Reformation to the present day.

53 **The Westminster Confession of Faith,** chap. 1, article 3.

It is likewise evident that the ecclesiastical recognition of the Apocrypha as canonical Scripture in the Greek Orthodox Church and the Roman Catholic Church in the face of clear and unanswerable historical evidence to the contrary is both anomalous and highly arbitrary. In the case of Rome it is another example of the many gross evils and errors admitted into the so-called "Church" through the monstrous doctrine that the decrees and decisions of the "Church" are as authoritative and binding as the inspired Word of God itself. The result? The hierarchy at will sets aside the Word of God by arrogation to itself of authority which is intrinsically not its pre-rogative.

Accordingly, Steinmueller, the Catholic scholar, epitomizes the absurd result in the case of the canon when he says: "Had the Church accepted the Palestinian Canon, this also would have been binding upon all Christians, but only because of the value placed upon it by her. The Church, however, did not receive this Canon, but rather the Alexandrian, which included the deutero-canonical books and passages, and she thereby showed that she is the only legitimate and final authority determining the extent of the Canon."[54]

2. *Canonical Claims of the Apocrypha Refuted By Internal Evidence.*

The question of the limits of the canon is a historical problem and as such must be settled mainly by historical or external evidence. This evidence, as we have seen, is overwhelmingly in favor of the canon of the ancient Jews and in opposition to an imaginary so-called "larger-canon" containing the Apocrypha, despite the ecclesiastical recognition accorded the latter by the Greek Orthodox and the Roman Catholic Churches.

54 **Op. cit.,** pp. 71f.

Although the historical or external evidence is quite deter-
minative, additional proof of the invalidity of the canonical
claims of the Old Testament Apocrypha is supplied by internal evidence. In this instance the value of the internal
evidence, though negative, is of such a nature as to be quite
decisive. Certainly a book that contains what is false in
fact, erroneous in doctrine or unsound in morality, is unworthy of God and cannot have been inspired by Him.
Tried under these criteria the Apocryphal books stand self-
condemned.

a. The Apocrypha Abound in Historical, Geographical and
Chronological Inaccuracies and Anachronisms.

This is true to such an extent of Tobit and Judith that they
seem to be pure fiction, not even resting upon a basis of
fact. They thus present fiction, which, though of an edifying
variety, is unparalleled in canonical Scripture as a literary
genre. In Tobit's youth, for instance, the Ten Tribes are said
to have revolted from Judah under Jeroboam (1:4, 5). This
would make Tobit almost two hundred years old in 722
B.C. at the time of the Assyrian Captivity (and he lived into
the reign of Esarhaddon 680-668 B.C.). But according to
14:11 he was only one hundred and fifty eight years old when
he died (according to the Latin text, one hundred and two).

"Nineveh," the city in which the author of Tobit lays the
principal action of his story, is not the real Nineveh on the
upper Tigris, whose location was utterly forgotten even by
400 B.C., but according to Torrey, Seleucia on the Tigris across
the river from Ctesiphon.[55] Nineveh, moreover, is fictitiously
said to have been taken by "Nebuchadnezzar and Ahasuerus"
(14:15) instead of correctly "Nabopolassar and Cyaxares."

The author of Judith takes pains to tell his hearers plainly,
if not humorously, that they are listening to pure fiction and

55 C. C. Torrey **Jour. Bib. Lit.,** 41 (1922), pp. 237-245. **The Apocryphal Literature,** p. 86.

not to a recital of actual historical events at all. Was it gross ignorance or subtle humor of the Jewish novelist that caused him to begin as he did: Once upon a time "when Nebuchadnezzar reigned over the Assyrians at Nineveh," and when "Arphaxad reigned over the Medes in Ecbatana" (1:1)? Here he gives his auditors a sly wink. It is just as though a modern story-teller should say: "It happened at the time when Napolean Bonaparte was king of England and Otto von Bismarck was on the throne of Mexico."[56]

Likewise all the principal characters of the Judith story are apparently fictitious, excepting perhaps "Joakim the high priest" who may be the one referred to in Nehemiah 12:10. Holofernes (Orophernes) was familiar in Palestine since the middle of the fourth century B.C. when a Persian general of that name led an army through Phoenicia into Egypt.

In the matter of topography and geography of the principal scenes the author of Judith deals with actuality rather than fiction, but the places he names are pseudonymous. "Bethulia" is a false name for Shechem and "Betomesthaim" (4:6) for Samaria.[57] I Maccabees contains historical and geographical errors, but is much more reliable than II Maccabees, which is replete with legend and fables. Baruch contains false historical statements. For example, the vessels of the Temple are said to have been sent from Babylon in the time of Jeremiah (1:8), though they were not actually returned till after the exile (Ezra 1:7). Bel and The Dragon is a fanciful and ridiculous legend.

b. The Apocrypha Teach Doctrines which are False and Foster Practices which are at Variance with Inspired Scripture.

56 Torrey, **The Apocryphal Literature,** p. 89.
57 Cf. Torrey, **op. cit.,** pp. 91 f.

The moral and spiritual tone of these writings is far below that of the canonical Scriptures. II Maccabees justifies suicide (14:41-46) and prayers and offering for the dead (12:41-45). Ecclesiasticus is filled with many excellent precepts, yet contains passages at variance with inspired Scripture. Almsgiving is said to make atonement for sin (3:30). Cruelty to slaves is justified (33:26, 28). Expediency is presented as a ground for obligation rather than single regard for what is acceptable to God (38:17). The Wisdom of Solomon evidently teaches the doctrine of emanation (7:25) and the pre-existence of souls (8:19, 20).

Judith's language and conduct are a continued course of deception and falsehood, represented as meeting with God's approval and assistance (9:10, 13). In the book of Tobit the ridiculous fiction of the demon Asmodaeus, who is represented as the jealous lover of a young woman and who murders seven young suitors, until he is finally magically exorcized by the heart and liver of a fish burned in a censer by the young man who eventually marries her, countenances the grossest superstition.

c. The Apocrypha Resort to Literary Types and Display An Artificiality Of Subject Matter and Style Out of Keeping With Inspired Scripture.

Both Judith and Tobit may be classified as edifying religious fiction, a favorite type of literature in pre-Christian Palestine. Both are fine examples of Jewish popular tales designed to entertain as well as instruct. Bel and The Dragon, The History of Susanna and the Rest of Esther may be classed as fiction. Although the Old Testament contains many types of literature—historical narrative, poetry, proverb, drama, essay, short story, lyric, idyl—it does not contain (the critics notwithstanding) folklore, myth, legend or fiction.

Some would erroneously read folklore, myth and legend into Genesis and classify the book of Jonah, for instance, as "prophetic fiction."[58] But folklore, legend, myth and fiction are incompatible with inspired truth and are not found in the sacred canon. The use of fiction as a literary genre places a gulf between these apocryphal books and Holy Scripture.

But artificiality of *subject matter* is not confined to the Apocryphal books which may be classified as "religious fiction." Much of the literature besides is legendary, extravagant and fabulous, containing much that is absurd. In the matter of style there are a noticeable lack of originality and weakness in comparison with the canonical Scriptures. II Maccabees, for example, "is written in inflated and tiresome Greek . . . an overloaded and artificial style, and an ill-judged striving after rhetorical effect, are not absent."[59] Baruch is a poor imitation of the style of Jeremiah.

Summary:

The internal as well as the external evidence is, accordingly, overwhelmingly decisive against the canonical claims of the Apocrypha. Their historical, geographical and chronological discrepancies, their inferior moral and spiritual tone in teaching false doctrines and fostering practices contradicting inspired Scripture and their fictional, legendary and artificial characteristics prove conclusively that there is a distinct line of demarcation between the Apocrypha and the canonical books of the Old Testament. The differences, too, to a considerable degree, can be felt rather than precisely defined.

Literature on the Apocrypha

For Greek text of Apocrypha see H. B. Swete's manual edition 3 vols. (Cambridge 1887-1894, and later editions) and Alfred Rahlf's *Septuaginta* (Stuttgart, 1935). Vols. I and II. For the English text see *The Apocrypha* Revised Version (New York, 1895).

58 Edward C. Baldwin, **Types of Literature in the Old Testament pp. 31 ff.,** pp. 186 ff.
59 Torrey, **op. cit.,** p. 78.

Thornwell, J. H., *The Arguments of Romanists From the Infallibility of the Church and the Testimony of the Fathers In Behalf of the Apocrypha Discussed and Refuted* (New York, 1845).

Fritzsche, O. F. and C. L. W. Grimm, *Kurzgefasstes exegetisches Handbuch zu den Apokryphen des Alten Testamentes,* 6 vols., (Leipzig, 1851-1860).

For encyclopedia articles see: H. E. Ryle in Smith's *Dictionary of the Bible* (1893); C. F. Porter in *Hastings' Dictionary of the Bible;* T. W. Davies, *Int. Standard Bible Encyclopedia,* "Apocrypha."

Swete, H. B., *An Introduction to the Old Testament in Greek* (Cambridge, 1900, revised by R. R. Ottley, 1914).

Schuerer, E., *Geschichte des juedischen Volkes im Zeitalter Jesu Christi* III, 4th ed. (1909), pp. 188-716.

Charles, R. H., (Editor), *The Apocrypha and Pseudepigrapha in English,* with Introductions and Critical and Explanatory Notes to the Several Books, 2 vol. (Oxford, 1913).

Burkitt, F. C., *Jewish and Christian Apocalypses* (London, 1914).

Marcus, R., *Law in the Apocrypha,* Columbia University Oriental Studies 26 (New York, 1927).

Moore, G. F., *Judaism In The First Centuries of the Christian Era,* I (1927) pp. 125-216, III (1930) pp. 40-60.

Lagrange, M. J., *Le Judaisme avant Jesus Christ, Etudes Bibliques* (Paris, 1931).

Oesterley, W. O. E., *The Books of the Apocrypha: Their Origin, Teaching and Contents* (London, 1914); *An Introduction to the Books of the Apocrypha* (New York, 1935); *Judaism and Christianity* Vol. I, *The Age of Transition* (New York, 1937).

Bonsirven, J., *Le Judaisme Palestinien au temps de Jesus-Christ* 2 vols. (Paris, 1935.)

Goodspeed, E. J., *The Apocrypha.* An American Translation (Chicago, 1938); *The Story of the Apocrypha* (Chicago, 1939).

Rowley, H. H., *The Relevance of Apocalyptic* (1914. 2nd ed. 1947).

Torrey, C. C., *The Apocryphal Literature* (New Haven, 1945).

Rylaarsdam, J. C., in *The Study of the Bible* . . . ed. by Willoughby (1947). pp. 32-51.

Stamm, R. T., "A Brief Introduction to the Apocrypha of the Old Testament" in *Old Testament Commentary* (Philadelphia, 1948).

Bentzen, A., *Introduction to the Old Testament* Vol. II (Copenhagen, 1949), 218-252.

Important is the series *Jewish Apocryphal Literature* with the first issue entitled, *The First Book of Maccabees* (Greek text by Adolph Rahlfs, English translation by Sidney Tedesche, Introduction and Commentary by Solomon Zeitlin, New York, Harper and Brothers, 1950). The second issue of this series will be *Letter of Aristeas* with English translation by Moses Hadas. Other volumes are to appear.

Pfeiffer, R. H., *History of New Testament Times with an Introduction to the Apocrypha* (New York, 1949).

Chapter V

THE TEXT
OF THE OLD TESTAMENT

Having set forth the phenomenon of divine inspiration and its results in the formation of the Old Testament canon, at the same time noting how and why the Apocrypha were excluded, it is now necessary to consider the text or the actual form in which the canonical books have come down to us.

The Old Testament, being an ancient document, some parts of which were written as early as the fifteenth century B.C., naturally underwent a long process of development before it attained its present form. It is not easy for us moderns, to whom writing is such a simple process, to understand this. But writing in the ancient world was far from the simple thing it is now. Not only were writing materials and implements woefully inadequate from our modern point of view, but many baffling difficulties existed of which the ancients were not even aware. That which to us seems so obvious, the necessity of separating letters into words, sentences, paragraphs and chapters for the sake of clarity, dawned upon them only gradually.

Those who first attempted to reduce human speech to writing did not at once perceive the chasm that separates the spoken words from the characters in which they are symbolized. They wrote as they spoke in unbroken succession, inscribing the letters in closest proximity to each other, without separating them into words, much less into sentences, paragraphs and chapters. Ancient scribes did not at once realize that the writer, if he would make himself clearly understood, had to use some device to compensate for the natural modulations of voice and the manipulations of the organs of speech to which the speaker commonly resorts.

Imagine, then, an ancient text consisting of one unbroken string of letters and, to make matters worse, only consonants. Ancient Old Testament texts employed only consonants. Not a single vowel was indicated till centuries after Moses, and a full system of vocalization was not devised until 600-800 A.D. Think, then, what the task of the reader and the copyist was! The men who supplied the vowelless jumble of letters with vocalization, separated them into words, converted them into readable sentences, arranged them into prose or verse, into paragraphs and larger divisions, etc., were the *sopherim* or scribes. The story of their labors is the history of the text of the Hebrew Scriptures. It is a thrilling account of the providential preservation of the divine Oracles century after century through the meticulously accurate and tirelessly active hand of the ancient scribe. The result of their painstaking effort is the Old Testament we possess today.

I. THE LITERARY VEHICLE OF THE OLD TESTAMENT

Frequently many who are untrained in literary criticism go to the Old Testament as an inspired source of spiritual truth and help and drink of its inexhaustible well of refreshment, but fail to see or appreciate its sublime worth from a purely literary point of view. On the other hand, many critics fully understand and highly evaluate the superlative excellence and sheer magnificence of the Old Testament as literature and willingly place its grander passages above anything penned by Homer, Plato, Shakespeare, Milton or mortal muse, yet completely miss its true greatness and the source of its universal appeal as the Word of God to the needy and often unlettered and ignorant heart of mankind. To the spiritually enlightened and instructed believer the two aspects, the spiritual and the literary greatness of the Bible, must go hand in hand. A knowledge of the literary vehicle of Scripture must be coupled with a knowledge of God, and vice versa.

1. The Languages of the Old Testament.

Hebrew is *the* language of the Old Testament, except for an inconsiderable portion (Daniel 2:4-7:28; Ezra 4:8-6:18; 7:12-26; Jeremiah 10:11) written in Aramaic. Both Hebrew and Aramaic belong to the Semitic or "Shemitic" (Genesis 10:22) group of languages. The four principal tongues of this family are East Semitic (Babylonian-Assyrian), South Semitic (Arabic) and North and Northwest Semitic (Aramaic and Hebrew).

2. The Origin of the Name of the Hebrew Language.

The language is not referred to as "Hebrew" in the Old Testament, but takes its name from the people who spoke it. It the Bible, Abram is the first person who is called a "Hebrew" (Genesis 14:13). Thereafter his descendants through Isaac and Jacob are called "Hebrews" (Genesis 40:15; 43:32; Exodus 2:11). The language they spoke came to be known as "Hebrew." In Scripture it is referred to descriptively as "the language of Canaan" (Isaiah 19:18) and "the Jews' language" (II Kings 18:26, 28; Nehemiah 13:24), but never as "Hebrew." The first documentary occurrence of the term referring specifically to the language is in the Prologue to Ecclesiasticus (132 B.C.).

The origin of the name "Hebrew" presents a tantalizing problem, not because there is no explanation at all, but because there is as yet no sure or certain explanation in the light of a number of highly plausible possibilities. The name, for example, may be derived from the prominent Semitic progenitor, Eber, the ancestor of Abraham (Genesis 10:21, 22). Again, "Abram the Hebrew" (Genesis 14:13) may be "Abraham who crossed the river (Euphrates) (Joshua 24:2, 3) on his way to Palestine, when Abram, a Syrian . . ." became

"Abram, the Hebrew" (Genesis 24:4,10; Deuteronomy 26:5).
Thus the Septuagint translates "Abram, the Hebrew" (*ha
'Ibhri,* from *'abhar* "to cross over," Genesis 14:13) as *ho
perates* "The one who crossed over."

Perhaps, still more appealing, both archeologically and linguistically, is the widely discussed question whether or not
the *Habiru* ('Apiru), so prominent in the Nuzian, Hittite, and
Amarna documents of the 15-14th centuries B.C. are not to be
identified, in part at least, with the Hebrews. Most critics are
undecided. Says Albright, "Until the question is decided, we
must content ourselves with saying that a Khapiru origin
would square extraordinarily well with Hebrew traditional
history and would clear up many details which seem otherwise inexplicable."[1]

3. *The Origin of the Hebrew Language.*

a. Hebrew Adopted From a Canaanite Dialect.

Hebrew takes its origin from the old Phoenician alphabet,
from which all alphabets in current use, Semitic and non-
Semitic, have been ultimately derived. The origin of this
proto-Semitic alphabet is still obscure,[2] although the earliest
samples of this rude script, discovered by the famous archeologist Sir Flinders Petrie at Serabit el Khadem in the Sinaitic
Peninsula in 1904-5, push alphabetic writing back before the
time of Moses and have recently been more precisely dated in
the "early fifteenth century B.C." by Albright.[3] It is of singular
significance, moreover, that this early "Sinai Hebrew Script,"
as it is sometimes called, was found in the very region where
Moses was told to write (Exodus 17:8-14).

But old Hebrew goes back before the time of Moses and the
Egyptian sojourn to the patriarchal age, and the vexing
question is often asked: Did Abraham find the Hebrew lan-

1 W. F. Albright, **From the Stone Age to Christianity** (Baltimore, 1940), p. 183.
2 Cf. R. Pfeiffer, **Am. Jour. of Archeology** 41 (1937), pp. 643 f., J. W. Flight,
Haverford Symposium on Archeology and the Bible, pp. 111-135; M. G. Kyle,
Moses and the Monuments (1920), pp. 70-74.
3 **Bull. Am. Sch. of Or. Res.** 110 (April 1948), p. 22.

guage in Palestine or did he bring it with him from Haran? The Hebrew patriarchs presumably spoke an Aramaic dialect while in Mesopotamia before their settlement in Palestine. But there, at an uncertain period, "they adopted a local Canaanite dialect which was not identical with the standard speech of sedentary Canaanites, as may be linguistically demonstrated."[4] This conclusion seems inescapable since Old Hebrew is practically the same as Phoenician.[5] It is apparently reflected in the traditional name of Hebrew, "the language of Canaan" (Isaiah 19:18), and is indicated by early Canaanite and Hebrew inscriptions.

b. Canaanite Origin of Hebrew Attested by the Inscriptions.

Comparison between the Canaanite and Hebrew inscriptions of this general period shows the close similarity of the languages. For example, the language spoken at Ugarit in North Syria and made known by the discovery of the famous Ras Shamra literature (1929 following) is strikingly akin to Hebrew and Phoenician and dates from about 1400 B.C.[6] Like Hebrew it is a simple alphabetic script and offers innumerable parallels to Old Testament vocabulary, syntax and poetic style. Since 1923 a number of important Canaanite inscriptions have been unearthed at the ancient city of Byblus (Biblical Gebal), including the sarcophagus of Ahiram, belonging probably to the eleventh century B.C.[7] After 900 B.C. there are Phoenician inscriptions from Cyprus, Sardinia, Carthage and other colonies in the Western Mediterranean.[8]

Inscriptional material in Hebrew from Palestine, while by no means abundant, is sufficient to show the close affinity of the language with Canaanite dialects. The oldest inscription is the Gezer Calendar, written in perfect classical Hebrew, dated about 925 B.C.,[9] followed by the famous Moabite Stone

4 Albright, **From the Stone Age to Christianity,** p. 182.
5 See Gesenius-Cowley, **Hebrew** Grammar (Oxford, 1910), pp. 9-11.
6 Albright, **Archeology and the Religion of Israel** (Baltimore, 1942), p. 38.
7 Albright, **op. cit.,** p. 40
8 **Bull. Am. Sch. of Or Res.** 83 (Oct., 1941), pp. 14-22.
9 **Bull. Am. Sch, of Or. Res.** 92 (Dec. 1943). p. 21.

set up by Mesha, king of Moab, about 850 B.C., written in the language of Moab which was so closely akin to Hebrew that it "was scarcely more remote from the dialect of the Northern Kingdom than the latter was from the dialect of Judah, which we call 'Biblical Hebrew.' "[10]

Next in order of Hebrew inscriptions, the Samaritan Ostraca, now dated in the reign of Jeroboam II (ca. 774-776 B.C.), instead of in the time of Ahab, prove that the alphabetic dialect the Hebrews adopted from the Canaanites was used for commerce as well as for religion. The six-line Siloam inscription (about 701 B.C.) cut in the rock conduit at the time Hezekiah improved the water supply of Jerusalem against siege, and the Lachish Letters (autumn, 589 B.C.) two years before the fall of Jerusalem to the Babylonians, add further epigraphic evidence of the close affiliation of Biblical Hebrew with Phoenician and other Canaanite dialects. The important thing is that God had a simple alphabetic language ready for recording the divine revelation instead of the unwieldy and cumbersome cuneiform scripts of Babylonia-Assyria, or the complex hieroglyphic writing of Egypt.

II. The Hebrew Text of the Old Testament Before A.D. 90

Modern editions of the Hebrew Old Testament differ in two important external respects from ancient Hebrew manuscripts, especially those before 200 B.C. First, they differ radically in *writing materials and the general format of the book*. Secondly, they differ in *the form and writing of the letters*.

1. The Writing Materials and General Format of Early Hebrew Manuscripts.

Archeology has not only demonstrated that Moses had at hand a ready vehicle of literary endeavor in the simple alphabetic script of the old Hebrew of his day, but it has shed

10 Albright, **Archeology and the Religion of Israel**, p. 41.

abundant light on the writing materials he had at his command.

a. Clay Tablets.

Soft, wet clay, impressed with a stylus in the form of wedge-shaped signs and symbols and set out in the sun to dry and harden, provided a widely used medium of writing from earliest historical times. Prevailing before the Mosaic era for at least a millennium and a half in the lower alluvial Tigris-Euphrates Valley, the so-called "cradle of civilization," this ancient mode of writing on clay was exceedingly popular in Palestine-Syria in the fifteenth and fourteenth centuries B.C., precisely at the time we believe Moses lived and the earliest books of the Bible were written, as the Ras Shamra documents written in alphabetic cuneiform and the Tell el Amarna clay tablets, written in syllabic cuneiform of an Akkadianized *lingua franca,* prove. Accordingly the great Hebrew lawgiver could have written the earliest drafts of the Pentateuch *in Old Hebrew on clay tablets.*

b. Leather.

Skins of animals were used at an early date in Egypt, at least by the time of the fourth dynasty (2550-2450 B.C.), and their use was widespread. Hides of sheep or goats were suitably prepared for writing upon one side. The skins were cut into sheets and sewed together end to end to make rolls of the required length. Leather rolls varied in length from a foot or two to perhaps a hundred feet according to the number of books which were written on *one* roll. The skin was either wound in a single roll (without a stick), or wound around two sticks, one at each end. In this case it was unrolled from one stick in reading and, at the same time, wound around the other stick. Not until the second or third century A.D. did the ancient roll give way to the *codex*[11] or book in the

---

11 Cf. Kenyon, **Recent Developments in the Textual Criticism of the Greek Bible** (Oxford, 1933), pp. 53-55.

form of leaves sewed together. These were made of specially treated fine leather called vellum.

c. Papyrus.

Papyrus rolls employed for writing were prepared in Egypt during the Old Kingdom (c. 2800-2250 B.C.), perhaps earlier, by cutting lengthwise strips of the pith of the papyrus plant which flourished along the Nile, and pressing two or three layers together crosswise. Egyptian papyrus rolls are still in existence from the end of the third millennium B.C. According to the *Story of Wen-Amon*,[12] papyrus rolls were exported from Egypt to Gebal in Phoenicia. Later, for this reason, the Greeks called the city "Byblus," meaning "papyrus," later "book."

The largest ordinary papyrus roll in common use was about thirty feet long, and some ten inches high, sufficient for the unvocalized Hebrew text of Isaiah. Egyptians in unusual cases used such enormous scrolls as the Papyrus Harris, which was one hundred thirty-three feet long and seventeen inches wide and a Book of the Dead, one hundred twenty-three feet long and nineteen inches wide. But among the Jews the common use of the standard-sized papyrus rolls made necessary the division of certain books, like the Torah of Moses, into five books. The books of Samuel, Kings, and Chronicles (and presumably Genesis and Isaiah) were partitioned into two books when translated into Greek, because Greek, which included vowels, required more space than the purely consonantal Hebrew text.

Original copies of the Old Testament writings perished within a century or two after they were written, but the Bible gives us an example of the preparation of one of the "first editions" of Holy Scripture (Jeremiah 36). Baruch evidently wrote down Jeremiah's prophecies on a papyrus roll, less likely on leather, using pen and ink. The reed or calamus, made

12 II:41.

from the hollow stalk of coarse grass or rush, was cut diagonally with a knife to form a thin flexible point, which was split at the end like the modern pen and clipped to a stub at the tip. To keep the pen point in good writing order the scribe carried a knife with him, hence the term "penknife" (Jeremiah 36:23). Ink was customarily made of soot or lampblack and gum, diluted with water. The text was divided into columns (Jeremiah 36:23), separated, according to Talmudic tradition, by a two-fingered space. Wide margins at the top and bottom facilitated ample annotations.

2. *The Form and Writing of the Letters of Early Hebrew Manuscripts.*

The almost complete change in the form of the Hebrew letters themselves constitutes one of the most radical differences between early Hebrew manuscripts and those after the fifth century B.C.

a. The Change to Square Characters.

Until the time of Nehemiah (444 B.C.) the old Phoenician alphabet with its characteristic prong-type letters[13] was used for books (rolls), but after this period there was a shift to the square-type letter with large open bosom. Thereafter the archaic form of the alphabetic letters survived only as a vestige on coins.

Modern Hebrew Bibles are printed in so-called "square Hebrew," a modification of Aramaic characters. The first known occurrence of this type of script dates from the early second century B.C in an inscription found in Ammon. The Nash Papyrus dating in the period 150-100 B.C.,[14] till recently the oldest Hebrew Biblical manuscript, is written in the square Hebrew characters. Apparently an even older document, written also in the square characters, is the recently discovered scroll of Isaiah, dating ostensibly from the second

---

13 See "A table of Alphabets by M. Lidzbarski" in Gesenius-Cowley, **Hebrew Grammar** (second English edition), p. X.
14 Cf. W. F. Albright, **Jour. Bib. Lit.** 56 (1937), pp. 145-176.

century B.C., and, unquestionably, "the most important discovery ever made in Old Testament manuscripts."[15]

It is quite certain, therefore, that already in the first century B.C. (or earlier) the Hebrew Scriptures were written in the square characters. Jesus made reference to the Hebrew letter *yod* ("jot") as the smallest of all the letters (Matthew 5:18). He, of course, had reference to the current square letters, as the *yod* was by no means the smallest character in the old Phoenician alphabet.

b. The Origin of the Square Characters.

Two views exist. Hebrew tradition (in this case most likely legend) maintains that Ezra in the fifth century B.C. introduced the square characters from Babylonia.[16] Despite the historical precariousness of this view, it was accepted as true by Origen, Epiphanius and Jerome. The second explanation is more likely. It holds that the Jews adopted the Aramaic script, from which the square characters were derived, when Aramaic became the vernacular in the fourth century B.C. It may be they first began to copy the Scriptures in Aramaic, and then after 200 B.C., in square characters.

The Hebrew text at this period consisted only of consonants. Vowels were not added until 600-800 A.D. There were also few indications of long vowels by the use of the weak or semi-vocalic consonants. These consonants (*aleph, waw* and *yod*) were called *matres lectionis* ("mothers," that is, "aids to reading") because even if only feebly (from our point of view) indicating vowels, they were nevertheless definite helps in facilitating reading.

III. THE HEBREW TEXT OF THE OLD TESTAMENT FROM A.D. 90 to A.D. 135

Everyone conversant with the historical facts will readily agree that our present Hebrew Old Testament differs radically

15 G. E. Wright, **The Biblical Archeologist** (May, 1948), p. 21.
16 Cf. L. Ginzberg, **The Legends of the Jews**, Vol. VI, pp. 443 f.

from ancient copies of the Holy Scriptures, especially those which belong to a date before 200 B.C., in certain externalities, such as writing materials, general format and the alphabetic form of the letters. Higher critics, however, insist upon a third difference, that of the contents of the Sacred Books, which, if allowed, is of far greater importance than these mere external differences.

1. The Critical Theory of Differences in the Contents of the Ancient Hebrew Manuscripts and the Modern Hebrew Text Refuted.

a. The First Claim: The Canonization of The Old Testament Books Constituted the First Main Stage in the Concern About the Text.

The importance of guarding the Scripture against all change supposedly "dawned only gradually upon the Jews." When it did so, says Pfeiffer, it was "too late to recapture the wording of the original writings."[17] He continues, "Before the books of the Old Testament reached their canonical standing the Pentateuch in 400 B.C., the Former and Latter Prophets in 200 B.C., and the Writings in A.D. 90, they were circulating more or less privately. The owners of the manuscripts felt free to annotate them . . . Moreover, through accidental or deliberate modifications, each new manuscript was a new edition . . ."[18]

Reply:

A conclusion based upon a faulty theory cannot be expected to be sound. Since the canonization of the Old Testament is mistakenly made a slow process covering centuries, the erroneous deduction is inevitable—concern for the text was also a slow process involving centuries.

But is this position, besides ignoring the claims of Scriptural inspiration, credible on common-sense grounds? The Jews were distinctly "a people of one book," and were familiar with

17 R. Pfeiffer, **Old Testament Introduction**, p. 74.
18 **Loc. cit.**

a passage anywhere in that book. What was true of the people at large was eminently true of their spiritual leaders. From the time of Ezra, and doubtless long before, there was a special guild of sopherim or scribes whose special business was to copy the Sacred Text and meticulously reproduce and hand down the correct reading.[19] In the light of these strict measures which were taken to insure that every fresh copy was an exact reproduction of the original, it is arbitrary and nonsensical to maintain that each new manuscript was "a new edition." Only the exigencies of the critical theory can obscure the fact that such measures had been taken, not only from the time of Ezra, but (and there is no reason to suppose the contrary) continuously from the times of Moses and Joshua on down. The nation which was providentially chosen to be the recipients and custodians of the Sacred Oracles was also providentially endowed with a veneration and concern for the text to insure its correct transmission.

b. The Second Claim: The Literary Activity of Rabbi Akiba and Jewish-Christian Polemics In the Period 90-135 A.D. Aroused Sudden Interest in the Text.

Concern for the text, which had been a slow development coeval with the gradual formation of the canon from 400 B.C. to 90 A.D. (Pfeiffer's dates), now, under Rabbi Akiba and the Jewish-Christian controversies, supposedly took a new and unprecedented spurt.

Reply:

However, since under the contentions of the higher critical theory itself the law and the prophets had been canonized centuries before the Council at Jamnia (90 A.D.), any sudden interest in the text must be logically confined to the writings. For is it sensible to assume that Scripture can be accounted canonical and no deep interest exist in its text? The confusion of the critical position can only be relieved by realizing the

19 Cf. S. Goldman, **The Book of Books: An Introduction**, pp. 34-38.

fact that the Jews *always* had a deep interest in the text of their Holy Writings and a genuine concern for their meticulous accuracy and authentic transmission, because they considered them the Word of God.

It is demonstrably erroneous to connect the final official closing of the Jewish canon at Jamnia with a supposed renewed "concern for the text." Official sanction did *not* create public opinion. It merely confirmed it. When rabbi Akiba and others occupied themselves with the preparation of an authoritative list of sacred books, not only the law and the prophets but the writings as well, had long since established themselves in the hearts of the faithful with an authority that neither could be shaken nor confirmed by the decisions of councils or the pronouncements of the schools. It was impossible for a deep and genuine interest in the text not to have existed long before the period 90-135 A.D. The special exigencies of this particular period merely brought it into clearer historical focus.

The first circumstance bringing interest in the text into clearer historical focus during this period was *Jewish-Christian Controversy*. The Council at Jamnia, besides its pronouncements concerning the Jewish canon, officially declared that the Gospels and books of the Christians were not sacred Scripture. But there were many Judeo-Christians called Nazarenes, who were believers in Christ but followers of Judaism, in the synagogues, against whose claims that Jesus was the Messiah the rabbis had to contend. These, however, were expelled from the synagogue after Bar-Cocheba's rebellion (A.D. 132-135). Christians, zealous to prove their doctrines, used their Bible, which was the Septuagint. When textual differences arose, which was right—the Hebrew or the Greek Bible? The result was that the natural interest in the letter of their Holy Scriptures received a new impetus, as Jews went to the Sacred Writings to set forth their doctrines and to defend the very foundations of Judaism against Christian attack.

A second circumstance bringing Jewish interest in the Sacred Text into bold relief was *the exegetical methods of Rabbi Akiba* (died 132 A.D.). Akiba undoubtedly used a minute system of exegesis which sought hidden meanings in particles, peculiarities of spelling and other minutiae of the text. The critical hypothesis holds that textual variants would preclude interpretations based on textual minutiae and that Akiba must have endeavored to standardize the text in its minutest components.

But there is no reason to suppose that this minute standardization had not been the aim of the Jews on down through the centuries from the appearance of the first inspired autographs. The theory of long separated intervals in the canonization of the law, the prophets, and the writings leads to the fallacy that such standardization must, to a large degree, be restricted to this period in the development of the text. Evidence at our disposal would justify us in concluding nothing more than that which had been going on all the while, only now received a special impetus in the economy of God, as Christians took the Old Testament to their hearts and with the Jews became its guardians and defenders.

Summary:

The critical notion that the text of our present-day Hebrew Bible differs substantially in contents from ancient Hebrew manuscripts is false, being the result of an unsound deduction based on the erroneous theory of the gradual development of the canon that concern for the Hebrew text developed only gradually, and that when it did, it was too late to recapture the wording of the original documents. Activities directed toward the minute standardization of the text in the period A.D 90-135, are evidences, accentuated no doubt by the exigencies of the time, of that which had been the aim of devout Jewish scholars and scribes all along.

Despite the activity of rabbi Akiba and of the later Talmudic rabbis and the Massoretes, there is no substantia difference in the contents of present-day Hebrew Bibles and ancient Hebrew manuscripts, or the autographa themselves. Whatever changes there are, they are not strictly in content, but are confined to reading aids, as diacritical marks, vowels, accents, variants in spelling, modernization of place names or an occasional gloss or copyist's error, which can be traced down to the original correct reading through a comparison of variant readings, or by use of the ancient versions. In other words, the text of our Hebrew Bibles is substantially that of the autographa, and whatever changes occurred are of minor importance, affecting no fundamental doctrine or question of faith.

IV. THE HEBREW TEXT OF THE OLD TESTAMENT IN THE TALMUDIC PERIOD (135-500)

Between the time of rabbi Akiba and the completion of the Talmud there were a number of reading aids or diacritical marks introduced into the Hebrew text, which did not change its contents, but merely expedited a more accurate reading and understanding of its message.

1. Subdivisions of the Text.

a. Verses.

Division of the Hebrew text into words apparently took place in the interval between the completion of the Septuagint translation (ca. 150 B.C.), which indicates the Hebrew from which it was translated contained no such word divisions[20] and the presumable date of the Isaiah Scrolls (125-100 B.C.),[21] which contain such word divisions. Verse divisions also occur early and doubtless arose in the custom of reading successively brief sections of the Hebrew Scriptures in the synagogue for translation into Aramaic. The custom is first mentioned in the Mishnah (A.D. 200), but may be considerably earlier.

Verse divisions varied considerably in Palestine and Baby-

20 Pfeiffer, *op. cit.*, p. 79.
21 John Trevor,"A Paleographic Study of the Jerusalem Scrolls," **Bull. Am. Sch.** 113 (Feb. 1949), p. 23.

lonia until Ben Asher, the greatest of the Massoretes, in the first half of the tenth century edited the text with the current verse division. The end of the verse, indicated by a Hebrew "period" (*Soph pasuq*) corresponding in form somewhat to our colon (:), probably originated in this period, but it is mentioned only after 500 A.D.

b. Paragraphs and Pericopes.

Although chapter divisions in the Hebrew text are comparatively late, being first adopted from the Latin Bible in the thirteenth century, there are two kinds of divisions, one *textual* and the other *liturgical,* which are ancient. The textual divisions correspond roughly to our paragraphs and follow the natural subdivisions of the text. For example, the Pentateuch is currently divided into 290 "open" and 379 "closed" *parashiyoth* (singular, *parashah*). The "open" marked by a *pe* (p) are paragraphs beginning a new line. The closed are shorter and are marked by a *samekh* (s) and preceded by a blank space in the line. The Mishnah (ca. 200) mentions these subdivisions, which doubtless existed much earlier. The Talmud (ca. 500) distinguishes between the open and the closed *parashiyoth.*

The *liturgical* division of the law and the prophets is likewise ancient, originating in the period of the rise of the synagogue (400 B.C-168 B.C.). The law was first read and divided into weekly lessons for public reading and by the time of Christ the prophets had been added to the Torah lessons (Luke 4:16-21).

2. *Other Punctuation Marks and Textual Phenomena of this Period.*

Beside word and verse divisions and paragraph arrangements, natural and liturgical in purpose, there are other diacritical marks to be noted.

a. A Heavy Dot Placed Over a Word or Letter.

This period-like mark indicates words or passages concerning which some problem existed in the opinion of the ancient scholars, as in Genesis 16:5 and Numbers 9:10, etc.

b. Paseq or "Divider."

A vertical stroke, occurring about 480 times, separates two Hebrew words. The sign is now obscure in its meaning. In Genesis 39:10 it separates two identical words. In Psalm 139:19 it separates the divine name from an adjoining word. In I Chronicles 22:3 it separates a letter from an identical letter.

c. The Inverted Nun.

The Hebrew *n* is simply written upside down. It occurs, for example, in Numbers 10:34-36.

d. Peculiar Writing of Certain Letters.

A *raised* letter may denote a variant reading (Judges 18:30) or perhaps in Psalm 80:14 the middle of the Psalter. *Enlarged* letters indicate the beginning of a book (Genesis 1:1), the middle of the Pentateuch (Leviticus 13:33), or an especially famous and well-known passage, like Deuteronomy 6:4. *Small* letters also occur (Genesis 2:4; Deuteronomy 32:18). The *broken* letter in Numbers 25:12 probably indicates a variant reading. *Closed* letters also occur like the *qoph* in Exodus 32:25. *Final* letters are used medially (Isaiah 9:6) and non-final forms of letters occur finally (Job 38:1; Nehemiah 2:13).

e. A Blank Space.

This vacant space was left in the middle of twenty-eight verses (e.g. Genesis 4:8; 35:22; I Samuel 14:19, Ezekiel 3:16), in some cases to note an omission. In Genesis 4:8, according to the Samaritan Pentateuch, the Septuagint, Syriac, Old Latin, Vulgate and the Jerusalem Targum after 'And Cain talked with Abel his brother" should be added, 'Let us go into the field." Similarly the Septuagint in Genesis 35:22 adds to the clause "And Israel heard it" the words, "and t was grievous in his eyes."

These examples and others illustrate with what extreme

reverence the Talmudic rabbis, as well as their predecessors, regarded the text. It was transmitted *exactly,* even when it seemed to be doubtful, and was considered inviolable. Actual consonantal change was practically precluded. Corrected readings were approved, *but the consonants as they stood in the text were not changed.*

f. The Removal of So-Called Obscenities.

Without changing the consonantal text the rabbis took steps to remove what came to be regarded as indelicate words by the substitution of euphemistic equivalents. For example, boils associated with sexual perversions, were changed to emerods (Deuteronomy 28:27; marginal reading in I Samuel 5:6, 9, 12; 6:4f.). Human excrement and urine were changed to more refined words of the same meaning (II Kings 18:27; Isaiah 36:12).

g. Elimination of The Names of Pagan Gods.

This practice was regularly followed in public reading and even in manuscript copies. It reflects with what horror the synagogue regarded idolatry. Names of heathen divinities, such as Astarte and Melek were read *bosheth* ("shame"), and were given the vocalization corresponding to this opprobrious designation—Ashtoreth, with plural form Ashtaroth and Molech (for Melek). Similarly Topheth appears for Tapheth.

In compounded proper names *ba'al,* meaning "master," and used innocently for Jehovah, was sporadically altered to *bosheth*—thus Mephibosheth (II Samuel 4:4; 9:6, 10) for original Merib-baal (I Chronicles 8:34; 9:40); Jerrubbesheth (II Samuel 11:21) for original Jerubbaal (Judges 7:1). Ishbaal (I Chronicles 8:33, 9:39) was turned unto Ishbosheth (II Samuel 2:8; 3:8, 14). Sometimes *El,* a divine name, was substituted for Baal. For example, El Berith (Judges 9:46) occurs for Baal Berith (Judges 8:33).

The word *shiqquts* (abomination) occurs as a written substitute for the *elohim* (gods) of pagans (I Kings 11:5, 7; II

Kings 23:13, etc.) and in the phrase "the abomination of desolation" (Daniel 9:27; 11:31; 12:11; Matthew 24:15).

V. THE HEBREW TEXT OF THE OLD TESTAMENT IN THE MASSORETIC PERIOD (A.D. 500-1000)

The work of the sopherim or scribes, extending (we believe) from the earliest times till it was taken up by the Talmudic rabbis in the period from about 200-500 A.D., was continued and brought to completion by the famous Massoretic scholars in the succeeding centuries of the first millennium A.D.

1. The Contributions of the Jewish Scholars In Babylonia.

Christianity triumphed in Palestine. The result was that Jewish scholarship emigrated eastward to Babylonia in the second century A.D. By the third century important academies of Jewish learning were founded until the tenth century. The precise contribution of the Babylonian schools, formerly known only from a list of "Eastern" variants in contrast to Palestinian or "Western" readings, has become more familiar in recent times through the discovery of important Biblical manuscripts from Yemen, in Arabia, and from Old Cairo and through the researches of the celebrated German textual scholar, P. Kahle.[22] The Babylonian variants are listed in the critical apparatus of the third edition of R. Kittel's *Biblia Hebraica* (1929-1937). A system of accents and vocalization was also developed by the Jewish scholars of Babylonia, but their system was not destined to prevail.

2. The Contributions of the Massoretic Scholars in Palestine.

The Moslem conquest of Palestine in the seventh century (638) brought about a revival of Jewish learning in Palestinian schools. Tiberias, a city on the western shore of the Lake of Galilee, built in the first century A.D. by Herod the Tetrarch in honor of Tiberias Caesar, became the seat of

---

[22] **Massoreten** des Ostens, Beitraege zur Wissenschaft vom Alten Testament, (Leipzig, 1913).

a flourishing school of Jewish scholars in the eighth and ninth centuries. These learned rabbis were called Massoretes because they were rigid adherents of the traditional readings of the Hebrew text and were compilers of the Massora (Hebrew, "tradition") consisting of marginal readings, comments, notations and so on, transmitted to them from the Talmudic scholars and the early sopherim.

After the decline of the Babylonian academies in the tenth century, the Tiberian School became the center of Biblical studies and fixed the authorized text of the Scriptures, both consonantal and vocalic, for Judaism in general. The specific contributions of the Massoretes are of paramount importance to the history of the Hebrew text.

a. They Preserved the Traditional Text of Preceding Centuries.

The Massoretes manifested the same spirit of deep loyalty and devotion to the Sacred Scriptures as the inspired and authoritative Word of God, which had been handed down to them, that had been characteristic throughout the centuries of the history of the nation chosen to be the recipients and the custodians of the Holy Oracles (cf. Romans 9:4, 5). Neither they nor their predecessors ever considered themselves innovators. It was not their business or intention to bring in something new or to introduce novelties into the sacred text. Their task was as precise and definite as it was important, namely: *to determine the exact text handed down to them from all available evidence and to hand it on to future generations without change.* This magnificent task they accomplished with superlative success.

b. They Standardized the Consonantal Text.

When they were compelled to choose between two seemingly equally attested readings, they did not discard one in favor of the other, but devised an ingenious method of transmitting both. One was called the *Kethiv,* that is, "written" in the consonantal text, but upon it were placed the vowel signs that did not fit it, but were "to be read" with the consonants of another or preferred marginal reading, called the *Qere*. The bulk of *Kethiv-Qere* readings evidently belong to the Massoretic period, but there are a number of examples before A.D. 500. Some, like the numerous substitutions of *Adonai* for Jehovah (Yahweh), go back to the pre-Septuagint period.

Gordis maintains that in some instances two readings were written separately, producing a conflate text.[23] As a result of their stupendous labors, the Massoretes fixed the authorized text of the Hebrew Bible and passed on to their successors a standard edition of the Scriptures which precluded any change or variation. From that day to this the Hebrew Bible has been the Massoretic Text.

c. They Vocalized the Consonantal Text.

This was their epoch-making contribution and the vital element in the standardization of the text. Vocalization of the text assured the fixation and perpetuation of the correct pronunciation. Before the vowel signs were added to the consonantal text in the seventh century of our era, the vocalization was fluid, varying considerably through the centuries and in various countries. A vocalized text is much easier to read and much less liable to variation in reading as well as pronunciation. In a number of instances, for example, the Septuagint and other ancient versions read the consonants of the Massoretic text, but vocalized them differently.[24] Little wonder that this was the case since numerous Hebrew words written without vowels may have two or more different meanings according to the manner in which they are vocalized.

As a result of evidence from Jerome (died 420), the Targums and the Talmud, it is quite certain there were no vowel pointings at the end of the sixth century. The system ac-

23 R. Gordis, **The Biblical Text In the Making**, pp. 41 f.
24 Cf. G. A. Cooke, **Ezekiel**, ICC, I, xliii, for examples in Ezekiel; See F. Buhl, **Canon and Text of the Old Testament**, p. 237, for other versions.

cordingly was developed between A.D. 600-900, with evidence pointing to the seventh century.

The vocalic system that triumphed by the end of the eighth century over earlier systems in Babylon and Palestine was the Tiberian, consisting of seven signs, written, above, below and in the bosom of the Hebrew characters. It was an improvement over preceding systems and has prevailed to the present day. It is the system appearing in present-day printed Hebrew Bibles.

d. They Also Introduced an Elaborate System of Accents.

Together with the vowel points the Massoretes introduced a variety of accents to aid in indicating the correct reading of the text. These marks point out the stressed syllable, serve as punctuation signs to join or separate words (conjunctive or disjunctive) and also serve as musical notations to facilitate cantillation in the synagogues. The accents of the three poetical books (Psalms, Proverbs and Job) differ from those of the other twenty-one books of the canon.

e. They Took Definite Steps to Insure the Exact Transmission of the Text.

Having fixed the written and pronounced text minutely, the Massoretes did not consider their task ended until they had taken steps to insure its exact transmission to future generations. This they did by monographs and annotations aimed at precluding the slightest change in the standard text.

The Monographs are early Palestinian manuals dating before the invention of the vowel points from perhaps the seventh century. These handbooks outlined precise instructions for the scribes in preparing acceptable copies of the Scriptures and were incorporated in the treatise called *Sopherim* ("Scribes") during the eighth century. Ben Asher of Tiberias (about 920 A.D.) not only prepared the Biblical text with vowels and accents which became standard, but also composed a number of grammatical and Massoretic comments. These were published later by S. Baer and H. L. Strack in the nineteenth century under the title *Diqduqe ha-Te'amim* ("grammatical rules of the accents"). Similar manuals were prepared later after the work of Massoretes had been completed. The most complete edition of the Massora is that by C. D. Ginsburg, entitled, *The Massorah Compiled from Manuscripts,* appearing in London (1881-1905) in four volumes.

The Annotations are marginal comments of the Massoretes classified variously. *The Initial Massora* deals with the first word or the name of a book. *The Small Massora,* usually written on the side margins, gives statistics concerning the occurrence of similar words, spellings or peculiarly written letters. *The Large Massora,* written on the top and bottom margins, enlarges upon the Small Massora and deals more in detail with similar matters. *The Final Massora* is written at the end of a book and contains similar data on vowel points, accents, spelling, etc. The *Massoretes,* in other words, in counting the verses, the words and the very letters of every book, and calculating the middle verse and the middle letter of each one, were interested in the minutest detail of a standard text. Their aim was to pass it on unaltered and unalterable to their successors.

3. Manuscripts from the Close of the Massoretic Period.

All the extant Hebrew manuscripts were produced on the basis of the work of the *Massoretes.* This is the reason why there is little or no variation in Hebrew manuscripts of the present day. This text, moreover, in the light of the phenomenal labors of the *Massoretic* scholars and their loyal devotion to traditional readings and to the Scriptures as the revered, inspired Word of God, inviolable and holy, may be considered as a faithful reproduction not only of the text of about 90 A.D., but of the autographic copies themselves.

a. Ben Asher's Standard Hebrew Text.

In the period 900-950 two rival scholastic authorities at Tiberias, Ben Naphtali and Ben Asher, prepared two standard copies of the Massoretic Bible. Ben Naphtali's standard edition was lost, but evidence has survived indicating that its differences from Ben Asher's text were usually confined to minor points that do not affect the meaning of the passages.

Ben Asher's text survived. The autograph itself was taken to old Cairo when Jerusalem was plundered in 1099. There it was studied by Maimonides (died 1204), who declared it to be the official standard text of the Hebrew Scriptures. It was eventually recognized as the standard text as other scholars added their testimony to that of Maimonides.

b. *Earliest Extant Hebrew Manuscripts.*

Manuscripts of the Hebrew Old Testament are comparatively late, probably none being earlier than 900 A.D. It is this fact that constitutes the discovery of the Jerusalem Scrolls containing the entire Hebrew text of Isaiah dating as early as 125-100 B.C. not only "the greatest manuscript discovery of modern times"[25] but makes the documents themselves "the oldest existing manuscripts of the Bible in any language."[26] This sensational find will doubtless have a most profound effect upon the history of the Biblical text when all the evidence it affords is studied and collated.

As far as the post-Massoretic manuscripts are concerned, the oldest dated document was the Leningrad Codex of the Prophets (916 A.D.). A British Museum document of the Pentateuch, undated, is to be placed perhaps somewhat earlier. A manuscript in the Cambridge University Library bears the date 856, and the correctness of the date has been maintained by at least one capable scholar.[27]

The oldest manuscript of the entire Hebrew Old Testament does not date earlier than the eleventh century, and the number of manuscripts of the entire Hebrew Scriptures is very

25 W. F. Albright, **Biblical Archeologist**, Vol. XI, no. 3 (Sept., 1948), p. 55.
26 John C. Trevor, **Bull. Am. Sch. Or. Res.** 113 (Feb., 1949), p. 23.
27 Ira M. Price, **The Ancestry of Our English Bible**, pp. 34 f. Sir F. Kenyon, **Our Bible and the Ancient Manuscripts**, pp. 44-45.

small. However, there are about 1700 partial or fragmentary documents.

VI. THE HEBREW TEXT FROM THE MASSORETIC PERIOD TO THE PRESENT

The work of the Massoretic scholars in preparing an official standard text of the Hebrew Scriptures and in assuring that text transmission without substantial change or alteration was a necessary and fortunate prelude to the invention of printing and the ministry of the printed Hebrew Bible in the modern world. The invention of the printing press in the middle of the fifteenth century was an event of incalculable importance. The long laborious process of copying out the Scriptures by hand with all its attendant evils of liability to error and variation in different manuscripts was ended. Printing not only made far greater accuracy possible, but assured a much wider publication of the Sacred Scriptures.

1. The Earliest Printed Editions of the Hebrew Bible.

The first part of the Hebrew Old Testament to be put into print was the Psalter in 1477, twenty-seven years after the invention of the printing press. It was printed with the rabbinical commentary of Kimchi, text and commentary alternating at each verse. During the next decade (1477-1487) some four editions, covering all of the Old Testament, appeared in as many cities.

In 1488 the first edition of the whole Hebrew Old Testament with vowels and accents was completed at Soncino, near Milan, Italy. It was reissued at Naples 1491-1493, and appeared a third time in the Brescia Bible in 1494. This is the Hebrew text translated by Martin Luther, whose copy is at Berlin. This text was reproduced substantially in D. Bomberg's manual editions (Venice, 1516-1517, 1521, 1525-1528), in the editions of S. Munster (Basel, 1536) and R. Stephanus (Paris, 1539-1544). All these editions appeared under the direction of Jewish scholars. Printed editions of the Hebrew Scriptures thus appear from 1477 to the present.

2. *Printed Editions of the Hebrew Bible Under Christian Auspices.*

a. The Complutensian Polyglot.

This massive opus carried the Hebrew, Septuagint Greek and Latin Vulgate in columns and the Targum of Onkelos on the Pentateuch printed at the bottom. It was edited by Cardinal Ximenes and printed at the University he founded at Alcala (*Complutum*), Spain, 1514-1517. Its critical value is slight because of its defects and frequent errors. It did illustrate, however, the value such an edition might have if it possessed critical accuracy.

b. The Antwerp Polyglot.

For the Old Testament (Vols. I-IV) appeared the Hebrew text, the Targums (except Daniel, Ezra-Nehemiah, and Chronicles) with a Latin version, the Complutensian text of the Septuagint with a Latin version and the Vulgate. Other volumes embraced the New Testament. The work was called *Biblia Regia* because its publication was financed by Philip II. It was printed at Antwerp (1569-1572).

c. The Paris Polyglot.

Volumes I-IV reproduce the Old Testament and its versions as found in the Antwerp Polyglot. Volumes V and VI deal with the New Testament. Volumes VII-X contain the Samaritan Pentateuch with its Targum, the Peshitta and the Arabic versions of the Old Testament, all of which are translated into Latin. It appeared in Paris, 1629-1645.

d. The London Polyglot.

This work, which still possesses critical value, is the most comprehensive and important of the three great polyglots. The six folio volumes of the polyglot proper are supplemented in Volume VII-VIII (1669), with a dictionary of Hebrew, Aramaic, Syriac, Samaritan, Ethiopic and Arabic, with a separate

Persian vocabulary and a comparative Semitic grammar. The scholarly prolegomena in Volume I is still invaluable. The work appeared in London from 1657-1669 and was financed by public subscription.

4. The Standard Printed Edition of the Massoretic Text.

This is the text of Jacob Ben Chayyim published at Venice 1525-1526 in four volumes. This venture was sponsored by D. Bomberg, who had previously sponsored his first Rabbinical Bible in 1516-1517. Ben Chayyim's text, essentially a recension of Ben Asher with only an occasional reading from Ben Naphtali, remained unsurpassed among the early editions and became standard. This is the so-called *editio princeps* of the Hebrew Bible, forming the standard edition of the Massoretic text. It was frequently reprinted in the sixteenth century. It was used by Rudolf Kittel in the first and second editions of his *Biblia Hebraica* (1905 and 1912), unhappily, however, with tacit emendations in the form of variants from the ancient versions. It was also used by C. D. Ginsburg (1894 and 1926).

The received text of our standard editions is substantially that of Jacob Ben Chayyim. It is the basis of the manual edition of J. Buxdorf (Basel, 1611) and, finally, of A. Hahn (1832, 1833, and 1868) and M. Letteris (Vienna, 1852), which was reprinted in 1866 by the British and Foreign Bible Society.

Critically important modern editions are those of C. D. Ginsburg and R. Kittel (first edition 1905, second, 1912, third 1929-1945, fourth 1949). Kittel's third edition contains Ben Asher's text in its purest form, and other scholars have contributed a critical apparatus of selected variants from manuscripts and ancient versions.

VII. THE SAMARITAN PENTATEUCH

The Samaritan Pentateuch is *not* a version of a portion of the Hebrew Old Testament, but a part of the *text itself.* Because it is an independent text of the Pentateuch which had its own distinct transmission by scribes from the fifth century B.C., without any known contact with the numerous Hebrew texts, it reaches farther back to the origin of the Hebrew text than the oldest translation (the Septuagint), simply because it is the text itself.

1. The Origin of the Samaritan Pentateuch.

The strange religious community of the Samaritans owes its existence to the governmental policy of the New Assyrian Empire established by Tiglath-pileser III (745-727). The emperor, a great conqueror, initiated the inhuman policy of deporting whole conquered populations to other parts of his realm and importing foreigners to take their place with the remaining residents of the land. This expedient, resorted to, to reduce chances of revolt, resulted in a commingling of foreign peoples and a fusion of strange customs.

a. The Origin of the Samaritan Race.

After Sargon II, king of Assyria, captured Samaria (721 B.C.), he put an end to the kingdom of Israel by sending many of its people into captivity. To discourage rebellion in those Israelites who remained and to insure their complete denationalization, Sargon followed the precedent established by his famous predecessor, Tiglath-pileser III, and imported heathen people from Eastern provinces of the Empire (II Kings 17:5, 6, 24) to take their place. These peoples of pagan background intermarried with the remaining Israelites, producing a mongrel race, later known as the Samaritans.

It is a mistake to assume from II Kings 17:23 and 18:11 that Sargon carried away *all* the people of the Northern Kingdom or that the transported people constituted the entire new population. This is not specifically said to be the case, and such an interpretation would be contrary to the king's own statement in his Annals. "In the beginning of my reign in my first year . . . Samaria I besieged, I captured; 27,290 persons of its inhabitants I carried captive . . . but the remainder of the people I allowed to retain their possessions. I appointed my governor over them, and the tribute of the former king I imposed upon them."[28]

b. The Origin of the Samaritan Religion.

After the Jews returned from the Babylonian captivity in 536 B.C., the Samaritans offered their aid in rebuilding the Temple. Being refused they took offence and became adversaries to the Jews, doing all in their power to hinder the work (Ezra 4). At the time of Nehemiah they continued their opposition, doing their utmost to stop the building of the walls of Jerusalem (Nehemiah chs. 4 and 6).

In the course of his program of reform, Nehemiah discovered that a grandson of the high priest Eliashib had married a daughter of Sanballat, the governor of Samaria and the bitter foe of the Jews. Such alliances with foreigners were strictly contrary to the Law (Leviticus 21:14). Nehemiah forthwith expelled the offender along with others who would not submit to the reformation (Nehemiah 13:28-30).

It is now generally agreed that this incident, which took place about 432 B.C., furnishes the historical background of the Samaritan schism. Josephus, who misplaces the story a century later in the time of Alexander the Great, actually names the expelled priest as Manasseh and adds that he took with him a copy of the Torah when he fled to Samaria and headed the rival worship established in the Temple built on Mount Gerizim.

This is undoubtedly a correct tradition and the basis of the religious aspect of the Jewish-Samaritan hostility, with rival temple and priesthood set up on Mount Gerizim at Shechem (Nablus) and a rival Torah, as the Sacred Book of the new religious system. An old untenable theory which exists to the effect that the Samaritan Pentateuch came down in the

28 Cf. Daniel David Luckenbill, **Ancient Records of Assyria and Babylonia** ol. II, sections 4 and 55.

line of transcription from the Pentateuch current in Israel at the time of the revolt of the ten tribes under Jeroboam, is now for good reasons, generally abandoned. This may likewise be said of the theory that holds that the Torah was brought to the Samaritans by the priests sent by Sargon to instruct the people after the fall of Samaria (II Kings 17:26-28).

2. *The Critical Value of the Samaritan Pentateuch.*

When the first copy of the Samaritan Pentateuch came to the attention of the modern scholarly world in 1616, great contributions to textual criticism were expected of it. However, it has generally failed to fulfill these high expectations. After a careful study of all variant readings in the light of the Massoretic text, Gesenius, the celebrated Hebraist, in 1815 came to the conclusion that in scarcely a single instance was the Samaritan reading to be preferred to the Massoretic. Although in recent years scholars have questioned the sweeping character of Gesenius' conclusions and show a tendency to give more consideration to Samaritan readings,[29] there are considerations which tend to minimize the critical importance of the Samaritan Pentateuch.

a. Extant Manuscripts of the Samaritan Pentateuch are of Late Date.

Kennicott, the eighteenth-century textual critic, collated sixteen Samaritan manuscripts. None of these is as old as the oldest Hebrew manuscripts. The oldest (in the New York Public Library) dates 1232 A.D. The first copy of the Samaritan Pentateuch to reach Europe after a millennium of oblivion (it was known to Origen, Eusebius of Caesarea, Epiphanius, etc.) was brought thither by the Italian traveler Pietro de la Valle, from the Samaritan community in Damascus. It was published in the Paris Polyglot (1645) and the London Polyglot (1657).

29 Cf. S. A. Cartledge, **A Conservative Introduction to the Old Testament.** p. 3

b. The Samaritan Pentateuch Covers the Best Preserved Part of the Old Testament.

The Torah is not only the best preserved part of the Hebrew Bible, but the best translated portion. It is, accordingly, that section which needs least correction and could benefit least from an independent text which had its own distinct transmission.

c. The Bulk of the Variations from the Hebrew Text are Unimportant.

Of the 6,000 alleged variations, in 1900 of which it agrees with the Septuagint against the Massoretic text,[30] a large proportion of these are quite insignificant as affecting the meaning of a passage. Only a few are really important. In many instances the Samaritans made orthographic and grammatical revisions which do not affect the words of the text. A. Sperber, explains some important grammatical differences under the theory that the Samaritan Pentateuch preserves North Israelite dialectal peculiarities, while the Massoretic text preserves a recension of the Judean dialect[31] in the form of explanatory glosses, removal of fancied verbal difficulties, conjectural changes, etc. Other variations are due to changes in the Samaritan text for dogmatic reasons. In Deuteronomy 27:4 "Ebal" is changed to "Gerizim" and this altered passage is interpolated after Exodus 20:17 and Deuteronomy 5:21.

It is evident that these differences are not invaluable in seeking the true text. Perhaps the main feature of the Samaritan Pentateuch, although separated for so many centuries from the Hebrew text, is its striking and substantial agreement with that text except in these mostly unimportant variations. This fact makes it a valuable witness of the substantial purity of the Hebrew text as we have it preserved for us in the Massoretic tradition.

30 P. Kahle, Theologische Studien und Kritiken 88 (1915), pp. 399-439.
31 Hebrew Union College Annual XII-XIII (1937-1938). pp. 151 f.

LITERATURE ON THE TEXT

Haevernick, H. A. C., *Introduction to the Old Testament,* (Edinburgh, 1852), pp. 225-293.

Wickes, W., *A Treatise on the Accentuation of the Three Poetical Books of the Old Testament* (Oxford, 1881); *A Treatise on the Accentuation of the Twenty-one Prose Books of the Old Testament,* (Oxford, 1887).

Wright, C. H. H., *An Introduction to the Old Testament,* (New York, 1890), pp. 16-39.

Loisy, A., *Histoire critique du texte et des versions de la Bible,* 2 vols., (Paris, 1892, 1895).

Ginsburg, C. D., *Introduction to the Masoretico-Critical Edition of the Hebrew Bible,* (London, 1897).

Cooke, G. A., *Text-book of North-Semitic Inscriptions,* (Oxford, 1903).

Strack, H. L., "Text of the Old Testament," *Hastings' Dictionary of the Bible,* (Edinburgh, 1898-1904).

Weir, T. H., "Text of the Old Testament," *The International Standard Bible Encyclopedia, V,* (Grand Rapids, 1939), and *A Short History of the Hebrew Text of the Old Testament,* (London, 1907).

Geden, A. S., *Outlines of Introduction to the Hebrew Bible,* (Edinburgh, 1909).

Wiener, H. M., *The Pentateuchal Text,* (London, 1914).

Naville, E., *The Text of the Old Testament,* (The Schweich Lectures, 1915), (London, 1916), pp. 1-78.

Bauer-Leander, *Historische Grammatik der Hebraischen Sprache,* I Band, (1922), pp. 1-55.

Gordis, R., *The Biblical Text in the Making: A Study of the Kethiv-Kere,* (Philadelphia, 1937).

Kenyon, F., *Our Bible and the Ancient Manuscripts,* (London, 1939), pp. 3-47.

Zimmerman, E., "The Perpetuation of Variants in the Massoretic Text," *Jewish Quarterly Review* 34, pp. 459-474.

Pfeiffer, R., *Introduction to the Old Testament,* (New York, 1941,) pp. 71-101.

Robinson, H. W., *The Bible in its Ancient and English Versions,* (Oxford, 1941).

Kahle, P., *The Cairo Geniza,* The Schweich Lectures of the British Academy, 1941, (London, 1947), Lecture II, "The Hebrew Text of the Bible," pp. 36-115; *Masoreten des Ostens,* (1913); *Masoreten des Westens,* (1927).

Bentzen, A., *Introduction to the Old Testament,* Vol. 1, (Copenhagan, 1948), "The Text," pp. 42-58.

Goldman, S., *The Book of Books: An Introduction,* (New York, 1948), pp. 33-38.

For the origin and pronunciation of the divine name YHWH see G. F. Moore in *Old Testament and Semitic Studies in Memory of W. R. Harper,* Vol. I, (Chicago, 1908), pp. 145-163; *American Journal of Theology* 12, (1908), 34-52; Arnold W. R. in *Journal of Biblical Literature* 24, (1905), pp. 107-165; W. F. Albright *Jour. Bib. Lit.* 43, (1924), pp. 370-378, 44, (1925), pp. 158-162; J. A. Montgomery *Jour Bib. Lit.* 25, (1906), pp. 49-54; D. D. Luckenbill *Am. Jour. Sem. Lang.* 40, (1924), pp. 277-283.

Driver, G. R., *Semitic Writing: From Pictograph to Alphabet,* (Schweich Lectures, London, 1944).

Chapter VI

ANCIENT VERSIONS
OF THE OLD TESTAMENT

A version, as applied to Scripture, is a translation of the Bible into another language. The term usually embraces the thought of a rendering from the original in which the Bible is written into another tongue. The Hebrew Old Testament enjoys the unique distinction of being the first book, or rather a library of books (for such it is), known to be translated into another tongue. This translation took place in the third and second centuries B.C. During this period the entire Hebrew Bible was put into the Greek language. This version, as well as various subsequent translations into other languages, was made to meet a definite need. As the Word of God with a vital message for all mankind, it was inevitable that the Scripture would be required in other tongues beside its own. For this reason the work of translating the Bible into other languages has continued unceasingly throughout the centuries and to a phenomenal degree in our present day.

An "ancient version" is one which was made before the invention of printing. After 1450 the term "modern version" is usually employed. There are four ancient versions of the Old Testament, which are of great importance because they were made directly from the Hebrew: the Greek *Septuagint,* the Aramaic *Targums,* the Syriac *Peshitta* and the Latin *Vulgate.* Of these the most important by reason of its age and because it was rendered into the same language in which

148

the New Testament was later written, and served as the Bible of the Apostles and the Early Church, is the Greek Septuagint.

I. THE GREEK SEPTUAGINT

This translation is also commonly abbreviated LXX ("Seventy") and known as the Alexandrian version, from the city of its origin. It is the oldest known rendition of the Jewish Scriptures into another tongue.

1. The Historical Circumstances Requiring A Greek Version of the Old Testament.

From the earliest period of the patriarchs Jews had periodically gone down to Egypt in times of famine, war or for other reasons. In 586 B.C., shortly after the destruction of Jerusalem, there was a migration thither (Jer. 43:5-7; 44:1). However, not until the time of Alexander the Great and the subsequent reign of the Ptolemies did the most favorable conditions develop for Jewish emigration to the land of the Nile.

a. Alexander's Favorable Policy.

Alexander, quickly conquering Phoenicia and Palestine, swept on into Egypt. There, in 332 B.C., he founded the important and remarkably cosmopolitan city of Alexandria, his namesake. The Greek language everywhere took firm foothold in the wake of Alexander's phenomenal conquests and became the harbinger of Greek culture. Alexander was especially favorably impressed by the intelligence and conduct of the Jews of Palestine. His generosity toward them caused many of them to accompany him to Egypt. Numbers of them settled in and about Alexandria.

b. The Generosity of the Ptolemies.

After Alexander's death, the Ptolemies, under whose sway Egypt came, continued Alexander's policy of liberality toward the Jews. Ptolemy I, Soter, (323-285) brought many thousands of Jews from Palestine to Alexandria, conferred full political and religious rights upon them, and granted them other favors. He made Alexandria a city of learning and culture, establishing a famous library, museum and college.

Ptolemy II, Philadelphus, (285-246) continued his father's educational and cultural program and also his beneficent attitude toward the Jews. By this time Greek had become the common language of trade and culture in Egypt. Accordingly, it became impossible for the Jews to maintain their social and business standing and, at the same time, cling to their Semitic speech. Just as they had dropped Hebrew for Aramaic, so they now abandoned Aramaic for Greek. Hence arose an imperative need for a translation of the Old Testament Scriptures into the Greek language both for the synagogue services and for private reading.

2. *The Traditional Origin of the Greek Version of the Old Testament.*

Being the first foreign tongue into which the Old Testament was translated, and eventually becoming the Bible of all the Greek-speaking countries of the Mediterranean world before and in the time of Christ and the early Christian centuries, and, in addition, being the mother text of several translations, the origin of the Alexandrian version is of the greatest interest and importance to students of the Bible.

a. Origin of the Term Septuagint.

The common designation of the Greek Old Testament is derived from the ancient tradition of its origin. The name comes from the Latin *Septuaginta,* "Seventy." According to the letter of Aristeas, the authenticity of which is now seriously doubted, the librarian of the royal library at Alexandria suggested to the king the importance of having a Greek translation of the Hebrew law made for the library. The idea pleased the king, who, it is said, freed all Hebrew slaves, and then sent an embassy with rich gifts to the high priest at Jerusalem begging him to send a copy of the Torah with scholars to translate it into Greek. The result was that six translators were selected from each of the twelve tribes. The story is gaudily furnished with other details. The translation is alleged to have been completed in seventy-two days on the quiet island of Pharos and endorsed by an assemby of Jews.

This obviously fictitious story was repeated by various writers, among whom were Philo, who believed the translators were inspired, Josephus and many of the Church fathers, including Irenaeus, Clement of Alexandria, Cyril, Augustine and others. The unauthentic elements in the letter of Aristeas were not only accepted without suspicion by many of the Church fathers, but several of them added to them. Jerome ridiculed these later inventions. From the sixteenth century on the letter of Aristeas has been doubted, until at the present time it has few defenders.

b. Factual Basis of the Septuagintal Tradition.

When the popularized and embellished story is carefully sifted, the following facts may legitimately be assumed to be genuine. The version was made at Alexandria, and by Alexandrian rather than Palestinian Jews. This accords with the general trend of critical opinion, because the translation, while often almost slavishly literal, is nevertheless in many places quite free, frequently departing from the Hebrew text, which would have been improbable in the case of Palestinian Jews, who held the sacred text inviolable. In addition, Palestinian Jews, much more traditionally minded and insensitive to the need for a Greek translation than their Alexandrian colleagues, would certainly have been adverse, at least at this time, to translating the sacred Hebrew Scriptures into a *pagan* language. Moreover, it may be noted that the translation displays an imperfect knowledge of the Hebrew, containing many words, phrases and idioms peculiar to the Greek used at Alexandria, including quite a few Egyptian words, besides showing a lack of accuracy regarding Palestinian place names.

It may be safely gathered also that the Law was first translated about 250 B.C. in the reign of Ptolemy Philadelphus, and that the translation was made to meet the need of the Greek-speaking Jews at Alexandria.

3. *The Quality of the Translation of the Greek Version of the Old Testament.*

In evaluating the Septuagint as a translation many factors must be taken into account, such as the general purpose and character of the work, the peculiar difficulties with which the translators were confronted and the general principles which directed them in the performance of their task. Taking these items into consideration, the following conclusions may be stated concerning the quality of the Septuagint version.

a. It Varies In Its Standard of Excellence.

The Pentateuch, for example, is on the whole "a close and serviceable translation," while "the Psalms and more especially the Book of Isaiah show obvious signs of incompetence."[1] Daniel at times is rendered so freely it becomes mere Midrashic paraphrase. The Greek is "unintelligently literal" in the later part of Jeremiah.[2] Internal evidence shown by the varying quality of the work and other phenomena demonstrate that the Greek Bible is actually *not* a single version, but a *series* of versions produced at different times by translators of varying abilities and ideals.

b. It Varies In Its Precise Purpose.

It seems obvious that the aim the Pentateuchal translators had in mind, namely, to supply the need of the Alexandrian synagogue, did not coincide precisely with that of the later translators of the prophets and the writings. It is possible, however, that as early as this the major prophets and the twelve may have been translated with the same general purpose of synagogical service as the law, but it is not necessary to assume as Swete does, that if the translators did so, they performed their task "under a diminished sense of responsibility."[3]

1 H. B. Swete, **Introduction To The Old Testament in Greek**, pp. 315 ff.
2 Cf. R. R. Ottley, **A Handbook to the Septuagint**, p. 110.
3 Swete, **op, cit**, p. 318.

Critics assume that the prophets were held in lower esteem than the law, and the hagiographa than the prophets, and that the varying quality of the translation is largely to be accounted for on this basis. This, of course, is the result of the erroneous theory of the gradual development of the canon and the concomitant growth of esteem and concern for the text. Large sections of poetry in the prophets (Isaiah and the Twelve, for example) and the difficult poetry of Psalms, Job and Proverbs, together with the varying ability of the translators and similar factors, with, perhaps, some variation in the precise purpose as an element in the total situation, constitute a sufficient explanation without resort to the unsound notion that the prophets and writings were not held to be as inspired and authoritative as the law, and hence not worthy of as much patience and skill in translation.

In addition, may it not be possible, consensus of critical opinion to the contrary notwithstanding, that the letter of Aristeas does preserve the true tradition that Palestinian, rather than Alexandrian Jews were the translators of the Torah? May this not be the reason, in part at least, for the superiority of its translation over that of the prophets and the kethubhim, which, on the other hand, obviously were rendered by Alexandrian Jews defective in their knowledge of Hebrew and Hebrew tradition?

c. It is Conditioned by Its Peculiar Difficulties.

It must not be overlooked that the Septuagint was a pioneer venture, involving, in addition, the Herculean task of translating a Semitic book into the language of the West and the delicate job of fitting Hebrew idiom into the mold of Hellenistic Greek. The translator of Ecclesiasticus complained of the difficulty of the assignment in his day (132 B.C.). If it is true that *all* the translators were Alexandrian Jews, they doubtless learned Hebrew from imperfectly instructed teachers, deficient in traditional textual minutiae. This lack of a sound tradition especially crops out in the poetical passages and books.

Critics customarily postulate a textual difficulty and maintain that the Hebrew text used by the Septuagint translators was materially different from that after A.D. 90, when they assume that a thorough revision of the Hebrew Bible took place. This position is to be seriously questioned, apparently being based upon insufficient and inconclusive evidence.[4] There are many possible explanations of the differences between the Hebrew text after A.D. 90 and the Septuagint-Hebrew text without resort to the unsound notion that the former was substantially changed *in content* when it was revised sometime during the period of rabbi Akiba.

The Septuagint translators, on the other hand, undoubtedly faced a paleographic problem. From evidence supplied by the Jerusalem Scroll of Isaiah (about 125 B.C.) and the Nash Papyrus (about 100 B.C.), both of which employ the square-type Hebrew characters, there is every reason to believe that the alphabet of the Septuagintal Hebrew manuscripts was a transitional one, between the archaic letters of the old Phoenician script and the later square Aramaic-type characters. This seems evident because the translators repeatedly confuse letters similar in the square characters, but not in the archaic script.

Besides this, it must be remembered at this period words were evidently not yet separated by any system of punctuation or spacing, and there were no vowel points. Taking all these factors into consideration, it is evident that the Septuagint translators faced grave problems which demanded great ingenuity and skill to solve.

d. It Displays Loyalty to the Original.

This is true in a general sense and sometimes to a degree that amounts to a fault. Greek idiom is frequently sacrificed,

4 See chapter V.

and the reader familiar with Hellenistic Greek is continually reminded that he has before him the translation of a Semitic writing. In some cases the translator is faithful to the conceived meaning of the Hebrew, even when it makes no sense in the Greek. Even when the original is correctly understood, it is often rendered in unidiomatic Greek with little attention to rhythm or style.

Over against this general loyalty to the text, however, is a concomitant freedom of treatment. The Septuagint translators frequently interpret, qualify or paraphrase. Even in the same context they render the same Hebrew word by more than one Greek equivalent. They amplify and occasionally omit. Their translation on the whole, is, accordingly, far from slavishly literal.

e. It Reveals a Large Number of Actual Mistakes.

These blunders are not due to a faulty unrevised Hebrew archetype used by the translators, as some critics imagine, but chiefly to the misreading or misunderstanding of the archetype at their disposal. Transpositions, omissions and other blunders occur. An insufficient grasp of Hebrew or the complete miscomprehension of a context often is evident. It must be remembered, too, that "no sharp distinction was made in those days between the work of translation and that of interpretation. Thus the Septuagint is in some places a translation, in others a paraphrase and in others a running commentary."[5]

With these deficiences in mind the Septuagint must be used with great caution and reserve, whether for textual or hermeneutical purposes. It is manifestly inferior to the Massoretic text of the Hebrew Bible under any consideration. But taken as a whole, and evaluated in the light of the difficulties and pioneer circumstances under which it was produced, it is not only a creditable job, but an invaluable witness to the pre-Christian text of the Old Testament.

5 J. H. Raven, Introduction to the Old Testament, p. 66.

4. The Immense Importance of the Greek Version of the Old Testament.

Despite its deficiences and limitations, the importance of the Septuagint, in Judaism among Greek-speaking Jews and in Christianity in its vital role as the Bible of the Early Church, can hardly be exaggerated. Religiously, spiritually, historically and critically the Alexandrian version is of first-rate significance.

a. The Importance of the Septuagint Religiously and Spiritually.

It met the religious and liturgical needs of Alexandrian Jews and Greek-speaking Jewish proselytes in the pre-Christian era, and was a vital force in Alexandrian Judaism and philosophy for several centuries. Much more important in the history of redemption, it released the great revealed truths concerning creation, redemption, sin and salvation from the narrow isolation of the Hebrew tongue and people and gave them to the world through the divinely prepared vehicle of the Greek language, the *lingua franca* of the Graeco-Roman Age (300 B.C.-300 A.D.). It thus bridged the gap between the Hebrew and Greek-speaking peoples of the ancient world.

In a vital sense the Septuagint prepared the way for the coming of Christianity and the New Testament by releasing the Old Testament revelation in the same universal language in which the New Testament was destined to be written. The result was that the completed divine revelation became available to all in the *one* international language of the period. This momentous ministry of bringing God's revealed truth to the people of that age the Greek Old Testament shared with the New Testament. Before the New Testament was written, it *was* the Bible of early Christianity, and after it was written, it was added to the Septuagint to form the completed Scriptures of Christianity.

b. The Importance of the Septuagint Historically.

As the first translation of the Hebrew Scriptures into a foreign language, the Septuagint gained great prestige. Philo quotes generously from the Old Testament and always from the Septuagint. Josephus largely employed it. Jesus and the New Testament writers quoted from it, as well as from the Hebrew. It was received and adhered to by the Jews of the dispersion until the early second century of the Christian era. However, in the schools and synagogues of Palestine the sacred Hebrew was venerated.

The early Christian Church received the Septuagint from the Jews, according it the same veneration, quoting from it and using it to establish doctrine and to buttress argument in controversy. It was the vehicle for early missionary work and furnished the text for the Old Latin, Egyptian, Ethiopic, Gothic, Slavonic and other versions.

c. The Importance of the Septuagint Critically.

Despite variation between the Septuagint and the Hebrew Bible, there is a substantial agreement, which attests the genuineness and authenticity of the ancient Hebrew Scriptures. What the Samaritan Pentateuch did in attesting the integrity of the Hebrew Pentateuch some four hundred years or more before Christ, the Septuagint did for the rest of the Old Testament some two hundred or more years later.

The earliest Septuagint manuscripts (Codex Sinaiticus, Codex Alexandrinus, Codex Vaticanus, and Codex Ephraemi Rescriptus) antedate the earliest Hebrew manuscripts (early tenth century A.D.) by more than five hundred years, with the exception of the new Jerusalem Scroll of Isaiah (late second century B.C.) and the fragment of the Nash Papyrus (100 B.C.). Despite the recent exciting manuscript discoveries, the Septuagint still remains the earliest witness to the original Old Testament text (except for the Samaritan text of the Pentateuch) and, excluding the Isaiah Scroll, was made between a thousand and eleven hundred years before the earliest dated extant Hebrew manuscripts. It represents a Hebrew text which is earlier than the present uniform text, but we do not believe this Hebrew text is materially different in content from that after A.D. 90.

The critical value of the Septuagint, on the other hand, despite the antiquity of its witness to the Hebrew text, is substantially reduced, as noted, because the translation varies in its standard of excellence and in its precise purpose, is conditioned by peculiar difficulties, manifests both a loyalty and a freedom in dealing with the original and is marred by a large number of inaccuracies and mistakes. Added to this, there is no homogeneous extant text. Septuagintal manuscripts became exceedingly corrupt in the course of transmission and it is now evidently impossible to recapture completely the original text.

5. *The Later History of the Greek Version of the Old Testament.*

a. Jewish Reaction Against the Septuagint.

An increasing hostility toward Christianity together with a growing resistance in Jewish schools against all non-Jewish culture combined to bring the Septuagint into general disfavor with Jews by the first quarter of the second century. To a large extent Christians had come to venerate the Alexandrian version as inspired and authoritative and were using it in controversy with Jews to prove the Messiahship of Jesus. This was particularly annoying to the Jews, inasmuch as errors had crept into the manuscripts of the Septuagint, which differed from each other as well as from the Hebrew Scriptures. Christian and Jew mutually accused one another of tampering with the text.

Seemingly, Jewish scholarship and the labors of the sopherim had resulted in a carefully reworked Hebrew text, which, although it did not differ in actual content from the present text, yet presented another argument for a new and more accurate Greek translation. When this was executed, the Jews cast off the Septuagint.

b. Aquila's Rival Jewish Version.

Made about 130 A.D., this slavishly literal Greek translation of the second century Hebrew text became the substitute for the Septuagint for Greek-speaking Jews. Aquila, who is said to have become a Christian and afterward to have gone into Judaism and who received a thorough training under Akiba and the rabbis, executed the translation. Its extreme literalness gives it value to Biblical criticism, since it shows the meaning which the interpreters of that day gave to the text.

c. Theodotian's Revision of the Septuagint.

Early in the second century, possibly before Aquila,[6] Theodotian, who was an Ebionite or Judaizing Christian according to Jerome, revised the Septuagint in order to bring it into harmony with the current Hebrew text. He was not a disciple of Akiba nor a slavish literalist. His version attained wide popularity among Christians. His rendering of Daniel prevails in all extant Greek manuscripts, except one, and in his version of the prophet he incorporates parts of an earlier Greek translation, known through quotations in the New Testament and in other first-century writings.[7]

d. Symmachus' Revision of Aquila.

Prepared probably toward the end of the second century, this translation is a reaction against the frequently incomprehensible literal renderings of Aquila's version, which was revised with the aid of the Septuagint and Theodotian and aimed at the sense rather than the letter.[8]

e. Origen's Hexapla.

By the time of Origen (185-254 A.D.) the text of the Septuagint had become woefully corrupt. There were said to have been as many different readings as manuscripts. Origen undertook the colossal task of correcting the textual corruption and

6 Cf. H. M. Orlinsky, Jewish Quarterly Review N. S. 27 (1936), p. 143.
7 Cf. J. A. Montgomery, Daniel, Int. Crit. Com., pp. 46-50.
8 Cf. Swete, op. cit., pp. 49-53.

unifying the text. Like Jerome, at a later date, the great scholar was convinced that the Hebrew text was the correct one. Accordingly, he mastered Hebrew to recover the correct text of the Greek Bible, which Christians of that day generally regarded as the inerrant transcript of divine revelation.

The result of Origen's incredible labor was the *Hexapla*—a magnificent achievement, which was not only "a textbook wherewith to learn the Hebrew language"[9] but also an effective textual apparatus for eliminating the discrepancies in the Septuagint manuscripts of the Old Testament. Precisely, it contained the Old Testament text six times, in six parallel columns. Hence the significance of its name, *Hexapla*, meaning "sixfold." The first column consisted of the consonantal Hebrew text then current. The other five columns were in Greek. The second column comprised the Hebrew text rendered in Greek letters, the third, Aquila's version, the fourth, Symmachus' version, the fifth, the Septuagint revised by Origen and the sixth, Theodotian's version.

In the psalter Origen added three more columns, giving a *fifth, sixth* and *seventh* Greek version known in his day.[10] There also existed a smaller handier edition, a *Tetrapla* ("fourfold"), which omitted the first two columns.

Origen's great work was placed in the library at Caesarea, and was accessible there until the Moslems burned the city in 638 A.D., when the priceless manuscript disappeared. The important fifth column, representing the great scholar's revision of the Septuagintal text, was recopied repeatedly, but when it became separated from the rest of the work, the critical symbols, which the other columns explained, became unintelligible to copyists, who were careless in their use or omitted them altogether. The result was that the versions were mixed, with no way of telling them apart, and became the means of defeating the very object the author had in mind.

9 Orlinsky, **op. cit.,** p. 149.
10 Eusebius, **Ecclesiastical History,** 6:16.

Fortunately, however, a Syriac translation of part of the fifth column with critical symbols is extant, containing the poetical and prophetical books. It is in the Ambrosian Library at Milan. Volume I containing the Pentateuch and the historical books was in existence in 1574, but since it has disappeared. Other smaller fragments of the so-called "Syro-Hexaplaric" version exist in the British Museum.

f. Other Revisions of the Septuagint.

Lucian, a scholar at Antioch (died 311) made a revision of the Septuagint. He supplied omissions and made other changes. His recension was used at Antioch and Constantinople. Hesychius about the same time also made a revision used in Egypt. Little is known of this revision.

Eusebius and Pamphilus around 300 A.D. copied Origen's Septuagint with his corrections and symbols. This copy had a wide circulation in Palestine. Constantine ordered fifty copies of this edition for the churches.

6. *The Important Manuscripts of the Greek Version of the Old Testament.*

Manuscripts of the Septuagint, which are the chief basis for a critical reconstruction of the Alexandrian version in addition to patristic quotations and versions based on the Greek Bible, are fortunately quite numerous in the world's libraries. Those dating from the third or fourth to the ninth century (the most valuable) are written in *uncials,* or large separate capital letters. Later manuscripts from the ninth century to the invention of printing (less valuable critically) are in a small flowing script and are called *cursives.*

At present there are about 170 known uncial manuscripts in existence. The oldest and most important of these listed in order of their critical importance for the Old Testament are The Codex Vaticanus (B), The Codex Alexandrinus (A), The Codex Sinaiticus (Aleph) and The Codex Ephraemi Rescriptus (C).

a. Codex Vaticanus (B).

Dating from about 325-350 A.D. and now in the Vatican Library, Rome, this famous manuscript undoubtedly offers for the Old Testament as a whole the best text of the Septuagint, although it gives an early fourth-century Egyptian version for Judges[11] and Theodotian's translation of Daniel and also of Chronicles-Ezra-Nehemiah, according to Torrey.[12] It contains both the Old and New Testaments and is the property of the Roman Catholic Church. The writing is small neat uncial. The material is fine vellum. It made its historical debut in 1481 when it first appeared in the Vatican Library catalogue.

Since the Roman or Sixtine edition, published at Rome under the auspices of Sixtus V in 1590, Codex B has been the basis of nearly all printed editions of the Greek Bible. Cardinal A. Mai edited the great manuscript in 1828-1838. It was issued in 1857, and a corrected edition put out in 1859. Another edition under the auspices of Pius IX appeared in 1868-1872. Not until 1889-1890 did the Vatican issue a photographic facsimile of the entire manuscript, making it accessible to the scholarly world at large. The text of Codex B is Egyptian, and in the main "reproduces a pre-Origenic text."[13]

b. Codex Alexandrinus (A).

Dated around 450 A.D. and stemming from Egypt, this important uncial codex gives the Old and New Testaments, except for some substantial lacunae, notably, Genesis, I Samuel and Psalms. Its general text seems to follow Origen's Hexaplaric edition of the Septuagint, capturing, however, some earlier readings. In 1078 it was presented to the Patriarch of Alexandria, thereby obtaining the name *Codex Alexandrinus.* In the seventeenth century the mansucript came into the pos-

11 G. F. Moore, Judges, **Int. Crit. Com.,** pp. XLV f.
12 C. C. Torrey, **Ezra Studies** (Chicago, 1901), pp. 66 f.
13 R. Pfeiffer, **Old Testament Introduction,** p. 113.

session of the British nation and is now in the British Museum.

c. Codex Sinaiticus (Aleph).

Discovered by Constantin Tischendorf in the Monastery of St. Catherines on Mt. Sinai in the middle of the nineteenth century, this manuscript, the text of which in general resembles that of Codex B, was written at the end of the fourth century or early in the fifth. The fragments were published at different times by their discoverer and were collated by E. Nestle in a supplement to the sixth and seventh editions of Tischendorf's *Vetus Testamentum Graece* (Leipzig, 1880, 1887). The codex is now in the British Museum, having been purchased for over a half million dollars from the Soviet Union in 1933, into whose hands it fell after the Russian Revolution.

d. *Codex Ephraemi Rescriptus* (C).

Stemming probably from the fifth century,[14] this codex is a palimpsest, now in the Bibliotheque Nationale in Paris. The Biblical text on its sixty-four Old Testament leaves (containing parts of Job, Proverbs, Ecclesiastes, Wisdom of Solomon and Canticles) has been erased to make room for a treatise of St. Ephraem of Syria in the twelfth century. Only with great difficulty can the underlying Biblical text be deciphered.

e. Other Septuagint Manuscripts.

Codex Cottonianus (D), a charred fragment of the fifth century, and the Bodleian Genesis (E), containing large intact portions of Genesis, are to be listed with the more important uncials. Other uncials and minuscule codices likewise contain only fragmentary portions of the Old Testament. Collations of large numbers of them are given in the still indispensable edition of R. Holmes and J. Parsons[15] and in the "Larger Cambridge Septuagint."[16] The new manual text

14 Cf. Swete, op, cit., p. 129.
15 **Vetus Testamentum Graece cum variius lectionibus**, 5 vols. (Oxford, 1798-1827).
16 Edited by A. E. Brooke and N. McLean, Vol. I, 1906, etc.

of the Septuagint entitled *Septuaginta* by Rahlfs[17] is based principally on the three great uncial codices, Aleph, A and B, with selected variants from other sources collated in a small critical apparatus, and is of primary critical importance.

II. THE ARAMAIC TARGUMS

The Targums, like the Septuagint, were made directly from the original Hebrew and are similar also in that both are renderings in the common language of the period to meet a definite need. However, unlike the Septuagint, the Targums are not, strictly speaking, a translation, but free paraphrastic renderings of the Hebrew Scriptures into Aramaic. The word itself comes from an Aramaic quadriliteral verb, *trgm,* meaning "to translate from one language to another" or "to interpret." In Ezra 4:7 the *pual* participial form of the verb *methurgam,* occurs, meaning "translated." From the same root we get our modern word "dragoman" (from "targoman"), meaning an "interpreter or traveler's agent."

1. *The Origin and Date of the Targums.*

The Targums came into existence by a gradual process which began in the post-captivity period when Hebrew began to fade out as the popular language of the Jews. As the synagogue developed and the law, and later, selections from the prophets were read, it was necessary to appoint, in addition to the reader, an officer called a *methurgeman* or interpreter, whose duty it was after the reading of each verse in the Pentateuch and after each three verses in the prophets, to render the passage freely in the language of the people.

For a long time oral, the Targums were finally written down. The original Palestinian Targums of the law and the prophets (those of the writings are late) date from the second century A.D. They were edited in Babylonia during the third century and are extant in the form of late recensions.[18]

---

17 2 vols. (Stuttgart, 1935).
18 E. Schuerer, **Geschichte des Juedischen Volkes,** Vol. I (Leipzig, 1901), pp. 147-156.

2. The Three Important Targums.

None of the Targums covers the entire Old Testament, but together give us Aramaic renderings of all the books, except Daniel and Ezra-Nehemiah. These were not translated into Aramaic because of the Aramaic portions of Daniel and Ezra, Nehemiah being classed with Ezra.

a. The Targum of Onkelos.

The oldest and best Targum on the Pentateuch is the one erroneously assigned to "Onkelos" by a confusion of the name with Aquila, the author of the Greek version. A rabbinic legend is current to the effect that this, the official Targum on the Torah, was dictated to Onkelos by two contemporaries of rabbi Akiba, Eliezer and Joshua by name. But scholars are now generally agreed that *Onkelos* is merely an Aramaic spelling of Aquila (*Akylas*). Onkelos is strictly literal except for a paraphrastic rendering of the poetic passages and some of the prose sections. Some critics maintain that it is a revision of an old Palestinian Targum in which the differences between this and rabbi Akiba's later so-called "official Hebrew text" were eliminated.[19] This, however, is largely conjectural and possesses no concrete proof. Some scholars think it was composed in Babylon.

Two later Targums on the Pentateuch, which seem to be survivals of the earlier paraphrastic Palestinian Targum antedating Onkelos, appeared in late enlarged editions called "Jerusalem Targum" and in a slightly different recension "Targum of Jonathan." The latter is frequently called the Pseudo-Jonathan because its name rests on a misinterpretation of the abbreviation "T.J.," which stands for "Jerusalem Targum" and not supposedly for the "Targum of Jonathan," who wrote the Targum on the prophets. The extant edition of "Pseudo-Jonathan" is not earlier than the seventh century. The Jerusalem Targum survives only in fragments and, like Pseudo-Jonathan, contains many legendary additions and is

19 Pfeiffer, **op. cit.**, p. 78.

far inferior to the Targum of Onkelos. Also a third Targum to the Pentateuch called the "Fragment Targum" exists, which may be another recension of the old Palestinian Targum.

b. The Targum of Jonathan On the Prophets.

This, the oldest and the official Targum on the prophets (Joshua-Kings, Isaiah-Minor Prophets), is traditionally, though doubtfully, assigned to Jonathan, the son of Uzziel, a pupil of Hillel, in the first century. It is much more paraphrastic than Onkelos and often becomes a mere running commentary. It was revised in Palestine, rewritten in Babylon in the fourth and fifth centuries and survives in a different recension in the codex Reuchlinianus, edited by P. de Lagarde in 1872. This so-called Jerusalem Targum contains revisions, which are later than the Targum of Jonathan.

c. The Targum On the Hagiographa.

There are several in this category—one on Psalms, Job and Proverbs. Another exists on the rolls (Song, Ruth, Lamentations, Ecclesiastes and Esther). Another is extant on Chronicles. The Targum on Esther appeared in three recensions, attesting its popularity. The Targums on the Megilloth (rolls) and on Chronicles seemingly belonged to an ancient Jerusalem Targum on the Kethubim.

These Targums are relatively unimportant, since they are late, largely the work of individuals, have no official recognition and are free and paraphrastic, sometimes to the extreme.

3. *The Critical Value of the Targums.*

Despite the paraphrase, explanatory insertions and other liberties taken, the Targums are not completely devoid of value in determining the text used by the translators.[20] They have a distinctive use, moreover, in revealing current Jewish exegesis and the meaning the Jews at that time attached to difficult passages.

20 Cf. S. A. Cartledge, **A Conservative Introduction to the Old Testament** (1944), p. 32.

4. The Targums and other Contemporary Jewish Literature.
In the same general period in which Aramaic renderings of the Old Testament came into existence other important Jewish Biblical literature, although neither translations nor paraphrases nor directly connected with the Targums, has a vital connection with the Hebrew Scriptures and the development of the Hebrew Text. This literature consists of the Talmud and the Midrash.

a. The Talmud.
This body of Hebrew laws, civil and canonical, is based on the Torah and represents the learning, opinions and decisions of Jewish teachers from about 300 B.C. until 500 A.D. The Talmud (meaning "teaching" or "doctrine," from the root *limmad* "to teach") consists of two parts, the *Mishnah* (signifying "repetition, explanation"), a collection or digest of "oral laws," traditions and explanations of Scripture, forming the text of the Talmud and the *Gemara* (denoting "supplement"), a commentary on the preceding part, the Mishnah.

The Mishnah or "Second Law," that is, the "oral law," the Pentateuch being the first or written law, was compiled officially around 200 A.D. and written in Hebrew. The Gemara was written in Aramaic. The Palestinian Gemara was completed about 200 A.D. The larger, more authoritative Babylonian Gemara was finished about 500 A.D.

b. The Midrash.
The formal doctrinal and homiletical exposition of the Hebrew Scriptures, written in Hebrew and Aramaic, the Midrash differs from the Targums in that it is a commentary, not a translation, and from the Talmud in that it deals with written law, the Scriptures, and not with oral law. It is broadly divided into two parts, the *Halakah* and the *Haggada*. The former signifies the further expansion of the Law (from *halak* "to go, proceed") and is confined to the Pentateuch. The latter (derived from *nagad* "to tell, to declare") covers the entire Old Testament. The Midrashim flourished about

100 B.C. to 300 A.D., and were first oral and later were reduced to writing. They were the "earliest synagogue homilies."[21]

III. THE SYRIAC PESHITTA

The spread of Christianity and the conversion of peoples outside of Palestine (cf. Acts 1:8) created a need for the Scriptures in the language of the people evangelized. Hence from the second to the tenth century there was a procession of prominent versions. Christianity early spread into Syria. Consequently, there soon arose a demand for the Scriptures in the Syriac tongue.

1. The Syriac Language.

Syriac is the name used to designate the language of Syria (Hebrew, *Aram*) north of Palestine and east of Phoenicia, extending to the Euphrates River. In a larger usage the term includes Mesopotamia proper to the Tigris River. Two prominent cities of Syria were Antioch, the center of Gentile Christianity, and Damascus. Syriac belongs to the Aramaic branch of the Semitic languages and might be termed "Christian Aramaic." Since the Jews applied the term "Aramaic" approbriously to the heathen, Christians rejected it in favor of the designation "Syriac."

2. The Peshitta Syriac Version.

The common Syriac Bible, corresponding to the Vulgate of the Latin, after the ninth century A.D. came to be known as the Peshitta, denoting that which is "simple," that is, presumably to differentiate it from the symbols and complexities of the Syro-Hexaplaric version, based on the Septuagint as found in Origen's Hexapla. It is obviously the work of many hands, and the date of its origin is unknown. It most certainly came into existence after the birth of the Syriac Church about 150. Probably most of the Old Testament Books were translated from the Hebrew by 200. The Pentateuch, seemingly

21 Pfeiffer, op. cit., p. 81.

translated first, follows clearly the Massoretic Hebrew text and resembles the Targum of Onkelos. Some critics suggest a Jewish or a Jewish-Christian origin for not only the Pentateuch, but the entire Peshitta.[22] The most likely opinion is that of Buhl that it "owed its origin to Christian effort, while, to some extent, fragments of older Jewish translations have been made use of in it, and for the rest, the translation was made by Jewish Christians."[23]

Some of the books of the Peshitta were revised to conform with the Septuagint, by virtue of the latter's prestige as the official Christian Bible. The revision was not systematic or thorough, however, and this feature impairs the value of the Peshitta as an independent witness to the original text. Yet, where the Septuagint revision has not been carried out, it offers invaluable testimony to the original of certain Old Testament passages.

By far the most important text of the Peshitta is the codex in the Ambrosian Library, Milan, dating from the sixth or seventh century and edited by A. M. Ceriani 1879-1883. The Syro-Hexaplaric, a slavishly literal version based on the Septuagint of Origen's Hexapla and made by the Monophysite Bishop Paul of Tella in 618, became the Bible of the Monophysites. The Peshitta was used by the Nestorians.

IV. THE LATIN VULGATE

By the time of the rise and spread of Christianity in the first half of the first century A.D. Roman society had become distinctly bilingual. Since Greece and Macedonia had become a Roman province (146 B.C.), there had been a constant influx of Greeks into Rome. When Christianity was brought thither probably before the middle of the first century, it was already set in Greek culture and found a Greek atmosphere awaiting it. Paul preached and wrote in Greek. If

22 Cf. C. H. H. Wright, Introduction to the Old Testament (New York, 1890), p. 49.
23 Frants Buhl, Canon and Text of the Old Testament (Edinburgh, 1892), p. 186.

there were any Latin-speaking Christians, who were un-acquainted with Greek, they were not numerous enough to require a Latin version.

However, the case was different in North Africa around Carthage. There, Latin was the official language and the language of civilization. There, Latin held sway. When Christianity entered Africa at an early date, a need for a Latin version was imperative for a strong Latin-speaking Christian Church and community were in existence.

1. Early Pre-Vulgate Latin Versions.

There were probably several Latin versions current before the rise of the Vulgate. The so-called Old Latin and perhaps another, called the Itala, are conveniently named to distinguish them from Jerome's Vulgate.

a. The Old Latin.

Whether this consists of one version or more than one, is not definitely known, for extant manuscripts differ to such an extent as to raise the question whether or not they had their origin in a single source. Since the Old Latin was soon displaced by the Vulgate, its extant manuscripts are few and incomplete. The Old Testament was put into the Latin tongue around 150. The version was made from the Septuagint and slavishly follows it, even to the extent of reproducing evident blunders. The Apocrypha were added unrevised to Jerome's Vulgate and are thus preserved. Tertullian, who died about 230, Cyprian (died 258) and Augustine (died 430) all wrote their works in the Latin tongue and quoted from the Old Latin version (or versions).

b. The Itala.

Augustine speaks of an "Itala version," which may indicate another Latin translation which appeared in Italy (Italia) at that time. However, many scholars deny the existence of the Itala and consider Augustine's statement to be simply a reference to the "Old Latin."[24] Others consider his words as simply a reference to the Vulgate, the New Testament of which had been published for about ten years when he wrote.[25]

2. *The Origin of the Latin Vulgate.*

The Latin Vulgate is the great version of the entire Bible translated by Jerome (*Eusebius Hieronimus*) at the end of the fourth century. The New Testament was translated (rather revised) first from 383 onward, and the Old Testament last from 390-405. For one thousand years or more, from about 500 to 1500 when Latin held sway as the language of Western Europe, Jerome's translation was *the* Bible of the Western World. In the thirteenth century the name "Vulgate," denoting the version in common use, came to be applied to it as the term *koine* had previously, for the same reason, been used of the Septuagint.

a. The Need for the Vulgate.

Damasus, Bishop of Rome (366-384), who was of a scholarly turn of mind, was greatly distressed by the appalling corruption which existed in the text of the Old Latin version of his day. A motley host of manuscripts were in circulation with scarcely two alike. Heresies were springing up. Jews in conflict with Christians made sport of the confusion existing in the text of the Christian Scriptures. A standard, scholarly, authentic edition of the Latin Scriptures was desperately needed. In 382 Damasus charged Jerome with the revision of the Old Latin version, and the great scholar, eminently fitted for the task, undertook the work of revision and translation.

b. Jerome and His Work as a Translator.

In the New Testament Jerome simply amended the Old Latin text from the original Greek, confining his revision only to passages, as he says in the *Preface to the Gospels*, "which seemed to change the meaning." He made two revisions of the

24 Wright, op. cit., p. 64.
25 Cf. Kenyon, Textual Criticism, second edition, pp. 213 f.

Psalter. The first, before he left Rome in 385 (following the death of Damasus), was a cursory revision of the Old Latin according to the Septuagint, called *Psalterium Romanum* (The Roman Psalter). The second, after 385, revised according to Origen's Hexaplaric text, was called the *Psalterium Gallicanum* (Gallican Psalter) because it came into common use in Gaul. Other Old Testament books were similarly revised from the Hexapla. Only Job has survived.

The final phase of Jerome's translation work is by far the most important. In 390 he began to translate the Old Testament *directly from the Hebrew*. Even before he left Rome, he had been laboriously perfecting himself in the knowledge of Hebrew and had secured portions of the Hebrew Bible with a view to their translation into Latin. His increasing knowledge of Hebrew as a result of study under rabbis in Palestine, enabled him to see the unsatisfactory condition of existing Septuagint and Old Latin texts and the substantial agreement among Hebrew manuscripts. With a renewed sense of the importance of his task Jerome began, it seems from his famous Introduction, *Prologus Galeatus,* with the books of Samuel and Kings in 390. By 393 he had completed besides these, Job, the Prophets, and the Psalms. From 394-396 he completed Ezra, Nehemiah and Chronicles. In 398 he translated Proverbs, Ecclesiastes and Canticles. In 405 he finished the Pentateuch, Joshua, Judges, Ruth and Esther. Jerome, hastily and only upon the urgent request of friends, translated the apocryphal books, Judith and Tobit, together with the Rest of Esther and the uncanonical additions to Daniel. He did not desire to translate any of the apocryphal literature because it was not in the Hebrew canon. He was opposed to its being recognized as canonical.

3. *The Reception and Final Triumph of the Vulgate.*

Jerome's Latin Bible in its completed form was thus a composite work. It consisted first of all of the translation of the Old Testament (except the Psalms) from the original Hebrew. Secondly, the Psalms in the Old Latin revised with the help of Origen's Hexaplaric text of the Septuagint. (Jerome's *Hebrew Psalter,* translated from the original Hebrew, the best of all, never became popular, and his *Roman Psalter,* a slight revision of the Septuagint, was also replaced by the *Gallican*). Thirdly, the Gospels consisting of the Old Latin revised from the original Greek. Fourthly, the rest of the New Testament more superficially revised. The Apocrypha were added, but Jerome did not consider them a part of the canon.

a. The Initial Reception of the Vulgate.

Despite his caution in the New Testament to make as few changes as possible that the familiar language of the Old Latin might remain as undisturbed as possible, Jerome's translation of the Gospels was severely criticized. The reaction to his more superficial revision of the rest of the New Testament was less hostile. The real storm of opposition burst forth when the translation of the Old Testament books from the original Hebrew began to appear. The great majority of both clergy and laity was satisfied with the existing versions, especially the Septuagint, which was regarded with an almost superstitious reverence. To bring out a rival version which gave little or no consideration to it (inspired and authoritative as it was deemed to be) was to most people an insufferable outrage.

Jerome defended the superior accuracy of the original Hebrew manuscripts. He justified his endeavor to put the Hebrew Scriptures as a source of New Testament quotations into the best and most intelligible rendering by demonstrating that not all these quotations were taken from the Septuagint, but that many were taken direct from the Hebrew. Few, however, were wise or honest enough to admit the necessity of having the purest possible text of the Bible. Even some scholars, who should have known better, protested against the sweeping changes which were necessary to restore a pure text.

b. The Final Triumph of the Vulgate.

The storm was beginning to abate when Jerome, intensely disappointed by the fierce criticism of his fellow churchmen, died in 420. In many quarters hostility was beginning to turn to praise. The reception, however, was uneven. Different Churches adopted different portions at various times. In the fifth and sixth centuries the Old Latin was used side by side with the Vulgate. In the seventh century the Old Latin became rare, and by the eighth Jerome's Bible had almost completely displaced it. From then on till the Reformation, the Vulgate was the Bible of Western Europe.

During the course of its long and wide ministry, it became corrupt and often had to be revised. In 1228, it was divided into chapters by Stephen Langton, Archbishop of Canterbury. In 1455, after the invention of printing, it was the first book printed with movable type. However, it was made from the current unrevised manuscripts of the time and contained many errors. Despite the decree of the Council of Trent in 1546 calling for a fresh revision, the venture was not accomplished until Pope Sixtus V urged the task on, resulting in the appearance of the Sixtine edition of 1590. This however was shortly recalled.

The Clementine Vulgate, differing in some 3,000 instances from the Sixtine edition, came out in 1592. It superseded the Sixtine edition and became the standard text of the Roman Catholic Church. In 1907, work on a critical edition of the Latin text was begun. Since 1926 various books in quarto have been appearing. This new revision is far more correct than the Clementine Vulgate and gives promise of rendering valuable service in the textual criticism of the Old Testament.

4. *The Importance of the Vulgate.*

Jerome wrote voluminously, yet the Vulgate is his greatest achievement. He is remembered best and his highest distinction is as a translator of the Bible.

a. The Historical and Religious Importance of the Vulgate.

Not only was the Vulgate the Bible of Christendom for over a thousand years, but it also served as the text for numerous translations. Portions of it were rendered into Anglo-Saxon, Early English and other languages. The famous Wycliffe version, the first complete English translation of the Bible (1380-1382), was made from the Vulgate, as well as the following other versions: French, Italian and Spanish, including the Douay English version (1582-1610).

Historically the Latin Bible served as a connecting link between the ancient Greek and Syriac manuscripts and modern translations. Moreover, England is especially indebted to the Latin Bible for her Christianity, which spread to America and elsewhere.

b. The Critical Importance of the Vulgate.

Jerome's aim to render "with complete fidelity what stands in the Hebrew," as he states in a note after Esther 10:3 and to render "not the letter but the meaning," as he avers in Epistle 57 to Pammachius, was bound to lead to happy results. However, he was hindered from adhering with uncompromising loyalty to his purpose and method by the pressure of public opinion of his day. He was forced to make some concessions due to the excessive reverence in which the Septuagint and Old Latin versions were held at that time so as not to shock the religious feelings of the faithful. Yet, his devotion to the Hebrew Scriptures gave his work in the Old Testament critical value and offered a sound basis for translation of the Vulgate into other tongues. Judged by the standards of his day, his Latin translation of the Hebrew Bible was a notable and, indeed, a magnificent feat. The work as a whole has always been acclaimed as eminently successful by unprejudiced critics.

V. OTHER ANCIENT VERSIONS OF THE OLD TESTAMENT

Besides the four most important versions made directly from the Hebrew, the Septuagint, the Syriac, the Targums and the

Vulgate, a large number of translations were made from the Greek, including the Old Latin, already discussed in connection with Jerome's Vulgate.

1. Ancient Versions Made from the Greek.

a. The Coptic Versions.

The conversion to Christianity of native Egyptians unfamiliar with Greek, beginning with the third century, resulted in the formation of a Coptic or "Egyptian" Church and created a need for a translation of the Bible into Coptic dialects. The earliest version, completed about 350, is in *Sahidic,* the dialect of Upper Egypt. Translations were also made into *Akhmimic* (also Upper Egypt), *Fayumic* (Middle Egypt), and *Bohairic* (around Alexandria). All of these versions were made from fourth-century Septuagint texts, but contain occasional earlier readings.[26]

b. The Ethiopic Version.

Christianity was introduced into Abyssinia by Syrian missionaries in the fourth century. The Kingdom of Axum, whose inhabitants were descendants of South Arabian immigrants and spoke a Semitic dialect called *Geez* or *Ethiopic,* embraced Christianity. Between the fifth and the eighth century the Bible was translated into Ethiopic. The text eventually became corrupt. It was later revised with the aid of Arabic translations. Accordingly, the Ethiopic Bible is not critically significant for the Septuagintal or Hebrew text.

c. The Arabic Versions.

The rapid expansion of Islam after the death of Mohammed (632) disseminated the Arabic language and created a need for an Arabic translation. Partial translations doubtlessly were made in the seventh century, but the first recorded version is that of John, Bishop of Seville, made in 724, a dozen years after the Moslems overran Spain. Saadia Gaon's version made from the Hebrew (tenth century) was the first and most im-

26 Cf. H. S. Gehman, Jour. Bib. Lit. 46 (1927), pp. 279-330.

portant Arabic version among the Jews. Two Arabic versions were current in Egypt, one from the Bohairic dialect and the other from the Sahidic. Both were influenced by the Hebrew and Samaritan texts.

d. The Armenian and Georgian Versions.

The Armenian Bible came into existence as a nationalistic and religious reaction against the use of Syriac in public worship, a language incomprehensible to the common people. At the beginning of the fifth century Mesrop, the inventor of the Armenian alphabet, and the Patriarch Sahak began a translation from the Syriac, according to Moses of Chorene, said to have been a nephew of Mesrop. However, according to Lazar of Pharphi, another Armenian historian of the fifth century, the translation was made, not from the Syriac, but from the Greek. This latter view is that adopted by F. C. Conybeare.[27] In general the Armenian Old Testament follows exactly the Hexaplaric recension, but occasionally was revised according to the Peshitta.

The Georgian Church separated from the Armenian at the end of the sixth century. Thus, the Georgian version of the Scriptures is closely akin to the Armenian. The original translator shows an Armenian-Syriac foundation, but indicates some Septuagintal influence.

e. The Gothic and Slavonic Versions.

Both of these translations are based on the Lucianic recension of the Septuagint. The Gothic Bible was prepared by Ulfilas (about 350), called "the Apostle to the Goths," a warlike Teutonic race living in Dacia, north of the Danube River and west of the Black Sea.

In the ninth century the Slavonic Version was made by Cyril and Methodius, two missionaries, for converted Slavs, a people from Asia who had settled in central and eastern Europe. The oldest copy of the entire Slavonic Bible is dated 1499.

27 Hastings' **Dictionary of the Bible,** Vol. I, p. 152.

LITERATURE ON THE ANCIENT VERSIONS OF THE OLD TESTAMENT
SEPTUAGINT

Geden, A. S., *Outlines of Introduction to the Hebrew Bible,* (Edinburgh, 1909) pp. 165-217.

Swete, H. B., *An Introduction to the Old Testament in Greek,* (Cambridge University Press, 1900, 2nd ed. 1902. Revised by R. R. Ottley, 1914, with a bibliography of earlier literature).

Ottley, R. R., *A Handbook to the Septuagint,* (London, 1920).

Burkitt, F. C., in *Cheyne's Encyclopaedia Biblica* IV, 1903, 5016-22.

Nestle, E., in *Hastings' Dictionary of the Bible* IV, 1902, 437-454 (with a bibliography of earlier literature).

Kenyon, F., *Recent Developments in the Textual Criticism of the Greek Bible,* (Schweich Lectures for 1925, London, 1933).

Meecham, H. G., *The Oldest Version of the Bible,* (London, 1932).

Orlinsky, H., "On the Present State of Proto-Septuagint Studies" in *Journal of the American Oriental Society,* LXI, (1941), 81-91. Various introductions, especially A. Bentzen, *Introduction to the Old Testament,* (Copenhagen, 1948), pp. 75-92.

Very important: P. Kahle, *The Cairo Geniza,* (The Schweich Lectures, 1941, London, 1947).

TEXTS:

Rahlfs, A., *Septuaginta,* (2 vols., Stuttgart, 1935), and H. B. Swete, *The Old Testament in Greek According to the Septuagint* I, (Cambridge, 1925). II (1922), III (1912); Concordance: Hatch and Redpath *"A Concordance to the Septuagint"* (2 vols.) and supplement, (Oxford, 1897).

THE TARGUMS

For general summaries and bibliographies see: E. Schuerer, *Geschichte des juedischen Volkes* (3rd and 4th ed., Vol. I, Leipzig, 1901), pp. 147-156 and T. Walker in Hastings' *Dictionary of the Bible,* IV, pp. 678-683. For a comparison of the Targum Onkelos and the Hebrew text see A. Sperber in *Proceedings of the American Academy for Jewish Research,* 6, (1934-35); on Targum Jonathan see P. Churgin, *Targum Jonathan on the Prophets* (pp. 55-65).

THE PESHITTA

The *editio princeps* is that of Gabriel Sionita in the *Paris Polyglot,* (1645), reproduced in the *London Polyglot,* (1657) and by S. Lee (London, 1823). Nestorian recension by J. Perkins (Urumiah, 1852). The Apocrypha were published by P. de Lagarde (Leipzig and London, 1861). Edition by Dominicans in Mosul appeared in

1887-1891. J. Bloch (*American Journal of Semitic Languages* 37, 1921, pp. 136-144) appraises these editions.

THE VULGATE

An excellent manual is that of F. Stummer, *Einfuehrung in die lateinische Bibel* (Paderborn, 1928). Two splendid articles: Westcott in Smith's *Dictionary of the Bible* (in loc.), and White in Hastings' *Dictionary of the Bible*. Cf. S. Angus, "Vulgate" in *International Standard Bible Encyclopedia* (3058-62). F. Kenyon, *Our Bible and the Ancient Manuscripts* (pp. 165 ff.) and his *Handbook to the Textual Criticism of the New Testament* (1941), pp. 114-119 (with bibliography) and H. B. Swete, *Introduction to the Old Testament in Greek*, revised by Ottley, 1914, with bibliography.

Part II

THE PENTATEUCH

CHAPTER VII

THE IMPORTANCE AND SCOPE
OF THE PENTATEUCH

THE PENTATEUCH is the first of the three divisions of the
Hebrew Canon. It is called the Law or Torah because it records the giving of those religious and civil institutions which
were the foundation of Israel's theocratic national life. This
section, consisting of five books, Genesis, Exodus, Leviticus,
Numbers and Deuteronomy, is traditionally attributed to
Moses, Israel's great leader and lawgiver.

The first book of the Bible may possibly have originally
existed in a five-fold division as it came from the hand of its
author, Moses. Since Genesis, Leviticus and Deuteronomy are
natural units in themselves, we may assume, as Edward J.
Young does, "that the five-fold division was the work of the
original author of the Law, namely, Moses."[1] However, if
this was not the case, and the five books were originally one
book, such a fivefold division became necessary in the course
of history for liturgical reasons to facilitate the reading of the
Law in the synagogue worship.

Ancient "books" were in the form of rolls. The Hebrews
using the standard size rolls, about thirty feet in length, and
not the huge rolls sometimes employed by the Egyptians, like
the Papyrus Harris and The Book of the Dead, could conveniently accommodate the unvocalized Hebrew text of Genesis
or Deuteronomy, for instance, but no more. Hence, for

1 Introduction to the Old Testament (Grand Rapids, 1949), p. 48.

183

practical reasons the book would automatically have come to have a five-fold division, if indeed that form was not original.

Both Philo[2] and Josephus[3] attest this five-fold division in the first century A.D. Its existence goes back at least to the Septuagint (third century B.C.), but it is not certain whether it can be traced to the times of Ezra and Nehemiah (cf. Nehemiah 8:2, 3, 8; Ezra 7:6-10:3). It is because of this division, however, that the first book of the Bible came to be known as the Pentateuch *he Pentateuchos* (supply *biblos*). This designation is derived from the Greek *pente* (five) and *teuchos* (a tool or implement), the term being applied later to a sheath or case such as that in which the five rolls were kept. The Greek term first occurs in the second century A.D. and was later used by Origen.[4]

In the Old Testament the first book of the Bible is variously designated by terms chiefly descriptive of is contents. It is called "the law" or "Torah" (Joshua 1:7), more fully "the book of the law" (Joshua 8:34), "the book of the law of Moses" (Joshua 8:31), "the book of the law of God" (Joshua 24:26), "the law of Moses" (I Kings 2:3) and "the book of the law of the Lord" (II Chronicles 17:9). In the New Testament it is called "the book of the law" (Galatians 3:10), "the law" (Matthew 5:17, Luke 10:26), "the law of the Lord" (Luke 2:23) and "the law of Moses" (Luke 2:22).

I. THE IMPORTANCE OF THE PENTATEUCH

Not only by reason of its position and antiquity as the first book of the Bible, the Pentateuch is of the highest importance to Bible students no matter from what angle it is considered.

1. The Importance of the Pentateuch Cosmically.

In the first two chapters of Genesis in an account unique in all ancient literature, the Pentateuch catalogues the creation

2 De Abr. 1.
3 Against Apion I:8.
4 John E. Steinmueller, A Companion to Scripture Studies II, New York, 1942, p. 7.

of the heavens and earth, and all plant, animal and human life. Other nations have their creation stories.[5] But these are important only by sheer contrast in accentuating the sublimity and grandeur of the inspired record.[6] Purged of the gross polytheistic perversions of the numerous non-inspired creation legends by virtue of its advanced monotheistic point of view, only the Genesis account arrives at the great First Cause in that incomparably magnificent opening word: "In the beginning God created . . ." (Genesis 1:1). Lifting the reader with one stroke out of the morass and confusion of the polytheistic accounts, in which primitive peoples in their naive efforts to explain the origin of the universe attributed each different phenomenon to a separate cause in the form of a deity, the Pentateuch conducts us at once to that which was totally beyond the grasp of the natural mind, the concept of the universe as a whole as the creative act of one God.

By inspiration the author of the Pentateuch has the secret which the polytheistic writers of ancient Mesopotamia blindly groped after, the unifying principle of the universe. In an age grossly ignorant of the first principles of causation, Genesis stands out all the more resplendently as a divine revelation. The discovery of secondary causes and the explanation of the *how* of creation in its ongoing operation is the achievement of science. How cause produces effect, how order and symmetry prevail, how physical phenomena and organic life are interdependent—these and simliar questions science has answered. But science can only go so far. The elements of the universe, matter, force, order, it must take for granted. Revelation alone can answer the *why* of creation. The Bible alone discloses that the universe exists *because God made it* and brought it into being for a definite purpose.

5 For the Assyrian story of creation see Sir Frederic Kenyon, **The Bible and Archeology** (New York, 1940), pp. 46 f. and Alexander Heidel, **The Babylonian Genesis** (Chicago, 1942).

6. Cf. Joseph P. Free, **Archeology and Bible History** (Wheaton, Ill., 1950), pp. 28 f. For a discussion of the better known cosmogonies see H. C. Leupold, **Exposition of Genesis** (Grand Rapids, 1950), pp. 27-30.

The account of the origin of the cosmos in Genesis, moreover, is not only incomparably superior in every respect to ancient cosmogonies and creation accounts, but what is all the more amazing in the light of the utterly unscientific age in which it was produced, is its scientific precision even when judged by the standards of our modern scientific age. Commenting on the account of creation which we find in Chapter I of Genesis, W. F. Albright calls the "sequence of creative phases" which it outlines as "so rational that modern science cannot improve on it, given the same language and the same range of ideas in which to state its conclusions. In fact, modern scientific cosmogonies show such a disconcerting tendency to be short-lived that it may be seriously doubted whether science has yet caught up with the Biblical story."[7]

2. *The Importance of the Pentateuch Religiously.*

The roots of both Christianity and Judaism strike deep into the Pentateuch. Not only does the first book of the Bible catalogue the beginning of the cosmos, but also the beginning of human life, the entrance of sin into the human family, the commencement of the revelation of God's grace in type (Genesis 3:21) and the first promise of the Divine Redeemer (Genesis 3:15). The three primary names of deity, Elohim, Jehovah and Adonai, and the five most important compound names occur in Genesis. With these begins the progressive self-revelation of God, culminating in Christ. Everywhere in the Pentateuch, in type, symbol and prophecy, the Divine Redeemer is set forth.

Some aspect of the character of the Messiah, for instance, is typified by each of the patriarchs. The line of Messianic descent is carefully traced throughout the successive books. Of the eight great covenants which condition human life upon the earth and outline man's salvation, four, the Edenic,

7 "The Old Testament and Archeology," in the Old Testament Commentary, H. C. Alleman and E. E. Flack (Philadelphia, 1948), p. 135.

Adamic, Noahic and Abrahamic, are found in Genesis, and six appear in the Pentateuch, including the Mosaic and the Palestinian.

Ethnically, Genesis catalogues the beginning of the nations. Special reference is accorded the call of Abraham and his descendants through Isaac to be the chosen nation and the depositories of the divine revelation through whom the Redeemer in due time was to come. Further the Pentateuch gives an account of the providential events whereby the descendants of Abraham became a nation, including their exodus from Egypt and the establishment of the civil and religious institutions under which they were organized in prospect of their entrance into the land of Canaan.

Intricately interwoven into the structure of the rest of the Old Testament and especially deeply inwrought into the fabric of the New Testament are the experiences of the nation Israel, its redemption out of Egypt and its religious and social institutions in the desert. These varied circumstances of God's ancient people typify the experiences of the people of God now and illustrate the varied ramifications of their redemption in Christ (I Corinthians 10:11). Thus it is evident that all the subsequent revelations of the Bible and the Gospel of Christ itself rest upon the foundation laid in the Pentateuch.

The same religious importance attaches to the Pentateuch in Judaism as in Christianity. Jews have always regarded the Law as the foundation of their religious and social economy both in ancient and modern times. The basic difference between Judaism and Christianity is that the latter embraces "him, of whom Moses in the law, and the prophets, did write" (John 1:45), while Judaism rejects Him.

3. *The Importance of the Pentateuch Historically*. The Pentateuch not only stands in closest connection with physical and ethnological science and with religious faith, but is vitally bound up with history and archeology. However,

neither the Pentateuch nor the Bible as a whole is a mere history, as we commonly use the term to describe the systematic record of past events. Holy Scripture in its entirety may rather be defined as a highly specialized history, the history of human redemption. The Pentateuch may be said to be the introduction or the opening chapters of that history.

The author of the Pentateuch had a definite plan. He did not apply himself to recording the story of human history. His task was rather to give an account of God's gracious provisions for man's salvation. The Pentateuch, accordingly, is history with a motive behind it, a deep, religious motive, which imbues the whole. The religious principle underlying it, on the other hand, does not render the events recounted any less historical. It merely gives them a permanent importance far transcending the times in which and about which they were written and far outreaching in importance their application to any one nation or people, investing them with an inestimable and abiding value for all mankind.

The Pentateuch is, however, more than history. It is history wedded to prophecy. It records the past as it centers in the Promised Redeemer. At the same time it supernaturally foretells the future as it will ultimately find its fruition in the Promised Redeemer. It is thus a Messiah-centered history combined with a Messiah-centered prophecy. On the other hand, in the highest sense of the term, it is a philosophy of history, more precisely "the philosophy of Israel's history."[8] As such the Pentateuch recounts the events connected with the beginnings of the Israelite people and their establishment as a theocratic nation, interpreting the whole in the light of the nation's relation to Jehovah and His redemptive program for the world.

Failure to comprehend the precise character and purpose of the Pentateuch has led many critics to deny its historicity

8 Cf. Herbert C. Alleman, "The Book of Genesis," in **Old Testament Commentary** (Philadelphia, 1948), p. 171.

altogether or to adopt low views of its reliability. If, for instance, the account of the Egyptian sojourn, the miraculous deliverance and the wilderness wanderings were fictitious, its vital connection not only with Hebrew history but with the whole Biblical plan of salvation raises the insoluable problem of how this extraordinary record could ever have been fabricated. In addition, archeology has espoused the defense of the historicity of the Pentateuch, and when due allowance is made for the exaggerated claims sometimes made in its name, there still remains substantial archeological proof of the historical reliability of the Pentateuch, which is constantly increasing.[9]

II. The Scope of the Pentateuchal Books

The Pentateuchal books are partly historical and partly legislative. Historically, they present a highly specialized account of human origins, of the beginning of the Hebrew race and the rise and early fortunes of the Hebrew nation. Legislatively, the Pentateuchal books catalogue the particular social and religious laws which formed the basis of the Hebrew theocracy.

GENESIS

Genesis as the book of origins stands traditionally at the head of the entire body of Hebrew sacred literature. Recording the beginning of the physical creation, of all plant, animal and human life, as well as all human institutions and social relationships, it is the logical introduction not only to the Pentateuch but to the whole body of revealed truth in general.

1. The Name.

The Book of Genesis takes its name from the title given to it in the Septuagint Version, which is derived from the heading of its ten parts, *he biblos geneseos* (2:4; 5:1; 6:9;

9 Cf. W. F. Albright, op. cit., p. 141 f. Also pp. 134-140.

10:1; 11:10; 11:27; 25:12; 25:19; 36:1; 37:2). The Jews, following the custom of designating a book by its opening word or words, called it *Bere'shith*, "In the beginning."

2. *The Purpose*.

The name is indicative of the purpose of the book, which is to trace the beginnings of redemptive history. Genesis illustrates (as does the whole Bible) the principle of selection. The narratives are chosen, not for their secular interest or purely historical importance, but for the vital relation they sustain to God's dealings with mankind in His great purpose of redemption. Hence the creation of the world and its inhabitants for His Own glory is narrated. This is closely connected with the temporary thwarting of the divine purpose by the entrance of sin into the human family and the operations of divine grace to rescue man from the fall.

The divine dealings are traced through representative names in the line of the promised Redeemer—from Seth to Noah, from Noah through Shem to Abraham. From Abraham through Isaac and Jacob the ancestry of Israel is presented and the circumstances whereby it was to become the chosen nation through which the world's Redeemer was to come are set forth. Genesis, in tracing the beginning of the universe, of man, of human sin and of redemptive history, is thus introductory and foundational to the Pentateuch in particular and the whole Bible in general.

3. *The Contents*.

Part I. Primeval History of Humanity (1:1-11:26).
    a. The creation (1:1-2:25).
    b. From the fall to the flood (3:1-5:32).
    c. The flood (6:1-9:29).
    d. From the flood to Abraham (10:1-11:26).

Part II. Patriarchal History of Israel (11:27-50:26).
    a. Abraham (11:27-25:10).
    b. Isaac (25:11-28:9).
    c. Jacob (28:10-36:43).

d. Jacob's sons, especially Joseph (37:1-50:26).

4. *The Literary Scheme.* The narrative of Genesis is fitted into a genealogical framework, marked by the formula which recurs ten times, "These are the generations of." In Genesis 2:4 the formula is applied metaphorically to "the heavens and the earth." By this plan the book of Genesis is arranged as follows: (1) the generations of the heavens and the earth (1:1-2:4 [4:26]); (2) the generations of Adam (5:1-6:8); (3) the generations of Noah (6:9-9:29); (4) the generations of the sons of Noah (10:1-11:9); (5) the generations of Shem (11:10-26); (6) the generations of Terah (11:27-25:11); (7) the generations of Ishmael (25:12-18); (8) the generations of Isaac (25:19-35:29); (9) the generations of Esau (36:1-37:1); (10) the generations of Jacob (37:2-50:26).

Critics recognize the unity of plan in the genealogical skeleton and in many other details of the book of Genesis. However, they insist that the book is the product of composite sources, which have been welded together by a late exilic or post-exilic compiler or redactor into a continuous whole. The narrative sections (designated J and E) were supposedly fitted into the skeletal history of the origin of the Jewish nation (to which the genealogical framework of Genesis belongs), called the Priestly Code (P). J, the Jehovist, is said to have used the name Jehovah (Yahweh), writing about 850 B.C. in the South (Judah). E, the Elohist, is said to have employed the name Elohim, flourished about 750 B.C. in the North (Ephraim). This documentary theory, though subtly developed, highly plausible and almost universally adopted among higher critics at the present time is an anti-traditional product of modern rationalistic skepticism, which is at variance with clear lines of historical and Scriptural evidence supporting the unity of the Pentateuch. This topic will be discussed later.[10]

10 See chapter IX.

5. *The Chronology.* The opening chapters of the Bible leave both the date of the creation of the world and of man an open question. Genesis 1:1 places the origin of the universe in the dateless past. Genesis 1:2, on the other hand, evidently presents a gap or extended time period, leaving ample room for all the geologic ages. The possibility of such a hiatus has been held by many competent Biblical scholars, including Wilhelm Karl Hengstenberg, *Franz Delitzsch, F. von Meyer, Stier, Kurtz and others.[11] This view was popularized during the last quarter of the nineteenth century by George H. Pember in his book *Earth's Earliest Ages.*[12]

The appearance of man upon the earth is set forth in the Genesis account as the result of a direct creative act of God, which took place at least over 4,000 years B.C. and perhaps as early as "seven or ten thousand years B.C., which," writes Laird Harris, "would be more in the spirit of the Biblical record than either Ussher's compressed chronology or the evolutionist's greatly expanded ages."[13] Byron Nelson, a conservative, argues for even greater antiquity of man,[14] but this, we believe, is unwarranted by the facts and out of focus with the perspective of the Genesis account.

However, in dealing with the genealogies of Genesis chapters 5 and 11, it must be pointed out that these lists are most certainly not intended to be complete, much less compiled as chronological data. B. B. Warfield demonstrated more than a generation ago that there are gaps in the Biblical genealogies.[15] The genealogies in Exodus 6:16-24, Ezra 7:1-5 and Matthew 1:1-17 contain omissions. To use the genealogical lists of Genesis to calculate the creation of man about 4004

11 For a list of those holding this view see George T. Ladd, **The Doctrine of Sacred Scripture,** 1883, Vol. I., p. 265.

12 Published by Fleming Revell Company, New York, c. 1876.

13 "The Date of the Flood and the Age of Man," in Bible Today, Vol. 37, no. 9, September, 1943, p. 579.

14 **Before Abraham, Prehistoric Man in Biblical Light** (Minneapolis, 1948), p. 95.

15 "The Antiquity and Unity of the Human Race," in **Studies in Theology** (New York, 1932), pp. 235-258.

B.C., as Archbishop Ussher has done, is not only unwarranted from the text of Scripture, but is incontrovertibly disproved by the well-attested findings of archeology.

The total length of the period from the creation of man to the flood and from the flood to Abraham is not specified in Scripture. That the genealogies in Genesis chapters 5 and 11 are most certainly drastically shortened and contain names that are highly selective is suggested by the fact that each list contains only ten names, ten from Adam to Noah and ten from Shem to Abraham. It seems evident that symmetry is aimed at in constructing Hebrew genealogical tables rather than the exhibition of the unbroken descent from father to son, in contrast to modern registers of pedigree. Such symmetry, with the omission of certain names, is obvious in the genealogy of Matthew 1:1-17.

Furthermore, it must be borne in mind that the Hebrew expressions "beget," "bear," "father" and "son" are used with great latitude of meaning in ancient Semitic languages in idiom foreign to English. Thus to beget a "son" may signify, as with us, to bear an immediate male descendant (Genesis 4:25), or, contrary to our usage, to bear a more remote descendant as a grandchild (cf. Genesis 46:25; II Kings 9:2, 20), or a great grandchild (Genesis 46:18). The Israelites were known as sons of Israel or Jacob for centuries after the death of the patriarch (Malachi 3:6). The seventy souls that "came out of the loins of Jacob" (Exodus 1:5) included grandchildren. Usage extends to tribes or countries (Genesis 10:2-22) and even to a non-blood relationship. Jehu, a usurper and the founder of a new dynasty in Israel and with no blood relationship whatever with the house of Omri is nevertheless styled the "son of Omri" in the Black Obelisk of Shalmaneser III of Assyria.[16] Nebuchadnezzar is called the "father" of Belshazzar, the last king of Babylon, who was actually the son of Nabonidus, a usurper (Daniel 5:2).

16 Daniel David Luckenbill, **Ancient Records of Assyria and Babylonia** I:590.

Accordingly, as Raven has pointed out,[17] in the regularly recurring formula "A lived — years and begat B. And A lived after he begat B — years and begat sons and daughters. And B lived — years and begat C —." B may not be the literal son of A, but a distant descendant. If so, the age of A is his age at the birth of the child from whom B was descended. Many centuries, therefore, may intervene between A and B.

The purpose of the genealogies of Genesis is *not* to show the age of man upon the earth, but to trace in outstanding representative names the line of the Promised Redeemer (Genesis 3:15) from Adam to Abraham and to show the effects of sin and the changed conditions caused by the judgment of the flood upon human vitality and longevity.

Further evidence that the genealogies in Genesis 5 and 11 contain extensive lacunae is shown by the fact that they allow only about 4,000 years from the creation of Adam to Christ, whereas modern archeology clearly traces highly developed sedentary pottery cultures, such as the Halafian, well before 4,000 B.C.[18] It is archeologically fantastic to place the Noahic flood so late as 2348 B.C., as would be the case if the Genesis genealogies are used for chronological purposes. The deluge certainly took place long before 4,000 B.C.

LITERATURE ON GENESIS

Bacon, B. W., *The Genesis of Genesis,* (Hartford, 1892).

Ryle, H. E., *The Early Narratives of Genesis,* (London, 1892).

Dillmann, A., *Genesis,* Vols. I and II, (Edinburgh, 1897).

Moore, G. F., "Genesis," in *Cheyne's Encyclopaedia Biblica,* (1899-1902).

Driver, S. R., *The Book of Genesis,* (the *Westminster Commentary,* 1907).

Mitchell, H. G., *Genesis,* (*The Bible for Home and School*), 1909.

Skinner, J., *A Critical and Exegetical Commentary on Genesis,* (New York, 1910).

---

17 John H. Raven, **Old Testament Introduction** (New York, 1910), pp. 132-135.
18 Cf. W. F. Albright, **From the Stone Age to Christianity** (Baltimore, 1940), p. 96 f.

Eichrodt, W., *Die Quellen der Genesis,* (Giessen, 1916).

Koenig, E., *Die Genesis,* (Guetersloh, 1919).

Morgenstern, J., *A Jewish Interpretation of the Book of Genesis,* (Cincinnati, 1919).

Humbert, P., "Die neuere Genesis-Forschung," (*Theologische Rundschau,* N. F. 6, 1934, pp. 147-160; 207-228, with bibliography).

Alleman, H., "The Book of Genesis," in *Old Testament Commentary,* (*Philadelphia,* 1948).

CONSERVATIVE LITERATURE ON GENESIS

Green, W. H., *The Unity of the Book of Genesis,* (New York, 1910).

Moeller, W., "Genesis" in *International Standard Bible Encyclopaedia,* pp. 1199-1214.

Heinisch P., in *Die Heilige Schrift des Alten Testamentes,* (Bonn, 1930).

Goldman, S., *The Book of Human Destiny: In the Beginning,* (New York, 1949).

Keil, C. F., and F. Delitzsch, *Pentateuch,* Vol. I, (reprint, Grand Rapids, 1949).

Leupold, H. C., *Exposition of Genesis,* Vols. I, II, (Grand Rapids, 1950).

Of great value for spiritual insight are:

Grant, F. W., *The Pentateuch* in *The Numerical Bible,* (New York, 5th. ed., n.d.).

Coates, C. A., *An Outline of the Book of Genesis,* (Kingston-on-Thames, n.d.).

Griffith-Thomas, W. H., *Genesis,* (London, n.d.).

Useful from a conservative scientific point of view:

Nelson, B. C., *Before Abraham, Prehistoric Man in Bible Light,* (Minneapolis, 1948), and other recent volumes by the same author: *After Its Kind* and *The Deluge Story in Stone.*

Stoner, P. W., "Astronomy and the First Chapter of Genesis" in *Modern Science and the Christian Faith,* (Wheaton, Ill., 1948).

Heidel, Alexander, *The Babylonian Genesis,* (Chicago, 1942), is valuable from an archeological point of view.

Special articles:

Warfield, B. B., "On the Antiquity and Unity of the Human Race," in *Studies in Theology,* (New York, 1932), pp. 235-258.

Free, J. P., "Abraham's Camels," *Journal of Near Eastern Studies,* (July, 1944), pp. 235-258.

EXODUS

Genesis is the book of origins. Exodus, which takes up the history of the Israelites where Genesis leaves off, is the book of redemption. Delivered out of Egyptian bondage, the newly constituted nation is given the law, priesthood and system of sacrifice as the provision for the worship and government of a redeemed people.

1. The Name.

The book takes its title from the Vulgate through the Septuagint. It signifies "outgoing" or "departure" (cf. Exodus 19:1; Hebrews 11:22). The Jews, following their custom of naming their sacred books from one or more of the opening words call it *we'elleh shemoth* ("and these are the names," or simply, *shemoth*, "names").

2. The Purpose.

The aim of the book of Exodus centers in the great experience of redemption from Egypt as the type of all redemption and the constitution of Jacob's posterity as a theocratic nation at Mount Sinai. God, connected heretofore with the Israelites only through His covenant with Abraham, confirmed to Isaac and Jacob, now brings them to Himself nationally through redemption. As the chosen people through whom the Redeemer was to come Jehovah also places them under the Mosaic Covenant and dwells among them under the cloud of glory. The institution of tabernacle, priesthood and sacrificial ritual is typical in minute detail of the person and work of Christ.

Called "the second book of Moses," Exodus follows Genesis in the closest possible relation and is second to no other Old Testament book in the history of redemption. Moses is set forth as the great deliverer and lawgiver. In a most emphatic sense Exodus is *the* book of Moses.

3. The Contents.

Part I. The Hebrews in Egypt (1:1-12:36).
  a. The Egyptian bondage (1:1-22).
  b. The preparation of the deliverer (2:1-4:31).
  c. The struggle with Pharaoh (5:1-11:10).
  d. The Passover (12:1-36).
Part II. The Hebrews in the Wilderness (12:37-18:27).
  a. The Exodus and the pursuit (12:37-15:21).
  b. The journey to Sinai (15:22-17:16).
  c. The visit of Jethro (18:1-27).
Part III. The Hebrews at Sinai (19:1-40:38).
  a. The giving of the decalogue (19:1-20:26).
  b. The giving of the various laws (21:1-23:33).
  c. The ratification of the covenant (24:1-11).
  d. Instructions concerning tabernacle and priesthood (24:12-31:18).
  e. Defection of the golden calf and renewal of the covenant (32:1-34:35)
  f. Erection of the tabernacle: institution of the priesthood (35:1-40:38).

4. The Contemporary Historical Scene.

The Exodus is without doubt the most memorable event in ancient Israelite history. The date of this great occurrence, which is the key to the whole contemporary historical scene of the book of Exodus, and a large part of the book of Genesis, has been the proverbial football of archeologists and the subject of endless speculation. However, despite the fact that not a single name of an Egyptian Pharaoh under whom the various events of the Egyptian sojourn occurred has been preserved in the Biblical record, the approximate date of the Exodus remains a matter of speculation *only* if some or all of the Biblical chronological notices are rejected.

According to I Kings 6:1, which critics customarily but unwarrantedly dismiss as a late and unreliable notation, Solomon began building the temple in the fourth year of his reign, which is said to be the 480th year after the Exodus from Egypt. The fourth year of Solomon's reign (which lasted forty years I Kings 11:42), was about 962 B.C. (following Begrich's date of 926 B.C. for the Division of the Monarchy).[19] Adding 480 to 962 gives 1442 B.C. as the approximate date of the Exodus, which falls within the last few years of the reign of Thutmose III, who died about 1436 B.C. This great empire-builder and conqueror, following the Scriptural chronological notices and allowing five or ten years' margin for error in the Egyptian chronology of this period, was evidently the pharaoh of the oppression, while his successor, Amenhotep II (c. 1448-1420 B.C.) was the pharaoh of the Exodus.

Thus a date for the Exodus which falls within a decade after the middle of the fifteenth century B.C. not only satisfies the Biblical chronology but important archeological requirements as well. Cities mentioned in Joshua and Judges and in the Amarna Letters (c. 1400 B.C.) flourished at that time. Garstang's excavations at Jericho show that the fall of the city to the Hebrews took place sometime between 1475 and 1300,[20] with a preferred date between 1400 and 1385 B.C.[21] This date also fits well into the chronological scheme which underlies the period of the Judges (1400 B.C.-1020 B.C.), which scheme Garstang not only shows to be consistent in itself, but also demonstrates with plausibility that the periods in which the land of Canaan enjoyed rest correspond to the times when Egyptian power was strong in the land.[22]

Israel's entrance into Canaan, following the chronological scheme of Scripture, accordingly took place in the Amarna Age around 1400 B.C. The Amarna Letters, despite minor

19 Joachim Begrich, **Die Chronologie der Koenige von Israel und Juda,** 1929, p. 155.
20 **Bull. Am. Schs. Or. Res.** 86, pp. 32-34. John Garstang and J. B. E. Garstang, **The Story of Jericho** (London, 1948), p. 135.
21 Garstang, **loc. cit.**
22 J. Garstang, **Joshua-Judges** (London, 1931). Cf. J. W. Jack, **The Date of the Exodus** (Edinburgh, 1925), pp. 211-216.

difficulties, reflect conditions quite similar to those presented in Joshua and the early chapters of Judges. The Merenptah Stela, which contains the only mention in any Egyptian inscription of the name Israel, shows that around 1229 B.C. the Israelites were listed among other strong and dangerous people in Western Palestine. They must have been settled there for a long time to have furnished a satisfactory background for this important Egyptian reference.

Notices in Exodus 1:11 indicate that the oppressed Israelites built Pithom and Raamses. Archeology has shown that these cities were constructed by Raamses II (c. 1301-1234 B.C.), who, by some,[23] is made the pharaoh of the Exodus, which in turn is dated 1290 B.C. with the conquest set at 1250 B.C. But Pithom (Tell Retabeh) and Raamses (Tanis) may merely have been rebuilt or enlarged by Raamses II, who notoriously took credit for achievements accomplished by his predecessors.

Since it is true that Tanis was called Per-Re'emasese (The House of Raamses) only for a couple of centuries (c. 1300-1100), the reference in Exodus 1:11 *must* be to the older city Zoan-Avaris, where the oppressed Israelites labored centuries earlier. Hence, the name Raamses is to be taken as a modernization of an archaic place name like Dan (for earlier Laish in Genesis 14:14). Since Zoan-Avaris was once a flourishing city before the expulsion of the Hyksos about 1570 B.C., there was plenty of time for the enslaved Israelites to build the earlier city, for they entered Egypt about 1870 B.C.

Archeological excavations at Lachish,[24] Nelson Glueck's surface explorations in Transjordan[25] and the problems involved in the references to Pithom and Raamses in Exodus 1:11 are supposed to be fatal to the date 1441 B.C. for the Exodus. However, the present writer fails to see that these difficulties offer sufficiently clear evidence to warrant dis-

23 Cf. W. F. Albright, **From the Stone Age to Christianity** (Baltimore, 1940), p. 194 f.
24 Albright, **Bull. Am. Schs. Or. Res.** 68, pp. 23 ff; 74, pp. 20-22.
25 **The Other Side of the Jordan** (New Haven, 1940), pp. 125-147.

regarding plain chronological indications of the Old Testament and the whole underlying time scheme of the book of Judges for a date of the Exodus a century and a half later than that indicated in I Kings 6:1.

LITERATURE ON EXODUS

Baentsch, B., in *Handkommentar zum Alten Testament,* (Goettingen, 1903).

McNeile, A. H., in *Westminster Commentaries,* (London, 1908).

Driver, S. R., in *Cambridge Bible for Schools and Colleges,* (Cambridge, 1911).

Toffteen, O. A., *The Historic Exodus,* (Chicago, 1909).

Mowinckel, S., *Le Decalogue,* (Paris, 1927).

Lucas, A., *The Route of the Exodus of the Israelites from Egypt,* (London, 1938).

Beer, K., in *Handbuch zum Alten Testament,* (Tuebingen, 1939).

Rowley, H. H., "The Exodus and the Settlement in Canaan," *Bull. Am. Schs.* 85 Feb., 1942, pp. 27-31.

Noth, M., *Die Gesetze im Pentateuch,* (Halle, 1940).

CONSERVATIVE LITERATURE

Mead in *Lange's Commentary on the Holy Scripture,* (New York, 1876).

Richardson, E. C., "The Documents of the Exodus, Contemporary, Original, and Written," (*Princeton Theological Review* 10), pp. 581-605.

Rawlinson, G., *Exodus* in a *Bible Commentary* Vol. I, (ed. by C. J. Ellicott, London, n.d.).

Jack, J. W., *The Date of the Exodus,* (Edinburgh, 1925).

Adams, J. McKee, *Ancient Records and the Bible,* (Nashville, 1946), pp. 207-238.

Wilson, R. D., "Critical Note on Exodus 6:3," *Princeton Theological Review* 22, pp. 108-119.

Moeller, W., "Exodus," in the *Int. Stand. Bible Encyl.,* (1056-1067), with bibliography.

LEVITICUS

Exodus tells how Israel was redeemed and constituted to be "a kingdom of priests, and a holy nation" (Exodus 19:6). Leviticus recounts the cleansing, worship and service of the redeemed people necessary for the realization of their priestly call and career.

1. *The Name.*

The book of Leviticus, from the example of the Septuagint (*Leueitikon*) and the Vulgate (*Leviticus*) acquires its name from its contents. The Jews, likewise stressing content, sometimes called it the "Law of the Priests," (the sons of Levi). As far as content is concerned, the name "Leviticus" fits the book exactly. It may be described as a handbook of the ritual of the Old Covenant principally associated with what is called in the New Testament the "Levitical priesthood" (Hebrews 7:11). The Jews, however, usually referred to the book from the first word, *wayiqra'*, "and he called."

2. *The Purpose.*

Leviticus, as the code intended for the priests, outlines the true method of approach to God to be followed by the newly constituted "priestly kingdom and holy nation." It sets forth the way of access to the Divine Presence in the dispensation of the Law, as its inspired commentary, the Epistle to the Hebrews, describes the means of approach in the dispensation of grace. Being a manual of Levitical ritual, there is little or no narrative in it. What little there is, such as the brief notice of the offering of strange fire by Nadab and Abihu (10:1,2), simply illustrates the observance or infraction of the laws given.

3. *The Literary Character.*

The traditional view of the authorship of the Pentateuch holds that all these laws were given through Moses and were recorded by him. "Fifty-six times in these twenty seven chapters is the claim repeated that Jehovah imparted these laws directly to Moses. The denial of their direct Mosaic origin, therefore, is an obvious challenge to the truth of these statements."[26]

26 G. T. Manley, G. C. Robinson, and A. M. Stibbs, **The New Bible Handbook** (Chicago, 1947), p. 138.

Notwithstanding, exponents of the documentary hypothesis commonly assign Leviticus entirely to the exilic (Driver[27]) or post-exilic (Bewer[28]) Priest Code, abbreviated P, the source to which all the Mosaic legislation from Exodus 25 to Numbers 10 is commonly relegated. Some critics think that Leviticus 17-27 is distinct enough from P to be distinguished as a separate minor source, called H (Holiness Code), which is assumed to have been combined with P to form our present book.[29] According to Julius Bewer, the Priest Code in its original form was completed about 500 B.C., or a little later, in order to stir up zeal for the post-exilic temple and its ritualistic worship, so that Judah, then a Persian province, might be organized "as a theocracy, which was to be symbolized and realized in a hierocracy."[30]

The critical theory of an exilic or post-exilic date for the so-called Priestly Code is replete with incredulities. First, there is the *moral issue* involved in the deliberate design of passing off the elaborate code as Mosaic, a procedure manifestly inconsistent with the moral standards of a prophet. Second, there is the *historical absurdity* of getting so late a concoction of laws not only accepted at all, but, what is more incredible, approved as given directly by God to Moses. Third, there is the *legal inanity* involved in the glaring unsuitability of the code in its Mosaic dress and wilderness framework to the urban post-exilic community. The whole was out of date and out of place. Nothing could be less appropriate for its supposed purpose of stirring up the post-exilic generation to organize "a theocracy which was to be symbolized and realized in a hierocracy."

---

27 **Introduction to the Literature of the Old Testament** (Edinburgh, 1913) p. 136.
28 **The Literature of the Old Testament** (New York, 7th ed., 1947), p. 259.
29 Robert Pfeiffer, **Introduction to the Old Testament**, pp. 239 ff.
30 Loc. cit.

4. The Outline.

Part I. Prescriptions for Access to God (1:1-16:34).
  a. Prescriptions for priestly sacrifices (1:1-7:38).
  b. Prescriptions for priestly consecration (8:1-9:24).
  c. Punishment of priestly violation (10:1-20).
  d. Prescriptions for Purification (11:1-15:33).
  e. Prescriptions for the day of Atonement (16:1-34).
Part II. Prescriptions for Fellowship with God (17:1-27:34).
  a. Prohibitions preserving holiness (17:1-22:33).
  b. Prohibitions governing religious festivals (23:1-44).
  c. Prescriptions for lamps, showbread, etc. (24:1-23).
  d. Prescriptions concerning sabbatic year and jubilee (25:1-26:2).
  e. Promises and warnings (26:3-46).
  f. Prescriptions concerning vows and tithes (27:1-34).

LITERATURE ON LEVITICUS

Kellogg, S. H., *The Book of Leviticus* in *The Expositor's Bible*, (London, 1891).

Driver, S. R., *The Book of Leviticus*, (The Polycrome Bible), 1898.

Baentsch, B., in *Handkommentar zum Alten Testament*, (Goettingen, 1903).

Chapman, A. T., and A. W. Streans, *Leviticus* in the *Cambridge Bible*, (1914).

Gray, G. B., *Sacrifice in the Old Testament*, (Oxford, 1925).

Schoetz, P. D., *Schuld und Suendopfer im Alten Testament*, (Breslau, 1930).

Kennedy, A. R. S., *Leviticus and Numbers, The New Century Bible*, (Edinburgh, n.d.).

Oesterley, W. O. E., *Sacrifices In Ancient Israel*, (London, 1937).

Morentz I. and H. C. Alleman, "The Book of Leviticus," in *Old Testament Commentary*, (Philadelphia, 1948).

CONSERVATIVE LITERATURE

Keil, K. F., *Introduction to the Old Testament*, (translated by G. Dougherty, 1892).

Fairbairn, P., *The Typology of Scripture*, Vol. II, (Edinburgh, 1864), pp. 317-460.

Stewart, A. *The Mosaic Sacrifices,* (Edinburgh, 1883).

Moeller, W., "Leviticus," (*Int. Stand. Bible Encycl.*) pp. 1870-1880.

Lange, J. P., *Commentary on the Holy Scripture,* (Leviticus), Grand Rapids, 1950.

Kelly, W., *Offerings of Leviticus* I-VII, (London, 1899); *Priesthood, Its Privileges and Its Duties: An Exposition of Leviticus VIII-XV,* (London, 1902); *Day of Atonement,* (London, 1925).

NUMBERS

The book of Numbers continues the history of Israel as a "kingdom of priests and a holy nation" where Exodus leaves off. As Genesis is the book of origins, Exodus the book of redemption, Leviticus the book of holy worship and fellowship, Numbers is the book of the service and walk of God's redeemed people.

1. The Name.

The book receives its name from the Latin Vulgate, *Liber Numeri,* through the translation of the title in the Septuagint *Arithmoi.* It is so called because it makes a double reference to the census of the Hebrew people (chapters 1-3 and 26). The Jews according to custom name the book *wayyedabber* "and He (Jehovah) said," from the first word, or more often from the fifth word *bemidbar* ("in the wilderness").

2. The Purpose.

Numbers describes the continuation of the journey commenced in the book of Exodus, beginning with the events of the second month of the second year (Numbers 10:11) and ending with the eleventh month of the fortieth year (Deuteronomy 1:3). The intervening thirty-eight years concern the abject failure of the redeemed people under divine testing. Despite every provision for their welfare and speedy entrance into their inheritance as a redeemed people, miraculous deliverance out of Egypt, ample prescriptions for holy worship and fellowship, divine guidance and miraculous interposition and minute order and discipline for the host (Numbers 1-10), the people failed miserably at Kadesh-Barnea (Numbers 14) and were punished with defeat and eventual death in the desert (20:1-33:49). Numbers is important in the history of redemption in typically setting forth the perils of unbelief and the destructiveness of apostasy.

3. The Literary Structure.

Those who deny Mosaic authorship maintain that Numbers is composed primarily from P and JE, and resembles Exodus in structure. JE is supposed to reappear by the side of P, though, considered as a rule, not so intimately interwoven with it. Chapters 1:1-10:28 are taken as a long extract from P, as well as miscellaneous laws interspersed throughout the book.

The essential unsoundness of the critical view reappears in the confessed difficulty in distinguishing between J and E, though critics are usually agreed that the distinction between the "prophetic" JE and the "priestly" P is marked. Subject matter, purpose and other factors, however, are sufficient to explain the difference in style, vocabulary etc., between so-called JE and P, and inadequate evidence is furnished that P ever had a separate existence from JE or is non-Mosaic in composition.

4. The Outline.

Part I. Preparation for Departure from Sinai (1:1-10:10).
   a. The people numbered (1:1-54).
   b. The camp arranged (2:1-34).
   c. The priest and Levites instructed (3:1-4:49).
   d. The people protected from defilement (5:1-31).
   e. The law of the Nazarite given (6:1-27).
   f. The gifts of the princes enumerated (7:1-89).
   g. The lighting of the tabernacle lamps commanded (8:1-4).
   h. The cleansing of the Levites prescribed (8:5-26).
   i. The observance of the Passover enjoined (9:1-14).
   j. The guidance of the camp provided (9:15-23).

k. The signal for calling and removing the camp described (10:1-10).

Part II. Journey from Mount Sinai to Moab (10:11-21:35).
    a. From Sinai to Kadesh-Barnea—unbelief (10:11-14:45).
    b. The desert wandering—divine chastening (15:1-19:22).
    c. From Kadesh-Barnea to Moab—the new start (20:1-22:1).

Part III. Events in the Plains of Moab (22:2-36:13).
    a. Balaam's oracles and the worship of Baal Peor (22:1-25:18).
    b. Miscellaneous instructions (26:1-31:54).
    c. Territorial distribution in East Jordan (32:1-42).
    d. Itinerary of the journey from Egypt (33:1-56).
    e. Instruction prior to entering Canaan (34:1-36:13).

LITERATURE ON NUMBERS

McNeile, A. H., in *The Cambridge Bible for Schools and Colleges* (Cambridge, 1911).

Gray, G. B., in the *International Critical Commentary* (2nd. ed., Edinburgh, 1912).

Binns, L. E., in *Westminster Commentaries* (London, 1927).

Greenstone, J. H., *Numbers with Commentary* (Philadelphia, 1939).

Albright, W. F., "The Oracles of Balaam," *Jour. Bib. Lit.* LXIII, 1944, pp. 207-233.

Anderson, C. A., "The Book of Numbers," in *Old Testament Commentary* (Philadelphia, 1949).

CONSERVATIVE LITERATURE

Keil, C. F., and F. Delitzsch, *The Pentateuch,* Vol. II Leviticus (Grand Rapids, 1949, reprint).

Hengstenberg, E. W., *Die Geschichte Bileams und seine Weissagungen* (1842).

Grant, F. W., *Leviticus* in *The Numerical Bible* (New York, 1887-).

Ellicott, C. J., in *A Bible Commentary for English Readers* (New York, n.d.).

Gaebelein, A. C., *The Book of Numbers* (*Our Hope,* New York, 1913).

Coates, C. A., *An Outline of the Book of Numbers* (Kingston-on-Thames, n.d.).

DEUTERONOMY

Completing the five books of Moses, called by the Jews the "five fifths of the Law," the book of Deuteronomy occupies a logical place. Numbers brings the history of Israel up to the events in the Plains of Moab. Deuteronomy appropriately closes the events of the Mosaic age with three farewell discourses of Moses before his death on the eve of Israel's entrance into the land of Canaan.

1. The Name.

The name in our English versions comes from the Septuagint through an inexact rendering of chapter 17 verse 18, which should be translated "This is the copy (or repetition) of the law." Deuteronomy, accordingly, does not contain a "second law" distinct from the Sinaitic legislation, as the title of the book might imply, but simply consists of a partial restatement and explanation of previous laws to the new generation of Israel, which had grown up in the wilderness. The Jews called the book *'Elleh haddevarim,* "These are the words," or simply *Devarim,* "Words." In the Massorah it is named from its contents *Mishneh Torah* "repetition" or "copy of the law" (Deuteronomy 17:18).

2. The Authorship.

The book itself most explicitly declares its Mosaic authorship and vouches for the careful provisions taken for its preservation in *written* form by the religious leaders of the nation, "And Moses wrote this law, and delivered it unto the priests the sons of Levi, which bare the ark of the covenant of the Lord, and unto all the elders of Israel" (Deuteronomy 31:9). "And it came to pass, when Moses had made an end of writing the words of this law in a book, until they were finished, that Moses commanded the Levites, which bare the ark of the covenant of the Lord, saying, Take this book of the law, and put it in the side of the ark of the covenant of the Lord your God, that it may be there for a witness against thee" (Deuteronomy 31:24-26). It is further declared that Moses spoke "the words of this song" (verse 30) contained in Chapter 32.

The Mosaic authorship of no other book of the Old Testament is so emphatically asserted. Its claims are either true or false. Critics set aside or ignore these claims and insist that Moses was merely the traditional promulgator of these statutes or the actual originator of a small nucleus of oral laws, which after centuries of oral transmission, were finally expanded and published as the Book of Deuteronomy.

But following the unequivocal claims of the book itself, supported by its internal evidence, we maintain that the recognized unity of the book was effected by a single writer, and that that writer was Moses. Moreover, since the Pentateuch is obviously a unit itself, effected by one writer or redactor, it is not unreasonable to assume that the author of Deuteronomy was the author of the rest of the Pentateuch.

The hortatory nature of Deuteronomy, its code of conquest, its character as a military law book of a pilgrim people about to enter Canaan and the general scope and spirit of the writing are eminently appropriate for the Mosaic age as we know it, and most inappropriate for any other age. Not only does the work most explicitly and emphatically claim to be Mosaic in authorship, but the words are Moses' direct words. He is mentioned about forty times in the book, in most instances as the authoritative author of the subject matter. The first person predominates. The language unequivocally purports to come directly from Moses. If it were not written until the seventh century B.C., in the time of Manasseh or Josiah, as the critics contend, it is a most subtle case of misrepresentation and an undeniable literary forgery scarcely worthy of canonical Scripture and, in the writer's opinion, utterly incompatible with the revealed truth of the inspiration of Scripture.

3. The Critical Theory of Authorship.

Deuteronomy occupies a most strategic place in the documentary hypothesis. Leading advocates of the partition theory of the present day in general follow the views of the nineteenth century rationalists and maintain that the traditional fifth book of Moses was written anonymously by a prophetic writer (but in the spirit of Moses) between 715-640 B.C. sometime during the reign of Hezekiah, Manasseh, Amon or Josiah. It was allegedly first published in the eighteenth year of Josiah to effect his great reformation (II Kings 22 and 23). The reason assigned for this late date is the claim that it is only after the seventh century that the history and literature of the Old Testament bear incontrovertible testimony to the influence of Deuteronomy, notably in the matter of the law of the central sanctuary (Deuteronomy 12:1-7). Hence before this date it is assumed to have had no existence.

However, in the interests of a highly artificial theory, the critics wilfully minimize or ignore clear evidence that the laws of Deuteronomy were not only known and observed but existed in the form of written codified statutes and exerted an influence from the very start of the Israelite possession of Canaan. For example, the "devotion" of city and spoil when Jericho was captured (Joshua 6:17, 18) follows Deuteronomy 13:15 ff. When Ai was taken "only the cattle and the spoil," did Israel take as booty (Joshua 8:27), in keeping with Deuteronomy 20:14. The body of the king of Ai was removed from the gibbet before nightfall (Joshua 8:29), in accordance with Deuteronomy 21:23. Joshua's altar on Mount Ebal (Joshua 8:30, 31) illustrates Deuteronomy 27:4-6. (Cf. Joshua 8:32 and Deuteronomy 27:3, 9; Joshua 8:33 and Deuteronomy 11:29; 27:12, 13). Joshua read the blessings and the cursings (Joshua 8:34, 35) in strict agreement with Deuteronomy 31:11, 12; 28:1-30:20.

But more important the law of the central sanctuary was

known early in Israel. It is forced and arbitrary to say that this "unique commandment" contained in Deuteronomy was unknown and unpracticed in Israel till Josiah's reform. That the law of the central sanctuary was known in the days of Joshua is proved by the fact that the East Jordanic tribes disavowed their memorial at the Jordan when accused by their fellow tribesmen of plurality of sanctuary (Joshua 22:29, 31 with Deuteronomy 12:5). In I Samuel 1:3, 7, 9, 21, 24 Elkanah went yearly to Shiloh, the central sanctuary of early Israel. After the destruction of the central sanctuary, Samuel sacrificed at Mizpah, Ramah and Bethlehem, but only took advantage of the law of Deuteronomy 12:10, 11 because of the time of war and stress.

Hezekiah removed the high places (II Kings 18:4, 22) and his reforms were unquestionably carried out with a knowledge of Deuteronomy and its "unique" law of the central sanctuary. Eighth century prophets knew the law also. Not one of these prophets recognized the "high places" as legitimate centers of worship. Many other evidences of the influence of Deuteronomy previous to the time of Josiah's reform might be cited. These are sufficient to show the essential unsoundness of the critical position on Deuteronomy and on the Pentateuch as a whole. Leaving the firm ground of the Mosaic authenticity of the Pentateuch can only land one in the quagmire of doubt, skepticism and uncertainty, where the theories of men clash with the plain statements of God's Word and cast suspicion and aspersion upon its integrity.

4. *The Outline.*

Part I. Moses' First Discourse: Historical (1:1-4:43).

    a. Historical introduction (1:1-5).

    b. Historical review of journey from Horeb to Moab (1:6-3:29).

    c. Practical appeal to the new generation to keep the Law (4:1-40).

d. Historical account of appointment of East Jordanic cities of refuge (4:41-43).

Part II. Moses' Second Discourse: Legal (4:44-26:19).

a. Superscription (4:44-49).

b. Exposition of the first commandment of the Decalogue and theocratic principles (5:1-11:32).

c. Exposition of the code of special laws (12:1-26:19).

Part III. Moses' Third Discourse: Prophetic and Minatory (27:1-30:20).

a. Inscription of laws on stone and promulgation of blessings and curses (27:1-26).

b. Prediction of blessings and curses (28:1-68).

c. Enumeration of God's benefactions and exhortations to fidelity (29:1-30:20).

Historical Appendices (31:1-34:12).

a. Moses' last words and the appointment of Joshua (31:1-30).

b. Moses' song and exhortation (32:1-47).

c. Moses' sight of the Promised Land (32:48-52).

d. Moses' parting blessing (33:1-29).

e. The death and burial of Moses (34:1-12).

Literature on Deuteronomy

Kuenen, A., *The Hexateuch*, (London, 1886).

Driver, S. R., *A Critical and Exegetical Commentary*, (*Int. Crit. Comm.*, Edinburgh, 1895).

Ryle, H. E., "Deuteronomy," in Hastings' Dictionary of the Bible, (1898).

Moore, G. F., "Deuteronomy," *Encyclopedia Biblica*, (1899).

Patterson, J. A., "Deuteronomy," *Encyclopedia Britannica* VIII, (1910).

Koenig, E., in *Kommentar zum Alten Testament*, (Leipzig, 1917).

Smith, G. A., *The Book of Deuteronomy in The Cambridge Bible*, (1918).

Steuernagel, C., in *Handkommentar zum Alten Testament*, (Goettingen, 2nd. ed. 1923).

Welch, A. C., The Code of Deuteronomy, (London, 1924); *The Framework of the Code,* (1932).

Bentzen, A., *Die josianische Reform,* (Kopenhagen, 1926).

Siebens, A., *L'Origine du code deuteronomique,* (Paris, 1929).

Winnett, F. V., *The Mosaic Tradition,* (Toronto, 1949), pp. 42-56; 118 ff., 163-171.

CONSERVATIVE LITERATURE

Vos, G., *The Mosaic Origin of the Pentateuchal Codes,* (New York, 1886).

Zahn, A., *Das Deuteronomium,* (Guetersloh, 1890).

Girdlestone, R. B., *The Student's Deuteronomy,* (1899).

Robinson, G. L., "The Genesis of Deuteronomy," in *The Expositor,* (Oct.-Nov., 1898, Feb. March, May, 1899), and "Deuteronomy," in *Int. St. Bible Ency.*

Orr, J., "The Question of Deuteronomy," in the *Problem of the Old Testament,* (New York, 1906).

Wiener, H. M., *The Main Problem of Deuteronomy,* (Oberlin, 1920).

Davis, J. D., "Deuteronomy" in *Davis' Dictionary of the Bible,* (1911).

Cameron, G. G., "The Laws Peculiar to Deuteronomy in *Princeton Theological Review,* I, 1903, pp. 434-456.
Articles on "Deuteronomy," in the *Illustrated Bible Dictionary,* (1908) and *Temple Bible Dictionary* (1910). Also articles in the *Princeton Theological Review,* "The Laws of Deuteronomy and the Arguments From Silence," (V, 1907, pp. 180-209), and "Deuteronomy and the Argument From Style," (pp. 605-630).

Commentaries of Keil, Delitzsch, and Lange and Introductions of Haevernick, Keil, Moeller, Raven and Steinmueller, *A Companion to Scripture Studies* II, pp. 57-63.

For spiritual insight:

Grant, F. W., in the *Numerical Bible,* (The Pentateuch).

Coates, C. A. C., *An Outline of Deuteronomy,* (Kingston-on-Thames, n.d.).

Gaebelein, A. C., *Deuteronomy,* (New York, 1913).

Chapter VIII

THE AUTHORSHIP
OF THE PENTATEUCH

The Pentateuch as it has come down to us in the Hebrew Bible is generally admitted to be a unity. Its unity was effected either by a single writer or, as many critics contend, by a single redactor or school of redactors. The traditional view, practically unchallenged until the rise of modern criticism from the eighteenth century until the present, is that the Pentateuch was written by a single writer, that writer being Moses. This position was universally held by the ancient Jewish synagogue, the inspired New Testament writers, the Early Christian Church and by virtually all commentators, both Jewish and Christian, until challenged by modern higher criticism.

The modern critical theory, on the other hand, maintains that the Pentateuch was composed from a number of documents dating many centuries after the time of Moses, but containing Mosaic traditions. As we have noted in the preceding chapter, the Yahwist (J) is placed about 850 B.C. The Elohist (E) about 750 B.C., and the combination of J and E in the seventh century B.C. with Deuteronomy dated 621 B.C. and the addition of P in the completed Pentateuch around 500 B.C.[1] These documents, it is claimed, were used by a redactor (or redactors) who introduced the order and arrangement into the Pentateuch, as we now have it in the Hebrew Bible.

1 Cf. Julius Bewer, The Literature of the Old Testament (7th. ed., 1947), pp. XV f.

213

It is frequently asserted by certain scholars who hold some form of the critical hypothesis that the theory of documentary sources is a theory of composition, not of origin, and that subscribing to the documentary thesis does not necessarily question the Mosaic *origin* of the Pentateuch. For example, P. I. Morentz and H. C. Alleman[2] accept the documentary theory of the Pentateuch and yet claim to hold to the Mosaic origin in the sense expressed by W. Robertson Smith: "Mosaic Law is not held to exclude post-Mosaic developments. That the whole Law is the Law of Moses does not necessarily imply that every precept was developed in detail in his days, but only that the distinctive Law of Israel owes to him the origin and principles in which all detailed precepts are implicitly contained. The development into explicitness of what Moses gave in principle is the work of continuous divine teaching in connection with new historical situations."[3]

Although critics disagree in particular concerning the material listed under the various documents, the so-called documentary theory is extremely popular at the present time. Advocacy of it, at least in its broader outlines, is now well-nigh a badge of intellectual respectability, and it is accepted today "by virtually every reputable Old Testament scholar."[4] This being the case, a careful critical examination of the claim of Mosaic authorship is necessary.

I. The Basis of the Mosaic Tradition

If Moses is not the author of the Pentateuch, history knows nothing of any other author. The documentary hypothesis is a child of modern, rationalistic, higher criticism, which, dealing with the date, authorship, and authenticity of the Biblical books is much more likely to be subjective than lower criticism, which is concerned with establishing the correct text of a document. Accordingly, much of the literature advocating the

2 Old Testament Commentary (Philadelphia, 1948), p. 245.
3 The Old Testament In the Jewish Church (2nd. ed., 1892), p. 313.
4 Cf. Morentz and Alleman, loc. cit.

theory of late documentary sources for the Pentateuch is highly speculative and subjective, and arbitrarily sets aside the concrete objective facts of history and the testimony of the ancient manuscripts themselves, which overwhelmingly favor the Mosaic authorship. William Henry Green aptly speaks of the "unflinching intrepidity" and "veritable audacity" of the higher critics, who, in pushing their theory to its last results, place it "absolutely beyond the reach of the *reductio ad absurdum* argument; for the most preposterous conclusions are accepted without hesitation, and paraded as genuine discoveries."[5]

Since until comparatively recent times the practically universal view among both Jews and Christians has been that Moses was the author of the first five books of the Bible, the correctness of a tradition so ancient and universal is not only important in itself, but demands and merits the most careful scrutiny before it is abandoned in favor of some ingenious and highly plausible substitute. This is especially so when the rejection of the time-honored position involves consequences that jeopardize any high and worthy view of the authority and credibility of the Bible as a whole.

1. The Pentateuch Itself Witnesses To Its Mosaic Authorship.

Pentateuchal texts directly assert that Moses wrote at least parts of the Pentateuch. A careful study of the context and scope of these passages clearly implies that these portions are considerable. While there is no warrant to conclude from this direct evidence alone that Moses wrote all the Pentateuch, neither is there reason to deny Mosaic authorship of all other parts for which such authorship is not specifically predicated, as modern critics commonly do, or to relegate the verses, in which Mosaic authorship is specifically asserted, to later

5 William Henry Green, **Moses and the Prophets** (New York, 1883), p. 47.

redactors. Such a procedure is highly arbitrary, lacking objective foundation.

The entire body of Pentateuchal Law, comprising mainly the portion extending from Exodus 20 through the book of Deuteronomy, in explicit and positive terms claims to be Mosaic. Moses is expressly asserted to have written the Book of the Covenant (Exodus 20-23), which embraces the ten commandments and the accompanying judgments and ordinances (Exodus 24:4, 7). The so-called Priest Code relating to the priesthood and the tabernacle ritual contained in the rest of Exodus (except chapters 32-34), the regulations contained in Numbers and the whole of Leviticus are declared to have been directly given to Moses by the Lord. The laws governing the building of the tabernacle and the establishment of its ritual recorded in Exodus 25-31 are presented as personal communications to Moses (Exodus 25:1, 23, 31; 26:1, etc.). The account of the erection of the Tabernacle is set forth as being according "as Jehovah commanded . . ." This or similar phraseology recurs many times in Exodus chapters 39-40. Both Leviticus and Numbers in the most unequivocal language represent the priestly legislation as directly communicated to Moses (Leviticus 1:1; 4:1; 6:1, etc.; Numbers 1:1; 2:1; 4:1, etc.) and Leviticus 26:46 and 27:34 connect these cultic laws with Sinai.

The third body of Pentateuchal law, the Deuteronomic Code, embracing the legal portions of the book of Deuteronomy, is expressly said to have been written by Moses and to have been delivered to the Levites for safekeeping (Deuteronomy 31:9, 24-26). Thus, according to the testimony of the Pentateuch itself, its entire law is Mosaic—the book of the Covenant and the Deuteronomic law expressly claiming to be of Mosaic authorship and the ritual law or Priestly Code directly mediated through Moses, though the lawgiver is not actually said to have written it.

As far as the narrative sections of the Pentateuch are concerned, Mosaic authorship is expressly attributed to two prominent passages. Moses was instructed to record the victory over Amalek "in a book" (Exodus 17:14) and to record the various stopping places of Israel in their wilderness journey (Numbers 33:2). The latter passage furnishes evidence that the writer of the list of stations was the author of the entire Pentateuchal narrative, since the section containing the itinerary cannot be adequately fitted into the documentary theory.[6] To Moses is attributed the Song and Blessing in Deuteronomy 32 and 33.

Although there are no explicit statements covering any other sections of the Pentateuchal narrative, it is evident that both history and legislation form an integral part of a unified work. The various books are most intimately bound together. Exodus continues the narrative of Genesis. Leviticus continues the ritual law of the latter part of Exodus. Numbers intersperses appropriate narrative with the ritual laws and Deuteronomy follows closely with a repetition of the law to the new generation previous to entrance into the land. If the laws contained in the Pentateuch are Mosaic, as they claim to be, the closely interwoven narrative was evidently put down by the same hand. The internal evidence points to the conclusion that the entire Pentateuch is what it has always claimed to be, the genuine production of Moses.

2. The Rest of the Old Testament Testifies to the Mosaic Authorship of the Pentateuch.

The law of Moses is given prominence in the book of Joshua and its authority is constantly appealed to, showing at that early date that the legal portions of the Pentateuch were in written form (Joshua 1:7; 8:32, 34; 22:5). At the time of the conquest certain Canaanites were permitted to dwell in the land "to prove Israel by them, to know whether they would hearken unto the commandments of the Lord, which he

6 Cf. W. H. Green, **The Higher Criticism of the Pentateuch** (New York, 1896), p. 38.

commanded their fathers by the hand of Moses" (Judges 3:4). When David bore the ark to Zion, he did so "as Moses commanded . . ." (I Chronicles 15:15). He charged his son Solomon to observe that which "is written in the law of Moses . . ." (I Kings 2:3). Solomon appointed the ritual of his Temple in accordance with "the commandment of Moses . . ." (II Chronicles 8:13).

The high priest Jehoiada in appointing the Temple ritual "as it is written in the law of Moses . . ." (II Chronicles 23:18), on the other hand, stipulated the singing as it was instituted by David (II Chronicles 23:18), a distinction militating against the common critical notion of "legal fiction," by which laws in general, even though recent, were attributed to Moses. The Northern Kingdom was taken captive because of the transgression of "all that Moses the servant of the Lord commanded" (II Kings 18:12). The Law of Moses is prominently connected with Hezekiah's reforms (II Kings 18:6; II Chronicles 30:16) and those of Josiah (II Kings 22:8; 23:25). During the captivity Daniel refers to matters contained in the Pentateuch as "written in the law of Moses" (Daniel 9:11, 13).

The prophets only occasionally refer to Moses by name. They do make more frequent allusion to "the law," however, thereby meaning the law of Moses (Isaiah 1:10; 8:16, 20; Jeremiah 2:8, Ezekiel 7:26). The post-captivity books of Ezra (3:2; 6:18; 7:6) and Nehemiah (1:7, 8; 8:14; 9:14; 10:29; 13:1) refer prominently to the Law of Moses. The final injunction of the last of the Old Testament prophets is "Remember ye the law of Moses my servant, which I commanded unto him in Horeb for all Israel, even statutes and ordinances" (Malachi 4:4).

3. *The New Testament Attests the Mosaic Authorship of the Pentateuch.* In a citation from Exodus 3 Jesus calls the Pentateuch in general and Exodus in particular "the book of Moses" (Mark 12:26). It is clear that the "writings" of

Moses (John 5:46, 47) to which Jesus frequently referred were the Pentateuch (Luke 16:29, 31). The Jews not only referred to the injunctions of the Pentateuch as that which "Moses commanded" (John 8:5), but Jesus habitually employs the same expression (Matthew 8:4; 19:7, 8; Mark 1:44; 10:3; Luke 5:14) when referring to Mosaic legislation as a whole, whether to the book of the Covenant, the Priestly Code or the Deuteronomic Law. Jesus (John 7:19) and the evangelists assert not only that "the law was given through Moses" (John 1:17), but that he also reduced it to writing (Mark 10:5; 12:19). When the Pentateuch was read the Apostles said "Moses is read" or preached (II Corinthians 3:15; Acts 15:21).

4. Tradition Confirms the Mosaic Authorship of the Pentateuch.

From evidence furnished by the Samaritan Pentateuch, which has been attributed to Moses up to the present time, it is plain that as early as the fifth century B.C. both Jews and Samaritans firmly believed that the Pentateuch was of Mosaic origin. The Jews of Palestine and of the dispersion were likewise unanimous in this conviction. Ecclesiasticus in the first half of the second century B.C. is the earliest apocryphal book to bear witness to the Mosaic authorship of the Pentateuch (Ecclesiasticus 45:6). The second book of Maccabees speaks of the "commandment of the law which was given us by Moses" (7:30). Both Philo[7] and Josephus[8] ascribe Mosaic authorship to the Pentateuch. Both the Palestinian and Babylonian Talmud view Moses with the greatest reverence as author and legislator.[9] In all the lists of canonical Scripture set forth by the Church Fathers, the Pentateuchal books are given special place and often referred to as the "books of Moses." Higher critics cannot deny the antiquity and practical

7 **Life of Moses** (3:39).
8 **Antiquities** IV:8, 48.
9 Cf. Strack-Billerbeck, **Kommentar zum Neuen Testament aus Talmud und Midrash** (Munich, 1928), pp. 435-450.

universality of the tradition that the Pentateuch is Mosaic in authorship. They confidently assert, however, that their documentary view is a modern discovery which shows the ancient tradition to be erroneous.

5. *Internal Evidence Attests the Mosaic Authorship of the Pentateuch.*

If Moses did write the Pentateuch, he wrote it in the desert, as an eyewitness, as one familiar with Egypt, but unfamiliar with Canaan, and as one who would likely employ some archaic expressions. Are there such internal evidences pointing to Mosaic authorship?

a. The Pentateuch was written in the desert.

Egypt was behind the Israelites. Canaan was before them (Leviticus 18:3). They are reminded that they had not yet entered the land which God was to give them (Deuteronomy 12:9; 15:4,7) and that the laws which were given them looked forward to the time when they would "come into the land" and "possess it" (Deuteronomy 17:14; Leviticus 14:34). Israel occupies a camp and lives in tents in the wilderness (Numbers 2:1 f.; Leviticus 14:8; 16:21, 22). Everyone is within walking distance of the tabernacle (Leviticus 17:3, 9). Aaron and his sons are spoken of (Leviticus 17:1, 2), but never the high priest and his sons.

b. The Pentateuch was written with the vividness of an eyewitness. The local color, the minute descriptions of persons and places and the genuine atmosphere pervading the books can scarcely be attributed to oral tradition. Elim, for instance, is minutely described as a place of twelve fountains and seventy palm trees (Exodus 15:27). The wood for the construction of the Tabernacle is not cedar or cypress, but acacia, not found in Palestine but in Egypt and the Sinaitic Peninsula. The "tahash" (R. V. "sealskins" or "porpoise-skins") is an expression seemingly referring to the dugong, a herbivorous sea-animal living in the Red Sea (Exodus 25:5). These and numerous other details must have been written by an observer, which would be natural, or forged by later editors, which would be highly improbable.

c. The Pentateuch was written by an author who knew Egypt.

The story of Joseph and the account of the exodus with its geographical notations, historical and social references and accuracy of detail, could only have been written by one thoroughly familiar with the Nile valley. Of particular significance are such allusions as the Nile irrigation system (Deuteronomy 11:10) and the distinction between overseers and taskmasters (Exodus 5:6), the latter of which has been attested by the monuments.

Carefully analyzing the Egyptian narratives in Genesis and Exodus in the light of the history and archeology of the Hyksos Period and the New Kingdom in Egypt (1750-1100 B.C.), Garrow Duncan shows the minute accuracy and authentic local coloring of the author of the Pentateuch.[10] Concluding his detailed examination of the Joseph story and the Exodus narrative, Duncan says, "Thus we cannot but admit that the writer of these two narratives on the Old Testament was thoroughly well acquainted with the Egyptian language, customs, beliefs, court life, etiquette and officialdom; and not only so, but the readers must have been just as familiar with things Egyptian."[11] W. F. Albright notes evidence for the Egyptian sojourn in the name of Moses and the names of a number of the Aaronids, and calls attention to the fact that "there are a great many correct and local antiquarian details which would be inexplicable as later inventions."[12] The marshalled evidence for the true-to-life character and au-

10 **New Light on Hebrew Origins** (London, 1936), pp. 73-179.
11 **Op. cit.,** p. 176.
12 **From the Stone Age to Christianity** (Baltimore, 1940), p. 184.

thenticity of the Egyptian narratives of the Pentateuch is quite convincing.[13]

The founding of Zoan (Tanis) is referred to in connection with the building of Hebron (Numbers 13:22). This furnishes an illustration of the writer's familiarity with Egypt. Places, however, in Canaan are not as well known. Goshen (Genesis 46:28), On (Genesis 41:45), Pithom, Raamses (Exodus 1:11), Pi-hahiroth, Migdol, Baal-zephon (Exodus 14:2) are simply listed as places quite familiar to the readers, while regions or towns in Canaan are often compared with places in Egypt. The "Plain of the Jordan" is said to be "like the land of Egypt, as thou goest unto Zoar" (Genesis 13:10). Minute acquaintance is also shown with the topography of the Sinaitic Peninsula and Transjordan (Deuteronomy 1:1), while places like Hebron (Genesis 23:2), Shechem (Genesis 33:18), and Mount Gerizim and Mount Ebal (Deuteronomy 11:29-31) are simply listed as places in Canaan.

d. The Pentateuch preserves archaisms.

Despite apparent modernization of spellings and place names effected during the centuries of its transmission, the persistence of certain ancient expressions reveal the antiquity of the original text. For example, archaisms may be seen in the retention of earlier forms—the masculine personal pronoun *hu'* is employed 195 times for the third person feminine singular *hi'*, the regular feminine form, which is found only eleven times. The masculine form *na'ar* is found twenty-one times for girl, whereas the feminine form *na'arah* occurs only once. Similarly *hallazeh* (this) becomes *hallaz* outside the Pentateuch, and *ha'el* (these) becomes *ha'elleh* (except in obsolete expressions as in I Chronicles 20:8). Other old expressions take the form of a change of consonants. *Tsahaq*, "to laugh," occurs in the Pentateuch for the common *sahaq; tsa'q* ("to cry out") for *za'aq; kesev* ("lamb") for *keves* (an inversion of consonants).

Archaic phenomena are relatively more abundant in the Pentateuch than in any of the other books of the Old Testament. While they do not *per se* denote Mosaic authorship, they do point to ancient forms in the Hebrew language, and offer strong evidence of the early origin of the passages in which they occur, and thus corroborate the tradition of Mosaic authorship.

6. *The Elementary Character of the Doctrinal Teachings of the Pentateuch Favor its Early Mosaic Origin.*

Compared with later Scriptures in which the same truths are dealt with, such doctrines as the resurrection, the future state, the millennium, providential retribution, angels and the first and second advents of Christ, show clearly that the Pentateuch belongs to an earlier period of progressive divine revelation than the Psalms, the book of Job or the Prophets.

Summary

Arguments for the Mosaic authorship of the books which bear Moses' name are thus supported by historical evidence and the internal witness of the Pentateuchal books themselves. The Pentateuch is ascribed to Israel's great lawgiver and prophet (Deuteronomy 18:15) by unanimous and unbroken tradition from the days of Moses himself through the entire Old Testament period and onward. The ancient Jewish synagogue, the inspired New Testament writers, and our Lord Himself sanctioned it. Both Jewish and Christian tradition in the Christian era fully support it. The historical evidence is practically unanimous until the documentary theory took its rise in the last two centuries, gaining influential prestige especially in the last seventy-five years.

The internal evidence of the Pentateuchal books agrees with the unanimous historical witness. The books indicated they were written in the desert by an eyewitness, who was thoroughly conversant with Egyptian life, and contain archaisms which point to the antiquity of the text. The elementary character of the doctrinal teachings furnish additional evidence of early composition, consonant with the Mosaic authorship.

II. The Dangers of Denying the Mosaic Tradition

As plausible and ingenious as the documentary hypothesis of the critics is, and despite the vast amount of learning expended in its defense and the halo of recognized scholarship which has been cast over it, its advocates have spent their energies in the interests of a mere theory the correctness of which yet remains to be proved. Despite the wide popularity and almost universal acceptance of the documentary view in critical circles, the devout student may well hesitate to jump on the critical "band wagon" as he pauses to consider the consequences of embracing a theory which involves such serious issues.

1. Espousing the Critical View Involves Rejecting all the Positive Evidence of Mosaic Authorship, both Biblical and Extra-Biblical.

One must be prepared to ascribe to later redactors those verses in which Mosaic authorship is specifically predicated, a procedure highly arbitrary and without objective foundation. He must also be prepared to view the ritual legislation or Priest Code, which in Leviticus and Numbers is repeatedly and unequivocally represented as directly communicated to Moses, as not given to Moses at all, but the words put in the mouth of the lawgiver by priestly scholars about 500 B.C.—almost a thousand years after the time of Moses. Further, he must be prepared to believe that the Deuteronomic Code was likewise by no means spoken and written by Moses, as it distinctly claims to be, but was composed many centuries later, shortly before Josiah's reform in 621 B.C., the words being ascribed to Moses to give them authority to produce the revival needed at the time.

To say that there was not the slightest intention of fraud or deception in the mind of the priestly scholars who produced the Priest Code (P) or the Deuteronomic writer who composed D does not relieve the shock of such arbitrary and irreverent handling of Sacred Scripture in the minds of believing scholars, nor clear the sacred writers of suspicion, who, in this case, were guilty at best of pious misrepresentation.

Notwithstanding the firm insistence of some critics that there is nothing in the documentary theory incongruous with a high theory of inspiration of Scripture,[14] there remain those who can never reconcile such attribution of pious duplicity to inspired Old Testament writers with the elevated New Testament description of their work, "For the prophecy came not in old time by the will of man: but holy men of God spake as they were moved by the Holy Ghost" (II Peter 1:21). Since all inspired writers of Scripture spake from God and "were moved by the Holy Ghost," who is pre-eminently "the Spirit of truth," (John 14:17; 15:26; 16:13; I John 4:6) to the devout student it is utterly incompatible with His gracious mission and ministry to attribute to Him the questionable activity demanded by the exigencies of the critical hypothesis.

But the problem goes deeper than this. To the Christian the difficulty involved is not confined to the Old Testament, but is a New Testament question as well. The fact must be faced that our Lord gave unequivocal testimony to the Mosaic authorship of the Pentateuch. Critics resort to various makeshifts to circumvent or undermine this witness, but none is adequate. It is commonly asserted that Christ did not know. He simply shared the current but mistaken opinions of His countrymen. Several New Testament passages are appealed

14 Cf. S. R. Driver, **Introduction** (9th. ed., 1913), p. VIII f.

to, such as His ignorance concerning the "day" and "hour" of His second advent (Mark 13:32) and the kenotic passage (Philippians 2:7). That Christ voluntarily limited His knowledge is evident from these passages, but it is also obvious from many other verses that this limitation by no means extended to merely human knowledge (Luke 5:22; John 1:48; Matthew 20:17-19, and so on). He chose to limit His knowledge of certain time features of His second advent. But it is to be noted that He kept silence concerning that of which He was voluntarily ignorant. Had He been ignorant of the authorship of the Pentateuch would He not likewise have remained silent on this point? Moreover, if His kenosis is extended beyond the precise delimitations of Scripture, Christ becomes a mere man, and He is no longer infallible in matters either of history or faith.

Again critics assert that Christ did know, but did not view it as a part of His mission to correct such erroneous beliefs as the Mosaic authorship of the Pentateuch. His domain was in the moral and religious sphere, they say, and it was not His business to rectify errors in science, history or criticism. This, of course, is true. But it must be remembered that when in the course of His ministry He did touch these spheres, it was necessary, by virtue of His person and work, to be absolutely accurate. It is unthinkable that Christ would have prejudiced men against His heavenly message by a careless inaccuracy on the human plane. Doubting Christ in minor matters like this always furnishes a gateway to doubting Him in spiritual matters, as He warned Nicodemus: "If I have told you earthly things, and ye believe not, how shall ye believe, if I tell you of heavenly things?" (John 3:12).

2. *Espousing the Critical View Involves a Serious Capitulation to the Foes of the Credibility of the Pentateuch and of Religious Supernaturalism.*

It is a notorious fact that the documentary hypothesis as it has crystallized in the so-called Graf-Kuenen-Wellhausen

School of modern Pentateuchal criticism has been invented and elaborated by a long succession of distinguished scholars, who were unbelievers in an immediate supernatural revelation. One who embraces the theory aligns himself with those who have endeavored to set aside the reality of miracles and predictive prophecy and attempt to explain the miraculous on a purely human plane. It is this inveterate antagonism toward the supernatural which has been aptly styled "the prejudice of criticism."[15] Since the supernatural is so intimately interwoven into the fabric of Pentateuchal history, it is not a mere literary question which the divisive criticism raises. It is not simply whether the Pentateuch was written by one author or another, while its historical reliability and divine authority remain intact. The truth and authenticity of the whole Mosaic history are at stake.

Did God actually reveal Himself to Moses as the Pentateuch claims? Are the foundations of Bible history divinely established? Was Christ wrong when He said Moses wrote of Him? The types with which the Pentateuchal history and the Mosaic institutions abound point in a most wonderfully detailed and descriptive way to the person and work of Christ. If the history is unreliable, if the Levitical institutions are not divinely ordained and if the prophetic types are spurious, the mere record of priestly usage, what becomes of the unmistakable witness they bear to Christ, so elaborately set forth and expounded in inspired New Testament passages?

If one maintains that "the contents of the Pentateuch . . . were not first transmitted as a book but as a tradition" and not reduced to writing till centuries after Moses, and then only as two often divergent traditions (J and E) were united with still later Deuteronomic and Priestly additions,[16] the admission is inevitable that the account of the "Mosaic" age set forth in the Pentateuch is fundamentally unreliable. No

15 W. H. Fitchett, **Where the Higher Criticism Fails** (New York, 1922), p. 99.
16 Cf. H. C. Alleman, **Old Testament Commentary** (1948), pp. 171 f.

theory that the later redactors who combined the documents J, E, D and P were "inspired" can alleviate the suspicion of historical unreliability, as such a theory is at variance with the internal evidence of the documents themselves, which ascribe at least two of the three legal codes and considerable narrative sections directly to Moses' pen.

Insisting on a long period of oral transmission before the two main traditions were written down and later combined are only naturalistic devices to explain the miraculous as popular legend and folklore. Supernatural facts, which stand irrefutable and unshaken in the Mosaic documents, impregnable to all other methods of attack, are dissolved like wax in the crucible of the critics, because it is purposely invented to dissolve them.

"Conservative" scholars, in subscribing to some form of the documentary hypothesis because of its present popularity, are making fatal concessions to a theory which is basically unsound and highly injurious to devout and constructive study of the Old Testament. The degree to which Mosaic history is discarded as unauthentic and unreliable under such treatment varies with different critics, from those like Kuenen, Wellhausen and Stade,[17] who view it as almost completely unreliable, to those more recent writers, like Alleman and Flack,[18] who would classify themselves as conservatives and allow the record to stand more or less unchallenged. The different reaction, however, is the result of the subjective state of the critic rather than any intelligible reasons dictated by the nature of the hypothesis itself.

3. *Espousing the Critical View Involves Surrender of Any High or Worthy View of Biblical Inspiration.*

There is little wonder that those who subscribe to the documentary hypothesis soon find that their doctrine of in-

17 A. Kuenen, **The Origin and Composition of the Hexateuch** (New York, 1886), J. Wellhausen, **History of Israel**, pp. 318 f. ; B. Stade, **Geschichte des Volkes Israel I** (1881), pp. 129 f.
18 **Old Testament Commentary** (Philadelphia, 1948), 171 f., 207 f.

spiration must be modified. The "once reputable doctrine of verbal inspiration of Scripture"[19] now becomes no longer reputable. No longer is it a question merely of the strict inerrancy in minutiae of history or matters of science or mode of inspiration. The question now becomes, "Can any reliance at all be placed upon the historical accuracy of the Bible—not, be it observed, in unimportant details of purely technical or antiquarian interest—but in major events and vital facts connected with divine revelation, theological doctrines and the general history of redemption?"

If the Pentateuch yields an unreliable account of what actually transpired in the era which it describes, as the critical theory maintains, the only way to arrive at the factual basis is to undo the work of the redactors, eliminate their well-meaning but misleading editorial dressing, distentangle the interwoven documentary sources and, as far as possible, restore them to their pristine form before they were combined. The result would be the conflicting traditions which had been handed down orally for centuries concerning the events in question. From these a thimble full of truth might be extracted and the rest left to conjecture.

This is what one must logically be prepared to face when he adopts the partition theory. This is the basic view toward that which is not only a part of the canon of Scripture, but that part which is introductory and foundational to the whole, and which Jesus said could not be "broken" (John 10:35), Paul declared was "inspired" (II Timothy 3:16) and Peter asserted did not come by the "will of man" but through men who "spake as they were moved by the Holy Ghost" (II Peter 1:20, 21). It is understandable how this theory appears wicked and ridiculous in the light of the high New Testament doctrine of inspiration. It is comprehensible, too, that those who embrace this hypothesis insist that the doctrine of plenary-verbal inspiration of the Scriptures requires drastic revision.

19 W. F. Albright, **The Archeology of Palestine** (Pelican Books, 1949), p. 255.

4. Espousing the Critical View Involves Being Cast Upon a Limitless Sea of Uncertainty and Conjecture Without a Guiding Course.

Discarding the Mosaic authorship, explicitly asserted and supported by the earliest evidence both Biblical and extra-Biblical, one is helplessly cast adrift upon an open sea of doubt with nothing to point out the course ahead. It may be asked whether the Pentateuch may not be from the Mosaic age, but from the pen of one of Moses' contemporaries? This is pointless. Unless the Pentateuch is denied origin in the Mosaic age, there is no valid reason whatever to ascribe it to any one but Moses. To refuse it to him is to begin to scan the centuries in a fruitless search for authors and to be swamped in conjecture. J, the Yahwist (about 850 B.C.) and E, the Elohist (about 750 B.C.), are as shadowy and uncertain in name as in date. Even doubt in the legitimacy of distinguishing between J and E in the narrative sections of the Pentateuch occasionally creeps out in the writings of zealous and thorough-going advocates of the theory.[20] The publication of Deuteronomy in 621 B.C., as well as the Holiness Code in the sixth century and the Priest Code about 500 B.C., according to the critical view, is largely conjecture in favor of the theory.

Supposing the legitimacy of the distinction between the documents J and E in the narrative sections and D and P in the legal portions is established. Supposing also that the authors of the several documents were infallibly inspired and the redactors who combined and edited them to form the Pentateuch as we now have it were divinely kept from error, would we not then have just as trustworthy a record, though the events were recorded at a comparatively late date, as if Moses himself wrote them down in the era in which they oc-

20 Cf. S. R. Driver, **Introduction** (9th. ed., 1913), pp. 116 f. J. Wellhausen, **Die Composition des Hexateuch** (3rd. ed.,) p. 22. A. Dillmann, **Genesis** (Edinburgh, 1897), pp. 6 f. Cf. also Kautzsch, Koenig, Gunkel, etc.

curred? The answer, of course, is "yes." But the difficulties involved are insuperable.

To begin, the above-mentioned suppositions are fanciful and impossible in the actual working out of the critical hypothesis. Some evangelical scholars in becoming infatuated with one form or another of the documentary theory seem not to realize this, nor the fact that the very foundations of the partition theory are constructed upon the assumption of the fallibility and, what is more subtle, the actual falsity of the documents. For example, the result of the development of the two independent lines of oral tradition over many centuries in the J and E documents and in different parts of Palestine, E (Ephraimitic, in the North) and J (Judaic, in the South)[21] can only be that these accounts, by the very necessities of the case, must be divergent and discordant, as critics freely confess. To claim inspiration for them that would assure them trustworthiness is a highly subjective attitude at variance with the assumptions and the spirit of the critical view.

Again, Deuteronomy (D) if not published till 621 B.C., yet professing to be from Moses' mouth and pen, cannot be cleared of the suspicion of pious forgery. The same may be said of the Priestly Code, not completed till about 500 B.C., but repeatedly professing to be directly and divinely commanded to Moses. Under these circumstances the honesty and integrity of the redactors can scarcely be unchallenged. Conservatives espousing the documentary theory may fondly dream that within the framework of this hypothesis "a redactor can be just as much inspired in editing certain inspired material as the inspired writer who wrote it."[22] This is true if we admit slight redactions or certain editorial additions to the Pentateuch, regarded as *authentically Mosaic*. This is not and *cannot be true* within the framework and under the basic assumptions of the critical position when evaluated in the

21 Cf. Driver, **op. cit.,** pp. 122 f.
22 P. I. Morentz and H. C. Alleman, **Old Testament Commentary** (1948), p. 245.

light of the doctrine of the inspiration of the Old Testament as presented in the New (II Timothy 3:16; II Peter 1:20, 21).

To say that the writer or writers of either J, E, D or P were "inspired" is of necessity to alter the meaning of the term "inspired" from its genuinely Biblical connotation. If J and E represent two independent lines of tradition, based upon long centuries of fluid transmission, and are, hence, necessarily divergent and discordant, in what sense can they be inspired? If D and P are similarly based upon oral tradition and yet profess to give the minutiae of legal provisions in an elaborate Mosaic setting, to be of any value as spiritual truth they would have to be "inspired" most miraculously. But how then shall we reconcile their inspiration under the critical theory with their spurious claim (D) or representation (P) of Mosaic authorship? In what senses were the redactors inspired when they used contradictory sources and *incorporated* the disagreements and contradictions into their composite narrative (according to the critics) in the form of historical inaccuracies, anachronisms, etc., or, on the other hand, allowed to be represented as Mosaic in authorship that which was not really Mosaic? To attempt to cast the halo of an adequate Biblical doctrine of inspiration over the documentary theory cannot obscure its essentially unbelieving and anti-supernaturalistic framework and presuppositions.

SUMMARY

The serious consequences of rejecting the Mosaic authorship of the Pentateuch in favor of the highly plausible and learnedly developed theory of documentary sources may well cause the Bible-believing critic and student to hesitate before doing so. Not only must he be prepared to abandon all the positive and definite Biblical and extra-Biblical evidence for Mosaic authenticity in favor of a modern brain-child which has no traditional or solid Biblical support, but he must also face the fact that he is making a far-reaching capitulation to the foes of the credibility of the Pentateuch and of religious supernaturalism in general. In addition, he must be assured that he is embracing a view which is essentially incompatible with the high view of the inspiration of the Old Testament as presented in the New and, at the same time, he must realize that he is launching upon a limitless sea of uncertainty and conjecture which offers no guiding course or sure stopping place, and which gives little hope that the view will ever be more than it now is, an unproved and unprovable theory. It is high time for professedly conservative scholarship to realize anew the essential unsoundness of the critical hypothesis and to cease trying to reconcile its potent unbelief with the tenets of historic evangelical Christianity and conservative Judaism.

LITERATURE ON THE PENTATEUCH
(See also titles in Chapter VII and Chapter IX).

Wellhausen, J., *Prolegomena to the History of Israel,* (Edinburgh, 1885).

Holzinger, H., *Einleitung in den Hexateuch,* (Freiburg, 1893).

Koenig, E., *Einleitung in das Alte Testament,* (Bonn, 1893).

Carpenter, J. E., and G. Harford-Battersby, *The Composition of the Hexateuch,* (New York, 1902).

Strack, H. L., *Einleitung in das Alte Testament,* (6th ed., Munich, 1906).

Cornill, C. H., *Introduction to the Canonical Books of the Old Testament,* (New York, 1907).

Chapman, A. T., *Introduction to the Pentateuch* in the *Cambridge Bible,* (1911).

Moore, G. F., *The Literature of the Old Testament,* (New York, 1913).

Eiselen, F. C., *The Books of the Pentateuch,* (New York, 1916).

Creelman, H., *Introduction to the Old Testament,* (New York, 1917).

Brightman, E. S., *The Sources of the Hexateuch,* (New York, 1918).

Gray, G. B., *A Critical Introduction to the Old Testament,* (2nd. ed., New York, 1919).

Eissfeldt, O., *Hexateuch Synopse,* (Leipzig, 1922).

Simpson, D. C., *Pentateuchal Criticism,* (London, 1924).

Sellin, E., *Introduction to the Old Testament,* (London, 1923).

Harford, J. B., *Since Wellhausen: A Brief Survey of Pentateuchal Criticism*, (London, 1926).

McFadyen, J. E., *Introduction to the Old Testament* (2nd. ed., New York, 1933).

Koenig, E., *Ist die moderne Pentateuchkritik auf Tatsachen begruendet?* (Stuttgart, 1933).

Weiser, A., *Einleitung in das Alte Testament*, (Stuttgart, 1939).

CONSERVATIVE LITERATURE

Green, W. H., *The Pentateuch Vindicated*, (New York, 1863).

Keil, C. F., *Manual of Historical-Critical Introduction to the Canonical Scriptures of the Old Testament*, (Edinburgh, 1869), pp. 71-201, and with bibliography of earlier conservative literature, p. 72.

Hengstenburg, E. W., *Dissertations on the Genuineness of the Pentateuch* (Edinburgh, 1847).

Haevernick, H. A., *General Historico-Critical Introduction to the Old Testament*, (Edinburgh, 1852), and his *Introduction to the Pentateuch*, (Edinburgh, 1852), pp. 71-201.

Green, W. H., "Was Moses the Author of the Pentateuch?" *Herzog's Encyclopedia* American ed, by Schaff *s.v.* "Pentateuch."

Aiken, Dr. *Special Introduction to the Historical Books of the Old Testament*, (The Princeton Press, 1899).

Moeller, W., *Are the Critics Right?* (New York, 1899), and his *Einleitung in das Alte Testament* (Zwickau, 1934).

Kyle, M. G., "Problem of the Pentateuch," in *Int. Stand. Bible Encyl.*, (Supplement, 1929) s.v. "Pentateuch."

Mangenot, E., *L'Authenticite du Pentateuque*, (Paris, 1907).

Mechineau, L., *L'Origine mosaique du Pentateuque*, (Paris, 1901).

Wiener, H. M., *Pentateuchal Studies*, (Oberlin, 1912), *The Origin of the Pentateuch*, (London, 1912).

Kyle, M. G., *Moses and the Monuments*, (Oberlin, 1920), *The Deciding Voice of the Monuments*, (Bibliotheca Sacra Co., 1924).

Philips, A., *The Failure of the Higher Criticism of the Old Testament*, (London, 1923).

Wilson, R. D., *A Scientific Investigation of the Old Testament*, (Philadelphia, 1922).

Goldman, S., *The Book of Books: An Introduction*, (New York, 1948), pp. 39-103.

For a general apologetic approach:

Machen, J. G., *Christian View of Man,* (reprint, Grand Rapids, 1947); *Christianity and Liberalism,* (reprint, Grand Rapids, 1946); *What Is Faith?* (reprint Grand Rapids, 1946).

Hamilton, F. E., *The Basis of the Christian Faith,* (New York, 3rd ed., 1946).

CHAPTER IX

THE MOSAIC UNITY
OF THE PENTATEUCH

THE PENTATEUCH as we possess it today is a coherent, logically developed document. That fact can scarcely be denied on any sober or rational grounds.[1] The question, therefore, is not whether the Pentateuch is a unity, but rather, *how was that unity effected?* Is it a natural unity, the result of a single author or redactor, or an artificial unity, the composite work of a number of writers and redactors (or schools of writers and redactors), whose labors extended over many centuries? The view that the unity of the Pentateuch was effected by a single writer, that writer being Moses, as we have noted from the preceding chapter, is supported by the most ancient tradition both Biblical and extra-Biblical, by the ancient Jewish synagogue, the New Testament, the Early Church and by practically all commentators, Jewish and Christian, up to the rise of modern criticism.

Despite doubts and denials by the pagan Celsus, heretical Nazarenes, the Gnostic Ptolemy in the Patristic period and a few unimportant names in the Middle Ages, together with the Jewish philosopher Spinoza and the Catholic Oratorian, Richard Simon, in the pre-critical modern period, the Mosaic tradition was firmly held. Even up to the middle of the nineteenth century, notwithstanding the critical views of Astruc,

1 Yet even this obvious fact is denied by some critics, e.g. A. Bentzen, **Introduction to the Old Testament,** Vol. II (Copenhagen, 1948), p. 12, and G. von Rad, who speak of its "Unfoermlichkeit" or "shapelessness" (**Theol. Blaetter,** 1935, col. 251).

Eichhorn, Ilgen, Geddes, Vater and De Wette, the challenge to the Mosaic unity of the Pentateuch was more or less isolated and uninfluential. With the advance of modern criticism in the last century, more and more of the Pentateuch has been denied Mosaicity, until now the almost unanimous critical opinion is that the present Pentateuchal text was not brought to final completion until about a millennium after Moses' death, and owes its unity to the work of various scholars and redactors, who used four principal documentary sources in producing the logical coherence and orderly recital of events, institutions and laws, which are found in the Pentateuch today.

I. The Mosaic Unity of the Pentateuch Defined

The critical position maintains that the *form* of the Pentateuch is such that it cannot be the continuous composition of one writer, but it is compacted of parts of diverse origin, the product of different writers, who wrote long after the Mosaic era. It is freely granted that it may contain Mosaic elements. It is claimed, however, that in its present completed *form* it could not have come from the pen of Moses, but must be placed in a much later period (not before 500 B.C.). The critical theory accordingly is directed against the Mosaic unity of the Pentateuch and only indirectly against its authenticity. It is necessary, therefore, to define precisely what is meant by the Mosaic unity of the Pentateuch.

1. The Mosaic Unity of the Pentateuch Means That It Is One Continuous Work, the Product of a Single Writer.

The conservative position is well summarized by Robert Dick Wilson, "That the Pentateuch as it stands is historical and from the time of Moses; and that Moses was its real author, though it may have been revised and edited by later redactors, the additions being just as much inspired as the rest."[2] In other words conservatives believe that the arrange-

2 A Scientific Investigation of the Old Testament (Philadelphia, 1926), p.11.

ment of its laws, the continuity of its narrative, the logical development of its plan, the coherence of its purpose and the philosophy of its religious history, are due to *one* guiding hand and one directing intelligence. This position does not preclude the possibility that under divine inspiration Moses may have used previously existing sources in the production of his work, either oral or written, or both. Nor does it deny that for his special purpose and under the influence of divine inspiration, he may have incorporated larger or smaller portions of his sources into his work in summarized or amplified form, either verbatim, or in substance.

The Mosaic unity of the Pentateuch, moreover, does not necessarily preclude the possibility of later redactions of the whole work, so as to render it imperative to hold that Moses wrote with his own hand or dictated to amanuensis all and everything contained in it. Edward J. Young expresses this fact pointedly: "When we affirm that Moses wrote or that he was the author of the Pentateuch, we do not mean that he himself necessarily wrote every word. To insist upon this would be unreasonable. Hammurabi was the author of his famous code, but he certainly did not engrave it himself upon the stele. Our Lord was the author of the Sermon upon the Mount, but He did not write it Himself. Milton was the author of Paradise Lost, but he did not write it all out by hand."[3]

It is accordingly possible to hold to the Mosaic authenticity of the Pentateuch and to grant the possibility that Moses committed the composition of the work itself, conceived by himself under the influence of divine inspiration, to some other writer or writers, but in such a manner that they faithfully recorded his own thoughts, omitted or added nothing, or wrote nothing contrary to his will, and that the work thus produced, approved by Moses as the principal and inspired author, was published under his name.

3 *Introduction to the Old Testament* (Grand Rapids, 1949), p. 51.

The important thing from the standpoint of the Mosaic unity of the work is that from whatever the source of the materials, or whoever the secretaries or writers under the author's supervision, the finished product *must* be cast in the mold of the writer's own thoughts, written from his point of view and arranged and executed upon a method and plan all his own, thus bearing his unmistakable stamp.

2. *The Mosaic Unity of the Pentateuch May Admit Post-Mosaic Additions or Changes Which Do not Affect the Authenticity or Integrity of the Text.*

It is not inconsonant with the Mosaic authenticity and integrity of the Pentateuch to grant later redactions of the whole work and to allow that, during the course of the centuries of the transmission of the text, certain modifications were introduced into the work, such as additions after the death of Moses, modernization of archaic expressions and place names, marginal glosses or explanatory scribal insertions, which eventually crept into the text, and textual errors due to inadvertent mistakes of copyists. The latter constitutes the legitimate domain of scholarly criticism.

Deuteronomy 34:5-12, which narrates the death and burial of Moses and records an encomium to his prophetic ministry, is an example of an obvious post-Mosaic addition. As early as the Talmudic period some Jewish authorities ascribed these verses to Joshua. Exodus 11:3 and Numbers 12:3, which praise Moses in such a manner as we might not expect him to have written these passages concerning himself, are sometimes classified as such later additions. If so, the result is inconsequential, since they constitute an infinitesimal part of the text. Glosses or scribal explanations which have crept into the text, it must be confessed by anyone conversant with the Hebrew Bible, are one of the phenomena of the Pentateuch.

An example of an evident gloss or early scribal explanation is Genesis 15:2,3. This passage also contains, it would seem, a haplography. Taking these factors into consideration, the meaning of the passage is greatly clarified and may be rendered: "And the 'son of my house' is the 'son of Mesheq'; which is Damascus . . . and behold the 'son of my house' shall be my heir." The phrase *hu' Dammeseq 'Eli'zer* is the obvious gloss, explaining to a later generation the meaning of the difficult idioms, "son of my house" (heir presumptive) and "son of Mesheq" (a native of Damascus), and indicating that Eliezer, Abraham's steward was meant. When Mesheq (an older and perhaps a poetical name of Dammeseq or Damascus) was no longer comprehensible to the reader, a scribe felt a marginal explanation was necessary. This subsequently (and perhaps inadvertently) was incorporated into the actual text by a copyist.

An example of the modernization of a place name is Genesis 14:14 and Deuteronomy 34:1, where Leshem is called "Dan," although apparently this place (if indeed it is the same place) did not receive its latter name until after the Mosaic age (Judges 18:29). Raamses (Exodus 1:11) seems clearly another example. Since it is true that Zoan-Avaris was called Per-Re'emasese (The House of Raamses) only from about 1300 to 1100 B.C., in the light of the early date of the Exodus, the reference must be to the earlier city Zoan-Avaris.

Some critics maintain that if a few post-Mosaic additions are admitted, why not many? But the logic of this position is faulty. There is no necessity under the requirements of the Mosaic unity and authenticity of the Pentateuch to postulate that an inspired redactor might not make such additions as would not conflict with the Mosaic unity of the work or effect such minor changes as modernization of place names to make them comprehensible to a later generation.

Thus James Orr, after his brilliant and detailed exposé of the fallacies of the critics' arguments against the Mosaic unity of the Pentateuch, summarizes his exhaustive study with a strong declaration in favor of "the unity, essential Mosaicity, and relative antiquity of the Pentateuch."[4] However, Orr emphasizes the fact that he does *not* conclude "that Moses himself wrote the Pentateuch in the precise shape or extent in which we now possess it; for the work, we think, shows very evident signs of different pens and styles, of editorial redaction, of stages of compilation . . . its composition has a history whether we are able to track satisfactorily that history or not."[5]

The "very evident signs of different pens and styles," which Orr notes and about which the critics make such ado, may be explained either as Moses' incorporation of his sources into his work, in summarized or amplified form, verbatim, or in substance,[6] or as the work of an amanuensis under his supervision and final approval, or, in some cases (very few we believe) as the result of later post-Mosaic redactorial additions or slight revisions.

Thus by the Mosaic unity of the Pentateuch we mean that the Pentateuch as it has come down to us is historical and dates from the time of Moses, the great lawgiver himself being its real or fundamental author, as the witness of Sacred Scripture leads us to believe.

II. THE MOSAIC UNITY OF THE PENTATEUCH DENIED

Prior to the rise of modern Pentateuchal criticism about 1750 there were a few mild and sporadic denials of the Mosaic authenticity of the Pentateuch from the Patristic period onward.[7] However, in the seventeenth century, just before the rationalists began to partition the Pentateuch, attacks upon the Mosaic unity were more pronounced. Cornelius a Lapide (1697), believed Moses wrote a diary which was expanded by

---

4 **The Problem of the Old Testament** (New York, 1931), p. 369.
5 **Loc. cit.**
6 The genealogies of Genesis 5 and 11 and the Table of the Nations (ch. 10) are evidently examples.
7 For a brief survey of this period see John E. Steinmueller, **A Companion to Scripture Studies**, Vol. II (New York, 1942), p. 26. For a more detailed discussion see Edward J. Young, **Introduction to the Old Testament** (Grand Rapids, 1949), pp. 109-124.

Joshua. Isaac de la Peyrère (died 1676) contended that the Pentateuch was redacted from Mosaic sources and other writings. Thomas Hobbes, the English deist (1651), asserted the Pentateuch was a document about Moses rather than by Moses, although he did not deny the Mosaic authorship of those passages directly attributed to Moses. Benedict Spinoza, the Jewish philosopher (died 1677), maintained the Pentateuch was a later compilation, probably by Ezra. Richard Simon, the Catholic Oratorian (1678), distinguished between the laws attributed to Moses and history, which was composed by the prophets.

1. The First Documentary Theory.

Modern Pentateuchal criticism may be said to have taken its rise with Jean Astruc,[8] a French physician. In 1753 he published a treatise entitled, *Conjectures Concerning the Original Memoranda Which It Appears Moses Used To Compose the Book of Genesis.* As the title of his work suggests, Astruc correctly held to Mosaic authorship. In asserting that Moses may have employed written documents in compiling Genesis, he doubtless hit upon the truth. His basic blunder, as well as that of all subsequent partitionists of the Pentateuch, was to imagine that we can isolate and recognize the extent of these documents. The futile efforts of higher critics for well-nigh two centuries since his day have not yet taught scholars that this is as impossible as it is to "unscramble eggs" or to separate the crumbs of a loaf of bread into its original kernels of wheat.

Astruc's basic criterion of separation is the different use of the divine names in Genesis, which he imagined indicated two principal sources, designated A (using Elohim) and B (employing Yahweh). In this idea Astruc was anticipated by H. B. Witter, who in 1711 had published *Jura Israelitarum in Palestina,* in which he had observed that the two parallel ac-

8 See Howard Osgood, "Jean Astruc" in the **Presbyterian and Reformed Review**, vol. III, 1892, pp. 83-102.

counts of creation (Genesis 1:1-2:4 and 2:5-3:24) were distinguished by the use of these different divine names. Besides these two main documents Astruc alleged that there were ten other sources of lesser content (C to M).

Astruc applied his theory to Genesis. In 1781, in his *Introduction to the Old Testament,* Johann Eichhorn extended the theory to the entire Pentateuch. In the first three editions of his book he defended the Mosaic authorship. He abandoned it in the fourth edition, asserting that the Pentateuch was a compilation of Mosaic and other documents edited at a later period. Karl Ilgen, Eichhorn's successor at the University of Jena, dissected Genesis into seventeen different documents assigned to three authors, the Jehovist and the two Elohists (subsequently called P and E).

2. The Fragmentary Theory.

This hypothesis, introduced by Alexander Geddes, a Scottish Roman Catholic priest, holds that the Pentateuch was compiled probably during the Solomonic era from many disconnected fragments, some of which were coeval with and some even anterior to Moses. He joined the book of Joshua to the Pentateuch, maintaining that it had been compiled by the same author. He thus concocted the critical vagary implied in the later widely used term, the *Hexateuch.* His views appeared in his *Introduction to the Pentateuch and Joshua* (London, 1792) and his *Critical Remarks* (London, 1800).

Geddes' views were developed and introduced into Germany by Johann Vater in his *Kommentar ueber den Pentateuch* (1802-1805). Vater split the Pentateuch into thirty-nine fragments, dating some from the Mosaic age, a large part of Deuteronomy from the Davidic-Solomonic era, and other portions from other periods. He put the compilation of these heterogeneous fragments at the time of the exile.

This unbelieving rationalism was carried still farther by Wilhelm De Wette in his *Beitraege zur Einleitung in Alte testament* (1806-7). De Wette contended that the many fragments were pieced together by different compilers. Notably he put Deuteronomy in the time of Josiah, and returned to a variation of the documentary hypothesis with regard to Genesis. He naturally rejected the historicity of the Pentateuch.

Anton Hartmann (1831), doubting the art of writing was known in Moses' day (the absurdity of which position has been fully demonstrated by modern archeology), placed the substantial origin of the Pentateuch between the Solomonic era and the exile. He viewed the Pentateuchal narratives as myths and legends.

3. *The Supplementary Theory.*

This hypothesis, which retains the Elohist and the Jehovist of the earlier fragmentary theory, however, was the result of a revolt against its inconsistencies and incongruities. It attempted to recognize a certain literary unity for the Pentateuch and accordingly postulated one basic documentary source of the entire book. This *Grundschrift* or fundamental writing, is the Elohist of the older theory, who first prepared his treatise after the period of Moses and Joshua in the eleventh or tenth centuries B.C. from earlier traditions. These traditions are assumed to have contained many gaps and were supplemented by the later Jehovist, who supposedly left intact the earlier work (E) and simply incorporated into it sections of his own of a strictly supplemental nature.

Despite such able defenders of the theory as Heinrich Ewald (1825), P. von Bohlen (1835), Friedrich Bleek (1836), Friedrich Tuch (1838), Caesar von Lengerke (1844) and Franz Delitzsch (1852-1880), the supplemental hypothesis contains a number of difficulties, and signally breaks down at one vital point. Since the supplementer is "J," it is natural for the Jehovah passages to contain allusions to the "E" passages. But the question how the "E" passages, purportedly written before the supplementer "J" began his work, contain allusions to or presuppose the contents of the "J" sections is left unanswered by the theory.

4. The Crystallization Theory.

This is a modification of the manifestly weak supplementary theory and designed to relieve its difficulties. Those engaged in supplementing are increased. The one supplementer of the previous theory now becomes a series operating successively at different periods. Raven aptly styles it as "the *reductio ad absurdum* of the supplemental hypothesis."[9] Heinrich Ewald, in switching to the crystallization hypothesis, at the same time helped to destroy the supplementary theory, which he had previously advocated. August Knobel (1861) and Eberhard Schrader (1869) taught simplified varieties of the crystallization hypothesis.

5 The Modified Document Theory.

Hermann Hupfeld in *The Sources of Genesis* published at Berlin in 1853 undertook to remove the difficulties of previous theories by a novel approach, which gained such favor that his views may correctly be said to form the foundation of the modern documentary theory. According to him the J sections of Genesis were not mere supplementary material to an earlier Elohistic source, but themselves formed one continuous document. The Elohistic sections, he maintained, were on the other hand not one continuous document but two. The first Elohist or the original writing practically concluded at Genesis 20, while the second Elohist was considered to begin there. Hupfeld's first Elohist was later termed P or Priestly. In this division of E he notably agreed with Ilgen (1798). Hupfeld postulated the elaborate activity of a redactor in piecing together the documents in their present form. With Eduard Riehm (1854) the idea began that Deuteronomy was also an independent source. Thus four separate documents were allegedly woven into the

9 John Raven, **Old Testament Introduction** (New York, 1910), p. 115.

Pentateuchal narrative, two Elohists (P and E), one Jahwist (J) and one Deuteronomist (D), the last being the latest.

Despite the weakness of the Hupfeld theory manifested in extensively employing a redactor to account for difficulties and in dividing E, which emphasized the essential unsoundness of using the divine names as criteria for distinguishing documents, the hypothesis was substantially adopted by Eduard Boehmer, (1860), Eberhard Schrader (1863), Theodor Noeldeke (1869), August Dillmann (1875), Franz Delitzsch (1880), Rudolf Kittel, W. W. Baudissin and others, and forms the basis of the modern theory.

6. *The Final Documentary Theory.*

As early as 1834 Eduard Reuss had maintained that the basic Elohistic document (the Priestly Code) was the latest of all the Pentateuchal documents and was elaborated by Ezekiel and the priestly school during the Babylonian exile, being inserted in the other documents to form the Pentateuch. Final redaction was made at the time of Ezra (445 B.C.).

Karl Heinrich Graf, a pupil of Reuss, undertook to give a scientific exposition of his professor's opinion in his critical researches on the historical books of the Old Testament (1866). Deuteronomy, Graf thought, was Josianic, and shows acquaintance with the Jahwist and Elohist but not with the Priestly Code. The order of the documentary sources was EJDP or JEDP rather than the earlier arrangement PEJD.

This hypothesis was buttressed by Abraham Kuenen's work in Dutch, *De Godsdienst van Israel* (1869-70), and by August Kayser's *Das vorexilische Buch der Urgeschichte Israels* (1874). However, it was the skilled literary defense of Julius Wellhausen from the appearance of his *Die Komposition des Hexateuchs* (1876-77) till his death in 1918 that won many followers for the theory and gave it the ascendancy. As a result, it is popularly called the "Wellhausen Theory." It is tragic how this destructive and unsound hypothesis with this minor variation or that has captivated present-day scholarship and pervades Bible histories, encyclopedias, commentaries, dictionaries, exegetical collections and introductions. It is not an exaggeration to see in this rationalistic skepticism of the eighteenth and nineteenth centuries in Europe the seed that bore its devastating harvest in the two horrible wars of the twentieth century and which in turn has produced the present world-wide chaos.

III. THE MOSAIC UNITY OF THE PENTATEUCH DEFENDED

In the minds of the preponderating majority of modern higher critics the defense of the Mosaic unity of the Pentateuch is such a long-lost battle that anyone who undertakes such a forlorn hope in the face of the learned and elaborately developed partition theories is either a naive ignoramus or a stubborn "fundamentalist."[10] Aage Bentzen thus refers to Hengstenberg, who was the leader of a great nineteenth century school of reverent, believing scholarship and a staunch defender of the Mosaic authenticity of the Pentateuch,[11] as "the die-hard Hengstenberg,"[12] and shows how the Wellhausen theory "has conquered the world,"[13] and "is still held by the majority of scholars."[14]

However, all is not well with the "world conqueror," as perforce some of its most enthusiastic protagonists must admit. Bentzen, for example, confesses that the new Documentary Theory "is tending toward self-dissolution" and repeating the fate of the older forms of Astruc and Eichhorn from about 1800.[15] And little wonder! The whole destructive and voluminous literature of the partitionists from the days of Astruc to Pfeiffer[16] and Hoelscher,[17] and the recent simplified theory

---

10 Cf. Aage Bentzen, **Introduction,** Vol. II, p. 16.
11 Cf. **Dissertations on the Genuineness of the Pentateuch** (Edinburgh, 1847).
12 **Op. cit.,** p. 14.
13 **Op. cit.,** p. 15.
14 **Op. cit.,** p. 18.
15 **Op. cit.,** pp. 14-16.
16 R. Pfeiffer, **Introduction to the O. T.** (New York, 1941).
17 **Die Anfaenge der hebraeischen Geschichtsschreibung** (Sitzungsberichte der Heideberger Akademie des Wissenchaft), 1942.

of Winnett[18] is such a veritable labyrinth of disagreement, uncertainty and interminable confusion that it is becoming apparent a return, at least in the direction of the traditional position of the essential Mosaicity of the Pentateuch, is the only satisfactory solution of the Old Testament problem. The partitionists' contention that the traditional position of Mosaic authorship cannot offer a satisfactory solution to this problem, which is threefold, literary, historical and religious, is false and must be refuted.

1. The Literary Difficulties of the Pentateuch Do Not Preclude Mosaic Authenticity.

Textual phenomena current in the Pentateuch, assumed by the critics to necessitate composite authorship and plurality of sources, are usually listed under three headings. First, the usage of divine names, second, the occurrence of parallel passages and third, differences in vocabulary and style.

a. The Variation in the Use of the Divine Names Does Not Rule Out Mosaic Authorship.

The common-sense view, unless one is bound by the exigencies of some false theory and accordingly prepared to abandon the domain of legitimate exegesis, is that the usage of the divine names is intentional and theologically significant. To the reverent and devout student of Sacred Scripture accustomed to fine distinction and purpose everywhere else in Holy Writ, in symbol, type and prophecy, it would be unthinkable that this case should be a glaring exception. But if by careful exegesis one comes to the conclusion, as the well-known Rabbi Jehuda Hallevi (twelfth century) did, that Elohim is the divine name in general, and that Jehovah specifies the God of revelation and covenant, he

---

18 F. V. Winnett, **The Mosaic Tradition** (University of Toronto Press, 1949). Prof. Winnett maintains Exodus and Numbers constitute one primary source, the Mosaic Tradition. Deuteronomy he dates in the seventh century B.C. P (the Jerusalemite priesthood) in the post-exilic period produced confusion by attempting to harmonize the original tradition with the Deuteronomic version. This understanding of the confusion, according to him, is the key to the Pentateuchal problem.

thereby gives up these names as criteria for distinguishing supposed sources.

The critical theories of the partition of the Pentateuch based on the variation in the use of the divine names, rest upon the shaky foundation of four untenable presuppositions. *The first assumption is that the original writers (EJP) did not depart in a single instance from the mechanical use of the divine name assigned to them.* The moment one admits, for instance, that their use was not dictated by pure habit and that they may have had an intrinsic reason to use Elohim in a certain place rather than Yahweh, the critical assumption collapses, and one returns to the orthodox position of the church fathers, that there is a real difference between Yahweh and Elohim, and that the variation of the divine names is deliberate. Under the position of the Mosaic unity of the Pentateuch, significance is given the divine names and highly improbable assumptions are rendered unnecessary.

The second assumption, as precarious as the first, is that the Redactors (R), who fitted the accounts together, were imbued with the same inexplicable respect for the status quo of the divine names. But the unanswerable question is, "Why should they have been if the divine names had no special significance?" If they were not so imbued with respect, the foundation of the structure collapses, for if they altered the name once, why not often?

Indeed, critics sometimes resort to this illogical makeshift to sweep aside the difficulties engendered by their alleged dual use of the divine names by asserting that R altered the name. In doing this they contradict the basic presupposition of their use of the divine names. Sometimes they assert the text is evidently corrupt. Again this is a mere means of avoiding the weakness of the theory. The hypothesis is supposed to be derived from the phenomena of the text as we have it. But if these phenomena do not suit the theory, they are arbitrarily rejected. If the text is unreliable, certainly the theory derived from it must also be unreliable.

On the other hand, under the position of Mosaic authenticity of the Pentateuch, one can satisfactorily explain in practically all cases the use of the divine names.[19] The divisive theories, however, besides being vexed with the difficulty of having Elohim occurring in J passages (Genesis 7:9; 33:5, 11, etc.) and Jehovah in P sections (Genesis 7:16; 14:22; 17:1, etc).[20] are plagued with the necessity of postulating a highly artificial and meaningless use of the divine names, which would scarcely be tolerated if not demanded by the exigencies of the critical position.

In addition, the fact that the critics in the course of time divided the Elohist into two, the first Elohist, P, and the second Elohist, E, and, while declaring the composite character of JE yet confess the great difficulty of separating E from J, is further evidence of the unsatisfactory nature of the divine names as criteria for the documentary analysis of the Pentateuch.

The third assumption of the divisive critics, usually considered more tenable, is that the divine names were a rigidly fixed element in the text and encountered no change or possible shifting in the course of many centuries of transmission. However, it is important to note that in the use of the divine names the Septuagint, according to Johannes Dahse,[21] differs from the Massoretic Text in not less than 180 places in Genesis to Numbers. H. M. Redpath,[22] H. M. Wiener[23] and especially Dahse who collated the abundant critical material on the text in the first volume of his *Textskritische Materialen* in 1912, maintain that the Septua-

---

19 See W. H. Green, The Unity of Genesis (London, 1902) pp. 547-8; Oswald Allis, The Five Books of Moses (Philadelphia, 1943) pp. 24 f.
20 For detailed discussion see Green The Higher Criticism of the Pentateuch (New York, 1896) pp. 89-99.
21 Archiv fuer Religionswissenschaft (1903) pp. 305-309.
22 Modern Criticism and Genesis (London, 1905).
23 Essays in Pentateuchal Criticism (Oberlin, 1909); Pentateuchal Studies (Oberlin, 1912).

gint readings are the original and should be preferred to the Massoretic Text. While the Massoretic Text is usually supported by the Samaritan Pentateuch, and is to be followed, except in those isolated cases where textual criticism can prove that the Septuagint readings are the original ones,[24] nevertheless, the studies of Dahse and others show "what a variable element of the text these very Divine names were, and how necessary a thorough-going critical investigation of the text is, before one may use them as a means for distinguishing sources."[25]

The fourth assumption of the divisive critics regarding the use of divine names, which is entirely baseless, is that Exodus 6:2, 3 (P) records the first instance of the revelation of the name Jehovah and that all previous sections employing the name, being in conflict with this statement, must be attributed to another writer (J), who in turn held that it was known from the earliest periods.

That this supposition regarding the meaning of Exodus 6:2, 3 is totally unwarranted and has no foundation outside the exigencies of the critical hypothesis is apparent *first, because of the clear distinction indicated in the passage itself*: "God spake unto Moses, and said unto him, I am the Lord: and I appeared unto Abraham, unto Isaac, and unto Jacob, by the name of God Almighty (El Shaddai); but by my name Jehovah was I not known to them." Significantly, the reference does not distinguish Jehovah from Elohim (occurring over 200 times in Genesis) but from El Shaddai (occurring five times in Genesis), the name denoting the particular character in which God revealed Himself to the patriarchs (Genesis 17:1; 28:3; 35:11; 43:14; 48:3).

Moreover, it must be noted, the passage does *not* concern itself *at all* with the occurrence or non-occurrence of the divine

24 Cf. J. Goettsberger, **Einleitung in das Alte Testament** (Freiburg, 1928) pp. 33 f.

25 A. Noordtzy, "The Old Testament Problem," **Bibliotheca Sacra** (Oct.-Dec. 1940) pp. 111 f.

name Jehovah in the pre-Mosaic era, and cannot legitimately be regarded as denying or affirming anything about its anti- quarian usage. It concerns itself solely with a *declaration of the revelation* of that name, not its occurrence. To make the revelation of a name identical with its first occurrence is a subtle fallacy obscured by the plausibilities of the critical hypothesis.

In addition, the peculiar Biblical idiom "to know a name" or "be known by a name" must be interpreted, not at the caprice of a critic to fit a false theory, but by the uniform usage of Scripture. Always a true understanding of the divine character and not a mere acquaintance with the word Jehovah as such is meant (Psalm 9:10; Isaiah 52:6, etc.). The meaning is clear in Exodus by the repeated statement that Israel (Exodus 6:7; 16:12), Pharaoh (7:17; 8:6 etc.) and the Egyptians (7:5; 14:4, 18) should *know that He was Jehovah.* Certainly the meaning is *not* that they should be told that this was His name, but that they should see the mighty manifestation of God's grace and power in *redeeming* His people from Egypt, the attributes, in other words, which *the name* denoted. That He was not so known by the patriarchs, therefore, can in- dicate nothing as to the existence of the name Jehovah then, but simply that while tokens of God's Almighty power had been granted them, no such disclosure had been made of His redemptive faithfulness indicated by His name Jehovah as was now to be vouchsafed to their posterity.

The critical assumption regarding Exodus 6:2, 3 is not only disproved by the clear distinctions in the passage itself but also *by the common-sense implications of the critics' own hy- pothesis.* According to them the redactor to whom they at- tribute the present form of Genesis and the Pentateuch as a whole, *did not* understand the Exodus passage as they do, and saw nothing inconsistent in it with the frequent use of the name Jehovah by the patriarchs. Otherwise he would either have changed the statement in Exodus or the name of Jehovah in Genesis, unless perchance he was an ignoramus and no editor at all or a prematurely born protagonist of the divisive theory, anticipating his modern colleagues by perhaps more than three millenniums. Surely whatever literary difficulties the position of Mosaic authenticity of the Pentateuch in the matter of the use of the divine names may have, they are slight in comparison to the absurdities of the divisive criticism and capable of rational explanation.

b. The Occurrence of Alleged Parallel Passages in the Pentateuch Does Not Preclude Mosaic Authorship. Critics maintain that the Pentateuch contains duplicate accounts of the same events and that these so-called doublets, often contradictory as well as supplementary, are due to separate accounts taken from different documents and disprove Mosaic authenticity. A few observations, unobscured by the straitjacket requirements of an unsound theory, however, will suffice to show the fallacy of this much-abused argument, which is carried to absurd and extravagant lengths by many of the devotees of the divisive hypothesis.

(1) Many of these alleged parallel passages are not such at all but refer to distinct events merely containing similar features.

Among some thirteen alleged doublets in the narrative sections, for instance, critics list the two expulsions of Hagar (Genesis 16:4-16 and 21:9-21). By every fair consideration these are two entirely distinct episodes taking place at different times, the first just before Ishmael was born, the second when he was a lad at least fifteen years of age. Yet because of certain superficial similarities in the events, such as the appearance in each case of the angel at the well or fountain of water in a general wilderness territory south of Beersheba, critics construe the two events as really only one and the discrepancies due to conflicting traditions preserved in different documents, Genesis 16:4-16 being parcelled out between J and P and Genesis 21:9-21 being relegated to E.[26]

Exactly the same pernicious procedure of identifying two distinct events is followed in the case of the alliance of Abraham (Genesis 21:22-34) and Isaac (Genesis 26:26-33) with Abimelech, king of Gerar. But nothing could be more natural than that a son should renew a covenant, which his father had found advantageous. In closer connection with this alleged duplicate account critics list another "doublet"—the two namings of Beersheba, by Abraham (Genesis 21:31) and by Isaac (26:33). The simple explanation is that this is not a doublet at all. Isaac reopened the wells which Abraham had dug and which the Philistines meanwhile had filled up. While Isaac was at Beersheba, Abimelech came and made a covenant with him, as he or his predecessor had done with Abraham. That same day Isaac's servants announced that they had reached water. "As in former like cases, Isaac piously revived the old name, calling the well Shibah . . . thus confirming and preserving the name Beersheba."[27]

If modern historians identified different events on the basis of their mere general resemblance as supposedly scientific Pentateuchal critics constantly and arbitrarily do, all history would be immediately thrown into confusion. The only rational explanation of this irrational practice is that underlying the whole critical theory, evident everywhere and especially in the matter of alleged doublets, is the baseless assumption that the sacred account is unreliable. This is not a conclusion established by the critical theory, but a presupposition upon which the whole elaborate structure is erected.

(2) Other alleged parallel passages do refer to the same

[26] This is C. Steuernagel's documentary designations in **Lehrbuch der Einleitung in das Alte Testament.**
[27] "Beersheba" in **The Westminster Dictionary of the Bible,** revised H. S. Gehman (Philadelpha, 1944) p. 64.

events but under a different aspect and for a different purpose.

For example, Genesis 1:1-2:4a (assigned to P) and 2:4b-25 (allotted to J) are not duplicate or parallel accounts of creation, as the critics insist, but one is a sequel or supplement of the other. The first account catalogues the creation of the heavens and the earth (Gen. 1:1). Man is included *only* as one of the features necessary to complete the picture. The second is *not* another account of the creation of the heavens and the earth but, as the introductory key phrase (2:4) indicates, is a record of the "*generations* of the heavens and of the earth . . ." that is the creation of man whose body, as verse 7 indicates, was "formed . . . of the dust of the ground (earth)" and whose soul was of heavenly origin, since it is specifically said, "the Lord God breathed into his nostrils the breath of life; and man became a living soul." The term "generations" (plural) applies specially to the creation of the first man (2:4-20), but includes the creation of woman (2:21-25) and the generations of their immediate descendants (3:1-4:26).

Of all the narratives of the Old Testament the story of the flood (Genesis 6-9) perhaps has appeared most obviously composite to the critics. Ewald says that it "shone as a gleaming star before all others on the horizon of the Jehovistic and Elohistic documents."[28] Eichhorn, who regarded repetitions in general and those in the flood narrative in particular to be clear evidence that Genesis is composite and that in the deluge we have two accounts of the flood combined into one, arrayed the alleged duplications in two columns. He pointed out that the repetitions are not only frequent and distributed throughout the narrative, but also when set down in two columns form a continuous narrative.

In the face of the critical contention can the unity of the flood narrative which, because of its alleged obvious com-

28 Cf. John H. Raven, **Old Testament Introduction**, p. 125.

posite authorship is in a sense a test case, be successfully defended? We believe it can. To begin with, it must be noted that there are two marked features of Hebrew style, which, when understood, offer an easy and natural explanation of Pentateuchal literary phenomena, but, when misunderstood, lend seeming support to the idea of documentary sources, which, when separated, give accounts more or less complete. The first is the exceedingly common syntactical use of the conjunction "and" employed loosely to connect members of a compound sentence and to join subordinate clauses. The second is the widespread phenomenon of elaboration and repetition. It is especially this feature of Biblical style, so apparent in the flood story, which critics abuse by wresting it out of its ancient idiom and squeezing it into the mold of modern diction to support an absurd theory.

Allis has made a significant contribution toward demonstrating the unity of the deluge narrative by showing that the repetition and elaboration, so obvious in the narrative, are not the result of a fusion of different sources but a literary device common in Biblical style to stress the three main emphases in the account, namely, the sinfulness of man as the cause of the flood, the destruction of all flesh as the aim of the flood and the saving of a righteous remnant as the result of the flood.[29] The repetitions and elaborations are shown not to extend to all the narrative nor to be meaningless, but to bear directly upon these emphases. These facts, when taken into proper account, offer a far more natural and rational explanation of the literary phenomena of the text than the artificial and arbitrary theory of the critics, who err in attempting to explain ancient literary idiom by putting it in the rack of a modern hypothesis, and distorting from it a confession contrary to truth.

Wellhausen, Dillmann and other critics, by means of alleged doublets, have pushed the partition of the Pentateuch

29 Oswald Allis, **The Five Books of Moses**, (Philadelphia, 1943), pp. 94-99.

to extravagant lengths. Minute paragraphs and even single clauses are cut up. Any repetition of thought for dramatic, didactic and literary effect may be ignored at the caprice of the critic and a section regarded as a variant statement of the same thing by another writer and assigned to a different source. Perhaps in no other phase of the partition hypothesis do its adherents so offend against common sense as in the case of alleged doublets. When the examples cited are carefully studied without presupposition that the account is unreliable, they are found capable of adequate explanation consonant with the Mosaic unity of the Pentateuch.

c. Alleged Differences In Vocabulary and Style In the Pentateuch Do Not Preclude Mosaic Authorship.

Besides the variations in divine names, which form the original basis for the partition of the Pentateuch into different documents, critics lay much stress upon other alleged secondary variations in style and diction in the Pentateuchal books to support their theory of sources in opposition to Mosaic authorship. First, it is maintained that the Pentateuch does not employ a uniform vocabulary suggesting one author but displays lexicographic variations resulting from diversity of sources. Secondly, the alleged occurrence of numerous Aramaisms in diverse parts of the Pentateuch supposedly point to a late date (at least for the P document). Thirdly, differences in style in the four documents prove the legitimacy of distinguishing and recognizing them as separate sources.

(1) Alleged differences in vocabulary in the Pentateuch constitute an inconclusive argument against its Mosaic integrity.

Critics assume that each source prefers its own individual words, phrases or ideas. All lexicographical phenomena in one of the supposed documents which do not happen to occur in the others are catalogued in a formidable list. But this unsound procedure proves nothing unless it can be shown that the writer had occasion to use these particular words or expressions or that this particular usage is unusual or rare. Surely common everyday words are not the peculiar possession of any one writer. By this unscientific approach a treatise of an author can be proved not to have been written by him when compared to another treatise of his, especially if the latter is upon a different subject. Or, for that matter, any part of one treatise may be used to prove that the remaining portion came from another pen.

A logical fallacy is evident. The critics argue in a circle. They first create their differences and then argue from them. Documents are first distinguished on the basis of certain assumed characteristic differences and their correspondences with these assumed characteristics are taken as proof of their objective reality.

The critical practise of positively allocating specific words and phrases to definite documents is attended by grave difficulties. In the first place, synonymous words which are *especially cited to prove a consistent division of sources offer a precarious basis for the assumption that they represent the usage of distinct authors*. It is an error to suppose that the usage of words with similar meaning is a matter of rote habit or arbitrary choice by a writer. There is frequently a distinction, more or less clear, which requires the use of one rather than the other in a particular connection. To cite an example, the shorter form of the first common singular pronoun in Hebrew, *'ani,* is assigned to P, (except in Genesis 23:4) the latest of the four documents and supposedly written during or after the exile, while the synonymous longer form *'anoki* is allocated to earlier J and E documents.

In this case archeology has shown the fallacy of this distinction. Both of these synonymous forms of the first personal pronoun occur in the now-famous Danel Legend of the Ras Shamra epic religious literature which is coeval with the

Mosaic period, without any apparent distinction drawn between them.[30]

A second difficulty besets the attempt of the critics to allocate specific words to precise sources. *This bold practice assumes a perfect knowledge of the development of Canaanite dialects in general and of the Hebrew language in particular.* The origin and development of Hebrew as a northwest Semitic dialect is still imperfectly known. It is difficult, if not impossible, to determine objectively what precise words or synonyms were employed at successive periods.[31] This is another illustration of what W. H. Green aptly terms "the marvellous perspicacity verging on omniscience, claimed by the critics, who undertake to determine with the utmost assurance the authorship not merely of books, or large sections of paragraphs, but of individual sentences and clauses and fragments of clauses."[32]

Another serious difficulty faces the scholar who tries to substantiate the practice of partitioning the Pentateuch on the basis of vocabulary. He must at all times face the possibility, utterly disconcerting to the advocates of the documentary theory, *that later writers intentionally followed the archaic forms and expressions of older documents, or, on the other hand, rendered archaic expressions, then perhaps no longer understood by the people, into current language and idiom.*

But the most insurmountable barrier of the critic who employs differences in vocabulary to sustain his position, apart from the shaky assumptions underlying the use of the divine names themselves, *is the utterly untenable and inconclusive methods of carrying forward the partition on the basis of parallel passages.* How can any precise work be done in the matter of lexicographical differences in supposed documents when these very documents are distinguished on the ground

---

30 Cf. A. Bea, "Ras Shamra und das Alte Testament", **Biblica XIX** (1939), p.444.
31 Cf. Zellig S. **Harris, Development of the Canaanite Dialects** (New Haven, 1939), pp. 81-90.
32 **The Higher Criticism of the Pentateuch** (New York, 1896), pp. 126 f.

of alleged doublets, which for the most part are nothing more than falsely assumed identifications of distinct events?

The Mosaic authenticity with all of its problems offers an explanation of the linguistic phenomena of the Pentateuch unencumbered by the difficulties and absurdities of the critical hypothesis, which frequently necessitates the most violent vivisection of Biblical passages to harmonize the text with its often ridiculous preconceptions.

The existence of Aramaisms in various parts of the Pentateuch is, moreover, no decisive argument against Mosaic authenticity, as the critics themselves confess. A close relationship between Hebrews and Aramaeans from patriarchal times (Genesis 31:47; Judges 3:8 ff., I Samuel 14:47; II Samuel 8:3 ff., etc.) offers sufficient explanation. Besides, E. Kautzsch[33] lists only twenty-three Aramaisms in the Pentateuch, most of which have common Semitic roots and need not be derived from the Aramaic language.

(2) Alleged variation in style offers no basis for rejecting the Mosaic integrity of the Pentateuch.

Another fundamental error of the critics is not only to restrict the vocabulary of each of the sources into which they divide the Pentateuch but to put a premium on "monotony of style and to regard variety as a liability, a suspicious feature suggesting diversity of authorship."[34] That this is a basically erroneous assumption is proved by the fact that if the same treatment were accorded many other well-written documents which are of considerable length, deal with a variety of subjects and employ a versatile diction, yet known to be the work of a single author, they could likewise be divided precisely as the critics partition the Pentateuch.

The whole practice, therefore, of dividing the text of the Pentateuch into various sources on the basis of style is extremely questionable. Many factors must be kept carefully

33 **Die Aramaeismen im Alten Testament** (Halle, 1902), pp. 99 f.
34 Oswald Allis, **The Five Books** of Moses (1943), p. 67.

in mind. First, *the varied nature of the contents of the Pentateuch must be considered.* Historical narratives, poems, genealogies, laws, sermons, exhortations and so on call for variety of vocabulary and versatility of treatment. Certainly Moses by education, gifts and culture was equal to the task of writing now as a narrator, now as an orator, now as a poet, now as a prophet or legislator. It is unreasonable to deny him the ability to modify his style and diction in accordance with the demands of his varying subject matter. The same erroneous theory of limiting one form of style to an author has led modern scholars to deny *Menexenos* to Plato and the *Dialogue* to Tacitus, *De Mundo* to Apuleius, etc.[35]

In the second place it must be remembered that *the entire Pentateuch was not written at one time.* Its composition as far as Moses is concerned likely extended over forty years. Exodus, Leviticus and Numbers were probably written years before Deuteronomy. Genesis doubtless incorporates a well-defined oral tradition or previously existing written records, which Moses himself or his secretaries may have revised for his use. This is a possible explanation for the diversity of style in some passages.

Lastly it must be observed that *Occidental methods of literary criticism must not be foisted upon an ancient Oriental book.* Modern criticism has grievously transgressed in this respect. The idiomatic use of elaboration and repetition and the peculiar free use of the conjunction "and" cannot be ignored as Semitic stylistic devices and prostituted to support the vagaries of the documentary theory. Neither the Code of Hammurabi (c. 1700 B.C.) nor the eleventh tablet of the Gilgamesh Epic (seventh century B.C.), which display the same stylistic phenomena as the Pentateuch, is divided into sources by the critics.

35 Cf. A. Bea, "Der Heutige Stand der Pentateuchfrage," in **Biblica XVI** 1935), p. 193.

CONCLUSION

A survey of the literary problems of the Pentateuch and the manner in which the modern critical hypothesis deals with them has demonstrated that the solution offered by the critics is not only inadequate, but increases rather than removes the difficulties, besides casting doubt and aspersion upon the historical reliability and authenticity of the Pentateuch itself. On the other hand, Mosaic integrity of the Pentateuch is not at all endangered by the critics' claim that variations in the use of the divine names, the occurrence of parallel accounts or doublets and diversity in vocabulary and style preclude it. The Mosaic integrity remains not only the best explanation of the problems of the Pentateuch, but the only position that does proper honor to these ancient writings and accords with the witness of the New Testament and the well-nigh universal tradition of both Jews and Christians.

2. *The Historical-Archeological Difficulties of the Pentateuch Do Not Preclude Mosaic Authenticity.*

In addition to the literary arguments the critics adduce historical-archeological data as evidence that the Pentateuch was written long after the time of Moses. Among Pentateuchal phenomena in this category supposedly disproving Mosaic authorship, emphasis is placed on alleged anachronisms, geographical peculiarities and personal difficulties.

(1) Alleged Anachronisms.

These are supposed misplacements in time of events, places, persons and so forth. When the critical list is carefully sifted, it is doubtful that few, if any examples commonly cited, can be definitely established as genuine anachronisms when isolated from the exigencies of the critical hypothesis and subjected to sound exegetical study. For example, the notice that "the Canaanite was then in the land" (Genesis 12:6; cf. 13:7) is said to presuppose that they had been driven out when this notation was made. But the notice in itself merely states that they were in the country in the days of Abraham, without any implication that they were not there yet.

Genesis 14:14 and Deuteronomy 34:1 refer to the town of "Dan," but in the Mosaic era, it is claimed, the town was known as Leshem (Joshua 19:47) or Laish (Judges 18:29). There is no definite proof that the "Dan" of Genesis 14:14 is the same city referred to in Joshua and Judges. However, if it is, it is the case of a later modernization of an archaic place name that had likely become wholly obscure to a later generation.

Genesis 36:31-39 catalogues a list of Edomite rulers. The notation "before there reigned any king over the children of Israel" (v. 31) is supposed to indicate that this list was not composed until the royal period of Israel. The simple meaning, unforced by the critical theory, is that the list of Edomite rulers is pre-Mosaic and Moses emphasizes the singularity that Jacob, who had the promise of kings in his line of descent (Genesis 35:11), as yet had none, although just beginning his national existence, while Esau, who possessed no such promise, already had a line of princes.

Deuteronomy 3:11 gives the dimensions of king Og's bed, which, it is assumed, could only have been an object of curiosity for later generations. But the bedstead is not spoken of as a relic from a former age, but as the memorial of a recent victory. The "Book of the Wars of the Lord" (Numbers 21:14) is claimed to be subsequent to the Mosaic era, but it was no doubt a contemporaneous work as well, recording God's mighty deliverances, in the form of a national chronicle.

Other examples can be satisfactorily explained. But suppose it could be indubitably demonstrated that certain verses or even paragraphs were post-Mosaic, the additions of scribes in the form of glosses, modernization of archaisms, etc. This would simply prove that such verses or paragraphs could not have been in the Pentateuch as it issued from Moses' pen, not that the work as a whole did not proceed from him. It is far simpler and more satisfactory to assume some slight additions in the form of glosses or explanations, or to allow that certain words may have been translated from the ancient into more recent language, than to set aside the multiplied concrete proofs and evidences of Mosaic authenticity for the absurdities and contradictions of the documentary hypothesis.

(2) Alleged Geographical Peculiarities.

These are geographical terms supposedly used in such a manner as to suggest that the author or redactor of the Pentateuch lived in Palestine, whereas Moses was acquainted only with the territories to the south and east of Canaan. Critics, accordingly, insist that the sections betraying this knowledge could not have been Mosaic.

"Beyond the Jordan . . . " (Deuteronomy 1:1), describing Moses position east of the river, has no implication that the writer (or redactor) was in Canaan. This is plain from the elastic meaning of the expression in Numbers 32:19, where it is used both of the east and west side of the Jordan. In other passages it is defined "beyond Jordan eastward . . ." (Deuteronomy 4:47, 49; Josh. 1:15) and "beyond Jordan westward . . ." (Deuteronomy 11:30; Joshua 5:1).

The term *Negebward* ("southward" toward the desert of Beersheba) is used by the Lord in speaking to Abraham (Genesis 13:14) and "west" is mentioned as "seaward" (Gen. 12:8; 13:14, etc.). Critics quibble over the question how Moses could have used these terms when the Negeb was to the north of him and the Mediterranean could hardly be considered to be to his west. The simple explanation is that the stereotyped expressions *Negebward* for southward and "seaward" for westward were technical terms which had been part and parcel of the Hebrew language since patriarchal times.

(3) Personal Difficulties.

Critics such as C. Steuernagel[36] exclude Mosaic authorship

36 **Lehrbuch der Einleitung in das Alte Testament** (Tuebingen, 1921), p. 124.

because Moses is frequently spoken of in the third person. However, by the same argument Caesar could be ruled out of his *Gallic War* or Xenophon out of his *Anabasis*. Passages such as "the man Moses was very great in the land of Egypt . . ." (Exodus 11:3) and "the man Moses was very meek, above all the men which were upon the face of the earth" (Numbers 12:3) may be interpreted to satisfy Mosaic authorship. Some construe them as glosses, which may be considered inconsequential, since they constitute an infinitesimal part of the text. The account of Moses' death in Deuteronomy 34 is generally ascribed to a later inspired author.

CONCLUSION

A survey of the historical-archeological difficulties of the Pentateuch has demonstrated the same bias and arbitrariness of the divisive critics as in their dealing with the literary phenomena. Like the numerous alleged doublets, the so-called anachronisms and geographical difficulties vanish in the light of sound exegesis of the text. From an archeological standpoint the Pentateuch has a loyal ally in modern scientific archeology, which has frequently vindicated it, from establishing the historicity of the patriarchs to resurrecting the Hittites and the Horites. Thanks to modern excavations evidence for the Mosaic authenticity of the Pentateuch has been greatly increased and strengthened.

3. *The Religious-Philosophical Difficulties of the Pentateuch Do Not Preclude Mosaic Authenticity.*

Besides literary and historical-archeological data critics with confident assurance advance religious and philosophical arguments to shelve the idea of Mosaic authorship. Advancing their theories ostensibly to solve "the problem" of the Old Testament, in no other phase of their work do they bungle so deplorably as in their religious and philosophical approach to the Old Testament. Instead of solving the so-called "problem" of the Old Testament by their utterly baseless and destructive presuppositions, they create additional problems which have no actual existence. Instead of shedding light on Pentateuchal difficulties, they plunge them into greater gloom. Instead of bringing forth order, they produce chaos. Amidst the error of their conclusions the Mosaic unity of the Pentateuch stands unscathed.

a. The Critical Assumption of the Progressive Evolution of Israel's Religion from Lower Forms to Monotheism Does Not Disprove the Mosaic Authenticity of the Pentateuch.

This bold presupposition regarding the development of Israel's religion, which from the very first verses of Genesis collides head-on with the testimony of the Pentateuch and of all the Old Testament and the New Testament as well (cf. Romans 1:21-32), has its far-flung roots in other widespread philosophic errors of the nineteenth century, such as the anthropocentric view of the universe, the evolutionary idea of development in history and culture and the merely subjective conception of religion and religious experience. These three dominant philosophical ideas became foci of conflict with the Old Testament and exerted a powerful influence in the devolopment of the higher critical theories of the nineteenth century.

It is obvious at the outset that the Old Testament is anything but anthropocentric. Rather, it is theocentric to the core. At its heart is a self-revealing God, who, as the eternally existing Creator of all things, is ineffably transcendent above any of His creatures and separate from them, yet at the same time immanent, working among them in redemptive grace and miraculous power. Nothing could be farther from the truth of the Old Testament than the rationalistic idea that man is the center and God is on the periphery. This dominant concept was bound to clash with the Bible and become a guiding principle in the development of the higher criticism of the Pentateuch.

Closely allied to the anthropocentric concept was the concomitant evolutionary doctrine of the nineteenth century. With the universe centering in man rather than God the thought was inevitable that man was the highest creature of the evolutionary force active in nature and history. This required the supposition that long periods of development took place from that which was lower to that which was higher and from that which was less developed to that which was more developed. It also inclined toward an optimistic view of man, who had developed (it is supposed) from lower forms of life to a human being and lifted himself from the cave-man to the civilized genius.

This idea the Pentateuch flatly contradicts in its opening chapters. Man's origin is theocentric. He is divinely created, not evolved. He is at the start made in the image and likeness of God. He does not have to tread a long road before he can be liberated from rudimentary forms of life. His story is one of retrogression rather than of progression. He sins and thus falls from his integrity. His reclamation is as theocentric as his creation. He becomes utterly ruined and incapable of self-salvation. The grace and mercy of God constitute his only hope as he trusts a divine Redeemer. The rationalists' optimistic view of man and the doctrine of his inevitable self development are diametrically contradicted by the Pentateuch. Hence any theory of the Pentateuch based on these false philosophic principles must aim to discredit its integrity and authenticity, which the partition hypothesis labors to do.

In addition to its anthropocentric and evolutionary views, prevailing philosophic thought of the nineteenth century came into conflict with the Old Testament in a third point which was influential in the final formation of the partition theory. This was the subjective conception of religion and religious experience. Following Kant and Schleiermacher, men were accustomed to speak of religion as a form of moral activity or a state of feeling, but to deny its objective value. Religious phenomena were regarded more or less as of equal value and, in any case, of purely relative worth. Religion was no longer held to be a manifestation of God's grace to the sinful human heart, but a human effort whereby man attempted to attain communion with God, or with the divinity in question. All religions were placed on the same level and all intrinsic differences eliminated.

Nothing could be more contrary to the Old Testament. Everywhere on its pages God chose His people. They did not choose Him. He elected Abraham and His descendants, chose Moses, the redeemer, and Israel, the redeemed.

The Wellhausen School undertook to remove the difficulties which existed between the Pentateuch and the commonly accepted philosophy of the day. The anthropocentric evolutionary assumptions of Hegel and the materialism of Darwin consciously or unconsciously became the basis of the critical preconceptions. Israel's beginning must fit the anthropocentric evolutionary mold of contemporary thought and her beginning was boldly declared to be in no wise different from that of other nations. The possibility of pre-Mosaic or Mosaic monotheism was denied. *Every* religion inclusive of the Jewish religion must have developed from lower to higher forms, first, *naturism,* in the forms of fetishism, magic or totemism, next, *animism* or *polydaemonism,* in which the spirits of the departed dead were worshipped and third, *polytheism,* or the worship of many gods.

With Moses or David a fourth phase of development is assumed to have been reached called *monolatry,* when Israel worshipped Jehovah the one God but recognized Baal, Chemosh, Molech and other gods of the surrounding nations as existing. The fifth phase of development called *monotheism* is said to have been inaugurated by the new concept of Jehovah presented by Amos and the writing prophets of the eighth century B.C. Now for the first time Israel is supposed to have considered Jehovah not merely as the national god, but as the one and only God. He is now the ethical God of the

Hebrews and appears in Deuteronomy, which critics put in the seventh century B.C. The capstone of this ridiculous distortion of Israelite history is that this monotheism is developed into a liturgical system during the Babylonian Exile (sixth century) and finds its expression in the book of Leviticus.

The reverent and believing student of the Scriptures will have no difficulty in rejecting the critical assumption of the progressive evolution of Israel's religion based as it is on false philosophical views which flourished particularly in the past century and which are utterly at variance with the testimony of Scripture. To him a theory which denies the objective reality and the setting of Old Testament historical books and bases their interpretation to a very large extent upon subjectivism offers no evidence against Mosaic integrity of the Pentateuch. To any devout student the denial that true monotheism existed among the Hebrews from the very beginning under Abraham (Genesis 18:25; 24:3) is so utterly ridiculous and fraught with such blatant unbelief as to be almost unworthy of consideration. The ample Scripture evidence that the prophets preached absolute monotheism and condemned idolatry as a violation of the Mosaic covenant is enough to show the *utter* fallacy of the critical assumption of the evolutionary development of Israel's religion.

b. The Critical Assumption that Supernatural Revelation and Divine Miracle are Incompatible with Authentic History Does not Weaken the Case for Mosaic Authenticity of the Pentateuch.

The words of Jesus to Martha at the raising of Lazarus express a universal and omnitemporal truth unbelieving critics can never know or understand, "*If thou wouldest believe,* thou shouldest see the glory of God" (John 11:40). The humblest believer can testify to the supernatural intervention of God in answer to prayer and faith. To him the critical fallacy of ruling out supernatural revelation and divine miracle in connection with authentic history is at once apparent. That Moses was renowned for faith is shown by the prominence given him (next to Abraham) in the gallery of the faithful in Hebrews 11. As a result he most assuredly saw "the glory of God." He recounts what under the circumstances we would expect him to recount, authentic history, which included supernatural revelation and divine miracle.

On the other hand the anthropocentric view and the evolutionary concept of Israelite history, which is basic to the divisive hypothesis, preclude the possibility of any revealed religion with miracles and prophecy. It is notorious that the long succession of able scholars by whom the documentary theory was elaborated, have been unbelievers in supernatural revelation and divine miracle. For example, Abraham Kuenen wrote, "So long as we attribute a part of Israel's religious life directly to God and allow supernatural or immediate revelation to intervene even in one instance, just so long does our view of the whole remain inexact, and we see ourselves obliged to do violence here or there to the well-assured content of the historical accounts. It is only the assumption of a natural development that takes account of all the phenomena."[37]

In his *De Godsdienst van Israel* (1869-70) Kuenen freely confesses that "the familiar intercourse of the divinity with the patriarchs" constitutes for him one of the "determining considerations" against the historical character of these narratives.[38] Wellhausen, in his *Israelitische und Juedische Geschichte*,[39] ridicules the miracles at Sinai in connection with the giving of the law with the scornful exclamation, "Who can seriously believe all that?" He fondly imagines he has dealt adequately with the account when he contends "this passage is dominated by the poetical desire to handle dramatically, in an elevated style, the constitution of the people of the Lord."

37 **De profeten en de profetie onder Israel**, Vol. I, p. 5.
38 Vol. I, p. 111.
39 2nd. edition, p. 12.

It is accordingly evident that the critical theory has been deliberately fabricated and foisted on Old Testament scholarship to explain away the supernatural, whether in revelation, miracle or fulfilled prophecy. This is its fundamental error succinctly and unwittingly stated by Kuenen when he contends that "it is only the assumption of a natural development that takes account of all the phenomena." In reality, this is precisely what the assumption of a purely natural development fails to do. It does *not* take into account *all* the phenomena of the case. It forgets that there is a supernatural realm of spiritual law in addition to a natural realm of physical law and that upon occasion these may interact.

The purely naturalistic scientist, however, is utterly intolerant and skeptical of any phenomena which do not exist for him. Because they do not exist for him, he hastily concludes that they do not exist at all. This is his basic error. They do not exist for him simply because he refuses to accommodate himself to the primary law of the supernatural realm—faith. In fact, he refuses even to take the first step in that direction and believe that the supernatural realm exists. Accordingly, he cuts himself off from a whole sphere of phenomena which would inevitably condition his thinking and without which his assumptions, reasonings and conclusions must necessarily be vitiated and distorted.

It is for this reason that the Old Testament and particularly the Pentateuch, in which the supernatural constitutes the warp and woof of the narrative, have suffered their worst abuse from some of the ablest and the best technically trained scholars. They, with all their other equipment, lack the one vital and absolutely indispensable qualification for sound and undistorted handling of the Sacred Scriptures, namely, spiritual discernment. The results of their work are valid only where they touch upon matters resolvable wholly upon the basis of human research and naturalistic science. The moment they attempt to deal with revelation, miracle and prophecy they begin to deal with a realm of reality into which they have never entered and about which they are accordingly totally ignorant. Attempting to enter it, however, as Graf, Kuenen, Wellhausen, Steuernagel, Pfeiffer and others boldly do, they become like the proverbial "bull in a china shop," smashing and destroying that which is choice and spiritually valuable, wherever they chance to turn.

The anti-supernaturalistic bias of the principal formulators of the partition theory and their extreme hostility toward revealed religion should be warning enough to professing evangelicals who look upon the hypothesis with favor or who adopt it in any form. Its *entire foundation* is unsound and must be uprooted. Since its assumptions are false, its conclusions cannot be true. It creates rather than solves difficulties and complicates and vitiates the general problem of the Old Testament, which can only fairly be dealt with on the basis of the Mosaic integrity of the Pentateuch.

CONCLUSION

A survey of the religious-philosophical difficulties of the Pentateuch has shown that these are largely the creation of the critics erected on the foundation of false philosophical assumptions, which flourished from the nineteenth century to the present, and intrinsically do not exist as such. These false presuppositions including the anthropocentric conception of the universe, the evolutionary theory of development and the subjective view of religious experience underlie the developmental concept of Israel's religion and the critical bias against the supernatural.

Analysis of the critical theory has shown that it was invented and promulgated to explain the supernatural in the Pentateuch on the plane of the purely natural. Moreover, it is the attitude toward the miraculous which constitutes the fundamental and abiding issue in Pentateuchal criticism.

Allis' observation is to the point. "Consequently while we

may rejoice that critics and archeologists of high rank are now prepared to admit that Moses was able to read and write and could have recorded the events of his time, exactly as, on the testimony of the Bible, Old Testament and New, the Christian Church has for centuries believed that he did, we cannot expect them to admit that Moses wrote the Pentateuch and that it is trustworthy history unless or until they are prepared to accept as trustworthy the account which it gives of God's wonders of old. If the wonders are incredible, the Pentateuch cannot be regarded as trustworthy history. The redemptive supernaturalism which pervades it is a stumbling block to the rationalist. When the critics praise the historical accuracy of the Pentateuch and at the same time summarily reject its statements where the supernatural is clearly involved, they make it unmistakably plain that they regard as impossible the very things which it represents as supremely important, those things which make it uniquely precious to the Christian believer, the record it gives of God's wonders of old."[40]

Conclusion Regarding Mosaic Unity

Mosaic unity has been defined to mean that the Pentateuch is one continuous work, the product of a single writer, Moses, but it is concluded that the concept may admit post-Mosaic additions or changes which do not affect the authenticity and the integrity of the text. Denial of Mosaic unity appears in the development of various documentary theories from 1750 to the present. Defense of Mosaic unity is undertaken against the literary arguments of the critics. The alternation of the divine names can be otherwise explained and can be harmonized with the partition theory only by the free use of a redactor, by the supposition of repeated textual alterations and by an arbitrary and fallacious exegesis of Exodus 6:3.

Moreover, the continuity of the supposed documents is disrupted by serious lacunae or maintained by dubious methods.

40 **The Five Books of Moses,** p. 245.

Alleged doublets or parallel passages upon careful examination are found not to be such at all, but either distinct events merely containing similar features, or the same events set forth under a different aspect and for a different purpose. Arguments from alleged differences in vocabulary and variations in style are invalid, based upon utterly fallacious assumptions and inconclusive methods and capable of simpler and more natural explanation.

Historical-archeological difficulties in the form of so-called anachronisms and geographical peculiarities are greatly overdrawn by critics. Few, if any, genuine anachronisms exist, and there is nothing inconsistent with Mosaic unity to explain any that might exist as later slight additions or glosses to the Mosaic text, or translations into more modern speech.

The religious-philosophical difficulties are largely manufactured by the critics as a result of the clash of their anthropocentric evolutionary rationalism with the theocentric redemptive revelation recorded in the Pentateuch.

Thus, it appears that all the arguments amassed by the critics to deny Mosaic unity, literary, historical, philosophical, signally fail. The positive evidence of Mosaic unity meanwhile remains in the Pentateuch itself and cannot effectually be overthrown. The genuineness and unbroken continuity of its history, the consistency of its plan, the sublimity of its purpose, the universality of its appeal, the omnitemporality of its message, the coherence of its subject matter, the naturalness and beauty of its literary quality and the spirituality of its meaning bind it together and demonstrate it to be the work of one great mind in vital contact with God.

It is preposterous to think that separate, independent and conflicting documents, mechanically pieced together centuries later under artificial circumstances, and with questionable intent (if we follow the critics), could produce such an appearance of unity and genuineness as prevails throughout the Pentateuch. It would be just as unreasonable to suppose that a beautiful marble temple could be constructed out of discordant fragments of dissimilar materials.

LITERATURE ON THE PENTATEUCH

(See also titles in Chapter VII and at the end of Chapter VIII)

Wellhausen, J., *Die Composition des Hexateuchs* (3rd. ed., Berlin, 1899.)

Smith, W. R., *The Old Testament In The Jewish Church* (1894).

Bacon, B. W., *The Genesis of Genesis* (1893).

Holzinger, H., *Einleitung in den Hexateuch* (1893).

Briggs, C. A., *The Higher Criticism of the Pentateuch* (1893).

Driver, S. R., *Introduction to the Literature of the Old Testament* (Edinburgh, 9th. ed., 1913).

Bewer, J., *The Literature of the Old Testament* (New York, 1933).

Oesterley, W. O. E., and T. H. Robinson, *An Introduction to the Books of the Old Testament* (London, 1934).

Eissfeldt, O., *Einleitung in das Alte Testament* (Tuebingen, 1934).

Robinson, H. W., *The Old Testament: Its Making and Meaning* (Nashville, 1937).

Barton, G. A., "The Present State of Old Testament Studies," in *The Haverford Symposium on Archeology and The Bible* (New Haven, 1938), pp 47-78.

Eissfeldt, O., "Modern Criticism," in *Record* and *Revelation* (Oxford, 1938), pp. 74-109.

Weiser, A., *Einleitung in das Alte Testament* (Stuttgart, 1939).

Pfeiffer, R., *Introduction to the Old Testament* (New York, 1941).

Winnett, F. W., *The Mosaic Tradition* (Toronto, 1949).

Bentzen, A., *Introduction to the Old Testament* (Vol. II, Copenhagen, 1949).

CONSERVATIVE LITERATURE

Dreschler, M., *Die Einheit und Echtheit der Genesis* (1838).

Vos, G., *The Mosaic Origin of the Pentateuchal Codes* (New York, 1886).

Beattie, F. R., *Radical Criticism* (New York, 1894).

Green, W. H., *The Pentateuch Vindicated from the Aspersions of Bishop Colenso* (New York, 1863).

Green, W. H., *Moses and the Prophets* (1883).

Green, W. H., *The Hebrew Feasts* (1885).

Green, W. H., *The Unity of Genesis* (1895).

Green, W. H., *The Higher Criticism of the Pentateuch* (1895).

Baxter, W. L., *Sanctuary and Sacrifice, A Reply to Wellhausen* (London, 1895).

Orr, J., *The Problem of the Old Testament* (London, 1906).

Raven, J. H., *Old Testament Introduction* (New York, 1906), pp. 85-128.

Fitchett, W. H., *Where the Higher Criticism Fails* (New York, 1922).

Storey, F. D., *The Higher Criticism Cross-Examined* (Philadelphia, 1905).

DuBose, Bishop H. M., "The Aftermath Series" (Nashville, 1923-24).

Finn, A. H., *The Unity of the Pentateuch* (London, 1917).

Noordtzy, A., *The Old Testament Problem* (*Bibliotheca Sacra*, nos. 388-390), reprinted by the Dallas Theological Seminary (Dallas, 1940-41).

Coppens, J., *The Old Testament and the Critics* (Paterson, 1942).

Steinmueller, J. E., *A Companion to Scripture Studies* (Vol. II, 1942), pp. 1-66.

Allis, O. T., *The Five Books of Moses* (Philadelphia, 1943).

Manley, G. T., *The New Bible Handbook* (Chicago, 1949), pp. 40-56; 115-153.

Young, E. J., *An Introduction to the Old Testament* (Grand Rapids, 1949), pp. 109-153.

Aalders, G. C., *A Short Introduction to the Pentateuch,* (Chicago, 1949).

Chapter X

THE FORMER PROPHETS

The second of the three divisions of the Hebrew canon is the Prophets or Nebhiim, consisting of Joshua, Judges, Samuel and Kings (four books), called the *Former Prophets* and Isaiah, Jeremiah, Ezekiel and the Twelve (four books), called the *Latter Prophets*. The *Former Prophets* are anonymous. They were so called by the ancient Jews not because they were regarded as particularly prophetic in content, but because their authors were viewed as having held the office of a prophet.

The importance of the *Former Prophets* is evidenced by the fact that they not only continue the interpretative history of the divine dealing with the theocratic nation where the Pentateuch leaves off, but trace the sequence of events important to the history of redemption to the Babylonian Captivity. By so doing, they form a connecting link with the *Latter Prophets* and furnish an indispensable introduction to their meaning and message.

Joshua

The book of Joshua in the Hebrew language and in all the versions takes its title from the great leader whose exploits it recounts. The name, which means *Jehovah saves* or *Jehovah is salvation,* aptly describes the nature of Joshua's career. Jehovah wrought salvation through His chosen instrument, Moses' successor, by vanquishing Israel's enemies and giving them the land of Canaan.

1. THE PURPOSE.

The aim of the Book of Joshua is to demonstrate God's faithfulness to His promises by leading Israel into the Land of Canaan as He had previously led them out of Egypt (Genesis 15:18; Joshua 1:2-6). The events recorded are evidently highly selective. Only those occurrences are stressed which are meant to illustrate God's special intervention in behalf of His people. Summary statements emphasizing that God did not fail to perform all that He had promised (21:43-45) seemingly embrace other conquests not specifically described in the book. Those which are included were deemed sufficient to accomplish the author's purpose of proving God's adherence to His promises. In the light of God's faithfulness to His people, Joshua, in his farewell address, solemnly warns God's people to continue faithful to Jehovah or suffer the dire effects of disobedience (23:11-24:28).

2. THE CONTENTS.

Part I. The Land Conquered (1:1-12:24).

   a. Joshua commissioned (1:1-9).
   b. Preparation made to cross the Jordan (1:10-2:24).
   c. The Jordan crossed (3:1-4:24).
   d. Israel circumcized, etc. at Gilgal (5:1-15).
   e. Jericho and Ai taken (6:1-8:29).
   f. An altar erected on Mount Ebal (8:30-35).
   g. The Gibeonites received (9:1-27).
   h. Southern Canaan conquered (10:1-43).
   i. Northern Canaan conquered (11:1-15).
   j. The conquest summarized (11:16-12:24).

Part II. The Land Divided (13:1-22:34).

   a. Joshua divinely instructed (13:1-7).
   b. The Eastern Tribes assigned (13:8-33).
   c. The Western Tribes assigned (14:1-19:51).
   d. Cities of Refuge provided (20:1-9).

e. Levitical Towns allotted (21:1-45).
f. The Eastern Tribes sent home (22:1-34).
Part III. Joshua's Farewell Address and Death (23:1-24:33).

3. AUTHORSHIP AND DATE.

Although there are problems connected with the authorship, we are warranted in viewing the book as a literary unit (distinct from the Pentateuch) dating from the period of Joshua and in all likelihood written in substance by Joshua himself. That the book was composed in substance by Israel's great general or a contemporary, or so soon after his time that the history it contains is authentic, is supported by internal evidence.

a. Large parts of the book apparently *are written by an eyewitness* (Cf. Joshua 5:1; 5:6; 15:4). The sending out of the spies (Joshua 2), the passage of the Jordan (chapter 3), the capture of Jericho and Ai (chapters 6-8), the league with the Gibeonites (chapter 9), the victory at Gibeon (chapter 10), etc. are described with such vividness and minuteness of detail that participation in the events is suggested. For this reason ancient as well as modern Jewish (cf. the Talmudic Tract *Baba Bathra*) and Christian authorities before the rise of the modern school of criticism have ascribed the work substantially to Joshua.

b. Parts of the book, at least, *are written by Joshua*. The aged leader is specifically said to have written the covenant made with the people "in the book of the law of God" (24:26) which embraces his last charge to Israel just before his death (24:1-25). To this certainly was added the survey of the land made at his request and described "by cities into seven parts *in a book*" (18:9).

c. Numerous indications *in the narrative show that it was written very early*. At the time of the author Rahab, the harlot, was still alive (6:25). The author's reference to the Jebusites dwelling "with the children of Judah at Jerusalem unto this day" (15:63) points to a pre-Davidic date, for the native inhabitants of the city were not expelled until the seventh or eighth year of David's reign (II Samuel 5:5-9). The reference to the Canaanites dwelling in Gezer (Joshua 16:10) is pre-Solomonic, because Pharaoh king of Egypt slew the Canaanite inhabitants and gave the city as a present to his daughter, Solomon's wife (I Kings 9:16). Jerusalem (earlier Jebusi) was not yet an Israelite capital (Joshua 18:16, 28). Canaanite cities are mentioned by their archaic names (e.g. Baalah, later Kirjath-jearim, 15:9; Kirjath-sannah, later Debir 15:49; Kirjath-arba, later Hebron). Sidon apparently was the most important Phoenician city (13:4-6; 19:28), whereas Tyre gained the ascendancy after the twelfth century. The Gibeonites were still "hewers of wood and drawers of water . . ." around the Tabernacle as Joshua had made them "unto this day . . ." (9:27), whereas in Saul's day they suffered massacre and their status had been changed (Cf. II Samuel 21:1-9).

d. Although the legitimate conclusion from internal evidence is that the book is a literary unity going back in substance to the period of Joshua, and that Joshua himself was very likely the author, yet the account *in its present form contains minor details which cannot be ascribed to Joshua's original work*. The account of his death (Joshua 24:29, 30) is a later addition, together with the statement that "Israel served the Lord . . . all the days of Joshua, and all the days of the elders that outlived Joshua . . . " (24:31). The book records a few events which apparently occurred *after* the death of Joshua but early in the period of the Judges, such as Caleb's conquest of Hebron, Othniel's capture of Kirjath-sepher (Cf. Joshua 15:13-17 and Judges 1:9-13) and the transmigration of the Danites to the north (Joshua 19:47; Judges 18:27-29). Moreover, the book makes several references which indicate retouchings of a later hand, such as the possible allusion to one of the Judges in "the towns of Jair" (Joshua 13:30) and the strange use of the terms "mountains of Judah . . ." and "of Israel . . ." (11:21), seemingly employing terminology characteristic of the period after the division of the monarchy upon the death of Solomon about 922 B.C. The reference to the book of Jasher (Joshua 10:13) does not constitute a valid argument that Joshua was written during David's reign or later since reference is made to the same book then (II Samuel 1:18). Almost nothing is known of the Book of Jasher, which may have been an anthology of national heroes expanded from time to time to include contemporary celebrities. Cases of alleged additions, especially those subsequent to the period of the Judges, must be rigidly tested as to their validity, and if found to be genuine, regarded as mere interpolations and not necessarily as proofs of the late date of the composition of the book.

4. RELATION TO THE PENTATEUCH.

Critics deny the traditional view that the book of Joshua is a literary unit, a product substantially of one author, and place it in closest literary connection with the Pentateuch, insisting that it originated from the same literary sources, JEDP. Practically discarding the traditional term Pentateuch, they have coined the expression *Hexateuch,* to fit their theory. J (c. 950-850) and E (c. 650 B.C.), the two primary sources of chapters 1-12, were supposedly revised and edited by a Deuteronomistic writer (c. 550 B.C.) who added his own conclusions to chapter 23. A later Deuteronomist (c. 400 B.C.) added the Elohistic conclusion of chapter 24. The apportionment of Canaan among the Israelite tribes (chapters 13-22) is said to be from a priestly source (P) and was added to JED (c. 400 B.C.). Further slight additions were made to the final canonization of the book about 200 B.C.[1]

That the term Hexateuch is purely a critical invention ap-

1 R. Pfeiffer, Introduction to the O. T. (New York, 1941), pp. 293-313. Cf. Oesterley & Robinson, An Introduction to the Books of the O. T. (London, 1934), p. 69 f.

pears from the following observations: (1) *The whole foundation of the documentary hypothesis of the Pentateuch is
unsound* and based upon false literary, historical, religious and
philosophical presuppositions.[2] The book displays evidences of
a well coordinated narrative complete in itself insofar as the
purposes the writer set out to achieve are concerned.

(2) There is *no historical evidence that Joshua was ever
considered as forming a unit with the Pentateuch.* The Samaritans
(late fifth or fourth century, B.C.) appropriated only the Pentateuch, which would have been inconceivable had Joshua at
that time been joined to it in a Hexateuch, and especially so,
when the book seemingly favors the Samaritans by its
references to Shechem (Joshua 24:1, 32). The Septuagint
(c. 250-150 B.C.) places Joshua among the *Nebhiim* and not
in the Torah. Ecclesiasticus (second century B.C.) distinguishes between the Law and the Prophets. Josephus
(*Against Apion* 1:7) in the first century A.D. clearly distinguishes the five books of Moses from the rest of the Hebrew
canon, as did our Lord and first-century Christians. Joshua
was never included in the synogical readings from the
Torah, and only included when selections from the Prophets
were added. Massoretic tradition distinctly notes at the end
of the Pentateuch that "the five fifths of Law are completed."

(3) *Certain pronounced linguistic peculiarities of the
Pentateuch are absent from the book of Joshua.* In matters
of style, vocabulary and certain grammatical forms the two
differ and indicate the two books were subjected to independent
methods of transmission at early periods. The Hebrew
archaism *hael* and the usage of *hu'* for the feminine are con-
spicuously absent from Joshua. The expression "Jehovah the
God of Israel" occurring fourteen times in Joshua is extremely
rare in the Pentateuch. The spelling of Jericho, for instance,
is different in the two books.

(4) *The idea of a Hexateuch involves difficulties even with-*

2 See chapters VII-IX.

in the framework of the critics' theory itself. Why P, which
in the Pentateuch is supposedly the foundational document,
should appear only in Joshua chapters 13-21 remains without
a satisfactory answer, if the alleged sources are continuous.

5. AUTHENTICITY AND CREDIBILITY OF THE BOOK.

As redemptive history Joshua continues the account of all
those events which happened unto God's ancient people as "en-
samples" and which "are written for our admonition, upon
whom the ends of the worlds are come" (I Corinthians
10:11). The detailed redemptive typology of the Pentateuch
recording the deliverance of Israel *out* of Egypt is expanded to
include the consummation of redemption *into* the Promised
Land. Redemption *out* of the bondage of sin (Egypt) has its
spiritual sequel in redemption *into* a place of victory and
blessing (Canaan). In a spiritual and typical sense Joshua
is to the Old Testament (Joshua 21:43-45) what Ephesians is
to the New, and Canaan was to the Israelite what "the
heavenly places" (Ephesians 1:3) are to the Christian—not a
figure of heaven, but an experience here and now of conflict and a place of victory and blessing through God's manifested power.

This accounts for the large number of miracles in the Pentateuch and Joshua. Redemption *out* of Egypt, sojourn in
the desert and redemption *into* the Promised Land could
only be expected by divine power. The same is true of
every phase of Christian experience from deliverance from the
penalty of sin to deliverance from its power in a life of
victory and blessing.

Critics, who have never experienced redemption, naturally
regard the large number of miracles in the book as legends
and the history as idealized or legendized. To the Christian
scholar, however, who has experienced God's miraculous power
in every phase of his Christian life, there is no reason to deny
that the narrative rests on solid historical grounds. The rest

of the Bible fully confirms it, and its typology is interwoven in the New Testament revelation of God's redemption in Christ (Hebrews 3:7-4:11: cf. 4:8). For example, the crossing of the Jordan (Joshua 3) is narrated in Psalm 114:3, 5. Joshua's curse upon Jericho (Joshua 6:26) is referred to in its fulfillment in I Kings 16:34. Hebrews 11:30-31 catalogues the destruction of Jericho and the preservation of Rahab (Joshua 2 and 6). In addition to the Bible the Amarna Letters confirm the general historical and political background of Syro-Palestine about 1400-1375 B.C.

LITERATURE ON JOSHUA

Keil, C. F., *Joshua, Judges and Ruth* (Edinburgh, 1863).
Blaikie, W. G., *Joshua* in *Expositor's Bible* (1893).
   See *Encyclopedia Biblica*, II, (1901) for bibliography of older literature, also *Hastings' Dictionary of the Bible*, II, (1899).
Robinson, H. W., in the *New Century Bible* (n.d.)
Cooke, G. A., in the *Cambridge Bible* (Cambridge, 1918).
Burney, O. F., "Israel's Settlement In Canaan", in *The Schweich Lectures* 1917 (London, 1918).
Garstang, J., *The Foundations of Bible History: Joshua and Judges* (London, 1931).
Noth, M., *Das System des zwoelf Staemme Israels* (Stuttgart, 1930) and in *Handbuch zum Alten Testament* (Tuebingen, 1938).
Steinmueller, J. E., *Some Problems of the Old Testament* (Milwaukee, 1936).
Albright, W. F., "The Israelite Conquest of Canaan In the Light of Archeology" in *Bull. of Am. Schs. of Or. Res.*, 74, 1939, pp. 11-23.
Wright, G. E., and F. Filson, "The Conquest of Canaan" in *The Westminster Historical Atlas to the Bible*, (Philadelphia, 1945). p. 39 f.

JUDGES

The book of Judges takes its name in the oldest Hebrew records and in the various versions from the charismatic military leaders (*shofetim*) who delivered and ruled over the twelve tribes of Israel in their national youth when they were only a loose confederacy or amphictyony without a stable central government and particularly subject to enemy incursion. The Hebrew word "to judge" (*shft*) not only denotes "to settle a dispute and to maintain justice both for the individual and the people," but has the added idea of liberating or delivering. Thus the Judges performed a twofold function. First, they personally delivered their people from enemy oppression. Secondly, they ruled over them and administered justice. In their ruling capacity they correspond to the Shufetim of Phoenicia and the sufetes of Carthage, akin to the Roman consuls.[3]

1. The Purpose.

The book is designed to continue the history of God's chosen people through the era intervening from the death of Joshua c. 1375 B.C. to the time of Samuel about 1075 B.C., a period of approximately three centuries. Special prominence is accorded certain periods in the general or local history of the tribes, the purpose, like that of the Pentateuch and Joshua, being religious rather than strictly historical. The general aim is to show that apostasy from Jehovah is followed by servitude and punishment. Repentance brings restoration. The events illustrating this spiritual principle are selective, sometimes coeval rather than in chronological sequence, with long periods passed over in silence. Some of the Judges, for instance, are mentioned only by name without any description of their career.

2. The Contents.

Part I. General Introduction to the Period of the Judges (1:1-2:5).

> a. Political conditions from Joshua to the rise of the Judges (1:1-36).
>
> b. Religious conditions from Joshua to the rise of the Judges (2:1-5).

3 See Z. Harris, **A Grammar of the Phoenician Language** (New Haven, 1936).

Part II. The Period of the Judges (2:6-16:31).

    a. General religious characterization of the entire period (2:6-3:6).

    b. General list of the Judges (3:7-16:31).

        (1) Othniel of Judah (3:7-11).

        (2) Ehud of Benjamin (3:12-30).

        (3) Shamgar (3:31).

        (4) Deborah of Ephraim and Barak of Naphtali (4:1-5:31).

        (5) Gideon of Manasseh and Abimelech (6:1-9:57).

        (6) Tola of Issachar (10:1, 2).

        (7) Jair of Gilead (10:3-5).

        (8) Jephthah of Gilead (10:6-12:7).

        (9) Ibzan of Zebulon (12:8-10).

        (10) Elon of Zebulon (12:11, 12).

        (11) Abdon of Ephraim (12:13-15).

        (12) Samson of Dan (13:1-16:31).

Part III. The Double Appendix (17:1-21:25).

    a. The idolatry of Micah and the Danites (17:1-18:31).

    b. The crime at Gibeah of Benjamin and its punishment (19:1-21:25).

3. The Chronology.

Chronological notices include a total of 410 years during which Israel was oppressed by enemies and ruled by various Judges. At first sight this appears an impossibly large figure in the light of I Kings 6:1 which places the fourth year of Solomon's reign (when he began to build the Temple) only 480 years after the Exodus. Allowing forty years in the wilderness (Numbers 32:13), twenty-five years for Joshua in Palestine, forty years for Eli, possibly forty years for both Samuel and Saul, forty years for David (II Samuel 5:4) and four years for Solomon (I Kings 6:1), a total of 189 years is the result which, when subtracted from the 480 years from the Exodus to Solomon's fourth year, leaves only 291 years for the Judges.

That this is not a discrepancy, but the result of a simultaneous rule of certain Judges in their respective tribes is indicated by the further chronological notice in Judges 11:26 which places the period of Israel's sojourn at Heshbon, which was a year or two at the most before the entrance into Canaan (cf. Numbers 21:25), and Jephthah's judgeship as 300 years. Allowing thirty-eight years from the Exodus to Heshbon, 300 years from Heshbon to Jephthah's second year (cf. Judges 10:8, 11:4, 9, 32, 33) plus approximately 144 years from Jephthah to Solomon's fourth year (five years for the rest of Jephthah's reign, forty years for Samson, Eli twenty years, Samuel twenty years, Saul about fifteen, David forty and Solomon four) a total of 482 years is reached, which closely approximates the 480 of I Kings 6:1. In addition to these chronological data there are other indications of the synchronous rule of the Judges. For example, Joshua 10:7 clearly implies that Jephthah and Samson ruled contemporaneously, since one delivered oppressed Israel from the Ammonites and the other from the Philistines.

That the synchronous rule of the Judges, which can easily restrict their activity to somewhat less than 300 to 350 years, is the correct explanation of the chronological problem of the book and not the critical theory of discrepancies due to various conflicting documents (J, E, E², P) is thus indicated by the internal evidence of the book itself. Garstang is correct in showing that the chronological scheme underlying Judges is consistent in itself, but he is wrong in resorting to alleged late and conflicting documentary sources to do so.[4]

Garstang has done a valuable service, however, in correlating the various Judges into the framework of contemporary Egyptian history on the basis of the early date of the Exodus

4 See J. Garstang, **Joshua & Judges**, (London, 1931) pp. 51-61.

under Amenhotep II (1448-1420).[5] To adopt the later dating under Raamses II (c. 1290) involves the grave difficulty of being compelled to compress the period of the Judges into less than 175 years, which forces one to discredit I Kings 6:1 and to explain away the whole time scheme underlying Joshua and Judges.

4. LITERARY COMPOSITION AND DATE.

Critics commonly view the bulk of the Book of Judges as consisting of old hero tales taken from two principal independent sources, commonly called J and E. In the latter half of the seventh century a redactor is supposed to have united these two documents, and to have made a few smaller additions, such as the minor judges (10:1-5, 12:8-15), to form substantially the present book. In the following century a Deuteronomist, it is claimed, superimposed upon the whole a pragmatic religious interpretation, which although "solemn, impressive, and effective" is yet (according to Bewer) "distorted and wrong" from "an historical point of view."[6] After still other minor redactions the book allegedly did not reach its present form until about 200 B.C.

This prevailing critical view, while not as intimately connected with Pentateuchal source criticism as the book of Joshua, nevertheless is built on many of the same fallacies. The internal evidence of the book of Judges and tradition, however, suggest an origin during the early years of the Hebrew monarchy, likely in the time of Saul (c. 1020 B.C.). That Samuel as a member of the prophetic school may well have been the author and compiler is suggested on the basis of the following reasons:

First, *the book displays the unity of a single author-editor.* It has a consistent plan. The heart of the book, recording seven apostasies, seven servitudes and seven deliverances, is

5 Op. cit., pp. 61-66.
6 J. Bewer, **The Literature of the O. T.** (New York, 1933) p. 230.

preceded by an orderly introduction to the twelve judgeships. It is followed by a logical appendix, complementing the description of the general political and religious character of the period. This unity and plan are based upon an intensely pragmatic religious interpretation which is not the product of a late so-called "Deuteronomistic Work of History",[7] but a very early development in Old Testament literature, the result of the Mosaic genuineness of the book of Deuteronomy, where blessing in Canaan is contingent upon obedience to Jehovah's law and punishment upon its infraction (Deuteronomy 28:1-68 etc.).

Secondly, *the author was in large measure a compiler.* He necessarily had to make use of earlier documents written by different authors at different periods, since he records Israelite history extending over several centuries and was not a contemporary of the events cited. For example, he selected the early poem, "The Song of Deborah" in Chapter 5, and also included a prose account (chapter 4). He gave great prominence (certainly because of their eminent didactic value) to the stories of Gideon and Samson, incorporating certain stylistic peculiarities of the former (e. g. *she* for *'asher*) (6:17, 7:12, 8:26), and employing the idiom "the Spirit of the Lord clothed Gideon" (6:34) but "the Spirit of the Lord came mightily upon Samson" (14:6, 19; 15:14).

Thirdly, *the book contains evidences of belonging to the age of Saul.* The statement that "the Jebusites dwell with the children of Benjamin in Jerusalem unto this day" (Judges 1:21) could not have been written after David's conquest of Zion in the seventh year of his reign (II Samuel 5:6-8). Reference to the Phoenicians as Sidonians points to a time previous to the twelfth century for many of the events, for after that Tyre became the chief Phoenician city. The expression, four times repeated, "In those days there was no king in Israel" (Judges 17:6; 18:1; 19:1; 21:25) with the twice added note,

7 cf. A. Bentzen, **Old Testament Introduction II**, p. 87

"Every man did that which was right in his own eyes" (17:6; 21:25), points to the early monarchic period. The seeming anomalous reference to the Assyrian deportation in 18:30, if the Massoretic Text is correct, is difficult, and the phrase "till the depopulation of the land," should either be emended as many scholars do to "the carrying away of the ark" (I Samuel 4:5), that is, about 1050 B.C. by the Philistines, or viewed as the hand of a later editor.[8]

Fourthly, *Hebrew tradition holds that Samuel was the author.* We are dependent upon Hebrew tradition and internal evidence for our knowledge of the date of the author. These two witnesses are in agreement. This is the opinion recorded in *Baba Bathra* (14b) and defended by many Christian conservative scholars.

Literature on Judges

Moore, G. F. in *International Critical Commentary* (1895).
Burney, C. F., *The Book of Judges with Introduction and Notes* (2nd ed. London, 1920).
Eissfeld, O., *Die Quellen des Richterbuches* (Leipzig, 1925).
Garstang, J., *Joshua: Judges* (London, 1937).
    For conservative literature: See C. F. Keil's Introduction (Edinburgh, 1859), Keil & Delitzsch (Edinburgh, 1869), F. W. Grant, *The Numerical Bible* (Joshua to II Samuel).

Samuel

I and II Samuel, originally a single book, were divided by the Septuagint translators into two books called I and II Kings, while the other books of Kings, which deal with a later historical period, were called III and IV Kings. This designation carried over into the Old Latin and the Vulgate. The same division was carried over into the Hebrew Bible in 1448, but with the difference, however, that each book retained the title which it bore in the Hebrew manuscript, and I-IV Kings became I-II Samuel and I-II Kings. Although there was an old Jewish tradition in *Baba Bathra* (14b) that Samuel "wrote

8 See **Int. Crit. Com.** in loc.

the book which bears his name," the name of the two books can only find a logical explanation in the fact that Samuel was the principal character in the first part and anointed the other two principal characters.

1. The Purpose.

I and II Samuel continue the closing years of the period of the judges to the establishment of the Kingdom under David. The books trace the personal history of Samuel, the last of the judges (Acts 13:20) and the first of the prophets. The moral failure of the priesthood and judgeship is recorded in the death of Eli and his house. The failure of the judgeship is further indicated in Samuel's unsuccessful attempt to make the office hereditary in his sons (I Samuel 8:1).

The rise of the prophetic office alongside of the kingly office is described. Samuel, the prophet as well as judge, is the founder of both. He established the schools of the prophets (I Samuel 19:20; II Kings 2:3-5; 4:38). He anointed Saul, and after his rejection, David, but died before God's chosen king came to the throne. The establishment of Israel's political center in Jerusalem (II Samuel 5:6-12) and her religious center in Zion (II Samuel 5:7; 6:1-17) are also recorded together with the great Davidic covenant (II Samuel 7:8-17) which forms a basis for the development of all subsequent kingdom truth. David in prophetic strain describes the millennial kingdom yet to be established (II Samuel 23: 1-7).

2. The Contents.

Part I. Samuel's Judgeship (I Samuel 1-7).
  a. Samuel's birth and boyhood (1:1-2:10).
  b. Eli's rejection and Samuel's call (2:11-3:21).
  c. The Ark among the Philistines (4:1-7:1).
  d. Samuel's activity as judge (7:2-17).
Part II. Saul's Reign (I Samuel 8-II Samuel 1).
  a. Israel's demand for a king (8:1-22).

b. The choice of Saul (9:1-11:15).

c. Samuel's farewell address (12:1-25).

d. Saul's war against the Philistines (13:1-14:52).

e. Saul's disobedience and rejection (15:1-35).

f. David's anointing and call to Saul's Court (16:1-23).

g. David's slaughter of Goliath (17:1-58).

h. David's flight from Saul's court (18:1-20:43).

i. David's wanderings (21:1-30:31).

j. Saul's death (31:1-13).

k. David's lamentation (II Samuel 1:1-27).

Part III. David's Reign (II Samuel 2-24).

a. David's coronation over Judah (2:1-7).

b. David establishes national and religious unity (2:8-6:23).

c. The Davidic covenant (7:1-29).

d. David's conquests (8:1-10:19).

e. David's sin and repentance (11:1-12:31).

f. Amnon and Absolom's crimes (13:1-14:33).

g. Absalom's rebellion (15:1-19:8).

h. David's restoration to power (19:9-20:26).

i. The famine and the revenge of the Gibeonites (21:1-14).

j. Heroes in war with the Philistines (21:15-22).

k. David's song and last words (22:1-23:7).

l. His heroes (23:8-39).

m. David's census and punishment (24:1-25).

3. COMPOSITION AND DATE. Critics who hold the documentary theory of the Pentateuch generally conclude that the books of Samuel consist of at least two principal sources: J, the earlier (about the tenth century B.C.), and E, the later (about the eighth century B.C.).[9] The relationship of these documents is supposed to be similar to J and E in the Pentateuch and

9 Cf. R. Pfeiffer, **Introduction to the O. T.**, pp. 341-365. "Midrash in the Books of Samuel" in **Quantulacumque**, pp. 303-316

Judges, if not actually a continuation of these documents, as K. Budde maintained. About the seventh century these two sources were united and allegedly display contradictions, duplications, fusions and differences in points of view, style and diction. Later a Deuteronomic editor of the sixth century deleted certain portions contrary to his religious convictions, but these were subsequently restored.

Otto Eissfeldt[10] dissects the text into three sources: L, J and E, which are considered as probably continuations of the sources of the Heptateuch. This theory, however, has not found wide critical acceptance.

The critical theory is to be rejected because *it is at variance with the evidences of the unity of the books*. The careers of Samuel, Saul and David are so interwoven that they present an orderly progressive narrative. Although events are not always recorded chronologically, a consistent plan is discernible throughout. This plan is most naturally explained as the result of one and the same writer (who, however, most certainly used documents) rather than as the result of later editors who simply combined conflicting sources.

The critical theory is to be rejected, moreover, *because it makes out the compiler (or editor) to be an incompetent simple-minded blunderer*. It is incredible that he could have included repetitions of the same events. It is more inconceivable that he should have left alleged contradictions and fusions stand in the text, when his precise task as editor was to eliminate such discrepancies. Even now respect for the ancient editor compels us to make an honest attempt to harmonize the accounts (what the modern critic so frequently fails to do). In most cases this is easily done when one's thinking is not biased by the higher critical theory. As in the Pentateuch, many of the alleged parallels are accounts of different events with merely similar features. Others are records of the same

---

10 **Einleitung in das Alte Testament**, 306-317: **Die Komposition der Samuelisbeucher**, (1931).

event from a different point of view. Others still are not parallel at all but brief allusions to events already related which are referred to again because they have a special connection in the progress of the narrative. Alleged contradictions are only apparent, and may in every case be satisfactorily explained.

For example, a duplicate account is said to exist in the fact that Saul is "twice deposed from the throne (I Samuel 13:14; 15:26-29), but continues to rule, his legitimacy unchallenged to the day of his death."[11] That this is one of numerous forced interpretations to support the critical theory of composition is evident that in the first instance Saul is simply told that his kingdom would not be "established . . . upon Israel forever" (I Samuel 13:13). Whereas in his second more serious offense, he himself is rejected by God and so far from "his legitimacy being unchallenged to the day of his death" he merely continues in office without the divine presence, proof enough of his rejection.

Regarding an alleged contradiction, II Samuel 21:19 apparently reports that "Elhanan . . . slew Goliath the Gittite . . ." while I Samuel 17:50, 51 (cf. 19:5; 21:9, 22:10, 13) asserts that David did so. Moreover, I Chronicles 20:5 reports that "Elhanan the son of Jairi slew Lahmi the brother of Goliath the Gittite . . ." If this glaring error was in the original the final redactors of Samuel were guilty of a most obvious and stupid blunder, and must be considered to be incredibly incompetent. The other alternative, clearly the solution of the difficulty considering the fact that the Hebrew text of Samuel is in a poorer state of preservation than any other part of the Old Testament with the possible exception of Ezekiel and Hosea, is that the passage in Samuel has suffered corruption in the course of transmission. Evidence furnished by a careful study of the original suggests that the reading in Samuel and Chronicles originally was either "And

11 Pfeiffer, Introduction, p. 340.

Elhanan the son of Jairi slew Lahmi the brother of Goliath"
or "And Elhanan the son of Jairi the Bethlehemite slew the
brother of Goliath." The obvious original of both passages indicates that David slew Goliath and Elhanan slew the brother
of Goliath.[12]

The critical theory *is unsound in insisting that differences of
viewpoint are evidences of variety of authorship.* Much is
made, for instance, of a supposed diametrically opposed attitude
to the monarchy in the accounts of its origin (cf. I Samuel
9:1-10, 16 with 7:2-8:22). But here again critics fail to see
that the divine condemnation of the people's lack of faith in
desiring a king is not inconsistent with God's glowing promises
to bless that king. It is another illustration of God's common
method of dealing with His people wherein He makes the
wrath of man to praise Him.

The critical theory that differences *in style and diction
indicate composite authorship is weak and inconclusive.* While
such stylistic differences exist they are more readily explained by the inspired author's method of compiling his account from his sources without thorough assimilation and
elaboration. On the other hand there is an underlying uniformity of diction running through I and II Samuel, which
binds them into one, which Driver admits.[13]

4. AUTHORSHIP. The author of the books is unknown.
However, since the work is uniform in character and possesses
plan and purpose, it is to be regarded as the labor of one
author or compiler who was in all probability a prophet under
the kings, who made use of earlier documents left by Samuel,
Gad, Nathan (I Chronicles 29:29) and possibly others, adapt-
ing his sources to suit his purpose. The date of composition
need not be placed later than the end of David's reign, notwithstanding references to Judah and Israel (I Samuel

12 For suggested emendations see E. Young, **Introduction to the O. T.,** p.
181 f. Cf. S. R. Driver, **Notes on the Hebrew Text of the Books of Samuel**
(Oxford, 1913) Also Int. Crit. Com. in loc. p. 354 f.
13 Cf. **Lit of the O. T.** (Edinburgh, 1913), p. 184 f.

27:6). The distinction between Judah and Israel existed in the Davidic period, before the consolidation of the monarchy (I Samuel 18:6; II Samuel 2:10; 24:1). That the book ends just before David's death suggests that it was likely written then.

LITERATURE ON SAMUEL

Smith, H. P., in *International Critical Commentary* (New York, 1904).

Kennedy, A. R., in *The Century Bible* (1905).

Dhorme, P., *Les Livres de Samuel* (1910).

Driver, S. R., *Notes On the Hebrew Text and the Topography of the Book of Samuel,* (2nd ed. Oxford, 1913).

Arnold, W. R., *Ephod and Ark* (Harvard, 1917).

Segal, M. H., "Studies in the Books of Samuel" *Jewish Quarterly Review* (N. S. 5-10; 1914-1920).

Eissfeldt, O., *Die Komposition der Samuelisbuecher* (Leipzig, 1931).

Rehm, M., *Die Buecher Samuel* (Wuerzburg, 1949).

CONSERVATIVE LITERATURE

Keil, *Die Buecher Samuel* (2nd ed. 1875) "The Books of Samuel" in his *Introduction to the Old Testament* (Edinburgh, 1869).

Boyd J. O., articles in *The Princeton Theological Review*: "Monarchy in Israel: The ideal and the Actual" (vol. 26, 1928). pp. 41-64; "The Davidic Dynasty" (vol. 25, 1927, pp. 215-239). "The Davidic Covenant: The Oracle" (pp. 417-443). "Echoes of the Covenant with David" (pp. 587-609).

Grant, F. W., in *The Numerical Bible*—Joshua to II Samuel (New York, 1932).

Gaebelein, A. C., in *The Annotated Bible* (Our Hope, New York).

KINGS

The book (originally a single volume in the Hebrew Bible like Samuel) takes its name from the opening word in the Hebrew text *wehammelek,* "And the king," and from the contents describing the history of the kings of Israel and Judah. It appears as III and IV Kings in the Greek and the Vulgate, but as I and II Kings after I and II Samuel in modern Hebrew Bibles.

1. THE PURPOSE.

The Books of Kings continue the narrative of Israelite history where the Books of Samuel leave off just previous to the death of David and carry the account of Israel to the fall of Samaria in 721 B.C. and the history of Judah until the thirty-seventh year of King Jehoiachin's captivity in Babylon (c. 972-560 B.C.)

2. THE CONTENTS.

Part I. The Reign of Solomon (I Kings 1:1-11:43).
  a. His anointing as king (1:1-53).
  b. David's charge to Solomon and his death (2:1-46).
  c. Solomon's marriage and choice of wisdom (3:1-28).
  d. Solomon's administration (4:1-34).
  e. Solomon's building activities (5:1-8:66).
  f. Solomon's wealth and splendor (9:1-10:29).
  g. Solomon's apostasy (11:1-43).

Part II. The Synchronous Reigns of the Kings of Judah and Israel (12:1-II Kings 17:41).

For a synchronized list of the Kings of Israel and Judah based upon recent research see the "Chronological Table of the Divided Monarchy" by W. F. Albright.[14] In accordance with the prophetic slant of Kings (in contrast to the priestly emphasis in Chronicles) special prominence is given to Elijah and Elisha, during this period.

Part III. The Reigns of Judahite Kings to the Babylonian Captivity (II Kings 18:1-25:30).
  a. Hezekiah (II Kings 18:1-20:21).
  b. Manasseh (II Kings 21:1-18).
  c. Amon (II Kings 21:19-26).
  d. Josiah (II Kings 22:1-23:30)
  e. Jehoahaz II (Shallum) (II Kings 23:31-35).
  f. Jehoiakim (Eliakim) (II Kings 23:36-24:7).

14 Bull. of Am. Schs., 100 (Dec. 1945), pp. 20-22.

g. Jehoiachin (Jeconiah) (II Kings 24:8-17; 25:27-30).
h. Zedekiah (Mattaniah) (II Kings 24:18-25:26).

3. COMPOSITION AND DATE.

Higher critics, who hold to the general principles of the Wellhausen School, place the original edition of the Book of Kings ending with the eulogy of Josiah (II Kings 23:25, 28) shortly after the death of the pious king (i.e. somewhere between 609 B.C. and 600 B.C.). The writer is claimed to be the *first* to use historical materials illustrating the philosophy and religion of the book of Deuteronomy, the original edition of which is assumed to have appeared in 621 B.C. Says Pfeiffer, "Thus Kings, and Kings alone, is from its very origin a Deuteronomic history . . . a religious and not a historical work."[15] The law of the central sanctuary (Deuteronomy 12) is said to be the criterion for judging each king, whether of Judah or of Israel. Thus the account is considered idealized and colored by the theological prejudices of the writer.

About 550 B.C. during the exile a second Deuteronomist continued the history to the liberation of King Jehoiachin from prison in 561 or 560 (II Kings 25:27-30) and made various additions to the first edition of the Book of Kings. This writer is to be identified (it is assumed) with the Deuteronomist who also redacted Genesis, Exodus (not Leviticus), Numbers, Deuteronomy, Joshua, Judges and Samuel. A few additions were finally made by a priestly writer (P) between the second edition and the time it was canonized about 200 B.C.

The critical position cannot be accepted for the following reasons. *It is of a piece with the unsound method of partitioning ancient Biblical literature that characterizes the critical treatment of the whole magnificent Genesis-Kings historical corpus, starting with the creation of the universe and going down into the exile.* The same erroneous historical, literary and philosophical presuppositions underlie higher Pentateuchal criticism as underlie the view of the Book of Kings. Prominent among them is the ethically objectionable and historically unsupported theory that the book discovered in the eighteenth year of Josiah's reign (II Kings 22:3-8) was Deuteronomy and that book alone and that this code was written shortly before its discovery as a pious fraud promulgated as the genuine Law of Moses. It is sufficient to say that there are many passages in the historical books which prove that the Deuteronomic laws were known from the time of their promulgation by Moses. To reject these passages as glosses, Deuteronomic redactions or editorial additions and then to insist that Deuteronomy was unknown and hence nonexistent before Josiah, is a glaring example of reasoning in a vicious circle and of brushing aside with impunity the clear testimony of the ancient Oracles when they chance not to fit the artificial and distorted mold of the **critical theory.**

Again, the critical theory cannot be accepted because *the Deuteronomic stamp of other Old Testament books is no less original with these books than it is with the Book of Kings.* Joshua, Judges and Samuel were originally *written* with Deuteronomic legislation *as a background.* To assert they were not is pure supposition, denying the testimony of their internal evidence and missing the *whole* point of their history. In the whole so-called historical corpus from Genesis through Kings, we do not have history in the commonly accepted scientific sense, that is, a strictly objective record of past events, but a highly specialized and purposive account of redemptive history, which, after the promulgation of the law of Moses, was to a large degree interpreted on the basis of its precepts. To imagine that it was orignally not so interpreted, but that such an interpretation was superimposed upon it at a much later date, and then on the basis of a pious forgery called **Deuteronomy,** is a pure invention of the critics.

It is true however, as the critics maintain, that the author of

Kings had no intention of displacing available secular histories through his book. He had a religious motive and molded his account to achieve his purpose. The account of the kings consists of a stereotyped framework containing a synchronism of the date of accession according to the reigning year of the contemporary ruler of the opposite kingdom, the length of the reign, a verdict of the general character of the king, a reference to the documentary source and a mention of the king's death and successor. Sometimes other details are included, such as the king's age at accession, his mother's name, etc.

4. The Author and His Sources.

According to the Talmud (*Baba Bathra,* 14b) Jeremiah was the author. This may be the actual case. Steinmueller supports this view, contending that the Jeremian authorship does not preclude the composition of the book at Babylon, since rabbinical tradition holds that Nebuchadnezzar took Jeremiah to Babylon after he had conquered Egypt in his thirty-seventh year (568), where he died an old man past ninety. Under this view Jeremiah wrote II Kings 25:27-30 as an old man in Babylon, although the rest of the book according to Steinmueller, may have been compiled long before that time.[16]

Whether the author was actually Jeremiah or not, he at any event was assuredly a contemporary of Jeremiah and also a prophet, who was deeply distressed at the apostasy of Judah. Writing of events long before his time, he made extensive use of sources, which he freely mentions, such as: "The Book of the Acts of Solomon" (I Kings 11:41), The Books of the Chronicles of the Kings of Israel (17 times), The Books of the Chronicles of the Kings of Judah (15 times).

5. The Chronology of the Kings.

The difficult task of harmonizing the contemporaneous reigns of the kings of Judah and Israel has occupied scholars

16 J. E. Steinmueller, **A Companion to Scripture Studies** II, pp. 98 f.

for many years. A great many factors such as coregencies, synchronisms, complicated calendaric reckonings, etc. must be taken into account as Edwin R. Thiele's illuminating study, "The Chronology of the Kings of Judah and Israel" has shown.[17] Albright[18] also observes coregencies and synchronisms in his reconstruction of the chronology of this period of the dual monarchy, reducing the reigns of Judahite kings in a number of instances and also the Israelite kings, especially in the case of the Omrides. As a result of recent research many vexing problems of chronology have been cleared up. Few of the dates of this period are yet absolutely fixed, but are in most cases perhaps not more than five years wrong.

LITERATURE ON KINGS

On chronology:

Kugler, F. X., *Von Moses bis Paulus* (Muenster 1922) pp. 134-189.

Begrich J., *Die Chronologie der Koenige von Israel und Juda* (Tuebingen, 1929).

Mowinckel, S., *Die Chronologie der israelitischen und juedischen Koenige* (Leiden, 1932).

Vogelstein, M., *Biblical Chronology*, Part I (Cincinnati, 1944).

Thiele, E. R., "The Chronology of the Kings of Judah and Israel," in *Journ. of Near Eastern Studies* III (1944), pp. 137-186.

Albright, W. F., "The Chronology of the Divided Monarchy of Israel," in *Bull. of Am. Schs, of Orient. Res.* 100 (Dec. 1945), pp. 16-22.

General:

Burney, C. F., *Notes on the Hebrew Text of the Books of Kings* (Oxford, 1903).

Skinner, J., in the *New Century Bible* (n. d.).

Barnes, W. E., in the *Cambridge Bible* (1911).

Benzinger, I., *Jahvist und Elohist in den Koenigsbuechern* (Stuttgart, 1921).

Binns, L. E., *Old Testament* (The Clarendon Bible) II, 1929.

Foerster, F. C., *First and Second Kings* in O. T. Commentary (Philadelphia, 1948).

Rehm, M., *Die Beucher der Koenige* (Wuerzburg, 1949).

Archeological:

---

17 **Journal Near Eastern Studies** III (1944), pp. 137-186.
18 "The Chronology of the Divided Monarchy" in **Bull. Am. Schs.** 100 pp. 16-22.

Montgomery, J. A., *Arabia and the Bible* (Philadelphia, 1934).

Albright, W. F. *From the Stone Age to Christianity* (Baltimore, 1940) pp. 221-240. *Archeology and the Religion of Israel* (Baltimore, 1942) pp. 95-175.

Finnegan, J., *Light from the Ancient Past* (Princeton, 1946) pp. 129-191.

Free, J. P., *Archeology and Bible History* (Wheaton, 1950) pp. 146-225.

CHAPTER XI

THE LATTER PROPHETS

THE SECOND PART of the second division of the Hebrew Canon is known as the *latter prophets*. The usage in the Hebrew arrangement evidently does not refer to historical chronology, but to the fact that this portion of the prophetic writings is placed after the *former prophets*. Like the former prophets: Joshua, Judges, Samuel and Kings, the latter prophets are four in number: Isaiah, Jeremiah, Ezekiel and the Twelve (the twelve minor prophets being counted as one).

The *latter prophets* are sometimes called, the *writing prophets*, since their authors wrote down their utterances (Isaiah 8:1; 30:8; Habakkuk 2:2) for preservation in permanent form (Jeremiah 30:2; 36:1-32). This basic fact is erroneously denied by the critics of the so-called school of *form-criticism*, who, following Hermann Gunkel's pioneer work in this field, assume (contrary to the internal evidence of the books themselves) that the prophet wrote practically nothing. Their sayings, it is supposed, were first presented orally and later committed to writing by their disciples or "sons," but only after the genuine words of the "father" prophet were swallowed up in a mass of additions and traditions by his "sons." However, although it is now impossible or very difficult to arrive at the *verba ipsissima* of the master, these incrustations by the "sons of the prophet" are supposedly related to the "father prophet" in the nature of a "corporate personality," one body dominated by one spirit.[1]

---

1 A. Bentzen, **Introduction II** (Copenhagen, 1949) p. 101 f. Cf. Sigmund Mowinckel: **Prophecy and Tradition: The Prophetic Books In the Light of the Study of the Growth and History of the Tradition** (Oslo, 1946), pp. 84-88.

The subjectivity and skepticism manifested in the pre-suppositions and methods of this school of criticism do not commend themselves to reverent and believing scholars. Rejection of the internal evidence of the prophetic books, which followers of this school may do at will by the subjective nature of their theory, and their inability to account for the beautiful unity and harmony of the prophetic writings justify the complete rejection of their methods and conclusions.

The latter prophets are commonly divided into major (Isaiah, Jeremiah, Ezekiel) and minor prophets (The Twelve).

I. THE CHARACTER OF OLD TESTAMENT PROPHECY

Because of superficial similarities between inspirational divination, widely practiced in the ancient Semitic world, and Old Testament prophecy, modern scholarship shows a tendency to reduce Israelite prophets to a common stature with those of surrounding nations. However, a comparison of Hebrew prophetism with divinatory phenomena of adjacent pagan peoples serves to bring into clearer focus the uniqueness of the prophetic feature of Old Testament religion.

1. Old Testament Prophecy Is Divine In Its Origin. The Hebrew prophet believed in one personal God, omnipotent and infinitely holy, whose spokesman he claimed to be. According to I Samuel 9:9 the prophet was in earlier Israel commonly called a *ro'eh*, that is one who perceives that which does not lie in the realm of natural sight or hearing. Another early designation of similar etymology was a *hozeh* "one who sees supernaturally" (II Samuel 24:11). Later the Hebrew seer was more commonly called a *nabhi'* (I Samuel 9:9). This popular name is to be related to Accadian *nabu*, "to call or announce", either passively, as Albright,[2] "one who is called" (by God), or actively with Koenig,[3] "an announcer" (for God), or preferably

2 From the Stone Age to Christianity, 1940, pp. 231 ff.
3 Hebraeisches und Aramaeisches Woerterbuch zum Alten Testament, 1936, p. 260.

with Guillaume,[4] who construes the term to mean that the prophet is the passive recipient of a message manifest in his condition as well as in his speech, and is "one who is in the state of announcing a message which has been given to him" (by God).

Accordingly, "Thus saith Jehovah" was the authoritative formula which stamped his inspired utterances with the finality and infallibility of a message directly from God. As God's mouthpiece he thus claimed special knowledge.

The pagan diviner, on the other hand, also claimed special knowledge as one in communication with superhuman spiritual beings (gods) who are revealed in Scripture to be demons (I Corinthians 10:20, 21). The source of Biblical prophecy is therefore divine, in contrast to the source of divination, which is demoniacal.

Gesenius,[5] over a century ago, plausibly but inconclusively connected *nabhi'* with the Hebrew root *nabha'* "to bubble forth". To the present day many scholars, building shaky arguments on the idea of ecstatic or excited utterance as the real basis of the prophetic message, erroneously overemphasize this element in Hebrew prophecy and put it on a par with the abnormal behaviour of a dervish.[6]

That ecstasy was sometimes present, especially in early Hebrew prophetism, cannot be denied. But it is a gross error to make it the predominant or even the common element in the behavior of the Hebrew seer. If the so-called "ecstasy" really contained confusion, it could not be by the Spirit of God, "for God is not a God of confusion" (I Corinthians 14:33). In such a case it must be attributed to the intrusive influence of the same demon power energizing heathen prophets and dervishes in their excesses. For it must ever be remembered

---

4 **Prophecy and Divination**, 1938, pp. 112 f.
5 **Thesaurus linguae Hebraeae et Chadaeae Veteris Testamenti**, II, 2, 1840, p. 838.
6 Cf. H. H. Rowley's sane criticism of this view in "The Nature of Prophecy in the Light of Recent Study," **Harvard Theological Review**, Vol. 38, Jan. 1945, pp. 1-88.

that the genuine prophet of the Lord, like anyone dealing in the spiritual realm, was exposed to demoniacal influence and consequent disorder and continually had "to prove the spirits" to see whether they were "of God" or not (cf. I John 4:1).

2. *Old Testament Prophecy Is Coeval With the Beginnings of Redemptive History.* Because the oracle of no prophet earlier than the eighth century B.C. is found in the second part of the second division of the Hebrew Canon, known as the "latter prophets," or the "writing prophets", the erroneous impression is frequently given that prophecy in the common use of the term was a later development in Israel. As a matter of fact, prophecy and written prophetical oracles go back to most ancient times and are coeval with the beginnings of divine revelation.

The *protevangelium* or "first prophecy" of a divine Redeemer (Genesis 3:15, 16) was spoken directly by God without the necessity of prophetic intermediation. Enoch, the seventh from Adam, was a prophet (Jude 1:14, 15); Noah uttered prophetic oracles (Genesis 9:25-27). The patriarchs, especially Abraham who is specifically called a *nabhi'* or "prophet" (Genesis 20:7; Psalm 105:12-15), were the recipients of visions and divine revelations. Moses was a prophet in a pre-eminent sense. While others from time to time received divine messages through dreams and visions, God spoke "face to face" with Moses (Numbers 12:6-8; Deuteronomy 34:10), who in his unique prophetic capacity was a type of the coming of the Prophet *par excellence,* The Lord Jesus Christ (Deuteronomy 18:18; cf. John 6:14; 7:40).

Revelation through prophecy from the Mosaic period onward was never absent from Israel (Deuteronomy 18:15). Even when prophetic revelation was rare, as in the time of the Judges, prophecy was not wholly dormant (Judges 4:4). From Samuel's time, whose prophetic activity stood out all the more clearly against the dearth of prophetic vision (I

Samuel 3:1), we hear of prophetic guilds or schools of the prophets (cf. I Samuel 10:10; 19:18-24 etc.). Until the close of Old Testament prophecy with Malachi, prophets appear continuously in Hebrew history. Prophecy rose to great literary heights in the pre-exilic oracles of Isaiah and Jeremiah.

3. *Old Testament Prophecy Is Moral and Spiritual in Its Purpose.*

The prophets, particularly those like Amos, Isaiah and Jeremiah, frequently appear in the role of social and political reformers, revivalists and stirring preachers of righteousness, in addition to prognosticators of judgment or blessing, as the occasion demanded. But the political and social aspect of the prophet's message was never primary. First and foremost his oracles were religious and spiritual, announcing the will of God to men, and calling for complete obedience to the divine word.

4. *Old Testament Prophecy Was Frequently Predictive In Its Content.*

The predictive element cannot validly be denied a vital, and often a large place in prophecy. Two common extreme views are to be avoided. Many modern writers tend to stress the other elements in prophecy so that sometimes they give the impression that prediction is not even an intrinsic element. On the other hand others present it as the sole element, or at least the only important element. This is equally fallacious. The prophet can, and often does, refer to the past and present, as well as the future, to establish the supremacy of Jehovah's word and the triumph of His will.

Although foretelling cannot be denied a very real place in prophecy, it was normally not prediction for its own sake or to establish the genuineness of the prophet, though this was occasionally the case (cf. Deuteronomy 18:22). Prophetic prognostication was rather a preview of the future arising from the exigencies of the present, either to warn the impious of judgment or to encourage the faithful in perseverance. Moreover it was always inseparably interwoven with the profoundly spiritual message the prophet was divinely commissioned to deliver.

Quite often, however, the prophet made prognostications of doom or blessing not arising out of the immediate events of his own times, or in certain cases, like Isaiah (chapters 40-66) or Ezekiel (chapters 40-48), he could be transported by the Spirit of prophecy to a future ideal standpoint, and see the more distant vistas from this vantage ground.

Despite their dark warnings of disaster and judgment, the prophets were ultimately optimists. They saw beyond the weary centuries of Israel's sin and chastisement to the establishment of the yet-future Davidic kingdom, the grand Golden Age, when Jehovah's will would be done and all Israelite hopes would be realized in the Messiah. They inspired confidence and hope because they themselves were supremely assured that the word they spoke was indeed the Word of God, and was consequently certain of fulfillment.

LITERATURE ON HEBREW PROPHECY

Wace, H., *Prophecy Jewish and Christian* (Milwaukee, 1911).

Hoelscher, G., *Die Propheten* (Leipzig, 1914).

Cornill, C. H., *Der israelitische Prophetismus* (13th ed., Berlin, 1920).

Robinson, T. H., *Prophecy and the Prophets in Ancient Israel* (London, 1923).

Graham, W. C., *The Prophets and Israel's Culture* (Chicago, 1935).

Guillaume, A., *Prophecy and Divination Among the Hebrews and Other Semites,* (New York, 1938).

Smith, J. M. P., *The Prophets and Their Times* (2nd ed. Chicago, 1941).

Rowley, H. H., "The Nature of Prophecy in the Light of Recent Study," in *Harvard Theological Review* (Vol. 38, Jan. 1945), pp. 1-38.

Alleman, H. C., and H. L. Creager, "Hebrew Prophets & Prophecy" in *Old Testament Commentary* (Philadelphia, 1948) pp. 53-64.

Elmslie, W. A. L., *How Came Our Faith* (New York, 1949) pp. 179-382.

Meek, T. J., *Hebrew Origins* (rev. ed., New York, 1950) pp. 148-183.

Rowley, H. H., editor, *Studies in Old Testament Prophecy* (New York, 1950).

II. The Major Prophets

This classification is based on the size of the books. Any one of the three major prophets is in itself larger than all the minor prophets combined. Daniel, usually reckoned as one of the major prophets in the English arrangement, appears in the third division of the Hebrew Canon—the Writings.

Isaiah

Isaiah (*Yesha'jahu*, Jehovah is salvation) is the greatest of the Hebrew prophets and orators. For splendor of diction, brilliance of imagery, versatility and beauty of style, he is unequalled. Correctly he has been called the "Prince of Old Testament Prophets."[7] His name gives the title to the first book among "the latter prophets." He lived and prophesied in Jerusalem from about 740 (the year King Uzziah died) till about 700 B.C. or somewhat later during the reigns of Uzziah, Jotham, Ahaz and Hezekiah, kings of Judah (1:1). He was married to a prophetess (8:3) and had two sons whose names were symbolic of emphases in his preaching (7:3; 8:3).

1. The Purpose.

Isaiah's mission centered in his efforts to save Judah from its idolatry and moral degeneracy. He did lay stress upon the social message as modern scholars correctly observe, but what they frequently fail to point out is that the prophetic emphasis went deeper than mere denunciation of the political corruption and moral depravity of the nation. As cause underlies effect, Isaiah struck at the root of the trouble and exposed the nation's basic sin, its wrong attitude and relationship to God re-

7 Cf. B. A. Copass, **Isaiah Prince of Old Testament Prophets** (Nashville, 1944).

vealed in its idolatry. Isaiah clearly perceived that a nation's social life is the direct product of its religious life, which he sought to purify and turn back to God.

Failing, however, to turn the nation Godward, as he was warned in his commission would be the case (6:9-12), he boldly announces the inevitable collapse of Judah and the preservation of a godly remnant (6:13). Through this small group would come untold blessing through the Messiah, who would effect world-wide redemption at His First Advent (9:2,6; 53:1-12, etc.), and national salvation and restoration for Israel at His Second Advent (2:1-5; 9:7; 11:1-16; 35:1-10; 54:11-17, etc.). It is because of the fact that Isaiah was imbued with the vision that his nation would one day be a Messianic nation to the world and a medium of universal blessing that he has been called the Messianic Prophet.

2...The Contents.

Part I. Prophecies of punishment and blessing from the standpoint of the Prophet's own time (1:1-35:10).

    a. Prophecies concerning Judah and Jerusalem (1:1-12:6).

        (1) General introduction (1:1-31).

        (2) Millennial blessing through cleansing (2:1-4:6).

        (3) Israel's punishment for her sins (5:1-30).

        (4) The prophet's call and commission (6:1-13).

        (5) Prophecy of Immanuel (7:1-25).

        (6) Prophecy of the Assyrian invasion (8:1-22).

        (7) Messianic prediction and warning (9:1-21).

        (8) Punishment of Assyria (10:1-34).

        (9) Millennial restoration and blessing (11:1-16).

      (10) Millennial worship (12:1-6).

    b. Prophecies against foreign nations (13:1-23:18).

        (1) Babylon (13:1-14:23).

        (2) Assyria (14:24-27).

        (3) Philistia (14:28-32).

(4) Moab (15:1-16:14).

(5) Damascus (17:1-14).

(6) Land beyond the rivers of Ethiopia (18:1-7).

(7) Egypt (19:1-25).

(8) Assyria's conquests in Egypt and Ethiopia (20:1-6).

(9) The desert, Dumah, Arabia, the valley of vision (21:1-22:25).

(10) Tyre (23:1-18).

c. Prophecy of the establishment of the Kingdom (24:1-27:13).

(1) The great tribulation (24:1-23).

(2) The character of the kingdom (25:1-12).

(3) The worship and testimony of restored Israel (26:1-27:13).

d. Prophecies concerning Judah in relation to Assyria (28:1-35:10)

(1) Prediction of the fall of Samaria (28:1-13).

(2) Warning to sinful Judah (28:14-29).

(3) Zion to be attacked (29:1-4).

(4) The attacker frustrated (29:5-8).

(5) Reasons for the trial (29:9-16).

(6) The blessing of final deliverance (29:17-24).

(7) Warning against an Egyptian alliance (30:1-14).

(8) Exhortation to rely on Jehovah for help (30:15-31:9).

(9) Deliverance from the Assyrian typifies future deliverance by Messiah (32:1-33:24).

(10) The Day of the Lord (34:1-17).

(11) Full kingdom blessing (35:1-10).

Part II. A historical connecting link (36:1-39:8).

Supplementary to the first part of the book and introductory to the last part, these chapters form a transition from the Assyrian to the Babylonian period.

a. Sennacherib's invasion (36:1-37:38).

b. Hezekiah's sickness and recovery (38:1-22).

c. Arrival of Babylonian envoys and Isaiah's prophecy of the captivity (39:1-8).

Part III. Prophecies of redemption and restoration from the idealistic standpoint of the Babylonian exile (40:1-66:24).

a. Comfort to the exiles in the promise of restoration (40:1-48:22).

(1) Message of comfort to the exiles prefiguring future Messianic restoration (40:1-11).

(2) The basis of comfort—God's incomparable character (40:12-31).

(3) The reason for comfort—Jehovah's vindication against idolaters by raising up Cyrus to deliver His people (41:1-29).

(4) The Comforter—Jehovah's Servant—His Person and work of redemption (42:1-25).

(5) The results of the comfort—the nation redeemed and restored (43:1-45:25); the downfall of the idols of Babylon (46:1-13) and Babylon itself (47:1-15).

(6) Exhortation of comfort to those who are to be delivered from the captivity (48:1-22).

b. Comfort to the exiles in the great prophecy of Messiah the Redeemer (49:1-57:21).

(1) His call and work as Israel's Restorer and the Judge of Israel's oppressors (49:1-26).

(2) His obedience and faithfulness (50:1-11).

(3) His assured redemption of Israel (51:1-52:12).

(4) His atonement and exaltation (52:13-53:12).

(5) His guarantee of Israel's restoration (54:1-17).

(6) His world-wide salvation (55:1-13).

(7) His warnings and promises (56:1-57:21).

c. Comfort to the exiles in the prophecy of the future glory of the nation (58:1-66:24).

(1) The obstacles to Israel's restoration and their removal (58:1-59:21).

(2) The glory of Jerusalem in the Messianic age (60:1-22).

(3) The blessings of Messiah's ministry for Israel and the world (61:1-11).

(4) The Divine solicitude for Jerusalem and its result (62:1-12).

(5) Messiah's conquest of Israel's enemies occasions grateful acknowledgement of past national deliverances (63:1-14).

(6) Prayer of the remnant (63:15-64:12).

(7) Jehovah's answer (65:1-25).

(8) Blessing of the Messianic kingdom (66:1-24).

3. *Authorship and Date.*

Until the period of the beginning of modern destructive criticism in the last half of the eighteenth century, the traditional belief in the Isaianic authorship of the entire book was practically universally held and unchallenged. Since J. C. Doederlein denied the Isaianic authorship of chapters 40-66 in his commentary in 1775, it has been a common practice to speak of an unknown or "second Isaiah," who supposedly wrote in the period immediately before the end of the Babylonian exile (c. 550-539 B.C.) B. Duhm in 1892 denied the unity of 40-66, postulating a Trito-Isaiah for 55-66, whose activity he placed in Jerusalem just before the time of Nehemiah. Duhm is followed with variations in date, notably by K. Elliger[8] and E. Sellin,[9] while numerous critics deny the unity of this section and resolve Trito-Isaiah into a school of writing, rather than attribute it to an individual. C. C. Torrey in 1928 in his book entitled *The Second Isaiah* adopted the position that chapters 34-66 (36-39 excluded) were by one author residing in Palestine, thus presenting a strong position for the unity of this section.

Critics substantially attribute the first part of the book

8 **Die Einheit des Tritojesaja** (Stuttgart, 1928).
9 **Neue Kirsche Zeitschrift** (1930), 73-93, 145-173.

(1-35) to Isaiah, except chapters 11, 12, 13:1-14:23; 21:1-10; 24-27, 32-35. The historical connecting link (36-39) is commonly viewed as inserted from II Kings 18:13-20:19, although it is more probable that the original was that found in Isaiah or that Isaiah was the author of both.

Critics claim that three independent lines of argument converge to demonstrate that chapters 40-66 are not the work of Isaiah but rather that of an unknown author toward the close of the Babylonian captivity. They argue from the internal evidence, the literary style and the theological ideas.[10]

a. The first critical claim that internal evidence showing that the standpoint of the writer of chapters 40-66 is the exile, precludes Isaianic authorship on the basis of the historic function of prophecy, is inconclusive. The argument is not that the standpoint of the writer is exilic. This is freely admitted. The question is whether under the influence of the Spirit of prophecy, a prophet may not be supernaturally projected into the future to describe coming events to a future generation. Critics who rule out the supernatural and admit at most a premonition or "brilliant intuition"[11] are compelled to deny the possibility of such an occurrence and must of necessity refuse Isaianic authorship to the second part of the book. But to do so on the basis of the *analogy of prophecy,* insisting that the prophets never throw themselves forward into an ideal standpoint in the future, except when the transference to that state is transient (e.g. Isaiah 5:13-15, 9:1-6 and 23:1, 14), is incorrect.

But the essential notion of prophecy, which is the direct operation of God's Spirit upon the faculties of man, cannot be circumscribed by time or space or understood at all apart from the supernatural. If such a transient projection into the future is admitted by the critics,[12] why may not so renowned a prophet as Isaiah have prophesied from such an ideal stand-

---

10 See S. R. Driver, **Introduction** (9th ed.), pp. 236-243.
11 Cf. Pfeiffer, **Introduction**, p. 423.
12 Cf. Driver, **op. cit.**, p. 237.

point throughout a lengthy section? Ezekiel does the same, being transported from Babylon in the twentieth year of the captivity and brought by divine revelation "into the land of Israel . . ." and "set . . . upon a very high mountain . . ." (Ezekiel 40:2) to behold from the idealistic future standpoint of the millennium, the extended vision of the millennial temple and Israel in the land during the future Kingdom Age (Ezekiel 40-48). Similarly, Ezekiel is brought "out in the Spirit of the Lord . . ." and set down in the midst of the valley "full of bones . . ." (37:1). In this case the prophet is projected into the ideal standpoint of Israel's final world-wide dispersion and regathering. John was evidently projected into the day of the Lord (Revelation 1:10) to behold in extended vision the events of that future period (Revelation 4:1-19:21). Paul was "caught up to the third heaven . . . into paradise, and heard unspeakable words, which it is not lawful for a man to utter" (II Corinthians 12:2-4).

To rule out the Isaianic authorship of chapters 40-66 on the basis that it violates the "historic function of prophecy" is unwarranted. The prophet, says Driver, "speaks always, in the first instance, to his own contemporaries; the message which he brings is intimately related with the circumstances of his time; his promises and predictions, however far they reach into the future, nevertheless rest upon the basis of the history of his own age and correspond to the needs which are then felt."[13]

The question is, were not the words of consolation of the so-called "Second Isaiah" appropriate for the faithful and evidently persecuted believers in the early reign of Manasseh? Certainly, to them the idea of the exile was by no means an unknown event. Isaiah had repeatedly foretold it (5:5, 15; 10:20-24; etc.). More than that, the process of the exile had already set in. It had received notable confirmation in Sennacherib's invasion of Judah, and, especially, in the fall of the Northern Kingdom (722-21 B.C.). Isaiah's glowing prophecies

13 **Op cit.**, p. 237.

of restoration, it must be remembered, embrace not merely the two southern tribes immediately threatened, but the ten northern tribes as well (Isaiah 11:11-13; 49:6) which were already in captivity.

With Jerusalem so lately on the brink of disaster in Sennacherib's invasion and the flagrant idolatry, profligacy and fiery persecution of Manasseh's reign bringing suffering and death to the faithful (II Kings 21:16), little wonder the aged prophet considered the exile as not merely imminent, but already begun, and devoted his closing years to a description of a glorious restoration to comfort the persecuted faithful remnant of his day. As was usual with the prophets, who did not always realize the time interval which had to elapse between prophesied events, it was not revealed to him that Manasseh's long reign and Hezekiah and Josiah's reforms would delay the impending exile almost a century and a half.

b. The second critical claim that differences in style between the two sections of the Book confirm the non-Isaianic authorship of chapters 40-66 is also inconclusive.

The literary argument is always precarious, for it assumes that a writer may not change his style, especially in the course of a long literary career (in Isaiah's case forty years or more), or that a different subject may not alter his choice of words and expressions. Moreover, it is frequently arbitrary and subjective and practically valueless by itself. We can only know an author's style by the book which bears his name. To derive our knowledge of his diction from only part of that book on the presumption that he wrote it and then to deny his authorship of the rest of it is reasoning in a circle.

To these difficulties in the matter of style another is added which casts further suspicion on the whole literary argument— the similarities between the two sections. To explain these, some critics have suggested that the "Second Isaiah" was a disciple of the first, filled with his spirit. According to some critics, these similarities caused the editors to append this section to Isaiah's genuine prophecies. But this is embarrassing to the critical contention. If the similarities are real, why require another author? Why not emphasize them and explain the differences?[14]

c. The third critical claim that differences in theological ideas of the two sections indicate separate authorship is the weakest of all.

These differences are not alleged to be contradictory to those of Isaiah, but broader and more elevated. God's majesty is supposedly emphasized by Isaiah, God's infinitude by the "Second" Isaiah. The prominent idea of a remnant in Isaiah (6:13; 37:31 f.) is supposedly unemphasized in the "Second Isaiah." But these and other alleged differences can be accounted for in the same way as matters of style, and when the theological conceptions of the "Second Isaiah" are found to be quite similar to those of his contemporary, Micah, the contention of the critics loses its force.

4. Unity of the Book.

Besides the weakness of the critics' arguments, there are other reasons for holding to the unity of the book which commend themselves to conservative Bible scholars.

a. The New Testament witnesses to the Isaianic unity of the entire book.

Passages from the second part of the book are quoted as Isaiah's by John the Baptist (Matthew 3:3; Luke 3:4; John 1:23), by Matthew (8:17; 12:18-21), in John (12:38-41), where quotations are made from both parts of Isaiah and explicitly attributed to the man Isaiah; by Paul (Romans 9:27-33; 10:16-21). The weight of this argument cannot be dismissed by saying that the New Testament writers do not go into matters of technical introduction. This is true, but the manner of quotation, as in John 12:38-41, is so direct and personal that the actual author is meant. It may not simply indicate

---

14 For differences see Driver, op. cit., pp. 238-240; similarities, J. Raven, Introduction, pp. 190-192.

that all these quotations were made from the book that was then circulating under the name of the prophet Isaiah. For believing scholarship the infallible witness of the New Testament is sufficient.

b. Implicit allusions to the second part of Isaiah in pre-exilic prophets sustain the Isaianic authorship.

Zephaniah 2:15 shows acquaintance with Isaiah 47:8, 10. Nahum 1:15 echoes Isaiah 52:7. Jeremiah displays knowledge of Isaiah's prophecies (Jeremiah 31:35 with Isaiah 51:15; Jeremiah 10:1-16 with Isaiah 41:7 and 44:12-15).

c. Unbroken tradition supports the Isaianic unity of the entire book.

Nowhere in the book itself, in the Bible or in Jewish or Christian tradition is there mention or even a hint of two or more authors. Like the "Hexateuch," the "Deutero-Isaiah" and "Trito-Isaiah" are figments of the modern critical school. As in our Bibles, so in Josephus' day (A. D. 90), Isaiah was one book, not two. The Jewish historian specifically states that Cyrus read about himself in the prophecies of Isaiah (Antiquities XI:1:1f. Isaiah 41:2f; 44:26-28; 45:1-6, etc.).

In Jesus' day the book was considered a unity, and also in the first century B.C. and earlier, as the Isaiah manuscript of the Dead Sea Scrolls shows and as the book of Ecclesiasticus (48:22-25) indicates. The words "He (i. e. Isaiah) comforted them that mourn in Zion" (Ecclesiasticus 48:24) employs the same word used in the Septuagint of Isaiah 40:1 and in the original the same Hebrew word as in Isaiah occurs. This, the earliest tradition concerning the authority of Isaiah, knows nothing of a "Second Isaiah," but does know "Isaiah the prophet," "who was great and faithful in his vision."

This testimony involves the critical argument in difficulty. If the "Second Isaiah" was so great, the greatest of the Hebrew prophets according to many, both from a literary and theological point of view, why did his reputation dwindle so suddenly till, by the second century B.C., he was lost in anonymity, and his great masterpiece confused with a much lesser light, Isaiah, whose stature had so phenomenally increased that Ecclesiasticus gives him such high praise?

d. Evidence that the author of Isaiah 40-66 was a Palestinian favors Isaianic unity of the entire prophecy.

Local color and familiar knowledge of the land and religions of Babylon expected of one who is supposed to have been among the captives is absent. On the other hand, mention is made of Jerusalem, the mountains of Palestine, native Palestinian trees (41:19; 44:14). Such passages as 41:9; 43:14; 45:22; 46:11 and especially 52:11 confirm the Palestinian point of view rather than the Babylonian. C. C. Torrey's *Second Isaiah*, although arguing for a different author for the second section, presents a valuable defense of the unity of chapters 40-66 and of Palestinian authorship.

e. Passages in 40-66, evidently pre-exilic in character, favor Isaianic unity.

Critics list those that they claim prove an exilic standpoint.[15] These are explainable on the basis of the ideal (not actual) standpoint of the prophet. On the other hand, there are other passages which could scarcely have been written during the exile, such as 62:6, which presents the walls of Jerusalem as standing, or 40:9, which portrays the cities of Judah as still in existence.

Conclusion

Taking all factors into consideration, the Isaianic authorship of the entire prophecy is the most constructive view and the position which is least encumbered by difficulties. The anonymity of the second part of Isaiah, and the uncertainty which characterizes the critical approach, besides the clash with the infallible testimony of the New Testament, are a standing embarrassment to those who attack the Isaianic unity of the book. Those who grant the supernatural in Biblical prophecy

15 See Driver, *op. cit.*, p. 237.

and comprehend the varied phenomena of its operation will find no valid reason to discard the traditional view of Isaianic authorship of the whole book in favor of modern views, *which are largely dictated by skepticism with regard to the supernatural.*

LITERATURE ON ISAIAH

Cheyne, T. K., *The Prophecies of Isaiah* (5th ed., New York, 1889); *Introduction to the Book of Isaiah* (London, 1895).

Gray, G. B., *Introduction and Commentary* (chapters 1-27); *Int. Crit. Com.* (1912).

Oesterley, W. O. E., *Studies in Isaiah,* 40-66 (London, 1916).

Smith, G. A., *The Book of Isaiah in the Expositor's Bible,* Vol. III.

Duhm, B., in *Handkommentar zum Alten Testament* (4th ed., 2 vols., 1922, 1925).

Torrey, C. C., *The Second Isaiah* (New York, 1928).

Simcox, C. E., "The role of Cyrus in Deutero-Isaiah" in *Jour. Am. Or. Soc.,* LVII (1937), 158-171.

Smith, S., *Isaiah,* Chapters XL-LV, *Literary Criticism and History* (Schweich Lectures, London, 1940).

Kissane, E., *The Book of Isaiah,* Vols. I, II (Dublin, 1941).

CONSERVATIVE LITERATURE

Delitzsch, F., *Biblical Commentary on the Prophecies of Isaiah* (2 Vols., Edinburgh, 1890).

Calvin, J., *Commentary on the Prophet Isaiah* (reprint Grand Rapids, 1948), Vols. I-IV.

Boutflower, C., *The Book of Isaiah in the Light of the Assyrian Monuments,* I-XXXIX (London, 1930).

Baron, D., *The Servant of Jehovah, Exposition of Isaiah 53* (London, 1922).

Kelly, W., *An Exposition of Isaiah* (London, 1916).

Jennings, F. C., *Studies in Isaiah* (New York, 1936).

Copass, B. A., *Isaiah Prince of Old Testament Prophets* (Nashville, 1944).

Alexander, J. A., *Commentary on the Prophecies of Isaiah,* Vols. I, II (Edinburgh, 1865).

Von Orelli, C., *The Prophecies of Isaiah,* (Edinburgh, 1899).

Smith, R. P., *Authenticity and Messianic Interpretation of Prophecies of Isaiah Vindicated* (1862).

Hengstenberg, E. W., *Christology of the O. T. and a Commentary on the Messianic Predictions*, Vol. II, 1856, pp. 1-354.
Gaebelein, A. C., *The Prophet Isaiah (Our Hope)*, (New York, 1911).

JEREMIAH

The book of Jeremiah's prophecies is named after the prophet himself, *Yirmeyahu* or *Yirmeyah*. A great deal is known about his career from his prophetic call (1:2, 3) in the thirteenth year of Josiah's reign to the eleventh year of Zedekiah (c. 626-586 B.C.). His ministry accordingly extended over the last tragic forty years of the Kingdom of Judah to the destruction of Jerusalem and the deportation of its inhabitants to Babylon. After the fall of the city, Jeremiah was allowed to remain under the protection of Gedaliah. After Gedaliah's murder, however, he went with some Jews to Egypt (43-44). There he spent the last years of his life.

1. The Purpose.

Jeremiah's prophecies are directed as a stern warning to Judah and Jerusalem to turn away from idolatry and iniquity in order to avoid the inevitable punishment of the Seventy Years' Captivity in Babylon (25:1-14). The prophet's messages, necessarily severe and iconoclastic (1:10), met with intense opposition from all classes of a society which had become honeycombed with evil and fanatically attached to pagan idolatry. Despite persecution and continued danger of death, Jeremiah faithfully proclaimed his message of condemnation and doom, by word, sign and symbol.

The prophet's ministry was exercised during a tense international situation involving a three-sided contest for world supremacy between Assyria, Egypt and Babylon. Predicting the triumph of Babylon and the consequent captivity of Judah, Jeremiah repeatedly warned against alliance with Egypt. The moral and spiritual causes of the captivity are plainly set forth in the dominant note of doom pervading his messages. On the other hand, Messianic passages of hope flash through his prophecies, pointing to a better day (cf. 23:5f; 30:4-11; 31:31-34; 33:15-18). Final restoration of Israel (not to be confounded with the return from Babylon) is to be accomplished after a period of unparalleled tribulation (30:3-10) through the manifestation of David's righteous Branch Jehovah—tsidkenu (23:6; 30:9). The prophecy is yet to be fulfilled (Acts 1:7; 15:14-17) in the future millennial kingdom (Roman 11:25-29).

2. *The Contents.*

Introduction: The Prophet's Call (1:1-19).

Part I. Prophecies against Judah and Jerusalem (2:1-45:5).

    a. During the reigns of Josiah and Jehoiakim (1:1-20:18).

        (1) First sermon—sin and ingratitude of the nation (2:1-3:5).

        (2) Second sermon—devastation from the north (3:6-6:30).

        (3) Third sermon—threat of exile (7:1-10:25).

        (4) Fourth sermon—the broken covenant and the sign of the girdle (11:1-13:27).

        (5) Fifth sermon—the drought (14:1-15:21). The sign of the unmarried prophet (16:1-17:18). The warning concerning the Sabbath (17:19-27).

        (6) Sixth sermon—the sign of the potter's house (18:1-20:18).

    b. At various periods till the fall of Jerusalem (21:1-39:18).

        (1) Punishment upon Zedekiah and the people (21:1-29:32).

        (2) Future Messianic Kingdom (30:1-33:26).

        (3) Zedekiah's sin and the loyalty of the Rechabites (34:1-35:19).

        (4) Jehoiakim's opposition (36:1-32).

(5) Jeremiah's experiences during the siege (37:1-39:18).
  c. After the fall of Jerusalem (40:1-45:5).
    (1) Jeremiah's ministry among the remnant in the land (40:1-42:22).
    (2) Jeremiah's ministry in Egypt (43:1-44:30).
    (3) Jeremiah's message to Baruch (45:1-5).
Part II. Prophecies against the nations (46:1-51:64).
  a. Against Egypt (46:1-28).
  b. Against Philistia (47:1-7).
  c. Against Moab (48:1-47).
  d. Against Ammon (49:1-6).
  e. Against Edom (49:7-22).
  f. Against Damascus (49:23-27).
  g. Against Arabia (49:28-33).
  h. Against Elam (49:34-39).
  i. Against Babylon (50:1-51:64).
Part III. Historical Appendix: Fall and captivity of Judah (52:1-30). Liberation of Jehoiachin (52:31-34).

3. *Authorship and Authenticity.*

That Jeremiah "the son of Hilkiah, of the priests that were in Anathoth in the land of Benjamin" (1:1) wrote the book which bears his name is supported by a number of valid arguments.

a. The internal evidence supplied by the book itself supports Jeremian authorship.

The prophet dictated to his secretary, Baruch, all his prophecies from the beginning of his ministry till the fourth year of Jehoiakim (Jeremiah 36:1-4), which comprise well over half of the prophet's ministry. After this roll was destroyed by king Jehoiakim (36:23), Jeremiah dictated another edition, which included many additions to the first roll (36:32). This is not the present book we have, since many sections of Jeremiah bear a later date in his prophetic career

(e. g. 21:1, 24:1, etc.) and others show evidence of being composed in the latter part of his ministry. Internal evidence points to the fact that the prophet is the author of the entire book with the possible exception of chapter 52, probably added to his prophecies, at his own suggestion, from II Kings 24:18-25:30 with which it is practically identical.

b. The apparent composite character of the book is explained by the nature of its composition.

It was written in several stages, as the book itself indicates. The earlier edition was destroyed, as we have seen, then reissued with additions. Later prophecies were collected and doubtless edited by Baruch. These factors suggest why the contents are not always arranged in strict systematic order or chronological sequence. On the other hand, the wide divergence between the Septuagint and the Massoretic Hebrew is not easy to explain and seems to point to two different forms of the book.

c. Jeremian authenticity of the book is certain and is supported by external proof.

There are explicit references to the prophecy in the Old Testament. Daniel alludes to the prediction of the seventy-year captivity (Daniel 9:2, Jeremiah 25:11-14, 29:10). This prophecy and the general period of Jeremiah and the exile are confirmed by II Chronicles 36:21 and Ezra 1:1. Extra-canonical evidence does the same. Ecclesiasticus attributes the destruction of Jerusalem to the rejection of Jeremiah's warning and prophecies (Ecclesiasticus 49:6,7). Josephus (*Antiquities* X, 5:1) and the Talmud (*Baba Bathra* 14b-15a) confirm the same fact. The New Testament makes both explicit and implicit allusions to the prophecy of Jeremiah. Matthew 2:17, 18 quotes Jeremiah 31:15. Matthew 21:13, Mark 11:17 and Luke 19:46 quote from Jeremiah 7:11. Romans 11:27 amplifies Jeremiah 31:33 f. Hebrews 8:8-13 quotes Jeremiah 31:31-34. To this evidence Christian tradition adds its continuous testimony to the authenticity of the book.

d. Modern critical theories fail to disprove Jeremian authenticity.

These are largely subjective. For example, Pfeiffer[16] imagines that Baruch, in preparing an edition of the book of Jeremiah, combined the prophet's book with his own, reworking many of the prophet's speeches in his own "deuteronomistic style." Even the book of Baruch was later extensively revised with both prose and poetic additions. Such a procedure on the part of a pious disciple like Baruch is incredible. Bentzen rejects the idea that Baruch was the author of the "deuteronomistic sections." He thinks that Jeremiah fell into the hands of "deuteronomistic zealots," who used him "in their propaganda."[17] Other critics such as H. Birkeland,[18] assume that the book contains several complexes of traditions of Jeremiah's words, some preserving the old poetical forms, others cast in the style of deuteronomistic preaching. The whole idea of a nucleus of traditions subsequently expanded is without foundation in fact. The critics have no valid substitute for Jeremian authenticity of the prophecy.

LITERATURE ON JEREMIAH

Cheyne, T. K., *Jeremiah, His Life and Times* (*Men of the Bible*) (New York, 1888).

Driver, S. R., *The Book of the Prophet Jeremiah* (London, 1906).

Peake, A. S., in *The New Century Bible* (2 vols., 1910-1912).

Streane, A. W., in the *Cambridge Bible* (1913).

Binns, L. E., in *Westminster Commentaries* (1919).

Lofthouse, W. F., *Jeremiah and the New Covenant* (London, 1925).

Welch, A. C., *Jeremiah, His Time and His Work* (Oxford, 1928).

Volz, P., *Der Prophet Jeremia* (3rd ed., Tuebingen, 1930).

Gordon, T. C., *The Rebel Prophet* (New York, 1932).

Krocker, J., *Jeremia* (Giessen, 1937).

Herntrich, V., *Jeremia der Prophet* (Guetersloh, 1938).

May, H. G., "The Chronology of Jeremiah's Oracles," *Jour. Near East. Stud.* (Oct., 1945), pp. 217-227.

16 **Introduction**, p. 505.
17 **Introduction** (1949), p. 119.
18 **Zum hebraeischen Traditionswesen** (1938), p. 42.

CONSERVATIVE LITERATURE

Keil, C. F., *The Prophecies of Jeremiah* (2 vols., Edinburgh, 1874).

Allis, O. T., "A Modernistic View of Jeremiah," in *Princeton Theo. Rev.*, Vol. 23, 1925, pp. 82-132.

Stewart, A., "Jeremiah—The Man and His Message," in *Princeton Theo. Rev.*, Vol. 26, 1928, pp. 1-40.

Vos, G., "Jeremiah's Plaint and its Answer," in *Princeton Theo. Rev.*, Vol. 26, 1928, pp. 481-495.

Ironside, H. A., *Notes on the Prophecy and Lamentations of Jeremiah* (New York, rev. ed., 1928).

EZEKIEL

This book, like the prophecy of Jeremiah, takes its name from the prophet whose writings it records. *Yehezkel* ("God is strong") was the son of a priest named Buzi and most certainly a priest himself (1:3). He was deported to Babylon in 597 B.C., together with king Jehoiakim. The prophet's wife died the day the siege of Jerusalem began, 588 B.C. (24:1, 15-18), at which time he was living in Babylonia at a place called Tel-abib (1:1; 3:15) by the river of Chebar, which was a great canal southeast of Babylon. A. Bentzen is of the opinion that Tel-abib was a concentration camp peopled with deported Jews used for forced labor in the irrigation system of Babylonia.[19]

In 593 B.C., the fifth year of the captivity of king Jehoiakim, Ezekiel began his prophetic ministry (Ezekiel 1:1-3:21), when he was perhaps thirty years old (cf. 1:1). He continued his active ministry for twenty-two years at least until March-April 571 (Ezekiel 29:17), his last dated utterance. It is uncertain whether he lived to see the liberation of king Jehoiakim in 560.

1. *The Purpose.* While Jeremiah was predicting the destruction of Jerusalem to those not yet taken captive, Ezekiel was unceasingly prophesying the same fate for the unrepentant city (chapters 1-24). However, unlike the other major

19. A. Bentzen, *Introduction II* (1949), Vol. II, p. 123.

prophets, Isaiah and Jeremiah, his ministry exercised in exile did not have the emphasis of social and political reformation. His dominant note was rather comfort and exhortation to the discouraged captives comprising "all the house of Israel" (cf. 37:11, 15-24). He was necessarily more a writer than a speaker.

Ezekiel's mission of consolation was directed toward showing that Jehovah was justified in sending his people into captivity. This is the dominant theme from chapter 8 to chapter 33, verse 20. The complaint of the discouraged exiles was "The way of the Lord is not equal (right or just)" (18:25, 29; 33:17, 20). Ezekiel's message from the Lord was "Hear now, O House of Israel, Is not my way equal? are not your ways unequal?" (18:25). Proof is presented that instead of blotting them out as God had done with other nations who had committed similar abominations, His dealings with them, His people, were preventive and corrective to teach them to "know that He was God," that the surrounding nations, who were jubilant over their fall, would be judged (25:1-32:32) and that the nation would finally be restored in millennial blessing (33:1-48:35).

The phrase "they shall know that I am God" occurs more than thirty times in the book from 6:7-39:28. This repeated declaration that their punishments would bring about this happy result was amply fulfilled. The Babylonian captivity cured the Jews of idolatry. Up to that time, despite everything, they continually fell into idolatry. From that day forward, however, whatever sins the Jews have been guilty of, they have not been idolaters.

2. *The Contents.*

Introduction: The Prophet's call and commission (1:1-3:27).

Part I. Prophecies against Judah and Jerusalem (4:1-24:27).

a. Their destruction predicted by sign, symbol (4, 5) and prophecies (6, 7).

b. Vision of Jerusalem's sin (8) and its punishment (9-11).

c. Necessity of punishment because of universal corruption (12-19).

d. Last warning before Jerusalem's fall (20-24).

Part II. Prophecies against surrounding nations (25:1-32:32).

a. Against Ammon (25:1-7).

b. Against Moab (25:8-11).

c. Against Edom (25:12-14).

d. Against Philistia (25:15-17).

e. Against Tyre (26:1-28:19).

f. Against Sidon (28:20-26).

g. Against Egypt (29:1-32:32).

Part III. Prophecies of the final restoration of Israel (33:1-48:35).

a. Events preceding the establishment of the Kingdom (33:1-39:29).

(1) The wicked are to be purged out (33:1-33).

(2) False shepherds to give way to One True Shepherd (34:1-31).

(3) Restoration of the land (36:1-15).

(4) Restoration of the people (36:16-37:28).

(5) Judgment of Israel's enemies (38:1-39:24).

(6) Vision of the restored nation (39:25-29).

b. Worship in the Kingdom (40:1-48:35).

(1) The millennial temple (40:1-43:27).

(2) The millennial worship (44:1-46:24).

(3) The millennial land (47:1-48:35).

3. *Authorship and Date.*

Until comparatively recent times, all schools of criticism, even the most radical, have not seriously denied the genuineness and unity of the book of Ezekiel. Except for sporadic exceptions, literary criticism accepted the book as it stands. As late as 1924 Gustav Hoelscher complained that the critical knife had been laid on practically all the prophetical books of the canon except Ezekiel.[20] Accordingly, following the method known from the Jeremiah commentary of Duhm, he proceeded arbitrarily to dissect the book, leaving not much more than one-tenth of it to Ezekiel—the comparatively few rythmical sections, plus part of the visions in 1, 8-9, 11:24-25, and part of the narratives in 4-6. The rest, the prosaic parts, he assumes to be the actual work of the real authors of the book, supposed to have lived in the fifth century. V. Herntrich,[21] although essentially rejecting Hoelscher's theses, follows the same approach to the book, as does W. A. Irwin, who rejects chapters 40-48 entirely and accepts as genuine only about 250 verses of the rest.[22] C. C. Torrey (1930) rejected the authenticity of the book, representing it as a pseudepigraph of Palestinian origin to be dated about 230 B.C.[23] N. Messel (1945) advocates a similar approach, placing the book also in Palestine, but sometime after the period of Nehemiah, about 400 B.C.[24] A. Bentzen says, "The book as it now stands is no authentic work of the prophet Ezekiel."[25]

The story of negative criticism is the same. It begins in doubt and ends in utter confusion and uncertainty, demonstrated by the varied and contradictory views of recent scholars. As Bentzen says with regard to Ezekiel, "We have, accordingly, come to a point in the history of research which has been reached in most of the O. T. books. Its authenticity has been given up."[26]

---

20 **Hesekiel, der Dichter and das Buch** (Giessen, 1924), p. 1.
21 **Ezechielprobleme** (1932).
22 **The Problem of Ezekiel** (Chicago, 1943).
23 **Pseudo-Ezekiel and the Original Prophecy** (New Haven, 1930), p. 150.
24 **Ezechielfragen** (Oslo, 1945) and in his commentary in the Norwegian translation of the Old Testament by Michelet, Mowinckel and Messel (Vol. III, 1944).
25 **Introduction** II (1949), p. 125.
26 **Loc. cit.**

The reverent Christian student, on the other hand, who firmly believes in and has a vital knowledge of the supernatural in his own experience, need not be swayed by the critics' futile attempts to solve the so-called "problem of Ezekiel," which is largely their own creation because of their unbelief in the supernatural. Since few books of Scripture are more replete with supernatural vision and apocalyptic imagery, which like the book of Daniel, seem to be extended in the book of Revelation, it was inevitable that the skeptical knife of criticism would sooner or later cut up the book, despite the manifold evidences of its genuineness and unity, which the older critics like Cornill, who is hardly to be accused of uncritical blindness, freely admitted.[27] The evident arrangement and plan, the careful and correct dating of the prophecies, the use of the first person and the clear-cut purpose all point to the traditional view that Ezekiel himself composed the entire book.

LITERATURE ON EZEKIEL

Cornill, C. H., *Das Buch des Propheten Ezechiel* (Leipzig, 1886).

Redpath, H. A., in the *Westminster Commentaries* (1907).

Davidson, A. B., in the *Cambridge Bible* (1916).

Burrows, M., *The Literary Relations of Ezekiel* (Philadelphia, 1925).

Buttenwieser, M., "The Date and Character of Ezekiel's Prophecies," *Hebrew Union College Annual VIII* (Cincinnati, 1930).

Harford, J. B., *Studies in the Book of Ezekiel* (Cambridge, 1935).

Matthews, I. G., Ezekiel (*An American Commentary to the Old Testament*), Philadelphia, 1939.

CONSERVATIVE LITERATURE

Fairbairn, P., *Ezekiel and the Book of his Prophecy* (3rd ed., Edinburgh, 1863).

Keil's *Commentary on Ezekiel* (Edinburgh, 1866).

Hengstenberg, *The Prophecies of Ezekiel* (Edinburgh, 1869).

Kelly, W., *Notes on Ezekiel* (London, 1876).

Boyd, J. O., "Ezekiel and the Modern Dating of the Pentateuch," *Princeton Theo. Rev.* (VI, 1908), pp. 29-51.

27 **Einleitung,** p. 176.

Gaebelein, A. C., *The Prophet Ezekiel* (New York, 1918).

Mackay, C. M., in the *Princeton Theo. Rev.*, "The City and The Sanctuary" XX, 1922, pp. 399-417, "Ezekiel's Sanctuary and The Wellhausen Theory" (XX, 1922, 661-665). "The City of Ezekiel's Oblation" (XXI, 1923, pp. 372-388); "Ezekiel's Division of Palestine Among The Tribes" XXII, 1924, pp. 27-45.

Grant, F. W., and J. Bloore, Ezekiel in *The Numerical Bible* (New York, n. d.).

Unger, M. F., "The Temple Vision of Ezekiel" in *Bibliotheca Sacra* 105 (Oct., 1948), pp. 418-432; 106 (Jan., 1949), pp. 48-64; 106 (Apr., 1949), pp. 169-177. "Ezekiel's Vision of Israel's Restoration" (Ez. 37) in *Bibliotheca Sacra* 106 (July, 1949), pp. 312-324; 106 (Oct., 1949), pp. 432-445; 107 (Jan., 1950), pp. 51-63.

III. THE MINOR PROPHETS

Besides Isaiah, Jeremiah and Ezekiel the second part of the second division of the Hebrew Canon called the *Latter Prophets* contains another book called *The Twelve,* making a total of four in this section, as in the former prophets. *The Twelve* had already been grouped together in the early second century B.C. at the time of the son of Sirach (Ecclesiasticus 49:10). Josephus refers to them as comprising one book (*Against Apion* I, 8, 3). Subsequent Jewish and Christian tradition allude to them as "The Twelve" or "The Book of the Twelve Prophets." From Augustine's time the Latin Church employed the title "Minor Prophets" with reference to their brevity in comparison with the "Major Prophets." The order in the Hebrew Canon is apparently partly chronological but other now-unknown factors entered the arrangement.

HOSEA

Hosea (Hebrew, *Hoshea,* "salvation"), who bore the name used once of Joshua (Numbers 13:16) and the same borne by Hoshea, the last ruler of the Northern Kingdom (II Kings 15:30), was a contemporary of Amos and Isaiah. The span of his prophetic ministry is indicated in the superscription to the book. "In the days of Uzziah (767-739), Jotham (739-

735), Ahaz (735-715), and Hezekiah (715-686), kings of Judah, and in the days of Jeroboam II, (781-753) . . . king of Israel" (Hosea 1:1). Hosea's activity extended well beyond Jeroboam's death into the period of assassination and civil war, in which Zachariah (753), Shallum (752), Menahem (752-741), Pekahiah (741-739), Pekah (739-731) and Hosea (731-722) reigned till the fall of the Northern Kingdom (722-21). Since there is no reference to the fall of Samaria, some scholars view the reference to Hezekiah and the other Judean kings in 1:1 as a later interpolation.[28] This is unnecessary for the recorded prophecies of Hosea are doubtless only a compendium of his activity, which extended, we may believe, into the early years of Hezekiah's reign (c. 715 B.C.). Whether the prophet was carried into the Assyrian Captivity, we do not know. Like the future Jeremiah in the case of Judah he was called to pronounce final judgment upon Israel and sing her funeral dirge.

1. The Purpose.

Hosea is the apostle of God's unchanging love for Israel. Despite the fact that the nation had sunk to the lowest depths of apostasy and idolatrous immorality, the prophet labored unceasingly to warn the people to repent and to show them that God *still loved them*. Although Hosea's theme is fourfold: Israel's idolatry, wickedness, captivity and restoration—God's enduring love for the nation is interwoven throughout. Israel is set forth as Jehovah's adulterous wife, shortly to be put away, but ultimately to be purified and restored. These momentous events are portrayed in the divine instructions to the prophet to marry an unfaithful woman. The offspring of this union are given names symbolic of Hosea's chief prophecies: Jezreel, the dynasty of Jehu is to be wiped out (fulfilled in the murder of Jeroboam's son, Zachariah in 753); Lo-ruhamah, "not shown mercy," a prophecy of the Assyrian captivity; Lo-ammi, "not my people," temporary rejection of the people; Ammi, "my people," final restoration of the nation in the end time (Hosea 1:2-2:23).

2. *The Contents.*

Part I. Repudiation and restoration of Israel, the faithless wife of Jehovah (1:1-3:5).

a. The first symbolic marriage (1:1-2:23).

(1) Israel rejected—birth of Jezreel, Lo-Ruhamah, Lo-ammi (1:1-9).

(2) Israel comforted (1:10-11).

(3) Israel chastised (2:1-13).

(4) Israel restored (2:14-23).

b. The second symbolic marriage (3:1-5).

(1) The marriage itself—Hosea told to marry an adulteress, but immediately separates himself from her until she amends her life (3:1-3).

(2) The symbolic meaning—by captivity the people will be prepared for restoration (3:4, 5).

Part II. The triumph of the divine love in the restoration of the repentant nation (4:1-14:9).

a. Israel's guilt (4:1-19).

(1) The general charge (4:1-5).

(2) Willful ignorance (4:6-11).

(3) Idolatry (4:12-19).

b. The divine displeasure (5:1-15).

c. The repentant remnant's call (6:1-3).

d. The response of Jehovah (6:4-13:8).

e. The final restoration (13:9-14:9).

3. *Authorship and Authenticity.*

The entire book is unquestionably the work of "Hosea, the son of Beeri . . ." (1:1). Its unity is commonly admitted even by the critical school. Two types of passages are, however, sometimes denied to Hosea by the criticism of the late nineteenth century, namely, those dealing with Judah and those promising restoration and blessing. But actually there is no sufficient reason for denying to Hosea any of the prophecy. The tendency of more recent criticism is to view fewer passages as later interpolations. Oesterley and Robinson, for example, while admitting the "possibility, even the probability" that certain passages in which Judah is mentioned may be later interpolations, by no means insist upon it, and, regarding the passages on restoration, assert that the evidence "does not justify us in dogmatically asserting that they are not the work of Hosea himself."[29] A. Bentzen follows a similar conservative trend.[30]

The divine authority and authenticity of the book is vouched for by numerous quotations found in the New Testament (cf. Hosea 11:1 with Matthew 2:15; Hosea 6:6 with Matthew 9:13; 12:7; Hosea 10:8 with Luke 23:30; Hosea 2:23 (Heb. 2:25), with Romans 9:25; Hosea 13:14 with I Corinthians 15:55; Hosea 1:9, 10 and 2:23 and (Heb. 2:25) with 1 Peter 2:10.

LITERATURE ON HOSEA

Pusey, E. B., *The Minor Prophets with a Commentary*, Vol. I (New York, 1885).

Harper, W. R., *Amos and Hosea* in the *Int. Crit. Comm.* (New York, 1905).

Batten, L. W., "Hosea's Message and Marriage" in *Jour. Bib. Lit.*, 48, 1929, pp. 257-273.

Brown, S. L., on *Hosea* in the *Westminster Commentaries* (1932).

Nyberg, H. S., *Studien zum Hoseabuche* (Upsala, 1935).

Feinberg, C. L., *Hosea: God's Love For Israel* (New York, 1947).

Bewer, J., Hosea in *The Book of the Twelve Minor Prophets*, Vol. I (New York, 1949).

JOEL

Joel ("Jehovah is God") was the "son of Pethuel" (1:1) and prophesied in Judah and Jerusalem. He was probably a priest as his frequent apostrophes to the priesthood might suggest.

---

29 **An Introduction to the Old Testament**, p. 349.
30 **Introduction II** (1949), p. 133.

1. Date.

Since the book is undated and there is sparse chronological evidence to aid the critic, the prophecy has been variously placed from the division of the kingdom (932) till the time of Malachi or even later. That the book is a unit, the product of one author, is freely admitted by most critics. The safest date is pre-exilic. The time of Joash (835-796) best fits the prophecy.

In favor of this view several reasons may be mentioned. The position of the book between Hosea and Amos suggests that Jewish tradition regarded it to be early. Moreover its spirit and style are unlike the post-exilic prophets, Haggai, Zechariah and Malachi, and clearly belong to the period of Hebrew classical literature. The language of Joel is reminiscent of Amos. It seems that the latter actually made use of Joel (Cf. Joel 3:16 with Amos 1:2; Joel 3:18 with Amos 9:13). Significant also is the absence of any mention of a king in the book. Mention is made of only priests and elders. This fact fits admirably into the circumstance that Joash was a minor under the guardianship of the high priest Jehoida. In addition, the enemies of Judah mentioned are the Phoenicians and Philistines (3:4), and the Egyptians and Edomites (3:19), not the Syrians, Assyrians and Babylonians, who were the chief foes of Israel from Amos' time to the exile.

The arguments of Driver, Merx, Cornill, Oesterley, Robinson and others for a post-exilic date are inconclusive. The reference of Joel 3:2 is said to allude to the exile, but this is clearly a predictive passage of Israel's present diaspora and not a reference at all to the Babylonian captivity. The mention of the sale of Jewish prisoners to the Greeks (Jevanim or "Ionians") does not call for a post-exilic date since these people are referred to in Assyrian records of the eighth century B.C. Much is made, too, of the lack of any reference to a king, idolatrous places of worship, or the Northern Kingdom.

But this argument from silence is pointless, since mention of these is also missing in Nahum, Jonah, Obadiah and Zephaniah.

2. *Authorship.*

The authorship of the entire book by "Joel the son of Pethuel" (1:1) was denied as early as 1872 by M. Vernes, who maintained that chapters 3 and 4 were not by the same author as 1 and 2. J. W. Rothstein, 1896, followed by Sievers, Duhm and P. Haupt, also denied the unity of the book. These views, however, have not met with general acceptance, being refuted sufficiently by the uniform plan and style of the book.

3. *Contents.*

Part I. A prophetic type of the day of the Lord (1:1-20).
    a. The prophet presented (1:1).
    b. An unprecedented locust plague depicted (1:2-7).
    c. The afflicted people exhorted to repent and pray (1:8-20).

Part II. The prophecy of the day of the Lord itself (2:1-32; *M.T. 2:1-3:5).
    a. The invading northern army (2:1-10).
    b. Jehovah's army at Armageddon (2:11).
    c. The repentant remnant in the land (2:12-17).
    d. Jehovah's response to the remnant (2:18-29; M.T. 2:18-3:2).
    e. Signs preceding the day of the Lord (2:30-32; M.T. 3:3-5).

Part III. The prophecy of the judgment of the nations (3:1-16; M.T. 4:1-16).
    a. Israel restored (3:1; M.T. 4:1).
    b. The nations judged (3:2, 3; M.T. 4:2, 3).
    c. The Phoenicians and Philistines specially condemned (3:4-8; M.T. 4:4-8).

* The M.T. referred to on the following pages is the Massoretic Text.

d. The nations challenged to war and judgment (3:9-16; M.T. 4:9-16).

Part IV. The prophecy of full kingdom blessing (3:17-21; M.T. 4:17-21).

    a. Jerusalem's exaltation (3:17; M.T. 4:17).

    b. Judah's Prosperity (3:18; M.T. 4:18).

    c. Egypt and Edom's desolation (3:19; M.T. 4:19).

    d. Jerusalem's exaltation explained (3:20, 21: M.T. 4:20, 21).

LITERATURE ON JOEL

See C. H. H. Wright, *An Introduction To The O. T.* (New York, 1890) pp. 204 f. for older literature.

Dennefeld, L., *Les Problemes du livre de Joel* (Paris, 1926).

Smith, J., W. H. Ward, J. Bewer, *Joel* in *Int. Crit. Comm.* (New York, 1911).

Kapelrud, A. S., *Joel Studies* (Uppsala, 1948).

AMOS

Amos ("burden"), the author of the book which bears his name, was a herdsman or shepherd and dresser of sycamore fruits by incision (7:14) from Tekoa (1:1), located about ten miles south of Jerusalem in the hill country. He was not of the priestly or prophetic line, but of a humble and obscure family, as we may conclude from the omission of his father's name. He was called from his rustic occupation to be a prophet to the whole family of Jacob (3:1, 13) but principally to the Northern Kingdom (7:14, 15), exercising his ministry chiefly at the main sanctuary of the Northern Kingdom at Bethel (7:10). Although he denounced sin also at Samaria (3:9-12; 4:1-3) and possibly at Gilgal (4:4; 5:4, 5), his denunciation of the sin of the Northern Kingdom and his prophecy of its destruction stirred up the wrath of the high priest Amaziah, who reported Amos to Jeroboam II as a traitor. It was doubtless shortly after his return to Tekoa that he reduced his chief prophecies to writing, which have survived in the book bearing his name.

1. Date.

The prophecy can be fairly accurately dated from the chronological data of the superscription (1:1) in the age of Jeroboam II of Israel (c. 782-753)[31] and Uzziah of Judah (c. 767-740). As these two kings were contemporaneous from about 767-753 a date between 765-755 B.C. would not be far afield for the prophetic ministry for Amos.

The period was one of great wealth and prosperity. As a result of Jeroboam's successful campaign against the Moabites and the Aramaeans, the borders of Israel reached their widest extent since the days of Solomon (II Kings 14:25; Amos 6:14). Luxurious living, idolatry and moral corruption were the subjects of the fiery denunciations of the simple rustic prophet.

Beyond the warning of judgment and final captivity upon the sinful people, the prophet envisions the glories of the yet-future millennial kingdom (9:11-15).

2. Contents.

Part I. Judgments upon surrounding nations including Judah and Israel (1:1-2:16).
    a. Superscription (1:1).
    b. Judgment upon six neighboring nations (1:2-2:3).
        (1) Upon Damascus (1:3-5).
        (2) Upon Philistia (1:6-8).
        (3) Upon Phoenicia (1:9-10).
        (4) Upon Edom (1:11-12).
        (5) Upon Ammon (1:13-15).
        (6) Upon Moab (2:1-3).
    c. Judgment upon Judah and Israel (2:4-16).
        (1) Upon Judah (2:4, 5).
        (2) Upon Israel (2:6-16).
Part II. Jehovah's indictment of the whole family of Jacob (3:1-9:10).
    a. Three addresses of condemnation (3:1-6:15).

---

31 Edwin R. Thiele's dates are used **Jour. Near East. Studies III (1944)** p. 184.

(1) Divine punishment certain (3:1-15).

(2) Past chastisements unavailing (4:1-13).

(3) Divine punishment imminent (5:1-6:15).

b. Five symbolic visions of punishments (7:1-9:10).

(1) The locust plague (7:1-3).

(2) The drought (7:4-6).

(3) The plumb line (7:7-9) with an historical insertion (7:10-17).

(4) The fruit basket with application (8:1-14).

(5) The Lord standing upon the altar (9:1-10).

Part III. Future kingdom blessing of restored Israel (9: 11-15).

a. Messiah's return and establishment of the Messianic reign (9:11, 12).

b. Millennial prosperity (9:13).

c. Restored Israel (9:14-15).

3. *Authenticity.*

Comparatively few critical questions are connected with the prophecy. Practically all critics concede its substantial integrity, except for 1:9, 10; 1:11, 12; 2:4, 5; three doxologies 4:13; 5:8; 9:5-6 and the Messianic passage 9:11-15, which are commonly regarded as later glosses or additions.[32] The assumptions upon which these passages are generally regarded as additions, however, are unwarranted and underlie an erroneous theory of the religious development of Israel. Oesterley and Robinson regard 9:11-12 as certainly presupposing the exile since it refers to the Tabernacle of David as having fallen.[33] But A. Bentzen is correct in pointing out that Amos considered the House of David as fallen "because it had lost the position which it had occupied in David's own time, not as a consequence of the events of 587, which he had not seen."[34]

The divine authority of the book is attested by the New

---

32 Cf. A. Bentzen, Introduction II (1949), p. 141.
33 An Introduction to the Books of the O. T. (London, 1934), p. 366.
34 Op. cit., p. 142.

Testament. Stephen in his speech before the Sanhedrin (Acts 7:42, 43) quotes from Amos (5:25-27). James, addressing the Jerusalem Council (Acts 15:16), also cites the prophet (Amos 9:11).

LITERATURE ON AMOS

Pusey, E. B., *The Minor Prophets* (1861).

Keil, C. F., *The Twelve Minor Prophets* (1888).

Schmoller, O., *The Book of Amos* (Lange's Commentary, 1874).

Cooke, G. A., and E. A. Edgehill on *Amos* in the *Westminster Commentaries* (1913).

Cripps, R. S., *A Critical and Exegetical Commentary on the Book of Amos* (London, 1929).

Weiser, A., *Die Prophetie des Amos* (Giessen, 1929).

Morgenstern, J., *Amos Studies* in *Hebrew Union College Annual* XI-XV (Cincinnati, 1936-40).

Gordis, R., *Harvard Theological Review* 33 (1940), pp. 239-251.

Bewer, J., *Amos* in *The Book of the Twelve Prophets Vol. I* (New York, 1949).

OBADIAH

The book of Obadiah (from the Hebrew meaning "The servant or worshipper of Jehovah") is the shortest prophecy and the smallest book of the Old Testament. The name itself is quite common from the time of David onward. The prophecy concerns itself wholly with the denunciation of Edom for its unbrotherly conduct toward Judah, with a prophecy of its utter destruction and Judah's salvation in the day of the Lord.

1. Date.

Great disagreement prevails concerning the date of the prophecy. Critics generally ascribe it to the Chaldean period after the fall of Jerusalem (586 B.C.) and deny the unity of the book. Pfeiffer holds that the original oracle against Edom is preserved in two editions (Obadiah 1-9 and Jeremiah 49:7-22). He dates Obadiah 1-14, 15b about 460 B.C. and 16-21, which he styles "apocalyptic fancies," even later. Oesterley and Robinson view the book as a collection of oracles from "almost any time between the end of the sixth and the middle of the second centuries B.C."[35] The commentary of Robinson in Eissfeldt's *Handbuch*, divides the prophecy into seven fragments issuing from various periods after 587 B.C.

It is best to hold to the unity of the prophecy and to date it during the reign of Jehoram c. 848-841 B.C. During his rule the Philistines and Arabians overran Judah and plundered Jerusalem (II Chronicles 21:16, 17 cf. Joel 3:3-6, Amos 1:6). At that time the Edomites were bitter enemies of Judah (II Kings 8:20-22, II Chronicles 21:8-20). This historical context meets all the demands of the prophecy. In addition, the prophet Amos (c. 760) shows acquaintance with Obadiah (Cf. Obadiah 1:4 with Amos 9:2; Obadiah 1:9, 10, 18 with Amos 1:11, 12; Obadiah 1:14 with Amos 1:6, 9; Obadiah 1:19 with Amos 9:12 and Obadiah 1:20 with Amos 9:14). Jeremiah, too, doubtless used the prophecy (cf. Obadiah 1:1-6 with Jeremiah 49:7-22). Then, too, the place of Obadiah after Amos, suggests a pre-exilic origin.

2. *Contents.*

Part I. Edom's destruction prophesied (1:2-9).

    a. Dislodged from her impregnable fortresses (1:2-4).

    b. Completely plundered and deserted (1:5-9).

Part II. The cause of Edom's downfall (1:10-14).

    a. Violence against Jacob (1:10-14).

Part III. The day of Jehovah (1:15-21).

    a. Judgment upon Edom and all nations (1:15, 16).

    b. Salvation of the house of Jacob (1:17-20).

    c. The millennial kingdom (1:21).

LITERATURE ON OBADIAH

Peckham, G. A., *An Introduction to the Study of Obadiah* (Chicago, 1910).

Robinson, T. H., "The Structure of the Book of Obadiah" (*Journ. Theo. Stud.* 17, 1916, 402-408).

35 **An Introduction, p. 370.**

Wade, G. W., on *Obadiah* in the *Westminister Commentaries* (1925).
Lanchester, H. C., on *Obadiah* in the *Cambridge Bible* (1918).

JONAH

Jonah ("dove") was the son of Amittai and a prophet of Gath-Hepher in Zebulon, north of Nazareth. He prophesied under Jeroboam II (c. 782-753, Thiele's dates) that Israel would regain its ancient boundaries (II Kings 14:25). The book which bears his name, unique in that it is not a collection of Jonah's prophecies, but a biographical account of Jonah's ministry in Nineveh, shows that God's grace reached beyond Israel to embrace the nations.

1. Literary Character.

The story has been variously viewed as myth, legend, parable, prophetic allegory or history. But there is not the slightest reason to stumble over the miraculous in the book and to regard the work as unhistorical. The marvels recounted, the storm, the sea monster, Jonah's experiences and others are not a whit greater or more incredible than those which honeycomb all Scripture, the exodus, the pillar of cloud and fire, manna from heaven, water out of the rock or the resurrection of Christ, which is directly connected with Jonah's experience in the great fish (Matthew 12:39-41; Luke 11:29-32).

The book is to be viewed as historical. The form of the book is unquestionably such (despite critical subterfuges to circumvent this) and is obviously designed to convey that impression to its readers. Jonah is undeniably an historical personage. It is highly artificial to maintain that Christ's words regarding Jonah in connection with His resurrection do not imply His belief in the historicity of the events, particularly since Jonah was an actual person. Ancient Jews regarded the account as historical (Josephus Antiquities IX, 10, 2). Jewish and Christian tradition has followed the same view. Neither Jonah's experience with the fish, nor the gourd (racinus), nor the conversion of the Ninevites, which is not said to be permanent, are incredible to enlightened faith.

The book is correctly evaluated not as mere history, for then it would have no proper place among the twelve minor prophets, but as *predictive* or *typical history*, written by a prophet and possessing a prophetic motif. As such it is of immense spiritual and prophetic value. Jonah in one aspect of his ministry typifies Christ in His specific character as The One sent by the Father, suffering entombment, raised from the dead and carrying salvation to the Gentiles. In another aspect of his mission Jonah foreshadows the nation Israel, a serious trouble to the Gentiles outside its own land, yet meanwhile witnessing to them, finally cast out by them, but miraculously preserved, in their future tribulation at the end of this age (Daniel 12:1) calling upon Jehovah, finding salvation and deliverance (Romans 11:25, 26) and then becoming missionaries to the Gentiles in the future earthly Davidic Kingdom (Zechariah 8:7-23).

2. *Author and Date.*

Under the view that the book of Jonah is predictive or typical history there is no reason to deny the tradition that Jonah himself was the author in the eighth century B.C. The presence of Aramaisms in the book, made so much of by Oesterley and Robinson and other critics, means nothing since such forms occur in early as well as late Old Testament books and are to be found in the Ugaritic epics dating from about 1400 B.C. Furthermore, the expression in 3:3 that "Nineveh *was* a . . . great city" does not imply a date after 600 B.C., as some contend, but simply indicates the size of the city as Jonah found it. Luke 24:13, which states regarding Emmaus that it "*was* from Jerusalem about threescore furlongs" is a parallel.

In addition, the period of Jonah coincides admirably with historical conditions at Nineveh. Under Semiramis, the queen regent and her son Adad-Nirari III (810-782) there was an approach to monotheism under the worship of the god Nebo somewhat comparable to the earlier monotheistic reforms of

Amenophis IV in Egypt. Either in the closing years of this reign or early in the reign of Assurdan III (771-754), Jonah appeared at Nineveh. Whether Jonah appeared later and the plagues recorded in Assyrian history in 765 and 759 and the total eclipse of 763 regarded as portents of divine wrath prepared the Ninevites for his message, we do not know. At any rate the period was propitious for such a reception of Jonah's preaching as we read about in the book.

3. *The Contents.*

Part I. Jonah's first commission and disobedience (1:1-2:10).

    a. The divine call and his attempted escape (1:1-3).

    b. The tempest at sea (1:4-7).

    c. His confession (1:8-12).

    d. His fate (1:13-17).

    e. His prayer and deliverance (2:1-10).

Part II. Jonah's second commission and its results (3:1-4:11).

    a. His obedience (3:1-4).

    b. Repentance of the Ninevites (3:5-9).

    c. The preservation of the city (3:10).

    d. The prophets wrath (4:1-4).

    e. The prophets reproof (4:5-11).

LITERATURE ON JONAH

Wilson, R. D., "The Authenticity of Jonah," in *Princeton Theo. Rev.* 16, pp. 280-298; 430-456.

Bird, T. E., *The Book of Jona* (London, 1938).

Trumbull, H. C., "The Reasonableness of the Miracle of Jonah" in the *Lutheran Church Review* (1911); *Jonah in Ninevah* (Philadelphia, 1892).

MICAH

Micah (*mikah* apparently abbreviated from *mikayahu* "who is like Jehovah") was a native of Moresheth near Gath (1:1) and was a younger contemporary of Isaiah. He was active under the reigns of Jotham (740-735); Ahaz (735-715), and

Hezekiah (715-687). Like Amos he was a simple villager and espoused the cause of the poor.

Micah predicted the fall of Samaria (1:5-7) as Hosea (1:5; 3:4; 5:9), Amos (2:6; 3:12, etc.) and Isaiah (7:8, 9; 8:4) also were doing. Like them he also foretold the inevitable desolation of Judah (Micah 1:9-16; Hosea 5:10; Amos 2:4; Isaiah 6:1, 11-13). Directed especially to Judah, Micah's prophesies nevertheless concern all Israel (1:1; 5-7).

1. Contents.

Part I. General prophecy of judgment (1:1-2:13).
Introductory (1:1).

   a. Judgment against idolatrous Samaria (1:2-8).

   b. Judgment against guilty Judah (1:9-16).

   c. Judgment upon oppressors (2:1-11).

   d. Mercy upon a remnant (2:12, 13).

Part II. The establishment of the Messianic kingdom (3:1-5:15).

   a. Preparatory judgment upon wicked rulers, false prophets and the nations (3:1-12).

   b. Character of the Kingdom (4:1-5).

   c. The setting up of the Kingdom (4:6-13).

   d. The first advent and rejection of the King (5:1-4).

   e. The interval between King's rejection and return (5:3).

   f. Events upon His Return (5:4-15).

Part III. The Lord's controversy with His people and His final mercy (6:1-7:20).

   a. The people's ingratitude and wickedness (6:1-7:6).

   b. The prophet's intercession(7:7-20).

2. Composition.

Critics of the negative school commonly deny the unity of Micah. Pfeiffer's view is characteristic. According to him chapters 1-3 consist of the prophet's own oracles, sections 2:12f., 4:1-5:15 (Hebrews 4:1-5:14) are interpolations, while

6:1-7:6 is viewed as a later anonymous prophecy with its own editorial appendix (7:7-20).

The theories of the critics are suggested by the fact that the theme of the book is not presented in close well-knit argument but consists of an extract, a mosaic of various discourses delivered by the prophet over an extended period of time and under different circumstances. This, however, is not a valid argument for denying authorship of the entire prophecy to Micah. There are numerous parallels in chapters 4-7 with writings in and near Micah's time.[36] Similarity of chapters 6-7 to Isaiah 40-66 indicates genuineness, rather than a late date, since Isaiah 40-66 was written by Isaiah, Micah's contemporary. The expression "Hear" (1:2, 3:1; 6:1), moreover, strongly suggests unity of authorship. The unsound theory of the evolutionary development of Israel's religious concepts, which erroneously insists that certain theological ideas found in Micah were not developed until a later date, has no objective evidence to support it. The careful conservative scholar will not allow his critical approach to be vitiated by this fallacy.

LITERATURE ON MICAH

Wade, G. W., on *Micah* in the *Westminster Commentaries* (1925).

Lindblom, J., *Micha, literarisch untersucht* (Helsingfors, 1929).

Sellin, E., *Das Zwoelfprophentenbuch* (*Kommentar zum Alten Testament*, 1929).

Robinson, T. H., *Die Zwoelf Kleinen Propheten* (O. Eissfeldt's *Handbuch zum Alten Testament*, 1938).

Copass B. A., and E. L. Carlson, *A Study of the Prophet Micah* (Grand Rapids, 1950).

NAHUM

Nahum ("consoler" or "comforter"), an Elkoshite, gives his name to this short prophecy. The location of Nahum's town, Elkosh, is uncertain. His prophetic ministry was exercised between the conquest of No-Amon (Thebes) in Egypt (3:8), regarded as a past event and which occurred 661 B.C. under Ashurbanipal and the destruction of Nineveh in 612 B.C.

---

36 See Raven Old Testament Introduction, p. 230.

Nahum's one subject is the destruction of Nineveh "the bloody city" (3:1). As C. H. H. Wright says, "The descriptions given by Nahum are exceedingly fine and vivid, and the book is deservedly classed among the finest productions of Old Testament literature."[37]

1. Contents.

Part I. A psalm of God's majesty (1:1-2:2).
    a. Superscription (1:1).
    b. God's vengeance upon sinners and goodness to His own (1:2-11).
    c. Restoration of Judah (1:12-2:2).
Part II. Prophecy of the fall of Nineveh (2:3-3:19).
    a. The siege and destruction of the city (2:3-13).
    b. Reason for Nineveh's fall (3:1-19).

2. Authorship.

Since about 1880 it has been customary in critical circles to deny 1:2-2:2 in substance to Nahum and to view 1:2-10 as the remains of a post-exilic acrostic poem later prefixed to Nahum's prophecy. Pfeiffer regards 2:3-3:19 (Hebrew 2:4ff.) as Nahum's triumphal ode and the intervening material in 1:11-2:2 (Hebrew 2:3) as partly redactional and partly an original section of the poem. The redactional part was supposedly added about 300 B.C. He denies that Nahum was a prophet and asserts that his poem on the fall of Nineveh was mistakenly viewed as a prophecy and preserved as a result of this misunderstanding.

The theory is too subjective to be taken seriously. If the introductory psalm was considered fitting by a redactor, why should it be arbitrarily denied the prophet? The acrostic idea of the psalm is based on violent emendations and rearrangements and the baseless assumption that the redactor wrote it from a faulty memory. Even if the acrostic arrangement could be proved, why deny it to Nahum?

---

[37] **Old Testament Introduction** (New York, 1890), p. 216.

LITERATURE ON NAHUM

Davidson, A. B., *Nahum* (*The Cambridge Bible*) 1905.

Arnold, W. R., "The Composition of Nahum 1:2 2:3" in *Zeitschrift fuer die altestamentliche Wissenschaft* vol. 21, pp. 225-265.

Smith, G. A., *Nahum* in *The Book of the Twelve Prophets* (*The Expositor's Bible*) rev. ed., 1929.

Haldar, A., *Studies in the Book of Nahum* (Uppsala, 1946).

HABAKKUK

The prophecy of Habakkuk takes its name from its author (1:1) of whom practically nothing is known, except that which may be inferred from his book. From the reference "to the Chief Musician on my stringed instruments" (3:19) combined with the reference to Habakkuk "as the son of Jesus of the tribe of Levi" in the apocryphal legend of Bel and The Dragon (1 f., Greek Version), some scholars such as S. Mowinckel[38] have concluded that the prophet was a member of the temple choir or a Levite.

1. Date.

It is not possible to date the prophecy precisely, but, because of the prophet's allusion to the Chaldean invasion (1:5, 6), the book can be placed in the general period of the rise of the neo-Babylon Empire around 625 B.C. Many critics prefer a date in the later part of Josiah's reign (c. 625-608) or in the reign of Jehoiakim (608-597). However, it is not impossible to place the book as early as the reign of Manasseh (687-642 B.C.), the son of Hezekiah, who foolishly showed the Babylonian envoys the treasures of Judah (II Kings 20:12-19) and thereby called forth Isaiah's prophecy of the Chaldean invasion. B. Duhm, E. Sellin and C. C. Torrey arbitrarily and without textual support alter *Kasdim* (Chaldeans) in 1:6 to *Kittim* (Cypriotes), asserting that the prophecy was directed against Alexander the Great and the Macedonians and date the book in that period.

---

[38] **Psalmenstudien III,** p. 109 f. Cf. also E. Sellin in his **Commentary** (2nd ed.).

2. Composition.

The book has suffered severely at the hands of exaggerated literary criticism. K. Marti, leaving only seven verses of the entire prophecy intact, is said by unconservative B. Duhm to treat the book just as cruelly as it is said in 3:13 Yahweh will treat the house of the ungodly. Although critics differ with regard to the unity of chapters 1 and 2, chapter 3 is more commonly derived from chapters 1 and 2 and dated in the fourth or third century (Pfeiffer). The theme of both is the same. Both contain linguistic similarities. Chapter 3 is specifically said to be a prayer of Habakkuk (3:1). The technical musical terms it contains need not be viewed as post-exilic, for they were evidently used in pre-exilic times with references to the Psalter.

3. Contents.

Part I. The prophet's two-fold complaint (1:1-2:20).
    a. The first complaint (1:1-11).
        (1) Israel's sin and God's silence (1:2-4).
        (2) God's response: the Chaldean invasion (1:5-11).
    b. The second complaint (1:12-2:20).
        (1) Chaldean cruelty and God's silence (1:12-2:1).
        (2) God's response: Israel's deliverance: Woes upon the Chaldeans (2:2-20).
Part II. The prophet's prayer (3:1-19).
    a. Title (3:1).
    b. Introductory petition (3:2).
    c. A theophany (3:3-15).
    d. An undisturbed trust (3:16-19).

4. Canonical Authority.

The prophecy has always enjoyed canonical authority both among Jews and Christians. The book is quoted prominently in the New Testament (compare Acts 13:41 with Habakkuk 1:5; Romans 1:17, Galatians 3:11 and Hebrews 10:38 with Habakkuk 2:4). The New Testament references give Habakkuk unusual importance theologically.

LITERATURE ON HABAKKUK

Walker, H. H., and N. W. Lund, "The Literary Structure of Habakkuk," *Jour. Bib. Lit.* 53, pp. 355-370.

Gruenthaner, M. J., "Chaldeans or Macedonians? A Recent Theory on the Prophecy of Habakkuk," in *Biblica*, VIII (1927) pp. 129-160; 257-289.

Bevenot, H., *Nahum and Habakkuk* (London, 1937).

Ward, W. H., *Habakkuk in Int. Crit. Com.* (1911).

ZEPHANIAH

Zephaniah ("Jehovah hides" or "protects") was likely a great-grandson of Hezekiah (1:1), although the omission of the words "the king" has caused some critics (i.e. A. Bentzen)[39] to deny this. However, if this is not the case, there is no adequate explanation of the prophet's departure from the usual custom of mentioning only the father in his superscription.

1. Date.

The prophet prophesied in the reign of Josiah (640-608 B.C.), evidently before the great reformation of 621 B.C. This is confirmed by such hints of historical conditions as the presence of foreign cults (1:4) and the allusion to Assyria (2:13). It is likely that Zephaniah had access to the court and was influential in helping to bring about the revival under Josiah. Nahum and Jeremiah were his contemporaries.

2. Contents.

Part I. The day of the Lord prefigured (1:1-3:7).

    a. In judgment upon Judah and Jerusalem (1:1-2:3).

    b. In judgment upon surrounding nations (2:4-15).

    c. In Jehovah's manifestation in the midst of sinful Jerusalem (3:1-7).

Part II. The establishment of the kingdom prophesied (3:8-20).

    a. The judgment of the nations (3:8-13).

    b. Israel's Messiah manifested as King (3:14-20).

39 **Introduction II** (1949), p. 154.

3. Composition.

Critics such as Stade, Kuenen, Wellhausen, Budde and Eissfeldt have questioned the authenticity of various parts of chapters 2 and 3, but on subjective and insufficient grounds. S. R. Driver says, "There is certainly no sufficient reason for questioning 2:1-3, 3:1-8, 11-13, the exhortation in 2:1-3, and the promise addressed to the remnant in 3:1-8, 11-13, are (to a prophet) the necessary complements of the denunciation in c. 1."[40] Oesterley and Robinson acknowledge that "the general authorship of the book has not been seriously doubted" although they note that different editors have found reason to suspect "considerable interpolations."[41] However, from a strictly objective view there is no reason to deny any of the prophecy to Zephaniah.

LITERATURE ON ZEPHANIAH

Pusey, E. B., *The Minor Prophets*, Vol. II (New York, 1892).
Smith, J. M. P., *Zephaniah*, Int. Crit. Com., 1912.
Davidson, A. B., *Zephaniah in Cambridge Bible*, 1920.
Smith, G. A., in *The Book of the Twelve* (Expositor's Bible), rev. ed., 1929.
Pilcher, C. V., *Three Hebrew Prophets and the Passing of Empires*, 1931.
Keil, C. F., *Minor Prophets*, Vol. II (reprint, Grand Rapids, 1949).

HAGGAI

Haggai (Hebrew, "Festal") was a contemporary of Zechariah and labored with him to encourage the returned exiles to finish rebuilding the temple, which, though began in the second year of Cyrus, 535 B.C., had been abandoned in despair because of difficulties and opposition.

In the second year of King Darius of Persia (520 B.C.), Haggai delivered his four prophetic messages, portions of which compose our present book. The first prophetic utterance (1:1-15) was delivered in August—September, 520 the second (2:1-9), September—October, 520, the third (2:10-19),

---

40 S. R. Driver, *Introduction* (9th ed., 1913), p. 843.
41 *An Introduction* (London, 1934).

November—December, 520 and the fourth (2:20-23), November—December, 520.

1. Contents.

Part I. Summons to rebuild the Temple (1:1-15).

Part II. Prophecy of the millennial Temple (2:1-9).

Part III. Promise of present blessing upon building the Temple (2:10-19).

Part IV. Prophecy of future destruction of Gentile world power (2:20-23).

2. Composition.

There are no convincing reasons why the entire book was not written by Haggai. Oesterley and Robinson, however, agree that these short addresses were originally spoken by Haggai, but they deny the book as it stands is from his hand, but is to be attributed very likely to a contemporary who recorded the salient points of the prophet's addresses. Two principal reasons are advanced to support this position. First, the addresses as we now have them are very greatly curtailed resumés; secondly, the prophet is always spoken of in the third person. Neither of these reasons are decisive. If Haggai wrote under inspiration, there is no reason why he might not have contented himself with short excerpts from his larger discourses, or used the third person.

LITERATURE ON HAGGAI

Perowne, J. J. S., *Haggai and Zechariah in The Cambridge Bible*, 1893.

Bloomhardt, P., "The Poems of Haggai," *Hebrew Union College Annual* V, 1928, 153-195.

Crafer, F., *The Books of Haggai and Zechariah* (Cambridge, 1920).

Morgan, F. C., *Haggai A Prophet of Correction and Comfort* (London, 1935).

ZECHARIAH

Zechariah (Hebrew, "Yahweh remembers") was the "son of Berechiah, the son of Iddo . . ." (1:1; Ezra 5:1; 6:14; Nehemiah 12:16). The name was common in Israel, being used also by an earlier pre-exilic prophet (II Chronicles 24:20; 26:5). Zechariah began his prophetic ministry two months after Haggai in October–November, 520 B.C. Their combined preaching resulted in the completion of the temple in 516 B.C. Haggai's total recorded prophetic ministry lasted but four months, Zechariah's about two years, the last dated prophecy being placed in November or December, 518 B.C. (Zechariah 7:1).

The last part of Zechariah's prophecy (chapters 9-14) is undated and must be put much later, probably after 480 B.C in the light of his reference to Javan or Greece. There is no serious reason against attributing a long ministry of some forty-five or fifty years to the prophet. He doubtless outlived Darius I The Great (522-486), whose exploits in saving the Persian Empire from civil war are recorded on the famous rock of Behistun. Zechariah began his ministry when Joshua was high priest and Zerubbabel civil governor.

1. Contents.

Introductory call to repentance (1:1-6).

Part I. Foregleams of the future Messianic kingdom (1:7-8:23).

    a. A series of eight night visions (1:7-6:8).
        (1) The man among the myrtle trees (1:7-17).
        (2) The four horns and smiths (1:18-21; M.T. 2:1-4).
        (3) The man with the measuring rod (2:1-13; M.T. 2:5-17).
        (4) Cleansing of the high priest (3:1-10).
        (5) The candlestick and the two olive trees (4:1-14).
        (6) The flying roll (5:1-4).
        (7) The woman in the ephah (5:5-11).
        (8) The four chariots (6:1-8).
    b. The symbolical crowning of the high priest (6:9-15).
    c. The answer to the question of the fasts (7:1-8:23).

(1) The question propounded and the Divine reply (7:1-14).

(2) The restoration of Jerusalem (8:1-5).

(3) The future return to the land (8:6-8).

(4) Future prosperity of the land and people (8:9-23).

Part II. Two prophetic burdens—the great Messianic future (9:1-14:21).

a. The first burden—first advent and rejection of Messiah-King (9:1-10:12).

(1) The advent (9:1-10:12).

(2) The rejection (11:1-17).

b. The second burden—second advent and acceptance of Messiah-King (12:1-14:21).

(1) Future deliverance and national conversion of Israel (12:1-13:9).

(2) The return of the Lord in glory (14:1-21).

2. *Character of the Book.*

George L. Robinson aptly describes Zechariah thus, "In the present writer's judgment his book is the most Messianic, the most truly apocalyptic and eschatological, of all the writings of the Old Testament."[42] While everyone may not agree with this appraisal of the general nature of the prophecy, it does point to a salient characteristic of the book. Zechariah abounds in prophetic allusions to the person, work and future glory of Christ, couched in symbolic and figurative language. He has more to say on this momentous subject than all the other minor prophets combined. Important Messianic predictions in Zechariah include The Branch (chapters. 3 and 6, cf. Isaiah 4:2, Jeremiah 23:5), Christ as King-Priest (6:13), Christ's triumphal entry into Jerusalem and coming Glory (9:9, 10), Christ as Shepherd betrayed (11: 12, 13), Christ crucified (12:10), the sufferings of Christ (13:7) and the second coming of Christ (chapter 14).

42 Int. Stand. Bible Ency., p. 3186.

3. Authorship.

The Zecharian authenticity of 1-8 is practically uncontested. Chapters 9-14, on the other hand, are subject to such wide contrariety of critical opinion that the resulting confusion should serve as a warning against too ready abandonment of the traditional view of Zecharian authorship. Some scholars assign all of chapters 9-14 to a pre-exilic author. Others stoutly maintain that the same section belongs to a late post-exilic period (Greek or Maccabean). Others just as confidently assign chapters 9-11 to one or more pre-exilic authors and chapters 12-14 to one or more post-exilic authors.

There are several reasons which favor the Zecharian authorship of the entire book. First, *this is the universal testimony of both Jewish and Christian tradition,* practically unbroken until Joseph Mede in 1653 opened the way for the interminable modern theorizings by concluding that chapters 9-11 were not the work of Zechariah. Secondly, *in both chapters 1-8 and 9-14 there are numerous quotations from and allusions to the earlier prophets. The second portion contains several references to the later prophets.* C. H. H. Wright has collated the references and shows that the second part of Zechariah[43] contains more references to the former prophets (Isaiah, Jeremiah, Ezekiel, Hosea and others) than the first portion. So overwhelming was the evidence for the post-exilic authorship of 9-14 that de Wette, who in the earlier editions of his *Einleitung* had adopted views contrary to the traditional view of Zecharian authorship, in later editions felt constrained to change his mind and admit that the evidence for post-exilic authorship was decisive. Thirdly, *the historical point of view of chapters 9-14 is post-exilic.* There is no allusion whatever to any reigning king of Judah or Israel. Messiah alone is recognized as king throughout, and the picture of the Messianic reign is essentially the same. Efforts to contrast Messiah's rule in 1-8 and 9-14 have been dismal failures. In both

43 **Zechariah and His Prophecies** Bampton Lectures, 1878, (London, 1879), pp. XXXV-XXXVIII.

portions of the book the house of Israel and Judah are regarded as one, a fact in accord with Jeremiah's time (cf. 1:19; 8:13; 9:10, 13; 10:6, 7). The reference to the sons of Greece (9:13) is post-exilic, but not necessarily post-Zecharian, as some critics maintain. The reference is to the Greeks of Zechariah's day (not the later Seleucids) and the picture is of defeat for Javan. The context is not a portrayal of an actual battle, but an apocalyptic vision of a future victory. It envisions the *end-time* defeat of Israel's enemies, resulting in the establishment of the kingdom. Fourthly, *similar rare expressions are found in both sections of the book.* For example, the unusual phrase "from passing through and returning" occurs in 7:14 and 9:8. The expression "saith the Lord" appearing some fourteen times in 1-8 appears in 10:12; 12:1, 4; 13:2, 7, 8 in the latter section. The phrase "Lord of hosts" is characteristic of both sections. The language of each part is pure Hebrew, markedly free from Aramaisms. The prosaic style of 1-8 in contrast with the poetic flourish of 9-14 does not necessitate a different author. As C. H. H. Wright aptly observes: "It is time . . . for modern critics to give up the assumption which is too often made that a writer who uses prose on one occasion may not also at another time be the author of poetry."[44]

Conservative Literature on Zechariah

Hengstenberg, E. W., "The Genuineness of Daniel and The Integrity of Zechariah" (Edinburgh, 1848).

Pusey, E. B., *The Minor Prophets* (New York, 1877).

Wright, C. H. H., *Zechariah and His Prophecies* (London, 1879).

Perowne, J. J. S., *Haggai and Zechariah* in *Cambridge Bible*, (1888).

Baron, D., *Visions and Prophecies of Zechariah* (London, 1918).

Robinson, G. L., *The Prophecies of Zechariah* (Chicago, 1896).

Gaebelein, A. C., *Studies in Zechariah* (New York, 1904).

Munro, W. D., "Why Dissect Zechariah?" *The Evangelical Quarterly* X. 1938, pp. 45-55.

Feinberg, C. L., *God Remembers* (Wheaton, Ill., 1950).

44 Op. cit., p. XLI.

MALACHI

Malachi (Hebrew, "My Messenger" or more likely a short-ened form of *malakiyah* "the messenger of Yahweh") is the last of the Old Testament prophets. Scarcely anything is known of his personal life. Critics are accustomed to deny that he was an historical person, assuming that the prophecy is anonymous and that *Malachi* is merely an appellative or sym-bolical expression for the mission of the real author, whose name was later suggested by the expression "my messenger" in 3:1. Despite the Septuagint, which renders 1:1 "by the hand of his messenger" (compare, however, "Malachias" in the title), and despite the supposition of Jonathan ben Uzziel in the Targum that Ezra the scribe is referred to, it is best to treat the ex-pression as a proper name, since none of the other major or minor prophetical books are anonymous, and this would be a strange exception. It is not necessary to assume that 1:1 is based upon 3:1, and concrete proof that this is the case is lacking.

1. Date and Authorship.

The book is obviously later than Haggai and Zechariah. The temple had not only been completed and sacrifices offered (1:7-10; 3:8), but enough time had elapsed for abuses and laxities to creep in, which Malachi unscathingly con-demns. Personal piety of priest and people had degenerated (1:6-8). Mixed marriages were contracted (2:10-12). Pay-ment of tithes had been neglected (3:8-10). A Persian gover-nor was installed in Jerusalem (1:8). This was scarcely Nehe-miah, who was recalled to the Persian court in 433. This period of Nehemiah's absence is accordingly a likely date for the composition of the book.

2. Contents.

Introductory appeal: God's love for Israel (1:1-5).
Part I. An oracle against the priests (1:6-2:9).
    a. Their neglect in liturgical functions (1:6-2:4).
    b. Their faulty instruction in the Law (2:5-9).

360 Introductory Guide to the Old Testament

Part II. Four oracles against Jewish laymen (2:10-4:3; M.T. 3:13-21).

    a. First oracle: charge of treachery (2:10-16).

    b. Second oracle: warning of judgment (2:17-3:6).

    c. Third oracle: call to repent (3:7-12).

    d. Fourth oracle: divine indictment (3:13-4:3; M.T. 3:13-21).

Part III. Concluding Warning (4:4-6; M.T. 3:22-24).

    a. To keep the law of Moses (4:4; M.T. 3:22).

    b. To look for the (second) coming of Christ (4:5, 6; M.T. 3:23, 24).

3. *Unity and Authenticity.*

The essential unity of Malachi has never been seriously questioned. Critics agree that editorial additions are few and slight. Cornill and Marti regard 2:11, 12 as a later interpolation, but their attack on the authenticity of these verses is not generally recognized as valid. On the other hand, 4:4-6 (Hebrew text 3:22-24) is more commonly taken by critics to be an interpretation of 3:1 and "probably a later commentary" (Bentzen). But this critical contention too is mere plausible fancy without objective evidence. The canonical and doctrinal authority of Malachi is attested by New Testament citation. Compare Malachi 4:5, 6 (Hebrew text 3:23, 24) and Matthew 11:10, 14; 17:11,12; Mark 9:10, 11; Luke 1:17. Compare Malachi 3:1 with Matthew 11:10; Mark 1:2 and Malachi 1:2, 3 with Romans 9:13.

LITERATURE ON MALACHI

Torrey, C. C., "The Prophecy of Malachi," *Jour. Bib. Lit.* 1898, pp. 1-15.

von Bulmerincq, A., *Der Prophet Maleachi*, Vols. I, II (Dorpat, 1926-1932).

Smith, J. M. P., *The Book of Malachi*, in *Int. Crit. Com.* (1912).

Part IV
THE WRITINGS

Chapter XII

THE MAJOR POETICAL BOOKS

THE THIRD PART of the Hebrew Canon, called the Writings (*Kethubhim*), comprises eleven books, three major poetical books, Psalms, Proverbs and Job, five Megilloth or Rolls, Song, Ruth, Lamentations, Ecclesiastes and Esther, and the three historical books, the prophecy of Daniel, Ezra-Nehemiah and Chronicles. In the Septuagint, the Writings are called Hagiographa. Job is reckoned among the historical books, being placed after Chronicles and before the Psalms, while Ruth follows Judges, and Lamentations comes after Jeremiah. The Septuagintal order was destined to determine the order of the books in later translations.

THE NATURE OF HEBREW POETRY

Although the Massoretes in editing our present Hebrew Bible recognized only three poetical books, Psalms, Proverbs and Job, the study of Hebrew versification in the past two hundred years has not only recovered poetic principles which have been lost for centuries, but has demonstrated that large sections outside these books, particularly in the prophetical writings, share in the form of poetry. In addition, the extensive archeological findings of the past century in Egyptian, Babylonian, Assyrian and Canaanite (Ugaritic) literature have placed Hebrew poetry in the illuminating background of general Oriental prosody and demonstrated that it shares many of the same forms and features of its neighbors. Although much is still far from clear, the general characteristics and forms of Hebrew poetry are gradually becoming better understood.

1. Hebrew poetry employs parallelism.

This basic relationship in Hebrew verse was first clearly defined by Robert Lowth in 1753,[1] although vaguely recognized earlier by Ibn Ezra (twelfth century) and Kimchi (13th century). It consists of a balance or distribution of thought sometimes called "sense rhythm," constituting thought-arrangement rather than word-arrangement as the basis of Hebrew versification. Lowth distinguished the three principal types of parallelism as synonymous, antithetic and synthetic.

Synonymous parallelism is the repetition of the same thought with equivalent expressions, the first line (stich) reinforcing the second, giving a *distich* or couplet:

"He that sitteth in the heavens shall laugh;
The Lord will have them in derision" (Ps. 2:4).

Antithetic parallelism is the repetition of a contrasting thought in the second line to emphasize or confirm the thought of the first:

"The young lions do lack, and suffer hunger:
But they that seek Jehovah shall not want any good thing" (Ps. 34:10).

Synthetic parallelism is the progressive flow of thought in which the second (or following) lines add something to the first or explain it:

"And he shall be like a tree planted by the streams of water,
That bringeth forth fruit in its season,
Whose leaf also shall not wither;
And whatsoever he doeth shall prosper" (Ps. 1:3).

Parallelisms may consist of couplets or distichs (Ps. 36:5), triplets or tristichs (Job 3:9), quatrains or tetrastichs (Ps. 1:3). This basic device of Hebrew poetry produces a musical effect pleasing to the ear and satisfying to the mind. It is invaluable

1 De sacra poesi Hebraeorum praelectiones academicae. English translation by G. Gregory, 1847.

as an aid to interpretation and in ferreting out textual corruptions.

Further refinements in parallelism have been made since Lowth's day.[2] *Emblematic* is a type in which the second or succeeding lines give a figurative illustration of the first (Ps. 42:1, 129:5-7). *Stairlike* parallelism consists of a repetition of part of the first line by the second or succeeding lines, which carry the thought forward (Ps. 29:1-2a). *Introverted* parallelism occurs in a quatrain when the first line is parallel to the fourth instead of the second, and the intervening lines are parallel (Ps. 137:5, 6; Ps. 30:8-10).

Important advance in the definition of parallelism was made by G. B. Gray in his *Forms of Hebrew Poetry* (1915). Gray carefully distinguished between *complete parallelism* (a, b, c, a', b', c',) as in Isaiah 1:3 and *incomplete parallelism* as in Psalm 29:1:—

"Give unto the Lord, O ye mighty,
Give unto the Lord glory and strength."

That is:

a. b. c. d.
a. b.   e. f.

Gray noted a wide variety of combinations in incomplete parallelism and thereby shed much light on the underlying causes of the beauty of Hebrew poetry.

2. Hebrew poetry possesses rhythm.

The work of such scholars as J. Ley, K. Budde, B. Duhm and others was foundational for later studies in Hebrew metrical forms. E. Siever[3] especially undertook the task of ascertaining the nature of rhythm in Hebrew poetry and attempted to deduce the existence of regular metre from it. The conclusion was that Hebrew versification was not qualitative in the strict sense of the term, in that it did not count syllables, but

---

2 See C. A. Briggs, **Int. Crit. Comm.** pp. XXXVI-XXXVIII (1907).
3 **Studien zur hebraeischen Metrik** (1901).

depended upon the number of accents. Lyric metre was found to be 2 plus 2 (Canticles), dirge or *qinah* 3 plus 2 (Lamentations) and epic or didactic 3 plus 3 (Job and Proverbs).

However a note or warning must be sounded with regard to the critical conclusions concerning metre. Modern scholars frequently assume that Old Testament poets had objective metrical rules in mind when they wrote. On the basis of this dubious assumption they justify radical textual emendations. But if we base our theory on the Hebrew text itself instead of superimposing an *a priori* theory of prosody upon it and altering the text to suit the theory, we shall be compelled to conclude that Hebrew poetry is rhythmical but not strictly metrical, in the sense of adhering to hard-and-fast rules governing balanced numbers of accented and unaccented syllables.

One must be extremely careful in using the term "metre" of foisting Occidental form of expression on an Oriental book, and using terminology which is analogous rather than precise. There is no evidence that the ancient Hebrew poets had a fixed code of prosody like the Greeks, although they wrote under deep emotion and expressed themselves rhythmically, unconsciously producing the phenomena which were later to develop into more definite ideas of metre. In other words, there is evidence that poetry in ancient Israel had a long career and preceded prosody.

Divisions of Hebrew poetry into stanzas, or strophes, is possible in some cases, as in most of the alphabetic acrostics, Ps. 119, Prov. 31:10-13, Lam. 1-4, but it does not follow that all Hebrew poetry is strophic. Early investigators held that strophes in a poem need not contain the same number of lines or verses, but must be symmetrical in arrangement. Recent scholars tend to assume that all the strophes of a poem must contain the same number of lines. Extensive alteration of the text necessitated by this assumption is an indication of its unsoundness.

3. Hebrew poetry is highly figurative.

Hebrew verse, especially, is rich in choice of words and vividness of imagery. It abounds in numerous rhetorical devices. Simile, metaphor, metonymy, synecdoche, hyperbole, alliteration and personification frequently occur and are used to great effect. The language itself, even in the form of prose, has a singularly rhythmic and musical quality admirably adapted to noble poetry.

In such a language we may well inquire what there can be to differentiate between prose and poetry. The answer is that in prose the rhythms are absolutely free. Those of poetry are evidently confined within certain limits. The extent and the precise definition of these limits is the task of the student of Hebrew poetical form, a study which despite substantial advance is still in its elementary stage.

LITERATURE ON HEBREW POETRY

Ley, J., *Die metrischen Formen der hebraeischen Poesie* (1886).

Ley, J., *Leitfaden der Metrik der hebraeischen Poesie* (Halle, 1887).

Sievers, E., *Studien zur hebraeischen Metrik* (1901).

Budde, K., "Hebrew Poetry," in *Hastings' Dictionary of the Bible*, IV (1902).

Duhm, B., "Poetical Literature," in *Encyclopedia Biblica* III (1902).

Cobb, W. H., *A Criticism of Systems of Hebrew Metre* (Oxford, 1905).

Gray, B. G., *The Forms of Hebrew Poetry* (London, 1915).

Dhorme, E., *La Poésie Biblique* (Paris, 1931).

Kraft, C. F., *The Strophic Structure of Hebrew Poetry* (Chicago, 1938).

McClellan, W., "The Elements of Old Testament Poetry," in *Catholic Biblical Quarterly* III (1941), pp. 203-213; 321-336.

THE PSALMS

The book of Psalms, Israel's ancient devotional treasury for temple and synagogue worship, nearly always stands first among the Writings. Its importance in New Testament times is attested by the fact that it could represent the entire third part of the Hebrew Canon (Luke 24:44). In Hebrew it is called *Tehillim* "Songs of Praise," or the fuller form *Sefer Tehillim,* "Book of the Psalms." The title "Psalms" is from the Greek, meaning music of a stringed instrument, or more generally a song adapted to such music.

1. Tradition of Davidic Authorship.

The Hebrew text contains 150 Psalms, arranged in five books according to an ancient pre-Septuagint scheme. Psalms 1, 42, 73, 90 and 107 mark the beginning of each book, which ends with a doxology. The general designation, "The Psalms of David," is due to the large number of the songs (seventy-three in all) which are expressly ascribed to David in the Hebrew titles.

Modern critics, however, are accustomed to deny the historical worth of the titles and the Davidic authorship of the Psalms in general. Julius Bewer expresses a common critical view when he calls the superscriptions "guesses," which "are without value" and asserts that "not one of them that can be accepted as correct."[4] O. Eissfeldt grants that one or two Psalms may have been written by David, but that this is not discoverable from the titles.[5] R. Pfeiffer maintains that none of the Psalms could have been written by David, not only because of supposed "anachronisms" but also because their "language, style, and religious conceptions . . . are radically different from those of his time."[6]

The radical conclusions, however, are based on an untenable theory of the evolutionary development of Israel's religion and highly subjective criteria of literary style. Alleged anachronisms upon fair treatment are found not to be such. For example, the Tabernacle of David's day is referred to in Psalm 68:35 (H. 68:36) rather than the Solomonic temple (cf. I Samuel 1:9; 3:3, II Samuel 12:20). Aramaisms in the light of the

4 The Literature of the Old Testament (New York, 1933), p. 342.
5 Einleitung in das Alte Testament (Tuebingen, 1934), p. 499.
6 Old Testament Introduction, p. 627.

Ras Shamra literature constitute no valid argument for a late date.

That David was the principal author of the Psalter, despite the contentions of negative criticism, is supported by the following reasons:

(a) *The historical books of the Old Testament give ample evidence of David's gifts as a musician and a poet.* His masterful lament over Saul and Jonathan (II Samuel 1:19-27) displays his remarkable poetical powers and the magnanimity of his heart. He is called "the sweet (excellent) psalmist of Israel" (II Samuel 23:1). He was a skilled harpist (I Samuel 16:16-18; 18:10). Amos, the prophet, praises him as a model poet and musician (Amos 6:5).

(b) *David was especially endued with the Spirit of God.* As a deeply spiritual worshipper of the Lord and in connection with his role as "the sweet psalmist of Israel," he is said to have been "raised up on high . . ." and to be "the anointed of the God of Jacob . . ." through whom "the Spirit of the Lord spake . . ." and whose word was in his tongue (II Samuel 23:1, 2). He was thus divinely empowered to write inspired psalms. The charismatic gift, which David enjoyed, is mentioned in various New Testament passages (Mark 12:36, Acts 2:25-31; 4:25, 26).

(c) *David's name is everywhere in the Old Testament closely connected with the origin, composition and publication of liturgical song* (II Samuel 6:5-15; I Chronicles 16:4; II Chronicles 7:6; 29:30).

(d) *The Psalter itself furnishes abundant evidence of Davidic authorship.* In most of the Psalms ascribed to David, events in the life of Israel's poet-king are clearly reflected. For instance, Psalm 23 reflects the experience of the youthful shepherd. Psalm 51 records the heart cry of the poet for cleansing after his sin with Bathsheba. Psalm 57 clearly contains the prayer of the future monarch when he fled to the wilderness from the murderous hate of Saul.

(e) *The Davidic authorship of certain Psalms is attested by the superscriptions.* These titles, anciently prefixed to the Psalms, are older than the Septuagint version and represent very ancient Hebrew tradition. They may not reasonably be set aside, except where valid proof can be adduced that they are not genuine. The Hebrew expression, *ledavid*, is normally taken to denote Davidic authorship.

(f) *Both the Old and New Testament cite certain Psalms as Davidic in origin.* Psalm 2 is so cited in Acts 4:25, 26; Psalm 16 in Acts 2:25-28; Psalm 18 in II Samuel 22:1, 2; Psalm 32 in Romans 4:6-8; Psalm 69 in Acts 1:16-20, Romans 11:9-10; Psalm 109 in Acts 1:20; Psalm 110 in Matthew 22:44, Mark 12:36, 37, Luke 20:42-44 and Acts 2:34.

Besides those assigned to David the ancient traditions preserved in the superscriptions ascribe other Psalms to Asaph (50, 73-80), the sons of Korah (42, 44-49, 84, 85, 87), Solomon (72, 127), Moses (90), Heman (88) and Ethan (89). According to the Massoretic text forty-nine of the Psalms are anonymous.

2. *Classification by the Titles.*

Besides the titles indicating authorship, many of the superscriptions indicate poetic characteristics. The term *mizmor* (translated "psalm") is applied to a number of the Psalms, and means a song to be accompanied by a stringed instrument. The term *shir* is the common word denoting a song. *Maskil* seems to denote a didactic poem. *Miktam* is thought to mean a "golden" psalm, but the meaning is uncertain. *Tephillah* denotes a prayer—*tehillah*, a praise. *Shiggayon* is uncertain.

Some of the titles indicate liturgical use. For example, in Psalm 92 the special day on which the Psalm was to be sung is prescribed in the expression "for the sabbath day." Psalm 30 was written to be sung at the "Dedication of the House." Psalms 120-134 are "songs of degrees" or ascents, evidently to be chanted by the people as they went up to the feasts at Jerusalem.

Other titles indicate the musical setting. The expression *lamenatsteach* probably means for the chief precentor, and *selah,* denotes probably, as Eissfeldt thinks, "an interlude."

3. Composition and Date.

To determine the precise date of individual Psalms is frequently difficult and in many cases impossible. Evidence from the Ras Shamra epic poetry from ancient Ugarit dating from the fourteenth century B.C. proves the antiquity of many ol the Psalms.[7] The reasonable view, unless one's perspective is distorted by the unsound presuppositions of the Wellhausen school, is to regard the bulk of the material of the Psalter as pre-exilic, going back to poems from ancient collections dating perhaps even before David's time. Even if it be allowed that the book of Psalms in the form we have it today is a post-exilic collection, there is no valid reason to maintain, as Pfeiffer does, that the great majority of the Psalms were written between 400 and 100 B.C., and that "the real question with regard to the Psalter is not whether it contains Maccabean psalms of the second century, but rather whether any psalms are pre-exilic psalms."[8] Fortunately, extravagant views of this sort are being more and more rejected even by those who labor under the fallacious assumptions of the Wellhausan view, as the archaisms, ancient literary forms, expressions etc. of many of the Psalms eloquently argue for a pre-exilic date.

Literature on the Psalms

Kirkpatrick, A. F., in the *Cambridge Bible* (3 vols., 1897-1901).

Koenig, E., *Die Psalmen eingeleitet, uebersetzt und erklaert* (Guetersloh, 1927).

Gunkel, H., and J. Begrich, *Einleitung in die Psalmen*, 2 vols. (Goettingen, 1928 and 1933).

7 Cf. J. Patton, **Canaanite Parallels in the Book of Psalms** (Baltimore, 1944).
8 **Introduction**, p. 629.

CONSERVATIVE LITERATURE

Hengstenberg, E. W., *The Psalms* (Edinburgh, 1869).

Perowne, J. J. S., *The Book of Psalms*, 2 vols. (London, 1873).

Grant, W. F., *The Psalms in the Numerical Bible* (New York, 1897).

Martin, C., "The Inscriptions of the Psalms," *Pres. Ref. Rev. XI*, 1900, pp. 638-653.

Thirtle, J. W. *The Titles of the Psalms* (New York, 1905).

Allis, O. T., "The Bearing of Archeology Upon the Higher Criticism of the Psalms," *Princeton Theo. Rev. XV*, 1917, pp. 277-324.

Wilson, R. D., "The Headings of the Psalms," *Princeton Theo. Rev. XXIV*, 1926, pp. 1-37; 353-395.

Gaebelein, A. C., *The Book of Psalms* (New York, 1939).

PROVERBS

The title of the book is *Mishle Shelomoh* ("The Proverbs of Solomon"). The word *mashal* is properly a similitude or comparison, but its use is extended to sententious sayings. The book of Proverbs is a part of the so-called "Wisdom Literature" of the Old Testament.

1. Contents.

The book is a collection not only of proverbs or pithy sayings of practical wisdom, but of didactic poems of longer and shorter length. The subject, however, is not confined to mere human wisdom. Divine Wisdom, or God in revelation as the creator and goal of all things, is treated as well.

To a large extent the unit of thought in the book is one verse. Divisions are suggested by internal indications of authorship.

Part I. The Proverbs of Solomon (1:1-9:18).

    a. The call of wisdom (1:1-33).

    b. The rewards of wisdom (2:1-7:27).

    c. Praise of divine wisdom (8:1-9:18).

Part II. Miscellaneous sayings of Solomon (10:1-22:16).

Part III. The words of the wise (22:17-24:34).

Part IV. Proverbs of Solomon copied by Hezekiah's scribes (25:1-29:27).

Part V. The words of Agur (30:1-33).
Part VI. The words of Lemuel (31:1-9).
Part VII. Acrostic poem of the virtuous wife (31:10-31).

2. Authorship and Date.

According to internal evidence, two sections are in explicit terms attributed to Solomon (10:1-22:16 and 25:1-29:27). However, unless we view the introduction 1:1-7 as a later addition (fifth or fourth century B.C.), as even some conservatives unwarrantedly do,[9] there is no reason for denying chapters 1-9 to Solomon. The third section (22:17-24:34) resembles the first (chapters 1-9). Since the expression "words of the wise" is not a title to a new section, but a part of the verse, it seems that no separate division on the basis of authorship was intended. The fourth section is said to have been copied out by Hezekiah's men (scribes) plainly from another old collection of Solomon's proverbs, and not composed by them. Accordingly there is strong scriptural testimony that Solomon was the author of chapters 1-29, that is, of the entire book, except chapters 30 (definitely said to be by Agur) and 31 by King Lemuel. This view is supported by I Kings 4:32 which ascribes "three thousand proverbs" to Solomon. It is also in accordance with Biblical notices of Solomon's fame for his divinely-imparted wisdom (I Kings 3:5-28; 10:1).

Critics commonly ascribe little or none of the book to Solomon. Otto Eissfeldt, for example, views Part I (1:1-9:18) as the latest portion of the book, dating from the third or fourth century, B.C.[10] He even dates 10:1-22:16, usually conceded the oldest nucleus of the book, after the exile, admitting, however, that it may contain older pre-exilic material.[11] His argument for a post-exilic date on the basis of Aramaic elements is invalid, as the mutual influence of Hebrew and Aramaic goes back to early times and Aramaisms occur in the earliest

9 Cf. Steinmueller, A Companion to Scripture Studies II, p. 190
10 Einleitung, p. 523.
11 Loc. cit., p. 524.

portions of the Old Testament. For example, the inscription of Zakir, king of Hamath (c. 800 B.C.) is written in a mixture of Hebrew and Aramaic.

The arguments commonly advanced by critics for a late date and non-Solomonic authorship are inconclusive. Greek philosophical influence is supposedly discernible, but such influence is purely imaginary, as the book is practical rather than philosophical. The close kinship between knowledge and virtue, for example, is certainly not a unique feature of Greek philosophy. It is reasonable to believe such a concept existed in Israel through divine inspiration long before the Greek era.

In the absence of historical indications in the book, because of the nature of its contents, it is futile for critics to cite a lack of nationalism, when the nation was supposedly under Persian or Greek domination. The obvious monotheism of the book requires a post-exilic date only under the unsound critical theory of the evolutionary development of Israel's religion. The absence of any challenge to idolatry does not require a post-exilic date as the early reign of Solomon was evidently free from idolatrous contamination.

The Proverbs of Amenemope of Egypt (dated variously between 1000-600 B.C.) bear such a striking resemblance to Proverbs 22:17-24:22, usually considered non-Solomonic, that critics customarily assume that the literary dependence of the latter is certain.[12] Albright, for instance, believes the Egyptian proverbs "were taken over, almost certainly through Phoenician intermediation."[13] However, it may be both the writer of Proverbs and the Egyptian author were influenced by a common third source, or, what is a much sounder view, the Biblical work is older, since Proverbs, chapters 1-24, were certainly regarded as Solomonic in Hezekiah's time (eighth century B.C.).

12 Cf. Eissfeldt, op. cit., p. 525.
13 W. F. Albright, Archeology and The Religion of Israel (Baltimore, 1942, p. 15).

LITERATURE ON PROVERBS

Berry, G. R., *The Book of Proverbs* (Philadelphia, 1905).
Eissfeldt, O., *Der Maschal im Alten Testament* (Giessen, 1913).
Oesterley, W. O. E., in the *Westminster Commentaries* (1929).
Gemser in Eissfeldt's *Handbuch* (1937).

JOB

The book takes its name from its central character Job, *Iyyob*, which extra-Biblically occurs in the Berlin execration texts as the name of a prince of the land of Damascus in the nineteenth century B.C.[14] and later in the Amarna Age as a prince of Pella (modern Fahil). The Biblical Job was a pious man who dwelt in the steppes eastward or southeastward of Palestine in the land of Uz (1:1), Teman, Shuah and Naama (2:11). There is no concrete reason for denying that Job was a real character or for maintaining that the events recorded are not historical. The reference to Job in Ezekiel 14:14, 20 and James 5:11 shows that he was a historical character. There is nothing in the book itself to suggest that the account is symbolic, either in the names, places or circumstances of the narrative.

1. Theme.

The book is a magnificent dramatic poem belonging to the philosophic or wisdom literature of the Old Testament. It treats of the profound question which has always perplexed mankind, why do the righteous suffer and how can their suffering be reconciled with an all-powerful and infinitely holy God?

Job's three friends present essentially the same answer (chapters 3-31). Suffering, they intimate, is always the result of sin. In desperation Job protests his innocence and in his dilemma is driven to assume that God must be dealing unjustly with him. However, he expresses the confidence that he will finally be vindicated. Thereupon Elihu appears as the

---

14 See W. F. Albright, **Jour. Pal. Or. Soc. VIII,** 239, **Bull. Am. Schs.** 83, 1941, p. 36.

Lord's messenger and forerunner in declaring the truth (so fully revealed in the New Testament) that afflictions are frequently a means of purifying and strengthening the righteous, the chastenings of a loving father, not in any sense the expressions of an angry and implacable God (32-37). Fittingly introducing God's speech to Job out of the whirlwind (38-41), Job is humbled and brought to abhor himself before the divine majesty (42:1-6). His self-abnegation and spiritual refining prepare the way for his restoration and blessing (42:7-17).

2. *Outline.*

Prologue: Job's test (1, 2).

Part I. False comfort by his three friends (3-31).

a. First cycle of speeches (3-14).

Job's speech followed by those of his three friends, each in turn answered by Job.

b. Second cycle of speeches (15-21).

Each friend addresses Job and is answered by him.

c. Third cycle of speeches (22-31).

Eliphaz and Bildad speak and are answered by Job.

Part II. Elihu's speeches (32-37).

a. His first speech: God instructs man through affliction (32, 33).

b. His second speech: God's justice and prudence vindicated (34).

c. His third speech: The advantages of piety (35).

d. His fourth speech: God's greatness and Job's ignorance (36, 37).

Part III. God's speeches (38-42:6).

a. God's first speech: creation's proclamation of God's omnipotence. Job's confession (38:1-40:5).

b. God's second speech: The power of God and human frailty. Job's humility (40:6-42:6).

Epilogue: Divine rebuke of Job's three friends and Job's restoration (42:7-17).

3. Authenticity.

Higher critics commonly deny that the following passages are parts of the original poem: (a) the prologue and the epilogue in prose, (b) the poem of divine wisdom (chapter 28), (c) the description of Leviathan and Behemoth (40:10-41:25) and (d) the speeches of Elihu (32:1-37:24).

a. There is no valid reason for ascribing the prologue (Chapters 1 and 2) and the epilogue (42:7-17) to a later author. As A. Bentzen correctly observes, "The dialogue cannot have had any independent existence. In 8:4 and 29:5 it presupposes the description of Job's illness as given in the narrative."[15] The combination of prose narrative and poetic dialogue is not unusual and has its analogy in Egyptian literature.[16] Without the epilogue it would appear that Satan had been victorious and that God had abandoned Job.

b. There is no compelling reason to reject the poem of divine wisdom (Chapter 28). The passage is admittedly loosely connected with its context, but so are other choice literary masterpieces of the book in accordance with the marvelous poetic powers of the author and under the principle of poetic license. If (as is certainly true) "the finest literary masterpieces are to be found among these incidental pieces and in digressions, rather than in the argumentative scaffolding of the book," as Pfeiffer admits,[17] why reject this passage and retain others, when "to remove even some of them would greatly reduce the value of the original poem and imply that the poetic genius of the supplementers was equal if not superior to that of the original poet?"[18]

c. The same answer may be given to the critical contention that the description of Behemoth (hippopotamus) and of Leviathan (crocodile) in 40:15-41:34 is a subsequent poetic addition. While the theme of this passage is confessedly

15 Introduction II, p. 175.
16 Cf. R. Renie Manuel d'Ecriture Sainte II, p. 376.
17 Introduction, p. 686.
18 Pfeiffer, loc. cit.

unique, it is not more so than the entire poetical masterpiece. Moreover, the language and ideas are related to the rest of the book (cf. 40:15 and 39:15 with 5:23; 41:9 with 3:9, etc.). The author, moreover, shows acquaintance with Egypt elsewhere (cf. 8:11 and 9:26).

d. Critics customarily reject the genuineness of the Elihu speeches because Elihu is not mentioned either in the prologue or epilogue, because his alleged "long-winded" speeches supposedly interrupt the argument, adding nothing to the position presented by Job's three friends, and because his style is thought to be inferior to the rest of the book.

In reply, it must be said that there is no reason why Elihu should appear in either the prologue or the epilogue. He enters the discussion as a chance listener and at a later time than Job's three friends, and, so far from merely repeating them, speaks in order to correct their error (32:3-5). He adds the momentous truth that affliction of the righteous is disciplinary, corrective and refining (33:16-18, 27-30; 36:10-12, etc.). Elihu's speeches answer Job's problem and prepare him for Jehovah's appearance and words from the whirlwind. The book would lack a vital part if Elihu's discourses were omitted, and God's appearance would be abrupt.

Elihu does not appear in the prologue because he had fulfilled his ministry and spoke the truth. Unlike Job's three friends, he needed no rebuke. The contention that Elihu's speeches are inferior is pointless as critics are compelled to admit many points of contact with the rest of the book. His contribution to the solution of the problem of the book renders rejecting his speeches as invalid.

4. Date.

Vast disagreement prevails regarding the date of the composition. The events are evidently laid in the patriarchal age, but critics date the composition of the poem anywhere from patriarchal times (Ebrard) to as late as the fourth (Eissfeldt,

Volz) or even the third century B. C. (Cornill). The most likely date is the Solomonic era (Franz Delitzsch, Keil, Haevernick) since it bears evidence of the creative beginning period of Wisdom Literature, and moves in a similar circle of ideas as parts of Proverbs (cf. Job 15:8 and chapter 28 with Proverbs 8).

LITERATURE ON JOB

Green, W. H., *The Argument of the Book of Job Unfolded* (New York, 1881).

Dhorme, P., *Le Livre de Job* (Paris, 1927).

Kissane, E. J., *The Book of Job* (Dublin, 1939), see pp. LX-LXIV for bibliography.

Stevenson, W. B., *The Poem of Job: A Literary Study With a New Translation;* Schweich Lectures, 1943 (London, 1947).

CHAPTER XIII

THE ROLLS

THE FIVE ROLLS or *megilloth* are shorter books, which are brief enough to be publicly read on anniversaries. The Song of Solomon heads the list because it was used at the first and greatest feast of the year, the Passover.

SONG OF SOLOMON

The designation "Song of Songs" is a literal translation of the Hebrew idiomatic name (1:1), denoting the superlative degree, that is, "The best or most exquisite Song." The Septuagint *asma asmaton* and Vulgate, Canticum Canticorum, like the English "Song of Songs," slavishly render the literal Hebrew without resolving the Hebrew idiom. The Authorized and American Revised rendering "The Song of Solomon" is likewise taken from the data of 1:1 ("The Song of songs, which is Solomon's"), but is not a translation.

1. The Literary Form.

Understanding the Song depends to a large degree on the view taken of its form. Three different views are generally held. The conservative (and we believe the correct view) is that it is a unified lyrical poem with the dramatic form of dialogue. Those holding the second view maintain that it is a drama or melodrama (Origen, Ewald, Koenig, Strack, Driver, Renan, Godet). Those holding the third view regard it as an anthology of loosely connected individual love lyrics (Herder, Goethe, Reuss, Lods, P. Haupt, Oesterly and

380

Robinson, Pfeiffer and others) recited during wedding festivities (Wetzstein, Budde, Cheyne, Goodspeed, Cassuto).

That the Song is a homogeneous lyric, not an anthology of various disconnected love poems without plan, is apparent for the following reasons:

a. Identical imagery and local color are found in all parts of the Song. For example, the bridegroom (beloved) is compared to a young hart in 2:9, 17; 8:14. Compare the similar figure of the doe (gazelle) in 2:7; 3:5; 4:5. The bridegroom feeds his flock "among the lilies," 2:16; 4:5; 6:2, 3. The bride is called "fairest among women" in 1:8; 5:9; 6:1.

b. The same refrain occurs in 2:7; 3:5; 8:4. Part of the same refrain in 2:17 and 4:6.

c. The same persons appear in all parts of the poem, the bride (1:5; 2:16; 3:4; 6:9; 7:10, 11; 8:2, 8), the bridegroom (1:7; 2:13; 4:8-5:1; 6:1; 7:11-13) and the daughters of Jerusalem (1:5; 2:7; 3:5, 10; 5:8, 16; 8:4).

The theory that the Song is a drama, though widely subscribed to in modern times, is scarcely tenable. The poem does not possess sufficient action, plot or dramatic sequence for classification under this category. The supposition that the book consists of a collection of detached erotic lyrics is unsatisfactory. The unity discernible in the poem militates against this view as well as the requirements of divine inspiration and canonicity. It is difficult to see how the faithful of antiquity would have persisted in regarding as divinely inspired a poem of mere human love, especially when it was on such a plane often considered unedifying, and actually forbidden by the Jews to be read by persons under thirty years of age.

2. *The Interpretation.*

Three common methods of interpreting this difficult book may be discerned in the commentaries, (1) the literal, (2) the allegorical and (3) the typical.

The *literal interpretation* construes the poem as a mere representation of human love without any higher or spiritual meaning. Recently, Edward J. Young has set forth a species of the literal interpretation which borders vaguely on the typical. He views the Song as didactic and moral, in that it celebrates the dignity and purity of human love, but justifies its position in the canon by making it a reminder that God who "has placed love in the human heart, is Himself pure."[1]

Most modern scholars, however, in adopting the literal interpretation justify the canonicity of the book by resorting to the shepherd hypothesis, in which a third main character is introduced as the shepherd-lover of the bride, whom Solomon, villain-like, tries to seduce from her lover. The poem thus becomes a triumph of pure love over lust, but under an obviously objectionable representation of Solomon. More serious, the shepherd has no tangible existence. He is, as Delitzsch correctly characterizes him, "nothing else than a shadow cast by the person of Solomon."[2]

The *allegorical interpretation,* common among the Jews from ancient times and introduced into the Christian Church by Origen, views the events as figurative rather than historical. To the Jews the poem represented Jehovah's love for Israel; to the Christian it represents Christ's love for His Church. Details were subject to extravagant explanations.

The view has much to be said in its favor. It gives point to the canonical recognition of the book, according it a higher spiritual meaning. Both in the Old and New Testament the relationship of the Lord's people is illustrated by the figure of marriage. In the Old Testament, however, Israel is presented as the wife of Jehovah (Hosea 2:19-23), in her sin and unbelief now divorced, but yet to be restored (Isaiah 54:5; Jeremiah 3:1; Hosea 1-3). On the other hand, the New Testament presents the Church as a virgin espoused to Christ

---

1 **Introduction to the Old Testament** (1949), p. 327.
2 F. Delitzsch **Commentary**, p. 8.

(II Corinthians 11:2; Ephesians 5:23-32; Romans 7:4; Revelation 19:6-8). The objections to the allegorical view are mainly that it unnecessarily rules out the actual historicity of the events and lends itself to extravagant, far-fetched interpretations.

The *typical interpretation* is a mediating view between the two extremes represented by the literal and the allegorical. It avoids the objections which may be lodged against the latter in that it neither denies the historical background of the Song nor encourages fantastic interpretations of details, since the type adumbrates the antitype in only a few salient points. It avoids the secularity of the literal view and finds an adequate purpose in the book, not in the triumph of virtue over imaginary seduction, but in the typical relation between Solomon, elsewhere a type of Christ, and the Shulamite, the type of the Church, the bride of Christ.

3. *The Author.*

Although the notice of 1:1 "The song of songs, which is Solomon's" may conceivably be translated "the song of songs which is *about* or *concerning* Solomon" (cf. 1:4; 3:7-11; 8:11), the Hebrew preposition *lamedh* is sometimes so rendered (Isaiah 5:1), yet the *natural* rendering is here (as in the Psalms) indicative of authorship. Various internal arguments also support Solomonic authorship. The local color, affluence and evidences of royal luxury suit Solomon's reign, as well as references to Jerusalem, Engedi, Sharon, Tirzah, Gilead, Lebanon, Carmel, Heshbon, Hermon, etc., which are made as if all these places were located in the same united kingdom. The poem gives abundant evidence that Solomon "spake of trees, from the cedar that is in Lebanon even unto the hyssop that springeth out of the wall: he spake also of beasts, and of birds . . ." (I Kings 4: 33). According to Steinmueller "into the 116 verses of the poem he introduces twenty-one varieties of plants and fifteen species of animals."[3]

3 John Steinmueller, A Companion to Scripture Studies II, p. 206.

The linguistic peculiarities of the book (the presence of one or two Persian and Greek words) need not rule out Solomonic authorship. At most these features may indicate that the poem in the precise form we have it cannot be earlier than the third century B.C. (Eissfeldt), but one may inquire if even these features might be original, as Solomonic commerce was incredibly widespread and there was inevitably an influx of foreign words. Little can be made of the Aramaisms as close affinities existed between Hebrew and Aramaic from earliest times, and inevitably in the Solomonic realm, which embraced Aramaic countries.

LITERATURE ON THE SONG

Jastrow, M., *The Song of Songs* (London, 1922).
Rowley, H. H., "The Meaning of the Shulamite," *Am. Jour. Sem. Lang.* 56 (1939), pp. 84-91.

RUTH

In the later Hebrew arrangement the book of Ruth stands second among the five *Megilloth* (scrolls). It is read publicly at Pentecost, the harvest festival, since its scenery is the harvest field. There is evidence that in the primitive Hebrew Bible, Judges and Ruth were closely united as the testimony of Josephus, Melito of Sardis, Origen and Jerome indicates. At the time of the Septuagint, Ruth was still classified among the historical books. During the Christian era the Jews placed it among the *Kethubhim* or Hagiographa.[4] It found second place among the Megilloth, possibly because of its special use in Hebrew feasts.

1. Authorship and Date.

The author of the work is unknown. The Babylonian Talmud ascribes the book to Samuel, but this seems unlikely in view of the fact that the book evidently was written during the reign of David (c. 1000 B.C.). The period of the Judges

---

4 Baba Bathra 14 b and 15 a. Cf. J. E. Steinmueller, **A Companion to Scripture Studies I,** 58 ff. II, 82.

is described as past (1:1) and the genealogy is brought up to David (4:17, 22). Had the book been written after David's death, Solomon's name would naturally appear.

Despite obvious evidences of an early pre-exilic date, recent critics such as Oesterley, Robinson, Pfeiffer and Eissfeldt, following in Wellhausen's footsteps, argue for a post-exilic date. Such a procedure, however, is precarious. Oesterley and Robinson "note that in the language of the book there are several indications of a comparatively late date—Aramaisms, one or two late forms, and some fairly obvious archaisms."[5] But the Aramaisms, even if they could be proved to be genuine, offer no concrete evidence for a late date, as such forms exist in the earlier parts of the Old Testament. The late forms are as uncertain as rare. The archaisms would normally indicate an early date for the original. In fact, it is difficult for even radical critics to escape the force of the argument for an early date presented by the general character of the Hebrew vocabulary, syntax and classical purity of style.[6]

2. *Authenticity.*

Critics own that "the story is simply and beautifully told, and there is no doubt but that it was written as a complete work in practically the form in which we now have it" (Oesterley and Robinson). Some, however, persist in supposing that the genealogical note at the end is a later addition. A. Bentzen is correct in noting that "it is quite impossible to assume that a later interpolation would fabricate the tradition of David's extraction from Moab."[7] After the exile such a marriage would have been discreditable, and could not conceivably have been invented. This circumstance and the simple straightforward recital of events as actual history evidences the historical character of the narrative, which critics notwithstanding commonly deny. Pfeiffer views the story as ideal-

5 **Introduction,** p. 84.
6 Cf. Pfeiffer, **Introduction,** p. 718.
7 **Introduction** II, p. 183.

istic fiction. This view is ruled out by the infallible witness of the New Testament, which lists Ruth as a historical person in the Davidic Messianic line (Matthew 1:5). The critical tendency is arbitrarily to give the book a late date and then conclude, as Bentzen does, that a work which "cannot be earlier than the later periods of the Israelite-Judean Monarchy, cannot be expected to give much reliable evidence concerning days so far off as the time of the Judges."[8] But the events themselves bear unmistakable marks of reliability and the critics' basis of dating of unreliability, as we have noted.

The local color, detailed circumstances and events of the narrative are strictly in conformity with the customs and times of the period of the Judges. Marriage with the Moabites was not absolutely forbidden (cf. Exodus 34:16 and Deuteronomy 7:3). Only later was the Law interpreted to include Moabites. The book also furnishes a logical historical explanation of David's friendly contacts with the Moabite king, when he fled from Saul, and sought an asylum in Moab for his parents (I Samuel 22:3, 4).

LITERATURE ON RUTH

Grimmelsman, H. J., *The Book of Ruth* (Chicago, 1930).
Rudolph, W., in *Kommentar zum Alten Testament* (1939).
Haller, M., in *Handbuch zum Alten Testament* (1940).
Rowley, H. H., in the *Harvard Theological Review* (1947, pp. 77 ff.).

LAMENTATIONS

This book, consisting of five elegiac poems lamenting the fall of Jerusalem and the attendant sufferings of her people, is termed *Ekah* (How!) in the Hebrew from its first word. The English name "Lamentations" is derived from the Latin. The Greek rendering is *Threnoi*. The versions usually add the name of Jeremiah as the traditional author.

1. Form of The Poem.

The first four elegies are alphabetic. In the first two (chapters 1, 2) each verse begins with a new letter of the Hebrew

8 **Introduction II, p. 185.**

alphabet and has three parts. In the third dirge (chapter 3) three verses are devoted to each of the twenty-two letters of the alphabet and every verse in each group of three begins with the same letter. In the fourth dirge one verse consisting of two members is distributed to each letter. The fifth dirge is unalphabetic but comprises twenty-two verses. Anomalously in chapters 2-4 the normal alphabetic order of *Ayin* preceding *Pe* (as in chapter 1) is reversed.

To express the anguish of the poet's soul a special elegiac meter is used in the construction of the verse called the *qinah*. The first member of the verse is longer than the second, sometimes called the "limping verse." Instead of being balanced and strengthened by the second, it is faintly echoed, making the whole verse seem to die away in a plaintive, melancholy cadence.

2. *Contents*.

Although each chapter is a separate poem, the contents of each is similar. The book throughout laments the woe and suffering sin had brought upon the people in the destruction of the city and the theocracy. The poet, on the other hand, realizes the Lord is righteous in punishing His sinning people, and calls upon them to repent. He also clearly discerns the wickedness of those who have destroyed the city and calls for their punishment. In the midst of despair, hope shines forth as the poet appeals for divine mercy.

3. *Authorship*.

Although there is no mention made of the authorship of Lamentations in the Hebrew text, the Jeremianic origin of the book is a sound conclusion for several reasons. *First*, strong and persistent tradition from the time of the Septuagint on (third century B.C.) maintains that Jeremiah wrote the book. The Greek translation is prefaced with a definite statement of Jeremianic authorship. The Vulgate, Targum of Jonathan and other ancient versions adopted this tradition, as did the

Church fathers (Origen, Hilary, Jerome and others), the reformers such as Calvin, and numerous modern commentators (Keil, Plumptre and others).

Secondly, the internal evidence of the book itself confirms the Jeremianic tradition. The scenes are evidently portrayed by an eyewitness, which Jeremiah was (Jeremiah 39) and hence written soon after the destruction of the city and the Temple in 586 B.C. (cf. Lamentations 2:12, 21; 3:10, etc.). Moreover, a comparison of Lamentations with Jeremiah's prophecy shows many similarities. The same sensitive temperament manifests itself in both, the national calamities are attributed in both to the same causes and similarities of language and expressions occur in both.[9]

Yet many scholars (Ewald, Cheyne, Eissfeldt, Bewer, Pfeiffer and others) deny the Jeremianic authorship. The general reason advanced is that the tradition is unreliable, being separated by at least three centuries from the age of the prophet. Internal evidence of style in comparison with Jeremiah's prophecy and one or two historical allusions supposedly rule out Jeremianic in favor of composite authorship.

In reply to the critics' arguments it is sufficient to say that, if Jeremiah is not the author, "there is absolutely no other writer living at the time to whom it can be ascribed with the slightest shadow of probability,"[10] and those who deny that Jeremiah wrote the book are (as would be expected) in utter disagreement as to who the author or authors might be. The tradition of Jeremianic origin, so long undisputed and so generally received, could scarcely have been founded on error. The argument from vocabulary and style is extremely precarious, especially in this instance, where important similarities occur. To say that differences in vocabulary between the prophecy and the Lamentations necessarily point to different

---

9 For a list of similarities see S. R. Driver, Introduction (9th ed., 1913), p. 462.
10 E. H. Plumptre, The Lamentations of Jeremiah, An Old Testament Commentary (ed. by C. T. Ellicott), Vol. V, p. 181.

authors, to say that one poet could not write five poems on one subject or to say that different expressions within the poems themselves prove composite authorship, displays little sound judgment. Yet critics constantly build their theories on such shaky foundations.

LITERATURE ON LAMENTATIONS

Wiessmann, H., in *Biblica VII* (1926), 141-161; 412-428; VIII (1927), 339-347; XVII (1936), 71-84.
Haller, M., in *Handbuch zum Alten Testament* (1940).
Lohr, M., in *Handkommentar zum Alten Testament* (2nd ed., 1907).

ECCLESIASTES

Ecclesiastes is the roll which was read at the Feast of Tabernacles. The superscription (1:1) describes the book as "The words of the Preacher, the son of David, king in Jerusalem." "The Preacher" is a translation of the Hebrew *qal* feminine participle *qoheleth,* and apparently designates one who holds or addresses an assembly (Hebrew *qahal*). This is the meaning evident in the Greek *ekklesiastes,* the Vulgate *concionator* and the English "preacher." The feminine is due to the fact that words signifying an office or title, or the like, are in several languages feminine (cf. Ezra 2:55, 57, Nehemiah 7:57 and Arabic *khaliph*).

1. Contents.

Part I. The theme: All is Vanity (1:1-3).
Part II. The theme proved (1:4-3:22).

    a. By the transitory nature of all things (1:4-11).
    b. By the presence of evil (1:12-18).
    c. By the emptiness of pleasure, wealth and work (2:1-26).
    d. By the certainty of death (3:1-22).

Part III. The theme expanded (4:1-12:8).

    a. In view of the inequalities of life (4:1-16).
    b. In view of wealth (5:1-20).
    c. In view of man's end (6:1-12).

d. In view of man's wickedness (7:1-29).

e. In view of God's inscrutable providences (8:1-9:18).

f. In view of the disorders of life (10:1-20).

g. In view of the vanity of youth and old age (11:1-12:8).

Part IV. The conclusion (12:9-14).

a. Fear God and keep His commandments (12:9-14).

2. *Authorship.*

Several views of authorship prevail. Since the days of Luther, who denied the Solomonic authorship, the tendency has been to attribute the book to a much later writer or writers until today, few, even among conservative scholars, defend the Solomonic authorship. However certain evidences may be cited that Solomon wrote the book. It is difficult to escape the fact that the title in 1:1 clearly attributes the book to Solomon. In fact, the first two chapters assume the form of a Solomonic autobiography. Many texts in the book have clear reference to Solomon's wisdom (1:16), wealth (2:8), his servants (2:7), pleasures (2:3), his building activities (2:4-6), etc. Morever, Jewish tradition ascribes the book to Solomon.[11]

On the basis of linguistic and philosophic arguments the book is usually assigned to an anonymous author of the post-exilic period. These arguments, however, are not always convincing. Unless one is prepared to admit that the author personates Solomon, as in the apocryphal Book of Wisdom (cf. Wisdom 6-9), one must adhere to the Solomonic authorship, which, however, need not be abandoned as incapable of scholarly defense. In recent times Hans Moeller and the Romanist scholars, Gietmann, Vigouroux, Cornely-Hagen and Schumacher have defended this position.

3. *Unity.*

Some of the Church fathers such as Jerome and Gregory the Great and medieval scholastics such as Thomas Aquinas de-

11 Megillah 7a; Sabbath 30.

fend the unity of the book and answer some seeming contradictions on the theory that it is a pro and con discussion in which the inspired author answers certain questions which are broached. Many critics (among them Winckler, Haupt, Kautzsch and Barton) deny unity of authorship and regard the book as composed of many later annotations to the original skeptical treatise to give the book an orthodox tone. But the language, style and dominant theme of the entire book are against this view. Sellin and Eissfeldt, for example, correctly defend the unity of the book.

Literature on Ecclesiastes

Hengstenberg, E. W., *Commentary on Ecclesiastes* (Philadelphia, 1860).

Gietmann, G., "Ecclesiastes" in *Catholic Encyclopedia* V, 244-248.

Odeberg, H., *Qoaelaeth, A Commentary on the Book of Ecclesiastes* (1929).

Galling, K., in *Handbuch zum Alten Testament* (1940).

Gordis, R., *The Wisdom of Ecclesiastes* (New York, 1945).

Esther

The book takes its name from its chief character, whose Hebrew name *Hadassah* (Myrtle) was changed to the Persian name Esther (probably meaning "Star"). It is called by the Jews *Megilloth Esther,* or the Esther roll, and read at the Feast of Purim.

1. Purpose.

The book is designed to show God's providential care of His dispersed people in their trials and persecutions and to explain the origin of the important Feast of Purim, first mentioned in II Maccabees 15:36.

2. Contents.

Part I. The danger of the Jews (1:1-3:15).

    a. Esther made queen instead of Vashti (1:1-2:23).

    b. Haman's conspiracy against the Jews (3:1-15).

Part II. The deliverance of the Jews (4:1-10:3).

     a. Esther's courage brings deliverance (4:1-7:10).
     b. Vengeance on the Jews' enemies (8:1-9:19).
     c. The feast of Purim (9:20-32).
     d. Mordecai's exaltation at court (10:1-3).

3. Historicity.

Numerous critics deny the historicity of the story, except as history may be woven into fiction. Accordingly, A. Bentzen calls the book a "historical novel," but is forced to confess that "the story teller knows something of the administration of the Persian kingdom, and especially of the construction of the palace at Shushan."[12]

However the critics' arguments against the historicity of the events are singularly weak in the face of the manifest historical intent of the author (cf. 10:2) and his undeniable knowledge of Persian life and customs. For example, it is alleged that Mordecai would have to be well over a hundred years old to have gone in the first deportation in 597 B.C. (2:6). The relative pronoun of this verse evidently refers to Kish, Mordecai's great-grandfather. Hence this difficulty evaporates.

It is also claimed that Vashti, Esther and Mordecai are unknown to secular history in the reign of Xerxes I (485-465 B.C.). Esther did not become Queen till the seventh year of Xerxes' reign (478 B.C.) after his return from his defeat in Greece (480 B.C.), when Herodotus specifically tells us he paid attention to his harem (IX, 108). Although the Queen is said to have been Amestris, certainly Xerxes, from what we know of him, may well have had other wives, if Solomon had "seven hundred wives, princesses, and three hundred concubines . . ." (I Kings 11:3).

4. Authorship and Date.

The author is unknown. Those who accept the historicity of the book place it sometime during or near the reign of Artaxerxes Longimanus (464-425 B.C.), which accounts also for its literary phenomena, since its diction is comparable to such late books as Ezra, Nehemiah and Chronicles. Critics who deny the historicity of the book place it later in the Greek (third century B.C.) or Maccabean period (second century B.C.), but on tenuous literary grounds.

LITERATURE ON ESTHER

Watson, W. S., "The Authenticity and Genuineness of the Book of Esther," *Princeton Theo. Rev.* I (1903), 62-74.

Hoschander, J., *The Book of Esther in the Light of History* (Philadelphia, 1923).

Chapter XIV

THE HISTORICAL BOOKS

Of the historical books of the Writings Daniel is more precisely historical-prophetical in contrast to Ezra-Nehemiah and Chronicles, which are straight history. These books appear in the third part of the Jewish Canon, rather than the second, because their authors were not official prophets. Daniel was a statesman, Ezra, a priest, Nehemiah, a governor, and the author of Chronicles, in all probability, was likewise a priest, since tradition names Ezra as the writer.

Daniel

Daniel's prophecy takes its name from the prophet (cf. Matthew 24:15). As a young man he was carried away with other promising youths as a hostage by Nebuchadnezzar II (604-562 B.C.) to be educated at the royal palace in Babylon. Early in the period of exile, while still a young man, he became famous for his godliness and wisdom (Ezekiel 14:14, 20; 28:3). Higher critics who legendize "Noah, Daniel, and Job" in the Ezekiel passages, insist that the reference to Daniel can scarcely be to Ezekiel's young contemporary, but is an allusion to the ancient Semitic legendary figure of Danel, who renders justice to the widows and orphans in the famous Danel Epic of the Ras Shamra poems of the fourteenth century B.C.[1]

This unsound conclusion is to be decisively rejected because it would be strange indeed if an etymologically transparent name like Daniel, which Tregelles renders as "God's judge,"

1 See H. H. Rowley, The Rediscovery of the Old Testament (Philadelphia, 1946), p. 79 f.

i.e. "one who renders judgment in the name of God,"[2] did not appear in Ugaritic (which is really only a dialect of Biblical Hebrew) especially to describe one whose chief role was to render justice. Daniel must certainly have been no unusual name in early Israel, being borne as we know by the second son of David (I Chronicles 3:1). It is undeniably remarkable that Ezekiel should compare a young contemporary with the ancients Noah and Job, but Daniel had had ample time to establish his truly great reputation, since Ezekiel did not begin his ministry until 592 B.C., over thirteen years after Daniel's deportation, and the latter was, likely thirty-five years of age or older at the time.

1. Purpose.

Daniel is one of the most important prophetic books of the Old Testament, and constitutes an indispensable introduction to New Testament prophecy, the chief themes of which are the apostasy of the church, the revelation of the man of sin, the great tribulation, the second coming of Christ, the resurrections and the establishment of the millennial kingdom. These (except the apostasy of the Church) are Daniel's themes also.

The prophecy specifically traces the course of "the times of the Gentiles . . ." (Luke 21:24) which extend from the captivity of Judah under Nebuchadnezzar till the Second Advent of Christ and the setting up of the Messianic kingdom.

2. Contents.

Part I. Daniel's visions under Nebuchadnezzar and his personal history to the reign of Cyrus (1:1-6:28).

    a. Reasons for Daniel's fame and prosperity (1:1-21).

    b. Nebuchadnezzar's image vision and its interpretation (2:1-49).

    c. Deliverance from the fiery furnace (3:1-30).

2 S. P. Tregelles, Gesenius' **Hebrew and Chaldee Lexicon** (reprint, Grand Rapids, 1949).

d. Nebuchadnezzar's tree vision and its meaning (4:1-37).

e. Belshazzar's feast (5:1-31).

f. Daniel's deliverance from the lions' den (6:1-28).

Part II. Visions under Belshazzar, Darius and Cyrus (7:1-12:13).

a. The vision of the four beasts and its interpretation (7:1-28).

b. The vision of the ram and the rough goat and its interpretation (8:1-27).

c. The vision of the seventy weeks (9:1-27).

d. The vision of God's glory (10:1-21).

e. Vision of events from Darius to the end time (11:1-12:13).

3. *Authorship and Date.*

Modern criticism views the establishment of a Maccabean date (about 167 B.C.) and the rejection of the traditional Danielic authorship as one of its assured achievements. These views, however, are erected upon a series of highly plausible fallacies and unsound assumptions.

a. *It is assumed that because Daniel's prophecy is placed among the Writings it was not in existence when the Canon of the prophets was closed between* 300-200 B.C. This assumption, as shown in the chapter on the Canon, is gratuitous, based upon an unsound theory that one section of the Hebrew Canon was closed before another was opened. It also fails to take into account the official status of the prophet as a determining factor in the formation of the Hebrew Canon. Daniel, although he had the prophetic gift (Matthew 24:15), everywhere appears as a statesman and an administrator at a foreign court, not as a preacher, social reformer and religious revivalist, which were dominant functions in the Hebrew prophet's ministry, whereas prognostication was only an incidental aspect, as critics also readily admit.

b. *It is assumed that because Daniel is not mentioned in*

the list of writers in the book of Ecclesiasticus (c. 180 B.C.) *that the book did not exist.* But this argument from silence is highly precarious as Sirach does not mention Asa, Jehoshaphat or Ezra. He plainly follows the order of the Hebrew books, Isaiah, Jeremiah, Ezekiel and the Twelve. He does not mention Daniel because the book was not classed with the prophets.

c. *It is alleged that the author of Daniel "makes erroneous statements about the history of the sixth century* B.C., *which would be incredible on the part of one who really lived during that period."*[3] For example, the opening statement of the book that Nebuchadnezzar came unto Jerusalem and besieged it "in the third year of Jehoiakim, king of Judah . . ." (1:1) is said to be in error. But this charge, as in the case of other supposed inaccuracies is based upon the precarious argument from silence and erroneously assumes that because this particular expedition against Jerusalem is not mentioned in the book of Kings and other extant sources that therefore it did not occur. In making a detailed survey of this problem, R. D. Wilson correctly concludes that the statement in Daniel "stands absolutely unimpugned by any testimony to be produced from any reliable source of information."[4]

Regarding the supposed contradiction between Jeremiah 25:1, which states that the *fourth* year of Jehoiakim was the first year of Nebuchadnezzar, whereas Daniel says that Nebuchadnezzar was king and made an expedition against Jerusalem already in Jehoiakim's *third* year, the explanation is simple. Jeremiah, living in Palestine evidently used the Palestinian system of dating the first year of a king's reign as the accession year, whereas Daniel, living in Babylon, used the system there of dating the first year as the year after the accession, corresponding to the Palestinian second year.

Daniel's use of the term "king" has often been alleged to

---

3 Oesterley and Robinson, **Introduction**, p. 335.
4 **Studies in the Book of Daniel** (New York, 1917), p. 59. cf. pp. 43-59.

be historically inaccurate. Perhaps the most notorious instance is Belshazzar. The very existence of this prominent personage in Daniel used to be denied, but is now fully proved by modern archeology. Belshazzar is called both "king" and "the son of Nebuchadnezzar" by Daniel (5:1, 2; cf. vs. 11, 18, 22). But in the inscriptions he is spoken of only as "the king's son" and the son of Nabonidus, a usurper, apparently without blood relationship to Nebuchadnezzar. But this notice is accurate according to Semitic idiom. In similar fashion, Jehu, the usurper, is called the "son of Omri" by the Assyrians as recorded on the Black Obelisk of Shalmaneser III, although without any blood relation at all, "son of" being used in connection with royalty in the broad sense of "successor of."

Belshazzar, moreover, is legitimately called king in Daniel because, being closely associated with his father, he exercised royal functions, such as issuing decrees, performing acts, etc. equal to those of a king. The Persian Verse Account actually states that Nabonidus entrusted the kingship to his son Belshazzar, and that he established himself at Tema in Arabia.

Other historical difficulties in Daniel still persist however, such as the existence or non-existence of the enigmatic Darius the Mede (5:31; 6:1). Although Darius' name has not yet been found extra-Biblically, the case of Belshazzar and that of Sargon (Isaiah 20:1), both of whom were formerly known only from the Old Testament, should warn critics of too hasty conclusions in denying the historical accuracy of canonical Scriptures.

d. *It is alleged that the literary features of Daniel prove that it was written long after the sixth century* B.C. The arguments based upon the use of Persian and Greek words and the special employment of Aramaic, however, are of doubtful validity. At most they indicate a late redaction of the present form of the book. There is no reason to deny Danielic authorship on the basis of Persian influence since Daniel's ministry continued into the Persian period. To say, as Driver does, that the three Greek words (the names of musical instruments) "demand" a date "after the conquest of Palestine by Alexander the Great (B.C. 332)" is exceedingly doubtful,[5] since it is becoming more evident that Greek culture penetrated the Near East at a much earlier date than formerly had been supposed. That Nebuchadnezzar's court was thoroughly cosmopolitan we may be sure. If the Jewish captives were required to furnish music (Psalm 137:3), would it be incredible to assume that Greeks from Cyprus, Ionia, Lydia and Cilicia were required to do the same? Although it is possible that the Hebrew and Aramaic portions of Daniel were modernized, possibly by Ezra and the Scribes, there is nothing in them as they stand that necessarily precludes authorship by Daniel.

e. *It is maintained that the developed theology of Daniel proves a post-exilic date.* Such doctrines as Messianism, angelology, resurrection and judgment appear elsewhere in earlier books of the Old Testament in hardly less developed form. The critical argument in this respect is weak.

The Danielic authorship, it may be said in conclusion, has its difficulties, but the arguments arrayed against this view are not strong enough to overthrow it, supported, as it is, by unanimous ancient Jewish and Christian tradition, and by abundant internal evidence of the book itself.

To these critics, like Pfeiffer, who rule out the miraculous and the supernatural "as belonging to the subjective rather than objective knowledge,"[6] the essential historicity of Daniel must of necessity be denied, and assumptions and theories invented to attempt to explain the supernatural on a natural plane. It must be remembered that even if the latest date assigned to the composition of the book of Daniel were proved correct, the prophecy yet displays a knowledge of the future which can only be ascribed to divine inspiration.[7]

5 Introduction, p. 508.
6 Introduction, p. 755.
7 Cf. C. H. H. Wright, Introduction to the Old Testament (1890), p. 196.

LITERATURE ON DANIEL

Montgomery, J. A., *The Book of Daniel, Int. Crit. Com.* (New York, 1927).

Charles, R. H., *A Critical and Exegetical Commentary on the Book of Daniel* (Oxford, 1929).

Dougherty, R., *Nabonidus and Belshazzar* (New Haven, 1929).

Bentzen, A., in *Handbuch zum Alten Testament* (1937).

Ginsburg, H. L., *Studies in Daniel* (New York, 1948).

Auberlen, K. A., *The Prophet Daniel and the Revelation of John* (Edinburgh, 1856).

CONSERVATIVE LITERATURE

Hengstenberg, E. W., *The Authenticity of Daniel and The Integrity of Zechariah* (Edinburgh, 1848). *Christology of The Old Testament* (Vol. III, 1858, pp. 77-264).

Anderson, Sir R., *The Coming Prince* (London, 1881); *Daniel in the Critic's Den* (New York, n. d.).

Pusey, E. B., *Daniel The Prophet* (New York, 1891).

Gaebelein, A. C., *The Prophet Daniel* (14th ed. New York, 1911).

Stevens, W. C., *The Book of Daniel* (Los Angeles, 1915).

Wilson, R. D., *Studies in the Book of Daniel* (Series I, New York, 1917); Series II (New York, 1938).

Ironside, H. A., *Lectures on Daniel The Prophet* (New York, 1920).

Young, E. J., *The Prophecy of Daniel* (Grand Rapids, 1949).

Kelly, W., *Notes on the Book of Daniel* (New York, 7th ed., 1943).

EZRA

In the ancient Hebrew Bible, Ezra and Nehemiah were treated as one book called "The Book of Ezra." Not until 1448 was the division into two books introduced into the Hebrew. Modern Hebrew Bibles commonly designate the two-fold arrangement as Ezra and Nehemiah, as in our English versions. There is evidence in the repetition of the list of returned exiles in Ezra 2 and Nehemiah 7 that this was a reintroduction of the original order and that their being counted as one may have been to make the total number of books identical with the number of letters in the Hebrew alphabet, or because Nehemiah continues the history of Ezra.

In the Septuagint, Ezra and Nehemiah (called Esdras B to

distinguish them from Esdras A, an apocryphal book) follow Chronicles. This seems the more logical and primitive order since Ezra and Nehemiah carry on the history at the point where Chronicles leaves off and since the Massoretic notes on the Kethubhim stand at the end of Nehemiah and not Chronicles. Critics commonly view Chronicles, Ezra and Nehemiah as originally a single work, but the reasons for their position are not completely convincing.[8]

1. Purpose.

Ezra, continuing the narrative where Chronicles leaves off, traces the history of the return from Babylon and the rebuilding of the temple. The author passes over the period from the completion of the temple 516 B.C. to his own journey to Jerusalem in 457 B.C. because it was obviously a period of declension and had no purpose in the author's aim to give a connected account of the restoration of the Jews to their land from a religious and priestly standpoint. Hence Ezra describes his task to teach the Law of God in Judah, to restore the temple service and correct the abuse of mixed marriages.

2. Contents.

Part I. Restoration Under Zerubbabel (1:1-6:22).
    a. First return of the exiles (1:1-2:70).
        (1) Edict of Cyrus (1:1-11).
        (2) List of the exiles (2:1-70).
    b. The restoration of public worship (3:1-6:22).
        (1) The rebuilding of the temple (3:1-6:15).
        (2) The dedication of the temple (6:16-22).
Part II. Reforms under Ezra (7:1-10:44).
    a. Second return of the exiles (7:1-8:36).
    b. Dissolution of mixed marriages (9:1-10:44).

3. Authorship and Date.

There is no compelling reason, despite the theories of modern critics, to abandon the traditional assumption that Ezra

8 For a summary of the reasons for this position, see Oesterley and Robinson, *Introduction,* p. 110 f.

is the author of the book which bears his name. While it is possible to assume that a later inspired compiler made use of Ezra's memoirs written in the first person (Ezra 7:27— 9:15), the probability is that Ezra himself employed these passages as a groundwork of the book and filled out the remaining portions written in the third person from other sources to make it a logical and unified whole. If Ezra according to tradition is also the author of Chronicles, as is by no means impossible, then the book of Ezra must have followed Chronicles anywhere from about 430 B.C. to 400 B.C., or a little later. Ezra's ministry is clearly to be placed in the reign of Artaxerxes I (465-424 B.C.), but he may have written Chronicles and the book of Ezra considerably later.

Modern negative criticism views the book of Ezra as a compilation dating at least a century or more after Ezra's time, and, therefore, of little historical reliability. Alleged historical discrepancies adduced to support this position, however, are only apparent and not real. For instance, the use of the title "King of Persia" (1:1, 2, etc.) is supposedly unidiomatic for a genuine passage dating from the Persian period, whereas in the genuine passages from the memoirs of Ezra and in contemporary inscriptions the term "the king" is used (but cf. 9:9). This argument is invalid. The terms, as common sense would suggest, are used interchangeably and occur in the same passages (Ezra 1:1, 2, 7, 8; 7:1, 7), as one would now refer to "the President" or "the President of the United States" without implying in the latter term that a new nation had superseded the United States. From the Jewish standpoint a heathen king, although a "king of kings," might naturally be designated "King of Persia" even if such usage is rare on the momuments. But the term does occur, for instance, on the Behistun Inscription.

Again critics make the charge of chronological confusion in Ezra 4:6-23, when events of the reigns of Xerxes (485-465 B.C.) and Artaxerxes (465-425 B.C.) stand before events of

Darius' reign (521-485 B.C.) in chapter 5. But this is an idle accusation. Ezra, like any other writer would do, is simply finishing one subject before proceeding to the next, even at the expense of chronological sequence.

Again, the decree of Cyrus recorded in Hebrew (Ezra 1:1-4) and in Aramaic (6:3-5) is supposed to involve contradiction, and the first branded as a "Jewish forgery." But the two decrees are both historical and authentic. The one transmitted in Hebrew was evidently made by Cyrus when he first conquered Babylon and naturally has a Jewish coloring. The second in Aramaic was evidently the formal record drawn up for the official archives at Ecbatana and naturally has a Babylonian coloring.

NEHEMIAH

The book is named from its main character and traditional author. The introduction is "The words of Nehemiah the son of Hachaliah" (1:1).

1. Purpose.

The book recounts the rebuilding of the walls of Jerusalem and the establishment of civil authority under Nehemiah as governor. It is more civil and secular than the book of Ezra, but is also written from the priestly standpoint. In its broader purpose Ezra-Nehemiah shows God's faithfulness in restoring His exiled people to their land through great heathen monarchs, Cyrus, Darius and Artaxerxes, on one hand, and through their own anointed leaders, Ezra, Nehemiah, Haggai, Zechariah, Zerubbabel, and Jeshua, on the other.

2. Contents.

Part I. Restoration of the Walls of Jerusalem by Nehemiah (1:1-7:73).

    a. Preceding providential events (1:1-2:20).

    b. The rebuilding of the walls (3:1-6:19).

    c. The appointment of watchmen and the taking of a census (7:1-73).

Part II. Religious reforms by Ezra and Nehemiah (8:1-13:31).
    a. Revival and renewal of the Covenant (8:1-10:39).
    b. Lists of princes, priests and Levites and dedication of the walls (11:1-13:3).
    c. Reforms of Nehemiah's second governorship (13:4-31).

3. *Authorship and Date.*

Jewish tradition and the title of the book assign the authorship of the work to Nehemiah (1:1). The section 1:1-7:5 is an excerpt from the author's memoirs, as the first person indicates, inserted apparently without change. Other such passages recognized by critics as belonging to Nehemiah's memoirs are 11:1, 2; 12:27-43; 13:4-31. The work also contains earlier documents which the author incorporated into his work, such as 7:6-73a. The rest of the book is based on historical sources.

Critics generally regard Nehemiah as the work of the so-called Chronicler. This priestly historian supposedly wrote I and II Chronicles and the book of Ezra-Nehemiah long after the time of Ezra and Nehemiah. The date is usually placed at the beginning of the Greek period around 330 B.C. Reasons advanced for this position, however, are not sound.

a. The mention of Jaddua in Nehemiah 12:11, 22, who, it is claimed, was high priest from 351-331 at the time of Alexander the Great, necessitates a late date. But the reference, it should be noticed, occurs in a list of priests and Levites, which, in an unessential part of the book, may easily be a later insertion. But since the reference to Jaddua is not to him as a high priest, but evidently to him as a youth known to Nehemiah (cf. 12:26), it is not necessary to assume a later scribal gloss. Jaddua was the great grandson of Eliashib, the high priest in Nehemiah's day. Nehemiah mentions a grandson of Eliashib as married in his time (13:28). It is quite possible that Nehemiah lived to see Eliashib's great grandson and mentioned him as in the high priestly line. This is not out of harmony with the tradition in Josephus that Jaddua was the venerable high priest when Alexander entered Jerusalem (332 B.C.) and died apparently not long afterward (cf. *Antiquities* XI. 8, 7).

b. The mention of "Darius the Persian" (Nehemiah 12:22) is said to be Darius Codomannus (336-332), a contemporary of Alexander the Great, and therefore demands a late date. The Darius is, however, evidently Darius Nothus (424-395 B.C.), a contemporary of the youthful Jaddua.

c. The expression, "the days of Nehemiah" (Nehemiah 12:26, 47), is adduced as evidence that the writer was viewing the distant past. But this is perfectly natural usage from the context, since Nehemiah is employing an expression parallel to "the days of Jehoiakim" (v. 26) and "the days of Zerubbabel" (v. 47).

There is no valid reason for rejecting the authorship of Nehemiah as tradition, usage of the first person and other internal evidences show. The passages employing the third person are probably state documents requiring the mention of Nehemiah by his official name and title. The book may be dated during the reign of Darius Nothus (424-395 B.C.).

LITERATURE ON EZRA-NEHEMIAH

Ryle, H. E., in the *Cambridge Bible* (1893).
Torrey, C. C., *The Composition and Historical Value of Ezra-Nehemiah* (Giessen, 1896); *Ezra Studies* (Chicago, 1910).
Batten, L., in the *Int. Crit. Com.* (1913).

CONSERVATIVE LITERATURE

Wilson, R. D., "The Title 'King of Persia' in the Scriptures," *Princeton Theo, Review* XV, 1917, pp. 90-145.
Boyd, J. O., "The Composition of the Book of Ezra," *The Pres. and Ref. Review* XI, 1900, pp. 261-297; "The Documents of the Book of Ezra," *idem* pp. 414-437, "The Historicity of The Book of Ezra," *idem* pp. 568-607.
Kelly, W., *Lectures on Ezra and Nehemiah* (London, 1921).
Wright, J. S., *The Date of Ezra's Coming to Jerusalem* (London, 1946).

Ironside, H. A., *Notes on the Books of Ezra, Nehemiah, and Esther* (New York, 1913).

CHRONICLES

The name Chronicles comes from Jerome, who suggested that the Hebrew title *divre hayyamim* ("Events or Annals of the days" (times), cf. I Chron. 27:24) might be better called "a chronicle of the entire divine history." In the Hebrew the two books were originally one great historical work. The two-fold division made by the Septuagint was not introduced into modern Hebrew Bibles until the printed edition of Daniel Bomberg in 1517. The Septuagint styled the two books inaccurately *Paralipomena*, i. e. "things passed over or omitted" (from the books of Samuel and Kings), as if Chronicles were merely a supplement to these works. In the Talmudic Canon and modern printed Hebrew Bibles, the books of Chronicles are listed in the last place in the Writings. In the Septuagint and the Vulgate they follow the books of Kings.

1. Purpose.

I and II Chronicles present a history of priestly worship from the death of Saul to the end of the Babylonian Captivity, at the precise point where the book of Ezra continues the account. In distinction to the prophetic standpoint of Samuel and Kings, the books of Chronicles, being written from the priestly point of interest, are not merely a parallel account or a supplement or complement to these earlier historical books. They constitute an interpretative history of the Jerusalem priesthood and its growth and development under the Davidic dynasty. Their "omissions" or additions (so-called when compared with Samuel and Kings) are not such at all. The writer gives prominence only to those aspects of history that illustrate the cultivation of the Mosaic ritual as a medium of spiritual blessing and prosperity in the kingdom. Great prominence is accordingly given to priestly genealogies, to the tribes faithful to the Davidic throne and to those kings who were favorable to the true worship of Jehovah at Jerusalem. Special emphasis is accorded David and Solomon because of their paramount role in establishing the temple service. Saul and the kings of Northern Israel are passed over as being in the unfaithful line and extraneous to the author's purpose. The history of Elijah and Elisha, featured in the books of Kings because of their importance in the development of prophetism, is omitted in Chronicles as being unconnected with the development of the priestly cult.

2. *Contents.*

Part I. Genealogies from Adam to David (1:1-9:44).
    a. From Adam to Jacob (1:1-2:2).
    b. Jacob's generations (2:2-9:44).
Part II. History of King David (10:1-29:30).
    a. The death of Saul (10:1-14).
    b. Capture of Zion and David's heroes (11:1-12:40).
    c. David's prosperous reign (13:1-22:1).
    d. David's accomplishments in behalf of ritualistic worship (22:2-29:30).
Part III. History of King Solomon (II Chron. 1:1-9:31).
    a. Solomon's wealth and wisdom (1:1-17).
    b. His building and dedication of the temple (2:1-7:22).
    c. His various activities and death (8:1-9:31).
Part IV. History of the Kings of Judah (10:1-36:23).
    a. From Rehoboam to Zedekiah (10:1-36:21).
    b. The edict of Cyrus (36:22-23).

3. *Date and Authorship.*

Tradition considers Ezra the author of Chronicles. While this is not subject to unanswerable proof, evidence is not lacking to support the validity of the traditional position. W. F. Albright[9] defends the thesis that the Chronicler is Ezra and that he wrote between 400 and 350 B.C. This is an

---

9 "The Date and Personality of the Chronicler," **Jour. Bib. Lit.** 40 (1921), pp. 104-124.

essentially sound position albeit at variance with the general implications of the Wellhausen theory. Most negative critics place the book between 350-250 B.C. Pfeiffer sees nothing precluding the date "about 250 B.C. or a few years before."[10]

But Pfeiffer himself confesses that definite clues are lacking to fix the Chronicler between Nehemiah in 444 and Ben Sira in 180. Accordingly, arguments advanced against authorship by Ezra around 400 B.C. (or somewhat earlier) are inconclusive.

a. The arguments for a late date derived from the language and spirit of the work are without force. The language of the Chronicler is acknowledged to be similar to that of Ezra-Nehemiah and to come from the same period. The style of these books is scarcely artificial and decadent because the author's vernacular was no longer Hebrew but Aramaic, as Pfeiffer imagines.

b. The argument for a late date based on the genealogy in I Chronicles 3:17-24 is pointless. As the critics themselves confess, the text as it stands does not permit us to determine whether five or eleven generations are listed after Zerubbabel, and, hence, whether the last generation belongs to a period around 400 B.C. or around 270 B.C.

c. Arguments for the late date of Ezra-Nehemiah, since critics affirm these books were also written by the Chronicler, are arguments for a late date of Chronicles. These are also insufficient to prove a late date, as we have noted.

4. Historical Value and Trustworthiness.

Critics who insist on a late date, who stress the variation of Chronicles from Samuel and Kings, especially in the use of larger numbers, customarily depreciate the religious and historical value of the Chronicler's work.[11] Archeology is vindicating the book of Chronicles. As W. F. Albright says, "Chronicles contains a considerable amount of original material dealing

---

10 **Introduction**, p. 812.
11 Cf. Oesterley and Robinson, **Introduction**, p. 118.

with the history of Judah which is not found in Kings and . . . the historical value of this original material is being established by archeological discoveries . . ."[12]

In addition, several other factors point to the reliability of the history. The writer's wide use of sources and his careful reference to them disprove the critical aspersion that he was a careless historian. The substantial agreement of Chronicles with Samuel and Kings is corroborating evidence of the trustworthiness of Chronicles. Seeming divergencies must be handled with extreme caution and fairness, since there are serious gaps in our knowledge of the period covered. Disagreements may be only apparent due to ignorance of the full picture. Other difficulties are due to the state of the transmitted text. Others are resolvable under fair handling.

The trustworthiness and value of Chronicles must not be impugned on the basis of its priestly slant. It must be evaluated, as W. A. L. Elmslie correctly states, as "invaluable for the light it gives on the post-exilic priestly standpoint toward the past."[13] The priestly tone of Chronicles, the prophetic tone of Samuel and Kings and the religious and didactic aim of all Old Testament history must be properly appreciated and cannot in fairness be urged against its historical and religious value.

LITERATURE ON CHRONICLES

Curtis, E. L., The Books of Chronicles, *Int. Critical Commentary* (New York, 1910).

Podechard, E., "Les references du Chroniqueur" (Revue Biblique 24, 1915), pp. 236-247.

Albright, W. F., "The Date and Personality of The Chronicler," *Journal Biblical Literature* 40 (1921), pp. 104-124.

Welch, A. C., *The Work of the Chronicler: Its Purpose and Date, Schweich Lectures* (London, 1939).

CONSERVATIVE LITERATURE

Macmillan, K. D., "Concerning The Date of Chronicles" in *Pres. and Ref. Rev.* XI, pp. 507-511.

12 **Bull. Am. Schs. Or. Res.** 100 (1945), p. 18.
13 **How Came Our Faith** (New York, 1949), p. 39.

Keil, C. F., in Keil-Delitzsch Series (1872): Zoekler in *Lange's Commentary* (1876).
   Articles in *Bible Student* (Oct., 1899 and subsequent numbers). "Is the Chronicler A Veracious Historian?"
Beecher, W. J., "Chronicles" in *Int. St. Bible Ency.*, I, 629-635. See also Beecher, *Reasonableness of Biblical Criticism* (1911) chapters 18 and 22.

INDEX

411

Hebrew Style, 256
Hebron, 222
Hegel, G., 268
Heman, 370
Hengstenberg, E. W., 247
Heptateuch, 295
Herntrich, V., 331
Hesychius, 161
Hexapla, 159-161
Hexateuch, 243, 283-4, 320
Hezekiah's Reform, 210
Hilary, 103
Hippo, 87, 104
History of Susanna, 88, 93, 111
Hittites, 43
Hittite Documents, 118
Hobbes, T., 242
Hodge, A., 31
Hoelscher, G., 247, 331
Holiness Code, 202
Holmes, R., 163
Holofernes, 110
Homologoumena, 84
Horites, 43
Hosea, Book of, 333-336
Hupfeld, H., 245
Hyksos, 199, 221
Ilgen, K., 237, 243, 245
Illumination, 24
Inspiration, 22-43; Biblical doctrine, 33-4; false theories, 34-36; results of, 36-43; 225, 228-9, 231
Inverted nun, 131
Isaiah, Book of, 67, 311-323
Isaiah Scroll, 123-4, 129, 154, 157, 320
Isidore, 105
Itala, 170
Jaddua, 404-5
Jamnia, 58, 72, 85, 126-7
Jasher, Book of, 17
Javan, 355, 358
Jehoiakim, 75
Jehovist (J), 191, 213, 227-8, 230-1; 294
Jeremiah, 102
Jeremiah, Book of, 323-328
Jericho, 198
Jeroboam I, 144
Jeroboam II, 120
Jerome, 83, 87, 90, 103, 107, 135, 151, 171-174, 390
Jerubbaal, 132
Jerusalem, 53
Jesus Ben Sirach, 93
Joakim, 110
Job, Book of, 375-379
Joel, Book of, 336-339
John the Baptist, 95
Jonah, Book of, 344-346
Josephus, 30, 49, 55, 57, 64, 71-2, 77, 90, 99, 143, 184, 219, 320, 326
Joshua, Book of, 279-286
Josiah, 61
Josiah's Reformation, 209, 225
Judaism, 15, 19, 85, 127, 159, 186
Judges, Book of, 286-292
Judith, 88, 91, 95, 109, 111
Justin Martyr, 101

Kahle, P., 133
Kant, E., 267
Kautzsch, E., 260
Kayser, A., 246
Kennicott, 144
Kenosis, 225-6
Kethiv-Kere, 134-5
Kimchi, 139, 364
Kings, Book of, 298-304
Kittel, R., 38, 133, 141, 256
Knobel, A., 245
Koenig, E., 306
Koine, 171
Korah, 370
Koran, 41
Kuenen, A., 228, 246, 170, 271-2; 353
Lachish, 199
Lachish Letters, 120
Lamentations, Book of, 386-389
Langton, S., 174
Language of Canaan, 117, 119
Latin, 170
Latin Church, 103
Latter Prophets, 305-360
Law, 55, 64
Law of Moses, 60, 61
Leather, 121
Leningrad Codex, 138
Leo X, 105
Leshem, 240, 263
Ley, J., 365
Leviticus, Book of, 200-204
London Polyglot, 140
Lowth, R., 364-5
Lucian, 161
Lucianic Recension, 177
Luther, M., 88, 106, 139
Maccabees I, 88, 90, 93, 110
Maccabees II, 88, 90, 110, 111, 112
Maccabees, 71
Maimonides, 57, 138
Mains, G., 34-5, 37
Major Poetical Books, 363-379
Major Prophets, 311-333
Malachi, Books of, 359-60
Manasseh, 64
Marti, K., 360
Massorah, 134, 137
Massoretes, 128, 133-138
Massoretic Manuscripts, 133-4
Massoretic Period, 133-138
Massoretic Text, 37-8, 133-138
Matres Lectionis, 124
Mattathias, 68
Mede, J., 357
Megilloth, 380-393
Melek, 132
Melito, 87, 101-2
Men of the Great Assembly, 56, 73
Merenptah Stela, 199
Merribaal, 132
Mesha, 120
Mesrop, 177
Messel, N., 331
Metre, 365-6
Metrophanes, 103
Micah, Book of, 346-348
Midrash, 167

SCRIPTURE INDEX

416

Printed in the United States of America